Latin: A Linguistic Introduction

Latin

A Linguistic Introduction

RENATO ONIGA

Edited and translated by
NORMA SCHIFANO

OXFORD
UNIVERSITY PRESS

Great Clarendon Street, Oxford OX2 6DP
United Kingdom

Oxford University Press is a department of the University of Oxford.
It furthers the University's objective of excellence in research, scholarship,
and education by publishing worldwide. Oxford is a registered trade mark of
Oxford University Press in the UK and in certain other countries

Italian edition *Il Latino. Breve introduzione linguistica* first published by
FrancoAngeli, srl
© FrancoAngeli, Milan 2007
English translation © Renato Oniga and Norma Schifano 2014

The moral rights of the authors have been asserted

This translation first published in 2014

Impression: 1

Published in the United States of America by Oxford University Press
198 Madison Avenue, New York, NY 10016, United States of America

British Library Cataloguing in Publication Data
Data available

Library of Congress Control Number: 2013956102

ISBN 978–0–19–870285–6 (hbk)
      978–0–19–870286–3 (pbk)

Printed and bound by
CPI Group (UK) Ltd, Croydon CR0 4YY

Contents

Preface to the English edition

The aim of this English edition is twofold. Firstly, this work represents one of the most comprehensive introductions to Latin grammar from a generative perspective ever attempted, and the translation makes it now available to a much wider audience than the original Italian edition. The necessity to translate *Il Latino* into English gave us the chance to revise and update some of the notions contained in the original Italian edition, in accordance with the most recent advancements in Latin linguistics. The result is not simply a translation of the original textbook, but rather a more extensive and accurate edition which combines the analysis of Latin phonological, morphological, and syntactic structures with a more detailed comparative view on English.

But this is not the only reason behind the choice of an English version. Throughout the history of English culture a great deal of attention has been paid to traditional grammatical studies. It is not by chance that, after the revival of classical studies which took place in the sixteenth century, Great Britain was the homeland of *Grammar Schools*, in which the main academic focus was precisely on the study of Latin grammar. English grammatical culture was the one which produced the best Latin grammars for centuries, from William Lily to Benjamin Kennedy, as the rigour of grammatical thought was perceived to be essential for the development of the Anglo-Saxon make-up.

The traditional perspectives of nineteenth-century *Latin Primers* have been largely abandoned nowadays, as schools and universities privilege the study of history and archaeology, in order to contextualize the learning of Latin. As a consequence, traditional Latin grammars have become more and more inaccessible to students, while the advancement of modern linguistic theories have unmasked their conceptual failures. However, we think that something good has been lost by abandoning the old grammatical tradition. Not only our comprehension of Latin but also our Western culture in general would be impoverished without a theoretically informed Latin grammar.

This is the reason why this textbook aims to present the essence of Latin grammar in a new and updated format, which combines the outline of traditional descriptions with the most recent advancements of language analysis. The generative framework has been elected as a reference model, cutting through any esoteric jargon and excessive technicalities which would be inappropriate for an introductory textbook and uninteresting for classical philologists.

Therefore, some important innovations have been introduced in the description of many phenomena, in order to make the formulation of rules simpler, clearer, and more theoretically informed. In contrast, many other innovations, which have largely been accepted by linguists, have been left aside as they would imply a more advanced discussion, which goes beyond the scope of the present work. For this reason, this textbook will appear to be closer to traditional Latin grammars than many other recent works, which have tried to apply different theoretical approaches to the study of Latin grammar.

Many Latin grammars exist today which have been developed to suit a wide variety of theoretical and pedagogical inclinations. What makes this handbook special is that it represents a 'bridge' between tradition and innovation. If it will help students to approach Latin with new intellectual curiosity, it will have achieved its task.

We would like to thank our anonymous reviewers at Oxford University Press, whose insightful comments and suggestions on content and language have considerably enriched this work. All remaining errors or inaccuracies are ours. We also wish to thank Julia Steer, commissioning editor for linguistics at Oxford, and Vicki Hart, assistant commissioning editor, for their generous and constant support through all the stages of the preparation of the manuscript. The translations of the Classical texts contained in this work have been inspired by the Loeb editions.

Renato Oniga   Norma Schifano
University of Udine   *University of Cambridge*

List of tables

Abbreviations

σ	any syllable
>	'becomes' (diachronic derivation)
<	'comes from' (diachronic derivation)
→	'becomes' (synchronic derivation)
*	unattested (ungrammatical or reconstructed form)
#	word boundary
+	morpheme boundary
Ø	zero
__	context of a rule
A	adjective
abl.	ablative
acc.	accusative
act.	active
adj.	adjective
Adv	adverb
AgrO	object agreement
AgrOP	object agreement phrase
AgrS	subject agreement
AgrSP	subject agreement phrase
AP	adjective phrase
C	(i) consonant (phonology); (ii) complementizer (syntax)
Conj	conjunction
ConjP	conjunction phrase
conjug.	conjugation
CP	complementizer phrase
D	determiner
dat.	dative
decl.	declension
Dem	demonstrative

DO	direct object
DP	determiner phrase
e	empty category
En.	English
fem.	feminine
Foc	Focus
FocP	Focus phrase
Fr.	French
fut.	future
Ger.	German
gen.	genitive
I	inflection
imper.	imperative
impf.	imperfect
ind.	indicative
inf.	infinitive
Infl	inflectional suffix
IO	indirect object
IP	inflection phrase
IPA	International Phonetic Alphabet
It.	Italian
Lat.	Latin
lit.	literally
mas.	masculine
N	noun
neut.	neuter
nom.	nominative
NP	noun phrase
O	object
P	preposition
part.	participle
PartP	participle phrase

pass.	passive
perf.	perfect
pers.	person
pl.	plural
pluperf.	pluperfect
PP	prepositional phrase
Pre	prefix
pres.	present
pro	null pronoun of finite clauses
PRO	null pronoun of infinitival clauses
pron.	pronoun
Q	quantifier
QP	quantifier phrase
Rom.	Romanian
S	subject
SC	small clause
sg.	singular
Sp.	Spanish
Spec	specifier
subj.	subject
Suf	suffix
t	trace
T	tense
Top	Topic
TopP	Topic phrase
trans.	transitive
V	(i) vowel (phonology); (ii) verb (syntax)
V̄	long vowel
V̆	short vowel
voc.	vocative
VP	verb phrase
X	lexical or functional head

X'   intermediate projection

X" or XP maximal projection

x, y, z variables

$x_i \ldots y_i$ x and y are co-referential

Latin authors are quoted according to the *Index* of the *Thesaurus linguae Latinae.*

1

Introduction: from traditional grammar to modern linguistics

Correct usage is a premise for moral clarity and honesty [...] Who knows how many things, how many cherished pleasures and joys are owed, all unwittingly, to the schoolteachers' red pencils.

Claudio Magris, *Microcosms* (trans. by I. Halliday)

1.1 The teaching of Latin

According to Quintilian, the study of grammar is divided into two parts: *recte loquendi scientiam et poetarum enarrationem* 'the art of speaking correctly and the interpretation of the poets' (*Institutio Oratoria* I 4, 2). This sentence summarizes the long debate by Greek and Latin grammarians about the status of their discipline. After two thousand years, this path is still there for all those who want to learn a foreign language seriously: first of all, one has to master its linguistic structures, then the reading of the literary texts of that civilization should follow.

Modern language teaching has added a further preliminary step, through a distinction between 'knowledge' and 'skill' (more precisely, the 'ability to do' with language). If a learner is aiming for practical results in a specific field, such as tourism or another profession, the first step of language learning should favour the 'ability to do' over 'knowledge', and practical skills over grammar. As for Latin, however, this preliminary step would be useless, since there is no 'Latin country' where one could be a tourist. Whilst it is possible to speak English without knowing the works of Shakespeare, the idea of speaking Latin without knowing the works of Cicero would be unwise. Latin is not a practical means for international communication, but rather the expression of a great literary civilization. There are no short cuts: methodologies which aim to quickly achieve the ability to interact with native speakers would not suit a language like Latin, which no longer has any native speakers. Therefore the aim of studying Latin must be 'reading in order to understand' instead of 'speaking in order to do'.

For this reason, when studying Latin it is necessary to turn one's attention to the grammar. Knowing grammar means mastering the instruments employed to analyse the language, which allows the learner to deal with literary texts from the correct perspective. In addition to this, one has to bear in mind that grammar is not only a utilitarian instrument. In this handbook, grammar will be presented as a scientific discipline with its own autonomous value. As is the case for all sciences, research will be done, old mistakes will be corrected, and new discoveries will be made, all without implying that we have resolved every issue once and for all. For this reason, exploring Latin grammar will be a highly intellectual and formative experience. In other words, we will present Latin grammar as an open working laboratory on language, trying to overcome many trivial notions that standard school practice still accepts, in a rather passive way, and aiming instead at the development of a critical and analytical way of thinking. Knowing grammar means being able to analyse linguistic structures and therefore being able to understand texts, because learners can understand what they are reading only if the structure is clear to them. With no regrets, then, we will leave aside that multitude of peculiar aspects and exceptions, which—for the most part—were justified only by the concerns of those who had to write a refined Latin.

Grammar is the foundation of linguistics, i.e. the science of language, and the development of linguistics as a scientific discipline is one of the greatest achievements of modern thought, as it led to the discovery of some important principles about the general functioning of language. However, the most recent scientific discoveries made by linguists have not yet reached the general store of knowledge shared by most educated people. The plurality of theories, the wide range of data, the necessary technicality shared by all scientific analyses, have all contributed to keep the general public away from modern linguistics. In particular, classicists have found it very difficult to become involved in the debate, since new linguistic studies have been driven by the need to free themselves from the old subordination to Latin and to question the adequacy of certain aspects of the traditional grammatical apparatus.

Therefore, quite paradoxically, progress made by modern linguistics has had negative rather than positive effects on the grammatical description of Latin. Although traditional grammar is now outdated, it has not yet been properly replaced. In the mainstream, a widespread scepticism forces us to keep relying on outdated textbooks. A possible way out of this is to bring Latin grammar back to its original high-level conception, one that is scientific, going beyond prescriptive rigidity and restoring the original theoretical tension. To this end, many branches of modern linguistics are potentially suitable, although they have not yet been fully exploited in the teaching field. Their advantage is that they satisfy the same needs as the traditional analytical and philosophical Latin grammar, taking advantage, at the same time, of new methods, which are suitable to the formulation of more precise analyses and theoretical generalizations.

1.2 A generativist perspective

In the light of the above discussion, the aim of this handbook is to present an innovative description and explanation of many phenomena, in the belief that we can achieve a better understanding of this language if we exploit the results of modern research. The theoretical framework adopted by this handbook largely coincides with the one developed in the generative tradition, which has attempted to explain some fundamental properties of universal grammar in a simple and straightforward manner.

At the same time, however, this handbook is firmly rooted in the traditional approach, in the belief that modern linguists and ancient grammarians are dealing with the same questions, which constitute the very heart of our discipline. Contrary to the common practice of many ostentatiously 'modern' textbooks, the author has tried, whenever possible, to avoid any false innovations. There is nothing more frustrating than those passages of modern linguistics which hide a conceptual vacuum behind an apparently innovative terminology, which most of the time is nevertheless merely obscure. Coversely, important concepts can often be found in traditional grammar, which can be recovered and developed in the light of the most recent research.

The methodology of this handbook is closely related to the one employed by scientific disciplines, based on abstraction and generalization. We will start from some 'primitives', i.e. concepts we cannot define but which we accept as intuitive notions. For example, concepts such as 'word' and 'sentence' in grammar are the equivalent of 'point' and 'line' in geometry. Starting from these basic notions, we will try to construct a consistent theory, as formalized as possible, in which other concepts will be defined in a more rigorous fashion, and each phenomenon will be explained in the most straightforward manner. A number of formal mechanisms will be introduced, in order to provide a more satisfactory explanation of the regularity of linguistic phenomena.

The very notion of 'rule' will not be interpreted in terms of rules imposed by prescriptive grammars, but will acquire the logical meaning shared by all scientific disciplines. Grammar rules will not be presented as obscure and arbitrary precepts that one has to memorize in a passive way, but rather as regular patterns which can be discovered by looking at the properties of empirical data. A rule is an explicative hypothesis, a formal model of the mental processes which produce linguistic data.

This 'language faculty', therefore, will be at the centre of every discussion. After all, Latin is a natural language. For this reason, as we explain various grammatical phenomena, we will try to compare Latin structures with English and other modern languages. In order to restore the idea of a renewed *scientia recte loquendi*, we will develop Latin grammar in a modern linguistic framework, which can lead learners to acquire a better awareness of their own native language and help them to orient themselves among the structures of foreign languages.

As was already clear to ancient philosophers, language is the main faculty setting man apart from animals. These latter can communicate only by means of a finite set of signals. Human beings, on the other hand, are able to produce and understand an infinite number of sentences they have never heard before. The question about the functioning of language is one of the most interesting ever posed. Grammatical research arose exactly from this question and since its very origins it has been strictly connected to philosophical enquiry. As is still the case today, the main task for grammar should be suggesting problems and posing questions, instead of giving standard answers. Strictly speaking, we have to admit that even now we can provide only partial and tentative answers to many questions, but it is for exactly this reason that the research enterprise is worthwhile.

There is one point, however, about which ancient scholars already had clear intuitions. As pointed out by the Latin poet Lucretius (*De rerum natura* V 1028–1090), the language faculty is innate to the human mind and it develops automatically in the child's mind, as is the case for other faculties in other animal species. Similarly, when Varro, in his *De lingua Latina* (IX 23–29), talks about *declinatio naturalis* 'natural declension', he wants to highlight the fact that in the inflection of words some spontaneous regularities can be found, similar to those which arise in other natural phenomena, like the rhythm of the tides or the orbit of the stars. The explicative hypothesis for these phenomena was provided by the Greek philosophical concept of *logos*: the very same rational structure, which can be expressed by means of mathematical proportions, can be found both in the nature of the universe and in human language.

The intuitions of these scholars form the basis of a very long line of thought, which goes from St. Augustine, Descartes, and Pascal to the *Port-Royal Grammar* (1660), finally reaching the school-teaching tradition of past centuries. However, this conception of grammar took a complete form only from the beginning of the second half of the twentieth century, thanks to a linguistic current called 'generative grammar', founded by the American linguist Noam Chomsky. In his view, language is a fundamental component of human nature, and it is ruled by an innate 'universal grammar', from which all the grammars of the different existing languages are derived.

One of Chomsky's most important arguments regards the so-called 'poverty of the stimulus', which is based on the observation that children are, surprisingly, able to develop a perfect knowledge of their own native language without any specific instruction, simply through their exposure to a limited and fragmentary set of linguistic data. Without postulating the existence of innate mental abilities, the inductive leap from such data to knowledge would be impossible. This implies that the speaker, in order to produce and understand a potentially infinite number of sentences, must have an internalized knowledge of language, namely a set of innate mental schemes or mechanisms. In this sense, the challenge for linguistic research is the formal description of this extremely complex set of general principles and specific rules, which constitutes the speaker's internalized grammar, by means of a limited number of premises.

The most recent discoveries in the field of cognitive science have confirmed this line of research, which, nevertheless, has not yet sufficiently spread, not even in schools and universities. Old conceptions of language still survive, which consider natural languages to be artificial products of history, arbitrarily varying one from the other, and superimposed on the human mind, thought of as a *tabula rasa*, which can be easily manipulated. These relativistic conceptions of language, and of human nature itself, have generated widespread scepticism towards grammar, which is itself considered to be an artificial product. Today some scholars still reject the scientific study of language, on the basis of trivial prejudices, such as 'language is not mathematics'. If it is the case that natural languages radically differ from formal languages, then this does not in itself imply that the logic of formal languages cannot be of any help in our understanding of the way in which the human mind exploits its computational abilities in the linguistic domain. Consider, as an example, the fact that mathematics provides us with models to describe how it is possible to make infinite use of finite means, using recursive operations (such as addition).

In short, the exercise of morphological or syntactic analysis requires a number of abilities in reasoning, abstracting, and generalizing, which do not significantly differ from those required for solving a mathematical problem. If the study of grammar is devoid of any scientific interest, its practical value cannot be supported. Grammar is, by its own nature, a theory: the denial of theoretical interest inevitably results in the abandonment of grammar itself, in the sense of a creative and critic analysis, in favour of the development of automatisms that one has to memorize, in a totally passive fashion.

In addition to this, a formal linguistic theory gives grounds for considering grammatical analysis a necessary preliminary to translation. In order to translate with awareness, it is necessary to reconstruct the abstract grammatical structure of a given language, and then go back to the actual form of the target language. Translating always implies non-trivial linguistic reasoning, which is extremely rich and complex, and which can be either implicit or developed in an explicit way by means of the tools of grammar.

We will conclude this Introduction with some remarks regarding the overall organization of this handbook. The grammar of any natural language has its own intrinsic structure, regardless of any possible descriptions one can propose.

First, as the Swiss linguist Ferdinand de Saussure pointed out at the beginning of the twentieth century, words are *signs*, which correspond to referents, i.e. objects in the world. The linguistic sign is the combination of two inseparable sides: a phonetic *signifier*, i.e. its phonological component, and a logical *signified*, i.e. its conceptual component. Therefore, when we study a word, we must always bear in mind the distinction between phonological form and meaning. The first component of grammar, therefore, will be phonology.

Second, we must always be aware of the fact that the core linguistic unit, where meaning is expressed, is not the single word but the entire sentence. In this sense, assigning a meaning to a word always implies assigning a complete grammatical analysis to it, i.e. related to the morphological structure of the word and to the way in which the word combines with other words in the sentence. These constitute the other two components of grammar, i.e. morphology and syntax.

Each of the three components of grammar, i.e. phonology, morphology, and syntax, will be considered as an autonomous system, consisting of a certain number of primitives and some formal operations. Starting from primitives, these operations are used to build a number of formal objects, which are able to identify the relevant relations between the elements. The phonological component, for example, consists of some minimal units, i.e. the phonemes, which are used to build syllables, words, and metrical structures. In a similar way, the morphological component consists of some minimal units, i.e. stems, affixes, and endings, and rules which combine such units in order to produce morphological structures. Finally, the minimal units of the syntactic component, namely words, are combined by means of other rules to produce the phrase structure of sentences. Therefore, it is not only for practical reasons that we have chosen to follow the traditional strategy, i.e. an expository order where phonology precedes morphology and syntax comes last.

Part I

Phonology

2

The Latin alphabet

2.1 Types of writing system

Most European languages, including English, still employ the Latin alphabet, with only a few national variants. Nevertheless there are in Europe some languages which do make use of different alphabets, such as Greek or Cyrillic. Other countries, which are far away from Europe but yet quite familiar to us nowadays, like China or Japan, have writing systems which look even more different. Generally speaking, there are four types of writing system: pictographic, ideographic (or logographic), syllabic, and phonemic.

Pictograms (or *pictographs*) were in use in prehistoric times, but today they have almost disappeared (some traces can still be found among American Indian, Inuit, and Oceanic peoples). They represent the content of a message in a figurative way, without any reference to its linguistic sound form. In other words, pictograms are a sort of signal, similar to modern road signs, and are not connected to the linguistic sound form that the word has in that language. In this sense, they differ from all the other types of writing system, which imply a certain degree of linguistic analysis instead. For this reason, most linguists do not consider pictograms a writing system at all, as this must have some degree of conventionalization, which is absent in pictography.

Ideograms (or *ideographs*), such as those used in Chinese and Japanese writing, substitute the acoustic image of a word with a graphic sign, so most linguists prefer the term *logograms* rather than ideograms because the signs represent words, not ideas. The linguistic intuition which lies behind this type of system is the one expressed by Saussure, according to which the linguistic sign consists of two inseparable sides: a phonetic *signifier*, i.e. its sound, and a logical *signified*, i.e. its conceptual component. Languages with little overt morphology (like Chinese) are better suited to ideographic systems. The main issue with this type of system is that it requires a large number of signs (theoretically speaking, as many as the number of words in the language).

Syllabic systems answered the need to reduce the number of signs of an originally ideographic writing system. The basic linguistic intuition which lies behind them is that words can be decomposed into smaller units and that the syllable is the smallest unit which can express a lexical meaning in isolation (as shown by the fact that there exist monosyllabic words and that all other words can be decomposed into syllables). In syllabic systems, therefore, each graphic sign corresponds to a syllable. This type of writing is typical of the great civilizations of the ancient Near East. Examples of syllabic systems include cuneiform writing and the most ancient attested Greek syllabary, i.e. the so-called linear B.

Segmental (or *phonemic*) *systems*, whose earliest examples are proto-Sinaitic scripts, dated to about 1800 BC, were spread over the Mediterranean world by the Phoenicians towards the end of the second millennium BC. These systems analyse the word into its minimal constituents, i.e. the segments or 'phonemes'. Therefore, using a segmental system implies understanding that the only difference between two words like *car* and *bar* is a minimal unit, i.e. the initial letter. This minimal unit, that linguists call a segment or phoneme (such as the /b/ in *bar*), does not have any meaning per se: its function is to *distinguish* the meaning of words. In a segmental writing system every graphic sign is associated with a segment. The number of segments used by a language is always smaller than the number of syllables. It was precisely this economy in the number of signs which caused the immediate success and rapid diffusion of the Phoenician writing system. While the Phoenicians generally indicated only consonant phonemes—although the so-called *matres lectionis* were also sometimes added to indicate vowel segments—it is the Greeks who are credited with adding vowel segments to the original phonetic repertoire. Starting from the Greek colonies of Southern Italy, and via the Etruscans, the segmental writing system finally reached Rome towards the end of the eighth century BC.

2.2 The letters of the Latin alphabet

Most of the graphic signs contained in the Latin alphabet coincide with the English ones. Table 2.1 represents the twenty-three signs of the Classical Latin alphabet, in small and capital letters, and the corresponding Latin names.

These rules of capitalization only apply to modern editions of classical texts. Ancient Romans used to write in capital letters only, as shown by inscriptions

TABLE 2.1. The Latin alphabet

A	B	C	D	E	F	G	H	I	K	L	M	N	O	P	Q	R	S	T	V	X	Y	Z
a	b	c	d	e	f	g	h	i	k	l	m	n	o	p	q	r	s	t	u	x	y	z
a	*be*	*ce*	*de*	*e*	*ef*	*ge*	*ha*	*i*	*ka*	*el*	*em*	*en*	*o*	*pe*	*qu*	*er*	*es*	*te*	*u*	*ix*	*hy*	*zeta*

and the most ancient manuscripts. The small letter, instead, was invented during the era of Charlemagne (whence its name 'Caroline minuscule' or 'Carolingian minuscule'). Its definitive shape was defined in the Renaissance, after the invention of printing. Rules are the same as in English, with capital letters employed both for proper nouns, e.g. *Gallia*, and for the corresponding adjectives and adverbs, e.g. *bellum Gallicum* 'Gallic war', *Gallicē* 'in the Gallic way'.

Notes

C   In the archaic stages of Latin, this letter used to indicate both the voiceless [k] and the voiced [gg] sound, possibly because of Etruscan influence. In Classical Latin, the use of the letter *C* to indicate the voiced sound survived only in the abbreviation of two proper nouns, i.e. *Gāius (C.)* and *Gnaeus (Cn.)*. Later on, the letter *G* entered the Latin alphabet, derived by adding a dash to *C*. Spurius Carvilius (third century BC) is credited with this innovation by the Latin tradition, although this attribution is disputed.

K   This letter comes from the most archaic Latin alphabet, where it was used before the vowel *a* instead of *c*. It survived only in the following nouns: *kalendae*, *Karthāgō*, and *K.* as an abbreviation of *Kaesō* (also spelt *Caesō*).

I   Unlike English, the Latin alphabet does not distinguish the vowel /i/ from the semivowel /j/ (this latter in English can be graphically rendered as *y*, in words such as *yet*, though spelling rules in English can be unpredictable, e.g. in a word like *pretty* the same grapheme *y* indicates the vowel /i/).[1] During the Renaissance, a scholar called Pierre de la Ramée (Lat. Ramus) (1515–1572) is credited with the introduction of new graphic signs in order to distinguish vowels from semivowels. However, the so-called 'Ramist' letters predated Ramus and were not entirely successful during the following centuries. The use of *J* and *j*, in particular, is now avoided in Classical Latin texts, since these letters have entered the alphabet of some modern languages instead, like English, where *J*, however, does not indicate the semivowel but an affricate consonant (as in *John*).

V   In Classical Latin the semivowel *V*, *v* is pronounced like [w] in the English word *wine*. Only in the humanistic pronunciation is the initial sound of a Latin word such as *vīnum* pronounced like the initial sound of the word *variety*, that is as a labiodental fricative. Romans did not distinguish the vowel /u/ from the semivowel /w/, but they employed the very same graphic sign for both, i.e. a capital *V* (later on, the Caroline minuscule *u* became the corresponding small letter). Some editions of classical texts still employ this distinction, so one can find words such as *uīnum* and *Vrbs*. However, most textbooks nowadays employ the two 'Ramist' letters, i.e. the capital letter *U* and the small letter *v*. Because of these innovations, it is possible to graphically distinguish

---

[1]   When a comparison between Latin and English sounds is made, the reference for English is to the Received Pronunciation. No other reasons but simplicity underlie this choice.

the vowel *U, u* from the semivowel *V, v*, including the distinction between small and capital letters, thus avoiding the ambiguities of ancient writing.

Y, Z   These letters are rarely used, since they do not belong to the original Latin alphabet but were introduced during the first century BC to transliterate Greek nouns, e.g. *lympha, zōna.*

3

Phonemes

3.1 Phonemes and sounds

From a linguistic point of view, it is important to avoid any confusion between phonemes, sounds, and letters of the alphabet. The aim of this section is to clarify these concepts.

We shall start from the *sound*. A sound is a physical phenomenon perceived by the human ear. It can also be recorded by means of microphones. More precisely, a sound is a wave moving through the air, which is produced by the vibration of some object (such as a bell). Linguistic sounds, in particular, are produced by the vibration of vocal cords and then modulated in various ways by the organs of speech (larynx, tongue, teeth, lips). The oral and nasal cavities function as a resonating chamber. Since linguistic sounds are the products of these anatomical organs, their number is limited and little variation is attested among natural languages.

The stream of speech is perceived as a sequence of separate units. These speech segments are called 'sounds' or 'phones'. The study of speech sounds is called 'phonetics'. Phonetics can be 'historical', i.e. concerned with the evolution of sounds over time, or 'descriptive', i.e. aimed at drawing up an inventory of the sounds of a given language, or a general inventory for all languages.

One of the main achievements of descriptive phonetics is the 'International Phonetic Alphabet' (IPA), in which each sound corresponds to one and only one symbol. In spite of its fair degree of approximation (it is impossible to express all the physical properties of a sound by means of a single symbol), the IPA is a 'perfect' alphabet, since each letter has a corresponding sound and vice versa. By convention, phonetic transcriptions are written between square brackets and make use of specific symbols, e.g. the phonetic transcription of the English word *college* is [kɒlɪdʒ].

All other historically attested alphabets, including the Latin one, are imperfect in the sense that there are many cases in which a single letter represents two different sounds (e.g. we saw in Section 2.2 that the Latin letter *V* can represent both the vowel [u] and the semivowel [w]), or cases in which the same sound is represented by two different letters (e.g. in Latin the sound [k] can be represented both as a *C* and as a *K*). Moreover, there are languages, like English, where the relationship between letters and sounds is even more complex.

In any scientific study of the sounds of a language, therefore, any reference to the *letters* of the alphabet should be avoided, except for those cases in which they coincide with those employed by the IPA. The reference to the letters of the alphabet in schools, on the other hand, can be maintained, provided that students are aware that they represent only an approximation.

If the sound is a physical phenomenon, the *phoneme*—on the other hand— is an abstract concept. Nevertheless, this latter is more relevant from the point of view of the language system because it is related to meaning distinctions. More precisely, the phoneme is the smallest sound unit that distinguishes the meaning of two words.

The definition of phoneme as the minimal distinctive unit comes from the technique used to identify the phonemes of a given language, which is based on the identification of so-called 'minimal pairs'. For example, from the English minimal pair *dog* and *fog*, we can infer the existence of two phonemes, i.e. /d/ and /f/ (by convention, these are written between slashes). The abstract phoneme should not be confused with the actual corresponding sound. In the last example, the phonemes /d/ and /f/ are realized by the sounds [d] and [f]. But if we take two other words, such as *pin* and *spin*, both containing the phoneme /p/, we will find that the very same phoneme /p/ has two different phonetic realizations, i.e. [pʰ] and [p], respectively. This shows that the very same phoneme can have phonetic variants, called *allophones*. These, in turn, can be in 'free variation' (e.g. in Italian, the phoneme /r/ can be freely realized as the dental trill [r] or as the uvular trill [R]) or in 'complementary distribu- tion', i.e. determined by the phonetic context, like the voiceless stops in English, which are aspirated when they are word-initial or at the onset of a stressed syllable and non-aspirated everywhere else (see the above example [pʰin] and [spin]). Finally, note that the notion of phoneme has been further revised by more recent research in phonology (cf. the theory of the 'distinctive features', according to which the phoneme can be decomposed into a set of more abstract features). However, given the introductory nature of the present handbook, we shall stick to the traditional notion of phoneme, which remains a useful tool for description and analysis.

3.2 Classification of the Latin phonemes

The conceptual distinction made in Section 3.1 allows us to understand why the inventory of linguistic sounds is universal, while the inventory of phonemes varies from language to language. This is the case because all human beings are capable of pronouncing the same number of sounds, but there may be a phoneme which is present in one language but not in another. For example, in Chinese there is no phoneme /r/. Similarly, the English interdental fricative /θ/, e.g. in *thin*, does not exist in Italian.

However, there is a second reason why the inventory of phonemes varies from language to language. The same sound can acquire the value of a phoneme in one language, and the value of a variant, or allophone, in another language. For example, English makes a distinction between two voiced labial phonemes, the stop /b/ and the fricative /v/, respectively, since *bat* and *vat* form a minimal pair. Conversely, in Spanish a single phoneme /b/ exists, which is realized by two different context-dependent allophones. In particular, if /b/ is word-initial, it is realized as a stop [b], e.g. *bien* [bjɛn] 'good', while in a word-internal position it is realized as a fricative [β], e.g. *caballo* [kaβaʎo] 'horse'. On the other hand, in Spanish the phoneme /v/ does not exist (the letter *v* is a graphic but not a phonetic variant), so that both *v* and *b* in *viento* 'wind' and *bien* are pronounced [b].

Another example comes from Italian, where the single phoneme /s/ is realized by two different regional allophones in intervocalic position, e.g. in a word like *rosa* 'rose', the phoneme /s/ is realized as a voiced fricative [z] in the north and as a voiceless fricative [s] in the south. Conversely, in English the voiceless /s/ and the voiced /z/ behave like two different phonemes, as shown by the minimal pair *price* [praɪs] and *prize* [praɪz]. In conclusion, we can argue that it is more important to study the inventory of Latin phonemes than a mere list of the letters of its alphabet.

3.3 Consonants

In all languages, consonants can be naturally classified according to their *place* and *manner of articulation*, namely where and how air is blocked before coming out from the mouth.

The place of articulation refers to the area where the air is blocked. Broadly speaking, most Latin school grammars distinguish only three places of articulation, i.e. *labial* (or, more precisely, *bilabial*, i.e. narrowing or closure of the lips: [p, b]); *dental* (or *interdental*, i.e. with the tip of the tongue either between or just behind the teeth: [t, d]); and *velar* (with the back of the tongue pushed up towards the soft palate, that is the muscular part of the roof of the mouth, behind the palate: [k, g]). Further distinctions, such as *labiodental* (with the upper teeth touching the lower lip: [f]), or *alveolar* (with the tongue just below or touching the tooth bridge: [l, r, s]) are not in use. Also note that Latin [t] is *dental*, as in Italian, and not *alveolar*, as in English.

The manner of articulation refers to the way in which the air is blocked: consonants are divided into *plosives* or *stops* (complete obstruction followed by an explosion: [p, b, t, d, k, g]), *fricatives* (the air is expelled with a little friction: [f, s]), *nasals* (the air comes out through the nasal cavity: [m, n]), *laterals* (the air escapes around the sides of the tongue: [l]), and *trills* (the air flows causing some vibration: [r]).

Another major distinction, i.e. *voicing*, is determined by the behaviour of the vocal cords, which, when the air flows between them, may vibrate (voiced consonants) or may not (voiceless consonants). The main phonemic consonants of Latin are summarized in the Table 3.1.

In the traditional terminology of school grammars, stops used to be called 'mute', voiceless consonants 'tenuis', voiced consonants 'medial', and fricatives 'spirant'; the fricative /s/ may still be called 'sibilant', while the lateral /l/ and the trill /r/ are both called 'liquids'.

The above inventory is completed by the following consonants, which are less common because they require a more complex articulation.

Labiovelar consonants are orthographically represented as *qu* and *gu* in the Latin alphabet and [k^w] and [g^w] in the IPA. In both cases, we are not dealing with the combination of a velar consonant and the vowel *u*, but rather with digraphs, that is, pairs of graphemes which refer to a single phoneme, /k^w/ and /g^w/, respectively, i.e. a velar consonant (either voiced or voiceless) with a labial appendix. Labiovelars are not very common cross-linguistically, e.g. they exist in Italian (cf. *questo* 'this'), but not in English or German.

The letter *x* is called a 'double' consonant, since it is used to indicate the sequence of a velar followed by /s/, i.e. either /k/+/s/ or /g/+/s/. An example is represented by the declension of *crux, crucis* 'cross', and *lēx, lēgis* 'law', where the *x* of the nominative form represents the combination of the phonemes /k/+/s/ and /g/+/s/, respectively.

TABLE 3.1 The consonants of Latin

Place	Labial		Dental		Velar	
Manner	Voiceless	Voiced	Voiceless	Voiced	Voiceless	Voiced
Stop	p	b	t	d	k	g
Fricative	f		s			
Nasal	m		n			
Lateral			l			
Trill			r			

The letter *z* was introduced in the Latin alphabet in order to spell Greek words such as *zōna* 'girdle, zone', which includes the voiced dental affricate [dz], unknown in Latin. Generally speaking, affricates are not common cross-linguistically (English also has two palatal affricates, the voiceless /ʧ/, e.g. *chess*, and the voiced /dʒ/, e.g. *jet*, which did not exist in Classical Latin). For this reason, the affricate [dz] also tends to become a fricative [z] in Late Greek and Late Latin.

3.4 Semivowels

Semivowels (or *approximants* or *glides*) are phonemes whose nature is halfway between vowels and consonants. This is the case for the palatal phoneme /j/, as in the English word *yet* [jet], and the labialized velar phoneme /w/, as in the English word *well* [wel].

Sometimes it may be useful to distinguish these phonemes in accordance with their distribution, so they are called 'semiconsonants' when they precede a vowel (cf. *yacht* [jɒt] and *woman* [wʊmən]) and 'semivowels' when they follow a vowel (cf. *bay* [beɪ] and *how* [haʊ]).

In word-initial position, semivowels behave like other consonants, e.g. *iactō* [jakto:] 'to throw' and *veniō* [wenio:] 'to come'. As mentioned above (Section 2.2), in the Latin alphabet the phonemes /j/ and /w/ are spelt with the characters which indicate the corresponding vowels, i.e. *i* and *u*.

One difficulty may be the presence or absence of the 'Ramist' letters, e.g. the possible alternation between *jactō* and *iactō*, or *veniō* and *ueniō*.

Moreover, there are a few cases in which *i* behaves like the vowel /i/ and not as the semivowel /j/, despite its placement in word-initial position. For example, in the Latin word (of Greek origin) *Iāsōn* [ia:so:n] 'Jason' or in the present participle form *i-ens* [iens], the *i* preceding a vowel is exceptionally a vowel itself.

3.5 Vowels

Vowels can be classified cross-linguistically in accordance with the position of the tongue within the mouth during the production of the sound. Their classification, therefore, takes into account a horizontal axis (front, central, or back) and a vertical axis (high, mid, or low), as shown in Table 3.2.

The vocalic system of Latin is very simple, if compared to the complexity of the English one. Following the horizontal axis, Latin vowels are divided into front or palatal, i.e. [i] and [e] (the tongue is moved forwards, towards the palate), central, i.e. similar to [a] (the tongue is kept in a central position), and back or

TABLE 3.2 The vowels of Latin

	Front (palatal)	Central	Back (velar)
High (close)	i		u
Mid	e		o
Low (open)		a	

velar, i.e. [u] and [o] (the tongue is moved backwards, towards the throat). Following the vertical axis, vowels are divided into high or close, i.e. [i] and [u] (the tongue being in a high position, air flows through a narrower space), mid vowels, i.e. [e] and [o], and one low or open vowel, i.e. [a] (the tongue being low, the oral cavity is more open).

The pronunciation of Latin [i], [e], [u], [o] is *roughly* the same as the vowels of the following English words: *six, pet, put, not*. The pronunciation of [a] is instead more similar to the Italian, French, or Spanish counterparts, while its nearest cognate in English could be a short [ɑ] (cf. its long realization in *arm*).

3.6 Quantity of vowels

In Latin the quantity of vowels, i.e. whether they are 'long' or 'short', is phonologically relevant. Consequently, there are not five Latin vowels but ten, since each vocalic sound corresponds to two autonomous phonemes: a long vowel V̄ and a short one V̆. Thus, Latin vocalic phonemes are the following ones: /ĭ/, /ī/, /ŭ/, /ū/, /ĕ/, /ē/, /ŏ/, /ō/, /ă/, /ā/. In this handbook only the long vowels will be systematically marked, by a macron, in the sections devoted to phonology and morphology, the diacritic sign for a short vowel being limited to those cases where some special phonological processes must be emphasized. Elsewhere, no vowels will be marked, in accordance with the current use in critical editions of classical texts.

The fact that in Latin the quantity of vowels is relevant for the distinction of phonemes is shown by the following minimal pairs: *dĭcō* 'I dedicate' / *dīcō* 'I say'; *pŭtet* 'he would think' / *pūtet* 'he stinks'; *vĕnit* 'he comes' / *vēnit* 'he came'; *nŏvī* 'something new' / *nōvī* 'I know'; *mălum* 'misfortune' / *mālum* 'apple'.

A similar phenomenon can be found in Hungarian, where every short vowel has a long counterpart, which is marked by a superimposed diacritic, e.g. *kor* 'age' vs. *kór* 'disease'. Vowel quantity can also be observed in English, e.g. *sheep* versus *ship*, although it could be argued that these vowels are not only quantitatively but also qualitatively different. Interestingly, it has been argued that in Classical Latin short and long vowels also tended to be associated with slight qualitative distinctions, which became more salient in Vulgar Latin. This hypothesis is supported by the fact that in Standard Italian, for example, original short close vowels ([ĭ, ŭ]) became open ([e, o]), e.g. Lat. *mĭttō; iŭgŭm* > It. *metto; giogo*, possibly as a consequence of the fact that in Latin long vowels naturally tended to be close, while short vowels tended to be open.

3.7 Diphthongs

A diphthong (from the Greek *díphthongos,* meaning 'two sounds') is perceived as a vowel changing its sound during the utterance. In other words, the vocalic sound perceived at the beginning is different from the one perceived at the end, e.g. [aʊ] in *cow.*

Traditional grammars usually make a distinction between 'rising' (or 'ascending') diphthongs, like [jɛ] in Italian *ieri* 'yesterday', where the sound rises from the first to the second element, and 'falling' (or 'descending') diphthongs, like [aɪ] in English *eye*, where there is a decline in sonority. However, according to modern linguistics, whether a sequence is diphthongal or not depends on how the sequence functions in the phonological process of a language. Thus, the sequence [jɑ] is clearly not a rising diphthong in English *yard*, but it could certainly be a diphthong in some languages if, for example, it patterned with long vowels in a stress assignment rule.

The most frequent diphthongs in Latin are *au, ae,* and *oe,* e.g. *causa* 'cause', *Caesar* 'Caesar', *poena* 'punishment', whereas *eu, ei,* and *ui* are much less frequent. In Latin, diphthongs are falling, i.e. the sound falls down from the first to the second element. For this reason, if the syllable is stressed, the stress always falls on the first vowel of the diphthong, e.g. *cáusa, Cáesar, póena.*

As a matter of fact, the actual phonetic value of the diphthongs *ae* and *oe* in Archaic Latin was [ai] and [oi], not [ae] and [oe], similar to English *night* [naɪt] and *boy* [bɔɪ]. This is witnessed by a number of phonetic spellings found in archaic inscriptions, such as *aidīlis* for *aedīlis* 'aedile', and by the fact that the Latin word *poena* corresponds to the Greek ποινή [poiné]. Cross-linguistic evidence shows that the second element of a diphthong is typically a semi-vowel (*j* or *w*), but rarely the vowel (*e*). Diphthongs such as *ai* and *oi* can be found in Italian, e.g. *mai* [mai] 'never' and *noi* [noi] 'we', as well as in Ancient Greek. Conversely, the diphthongs *ae* and *oe* are not attested in any of these languages. In this respect, the pronunciation [ae] and [oe] of Classical Latin may be considered the result of the evolution from the archaic forms [ai] and [oi]. This is quite similar to a well-known phenomenon in Southern American English, where RP /aɪ/ is rendered quite like [ae].

During the Late Latin period, but also in the sociolectal spoken language of the classical era (cf. the so-called 'rustic' pronunciation or 'vulgar' speech), the diphthongs *ae* and *oe* further evolved and became monophthongs, that is they were reduced to the phonetic value of one single vowel. In particular, *ae* became [ɛ:] (e.g. Italian *cielo* 'sky' comes from Latin *caelum* through the intermediate reconstructed stage **kɛ(:)lo*), while *oe* became [e:] (e.g. Italian *pena* 'pain' comes from Latin *poena* through the intermediate reconstructed stage of **pe(:)na*). For this reason, in the ecclesiastical pronunciation of Latin, the original diphthongs of *caelum* and *poena* are pronounced as their Italian counterparts. On the other hand, the diphthong *au*—whose reduction to a monophthong is attested as well in rustic Latin, e.g. *caupō > cōpō* 'innkeeper', and in some Italian derivations, e.g. Lat. *aurum* > It. *oro* 'gold'—survived in literary Latin until the late period, and it has been preserved in some varieties of Romance, including, among others, southern Italian dialects, most varieties of Rhaeto-Romance, and Romanian, e.g. Lat. *taurus* 'bull' > Rom. *taur* (but It. *toro*).

4

Pronunciation

4.1 National pronunciations of Latin

The main problem with pronunciation is linked to the vitality of Latin as a spoken language. In past centuries, Latin was perceived as a living language and was commonly employed in many intellectual fields, e.g. science, culture, and religion. As a consequence, 'national' pronunciations of Latin arose, which were characterized by an increasing level of accommodation to the speaker's mother tongue. Until the mid nineteenth century, schools and universities around Great Britain used to employ a variety of local pronunciations of Latin, which were largely influenced by English phonology. A case in point is represented by France, where the placement of the stress on the last syllable of Latin words ending in a vowel—in accordance with the French pattern but different from the Latin—is still common today (sometimes, even lecturers apply this pattern to expressions such as *lingua Latīna* 'Latin language', rendered as *linguà Latinà*).

The most successful national pronunciation of Latin was the Italian one, because of its closeness to the original Late Latin pronunciation and because of the adoption of Late Latin pronunciation as the official pronunciation of the Roman Catholic Church. For this reason, the so-called 'ecclesiastical' or 'humanistic' pronunciation is still largely employed in some countries, such as Italy.

In contrast, the so-called 'classical' or *restitūta* 'restored' pronunciation has been spreading across universities all over the world during the last decades, as an attempt to restore the original pronunciation of Classical Latin, on the basis of strong arguments provided by historical linguists.

Today, although teachers should have a good knowledge of both pronunciations, i.e. classical and humanistic, it is advisable that they choose one or the other, in accordance with the cultural context of teaching, in order to avoid any confusion between the two. However, the problem of pronunciation is arguably minor: as we have seen, learning the phonemes of a language is the most important thing, the possible variation in their pronunciation being a secondary matter.

4.2 Classical pronunciation

The 'classical' pronunciation is the product of a process of historical reconstruction aimed at reproducing the use of the educated classes of Rome during
the classical period, i.e. around the first century BC. Because of the lack of any
actual recordings, this reconstruction cannot represent anything more than a
fair approximation of the ancient pronunciation. Some of its most salient
features are reported below:

- The pronunciation of the diphthongs *ae* and *oe* is [ae] and [oe],
  respectively.
- The velar stops *c* and *g* remain velar in all contexts, i.e. [k] and [g],
  respectively.
- The sequence *ph* is an aspirated stop, i.e. [pʰ].
- The aspirated consonant *h* is pronounced, as in English *how*.
- *s* is voiceless in all contexts.
- *v* is rendered as a labiovelar semivowel, i.e. [w], as in English *wine*.

4.3 Humanistic pronunciation

The 'humanistic' or 'ecclesiastical' pronunciation, which spread over Europe
from the Late Latin period until the period of Humanism, is based largely on
the native articulation habits of Italian speakers. A complete description of this
type of pronunciation would imply an in-depth analysis of Italian phonology,
which is outside the scope of this handbook. However, some salient features of
this pronunciation are listed below, which can be of interest to those who
study Christian, medieval, and humanistic Latin.

- The diphthongs *ae* and *oe* are pronounced as a monophthong, i.e. [e].
  However, when the diphthong *oe* appears in word-final position in Greek
  words, it is exceptionally pronounced [oe], e.g. *adelphoe* [adélfoe] 'broth-
  ers'. However, if the vowels of *ae* and *oe* are simply juxtaposed and
  actually belong to two distinct syllables, they are not pronounced as a
  monophthong. In this case, the second vowel is marked with a diaeresis,
  e.g. *aër* [á:e:r] 'air', *coërceō* [koértʃeo:] 'to shut up'.
- The voiceless dental stop [t] is pronounced as the corresponding affricate
  sound, i.e. [ts], when it appears before unstressed *i* and is not preceded by
  another *t* or by *s* or *x*, e.g. *grātia* is pronounced [grá:tsia], similarly to the
  Italian corresponding form *grazia* 'grace', as opposed to *tōtius* 'of whole',
  which is pronounced [to:tí:us], as *t* precedes a stressed vowel. Similarly,
  in words such as *Cottius* 'Cottius', *vestiō* 'to dress', *mixtiō* 'admixture', the

pronunciation of *t* is not altered as it is preceded by another *t*, by *s*, and by *x*, respectively. The same is true also for some words of Greek origin, such as *tiāra* 'tiara'.

- The velar stops *c* and *g* remain velar [k] and [g] when they precede the vowels *a*, *o*, and *u*, e.g. *columna* [kolúmna] 'column', but they become palato-alveolar affricates [ʧ] and [ʤ] before the vowels *e* and *i*, e.g. *Cicerō* [ʧíʧero:] and *Gigās* [ʤíga:s].
- The sequence *ph* is pronounced as the labiodental voiceless fricative [f], just as in Modern English, e.g. *philosophus* [filósofus] 'philosopher'.
- *h* is never pronounced.
- *s* is pronounced according to the use of standard northern Italian, where it is voiced [z] in intervocalic position, e.g. *rosa* [roza] 'rose'.
- *v* is rendered as the labiodental voiced fricative [v], as in Italian *vino* 'wine' or English *very*.

Note that the classical pronunciation tries, in a way, to be closer to the original value of the Latin phonemes. The humanistic pronunciation, however, is the result of a later evolution of Latin, which introduced many innovations, such as the monophthongization of the diphthongs, the fricativization of the stops in some contexts, the lack of aspiration, the voicing of the sibilant in some contexts, and the fricativization of the semivowel.

5

Prosody and metrics

5.1 The syllable

From a hierarchical point of view, the syllable is the phonological unit which immediately includes the phoneme, i.e. it is the set of one or more phonemes. Although it is difficult to give a formal definition of a syllable, the concept is rather intuitive. A syllable is the *minimal phonetic unit which can be pronounced on its own*. Note that not all phonemes can be pronounced in isolation: by 'pronounced' here we mean the possibility of producing a (monosyllabic) word, not a pure sound. In English, for example, some vowels can be pronounced in isolation and constitute a word, e.g. the indefinite article *a*, but stop consonants are rarely pronounced on their own and cannot constitute a word, e.g. *t*.

The vowel, therefore, is the *nucleus* of the syllable. However, a simple vowel is usually not sufficient to create a syllable. The prototypical syllable, i.e. the first one employed in children's babbling, is formed by a consonant followed by a vowel (CV), e.g. *da-da* 'dad'. A syllable can also be formed by a vowel followed by a consonant (VC, e.g. *at*), or by the sequence consonant—vowel—consonant (CVC, e.g. *top*).

It is interesting to note that a syllable is not a linear sequence of phonemes, but has its own internal structure. In particular, it is divided into three parts, which in technical terms are called the *onset*, the *nucleus*, and the *coda*. The nucleus and the coda form a sub-set which is called *rhyme* (or *rime*). The structure is illustrated in (1) with the Latin word *cum* 'with':

(1)

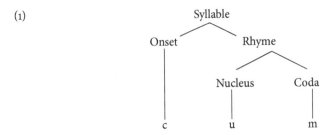

Some observations can be made about the structure in (1). First of all, a syllable always requires a nucleus. As we have already seen, the nucleus is usually a vowel, and if the vowel is long, we assume that the syllable has a bimoraic nucleus (cf. the discussion in Section 5.6). However, in some West Slavic languages, the nucleus can also be formed by a set of special consonants, called *sonorants* (*l*, *r*, *m*, *n*). An example is the name of the Czech city of *Br-no*, where the sonorant /r/ constitutes the nucleus of the first syllable. In English too, /m/, /n/, /l/, and /r/ can be the syllabic nucleus in an unstressed syllable following another consonant, especially /t/, /d/, /s/, or /z/, e.g. *prism*, where the sonorant /m/ constitutes the nucleus of the second syllable. Another well-known case of syllabic consonants is represented by the Tashlhiyt dialect of Berber, where the nucleus can consist of any consonant, including obstruents, such as stops and fricatives, e.g. *tqs.sf* 'it shrunk'. By the same token, the onset and the coda are usually constituted by consonants, but sometimes the onset can be formed by a semivowel and the coda by the second element of a diphthong, as in the Latin interjection *vae!* 'woe'.

Secondly, the onset and the coda can be formed by one or more consonants. This means that we can add CCV, CCVC, VCC, CVCC, and so on, to the types of syllables already mentioned (V, CV, VC, CVC).

5.2 Syllable division

The division of the word into syllables is part of that set of elementary operations which constitute the speaker's linguistic intuition. Although the principles of syllabification are largely universal, it is worth reviewing how they apply to Latin. The first thing to note is that syllabification in Latin is more straightforward than in English. While in English written syllable division is based mostly on etymological rather than phonetic principles, due to the weak correspondence between phonemes and graphemes, in Latin it follows a number of simple rules, which are discussed here.

The nucleus of the syllable is the vowel, which means that typically in a word there are *as many syllables as vowels*, e.g. the word *pānis* has two vowels and therefore two syllables: *p* is the onset of the first syllable, whose nucleus is *ā*, while *s* is the coda of the second syllable, whose nucleus is *i*. But what about *n*? Is it the coda of the first syllable or the onset of the second one?

This problem is solved by a fundamental principle which governs syllabification, i.e. the *Maximal Onset Principle*. If a phoneme, like the *n* in *pānis*, can be either the coda of the preceding syllable or the onset of the following one, it must be assigned to the onset. The correct syllabification is then *pā-nis*. Thus, the preferred syllabic structure in Latin, as in most languages, is CV, which means that most syllables begin with a consonant, e.g. *mī-les* 'soldier'.

If two or more consonants are placed between the two vocalic nuclei, the extent of the maximal onset will depend on the specific language. In Latin, it is sufficient to check whether it is ever attested in word-initial position. For example, in a word such as *summus* 'highest', it is not possible to put both consonants in the onset of the second syllable, since a syllable with an onset formed by two occurrences of the same consonant (*mm-*) is not admitted in Latin. The division therefore must be *sum-mus*. This means that double consonants are always syllabified separately, e.g. *mit-tō* 'to send'.

In contrast, in *patrem* 'father' (accusative), both consonants can be put in the onset of the second syllable, since a *tr-* onset is attested in word-initial position, e.g. *tractō* 'to handle', *tribus* 'tribe'. The division, therefore, should be *pa-trem*. This is in fact the invariable rule for Plautus and the most common procedure of syllabification in Classical Latin. Splitting only occurs under Greek influence and was first attested in Ennius' *Annales*. In Classical Latin poetry too the sequence '*mūta cum liquidā*', as Latin grammarians call it (today we would rather say 'stop plus liquid'), is exceptionally divided between the two syllables, e.g. *pat-rem*.

Another issue worth mentioning is the so-called 'impure *s*', i.e. an *s* followed by another consonant. This type of onset is not admitted in all languages. In Spanish, for example, the nexus *s*+stop can never occur in word-initial position, as shown by the fact that in Spanish words derived from Latin an initial vowel must be added, e.g. *estudio* 'study', whose correct syllabification is *es-tudio*. In Latin, the nexus *s*+stop can be found in word-initial position (*studium* 'zeal'), but not in a word-internal position (*magis-ter* '(school)mas-ter'). Therefore, when we divide a Latin word with an impure *s* into syllables, we must follow the Spanish rule (*magis-trum* 'accusative of *magister*') and not the Italian one (*mae-stro* 'teacher').

Issues such as the '*mūta cum liquidā*' and the 'impure *s*' show that the universal principles of syllabification are applied in accordance with parameters which may vary from one language to another, or even within the very same language, according to the stylistic register, e.g. prose or poetry. In conclusion, division into syllables is not a trivial task, as is also shown by the fact that sometimes different syllabifications are possible for the very same word.

5.3 Syllable quantity

The structure of the rhyme constitutes the basis for a fundamental concept in Latin phonology, i.e. the distinction between *open* and *closed syllables*.

A closed syllable has a rhyme with a coda, whereas the rhyme of an open syllable ends without a coda. This definition is more precise than the traditional one, i.e. an open syllable ends in a vowel, a closed syllable ends in a consonant. The reason is that there are also syllables ending in a diphthong, which is neither a proper vowel nor a proper consonant. However, if we take into account that the second element of a Latin diphthong is a coda, the problem is solved: syllables ending in a diphthong have a coda and are therefore closed.

The distinction between open and closed syllables is useful in order to understand a concept which is fundamental in Latin phonology, i.e. syllabic quantity. We have already considered vowel quantity and we know that Latin vowels are intrinsically long or short, e.g. /ĭ/ is short, /ī/ is long, and the same holds for /ŭ/, /ū/, /ĕ/, /ē/, /ŏ/, /ō/, /ă/, /ā/.

As we shall see in Section 5.6, in Latin it is important to recognize not only vowel quantity, but also syllable quantity, in order to place the accent in the correct position.

Establishing syllable quantity is pretty straightforward, i.e. *a short syllable is an open syllable with a short vowel*. All other syllables are long.

5.4 Accentuation

Accent or *stress* (the two terms will be used interchangeably) is a *suprasegmental* phenomenon, i.e. it belongs to the level of organization above the single segments which make up a syllable. In other words, accent is a phenomenon whose domain is the entire syllable, and not only the stressed vowel. First of all, we shall again distinguish between the phonological and the phonetic level.

From a phonological point of view, the concept of accent is pretty straightforward: accent has a *culminative* function, i.e. it 'emphasizes' one specific syllable.

From a phonetic point of view, however, accent is a more complex phenomenon, as it involves the combination of different physical parameters, such as length, frequency, and loudness. A stressed vowel tends to be universally longer than an unstressed one. Moreover, a stressed vowel tends to have a higher frequency, i.e. it is a higher-pitched sound. Finally, a stressed vowel tends to have a higher intensity, i.e. it is a louder sound. These phonetic features always co-occur within accent in all languages, albeit in different proportions, but they have a different phonological value.

In some languages the phonological value is associated with loudness, while in others it is associated with frequency. Consequently, we can distinguish languages with a stress accent (such as Italian or English) and languages with a pitch or musical accent (such as Ancient Greek and Japanese). Latin is a case in point in showing that the two typologies are not totally unrelated, but that there may be a change from one type to the other in the course of language evolution. Classical writers used to describe Latin as a language with a pitch accent. However, all Romance languages witness the fact that in Late Latin loudness began to prevail over pitch. As a matter of fact, two opposite hypothesis developed around this topic, supported by the French and German schools, respectively. The former argues in favour of a pitch stress in classical times, while the latter argues that Latin has always had a stress accent (according to this latter hypothesis, classical grammarians have allegedly made a mistake in describing their accent, because of a misapplication of the original Greek terminology).

5.5 Contrastive and predictable stress

Another fundamental issue arises in the distinction between different language typologies, that is the opposition between contrastive and predictable stress. In some languages, stress has a contrastive value, as its different placement is associated with different meanings. In Italian, for example, stress distinguishes the meaning of words such as *áncora* 'anchor' and *ancóra* 'still/again', or *cápitano* '(they) happen', *capitáno* 'captain' and *capitanò* '(he) headed'. English also has contrastive stress, as shown by minimal pairs such as *cónvert* (noun) and *convért* (verb).

There are languages, however, in which stress is not contrastive, but rather *predictable*. In Hungarian, for example, stress always falls on the first syllable, in French it always falls on the last syllable, and in Polish on the penultimate. When stress is predictable, it does not fulfil a distinctive function, but it helps to mark word boundaries, as it always falls on a precise position within the word. Latin is particularly interesting in this respect, in that it shows that predictable stress does not necessarily occupy a fixed position.

5.6 The Latin accent rule

The placement of the Latin accent is based on a phonetic principle which applies to other languages as well, such as Classical Arabic, by virtue of which there exists a necessary relationship between stress and syllabic quantity. This principle works as follows: *a short syllable is not suitable to bear a stress*. The reason for this is quite straightforward. Cross-linguistically, a stressed vowel tends to be longer than an unstressed one. Therefore, a stressed short syllable runs the risk of becoming long, affecting the distinction between long and short, which is fundamental for the quantitative system of Latin phonology.

A first consequence of this principle is that a monosyllabic word must consist of a long syllable in order to bear its own stress, i.e. it should be a closed syllable or an open syllable with a long vowel, e.g. *dăt* 'he/she/it gives', *rē* 'thing' (ablative). Short monosyllables are clitics instead, which do not bear an autonomous accent by definition (cf. Section 5.7), e.g. *-quĕ* 'and'.

In disyllabic words the stress always falls on the first syllable. This fact highlights another important feature of Latin phonology, that is the so-called 'trochaic rhythm', i.e. in a sequence of two syllables, the prominence is on the first one.

As for polysyllables, the fundamental rule governing the placement of the accent is called the 'Penultimate Law'. The law says that *the accent falls on the penultimate syllable if this is long, otherwise on the antepenultimate*. Note that this rule makes reference to syllable quantity, not to vowel quantity. For example, a word like *rēgīna* 'queen' is stressed *regína*, because the penultimate syllable is long. In a parallel fashion, a word such as *sepŭltus* 'buried' is also stressed *sepúltus*, because the penultimate vowel (*-ŭ-*) is short, but the syllable itself (*-pŭl-*) is long.

If, however, the penultimate syllable is short, i.e. if it is an open syllable with a short vowel, it is not suitable to bear the stress. For this reason, the stress moves to the preceding syllable, i.e. the antepenultimate, e.g. *facĕre* 'to do' is stressed *fácere*.

One could argue that a short antepenultimate syllable is not suitable to bear the stress either. This is indeed the case in some Uralic languages, such as Cheremis or the Mari language, where the stress keeps moving backwards until it finds a long syllable or the beginning of the word. However, the Latin accent is not allowed to move backwards beyond the antepenultimate syllable. Traditional grammars do not provide any explanation for this fact, but simply invoke a rule called the 'Trisyllabic Law', which states that the accent can fall on any of the last three syllables only.

Modern phonological theories have suggested a more explanatory account, which is based on the notion of *mora*. A short syllable comprises one *mora* [μ], while a long syllable or the combination of two short syllables comprise two *morae* [$\mu\mu$]. Furthermore, according to Latin 'trochaic rhytm', a bimoraic structure [$\mu\mu$] bears the accent on the first *mora* and is called a 'moraic trochee'.

From this perspective, it is possible to express the fundamental rule for the placement of Latin accent in an unitary way, i.e. *the accent falls on the moraic trochee before the final syllable*. This rule can be easily tested by parsing the four possible combinations of long and short syllables that can occur before the final syllable, as shown by examples (2a—d):

(2) a. ‾ ‾ <x>   laudāre 'to praise'
     b. ˘ ‾ <x>   favilla 'ash'
     c. ˘ ˘ <x>   facere 'to do'
     d. ‾ ˘ <x>   auferō 'to carry away'

In all these words, the final syllable is considered to be 'extrametrical' and is parsed as an *elementum indifferens* <x>, which means that it is always excluded from the metrical count, regardless of its quantity.

In examples (2a) and (2b), the final syllable is preceded by a long syllable. As mentioned above, a long syllable consists of two *morae* [μμ] and is therefore a perfect moraic trochee. Accordingly, the accent falls on the long syllable, i.e. *laudǎre* and *favílla*.

In example (2c), the last syllable is preceded by two short syllables. The combination of these two syllables also forms a perfect moraic trochee [μμ], so the accent falls on the first of the two short syllables, i.e. *fácere*.

In example (2d), the last syllable is preceded by a single short syllable, which cannot bear the accent, and a long syllable, which can form a moraic trochee and therefore bears the accent. Note that, if the accent falls on a diphthong, the prominent *mora* is always the first one, i.e. *áuferō*, according to the moraic structure of the trochee.

To sum up, the rule of the moraic trochee states that accent in Latin has a fixed position, which is not based on the number of syllables, but rather on their quantitative structure. As we shall see in Section 5.8, quantitative metrics is a distinctive feature of Latin poetry too.

The validity of a metrical approach to Latin accent is also supported by an additional piece of evidence. In the so-called 'iambic words', i.e. disyllabic words formed by a short syllable followed by a long syllable, the last syllable tends to shorten, as in (3):

(3) a. ămā>ămă 'love' (imperative)
     b. mălē>mălĕ 'badly'

In classical philology, this phenomenon is known as 'Iambic Shortening' or 'Brevis Brevians'. Interestingly, the final syllable does not undergo shortening if it is preceded by a long syllable, e.g. *mandā* 'commit'. This shows that this phenomenon is not a case of mere shortening in final position, but is rather conditioned by the metrical shape of the word.

Why should iambic words undergo shortening? Even if we are dealing with a complex phenomenon, which is sensitive to many linguistic and stylistic factors, a quite straightforward answer can be offered, if we accept the hypothesis that the Latin accentual system was based on the moraic trochee. Indeed, it would be very difficult for an iambic word to create a moraic trochee, and consequently the word would run the risk of not getting the right stress. In other words, if we consider the last syllable of an iambic word to be extrametrical, we are left with a single short syllable, which cannot bear any stress. Even if we suspend extrametricality, the problem remains, as we would obtain a trimoraic sequence with final prominence, contrary to a general trend of Latin, where stress usually avoids the final syllable. Therefore, iambic shortening may be considered a mechanism which is able to reduce the irregular shape of an iambic word into a regular moraic trochee, formed by a sequence of two short syllables with the accent on the first one.

5.7 Clitics

The vast majority of languages have words with a reduced phonetic body (usually monosyllabic), which do not bear an autonomous stress but rather depend upon the preceding or following word. These elements are called 'clitics', from the Greek word *klíno*, meaning 'to lean on'. Grammars usually draw a further distinction between 'enclitic' elements, i.e. those which depend on the preceding word, and 'proclitic' elements, i.e. those which depend on the following one. In a language such as Italian, clitics are very common, e.g. articles are proclitic elements (*la sedia* 'the chair'), while some personal pronouns are enclitic elements (*chieder-ti* 'ask-(to)-you'). An example of a clitic in English is the indefinite article *a* when it occurs in an unstressed context, e.g. *I need a new càr*.

In so far as the phonology of Latin is concerned, enclitics are the most interesting. The most common ones are *-que* 'and', *-ne* 'whether', *-ve* 'or'. When they get attached to a word, a peculiar phenomenon takes place, called 'Enclitic accent', i.e. when a clitic is attached to a word, the word loses its original accent and the accent of the whole word+clitic set is placed on the syllable preceding the enclitic one. The word *rēgīna* 'queen', for example, bears its stress on the penultimate syllable because that syllable is long. However, if we add an enclitic to it, such as *-que*, the stress will fall on the syllable preceding the enclitic syllable, i.e. *rēgīnáque*. Note that the Enclitic accent rule prevails over the Penultimate Law, as shown by the fact that the penultimate syllable is short but still bears the stress.

One exception to the Enclitic accent rule is represented by the enclitic forms *-dem* and *-nam*, which count as part of the word they get attached to. Consequently, in these cases the Penultimate Law prevails on the Enclitic accent rule, e.g. *índĭdem* 'from the same place', *útĭnam* 'if only'.

In fact, there may be some cases in which the presence of enclisis is unclear: ancient grammarians used to make a distinction between an enclitic structure such as *ităque* 'and so', where the adverb *ita* '*so*' is overtly combined with the conjunction *-que* 'and', and the corresponding structure which does not exhibit enclisis, *ítăque* 'therefore', where the conjunction is no longer overtly visible and the whole structure behaves as a single adverb. Due to the lack of native speakers, it is now almost impossible for us to distinguish such cases. For this reason, we will posit that if an adverb is listed in the vocabulary attached to the *-que,* then it counts as a simple word, e.g. *dénĭque* 'finally'; in contrast, if the *-que* form is not listed in the vocabulary, then that counts as enclisis, e.g. *sinéque* 'and without' is an example of enclisis because only *sine* 'without' appears in the dictionary.

5.8 Metrics

The unit which is immediately higher than the syllable is the foot. In its simplest form, the foot is composed by the union of two syllables:

(4)

                              Foot

          Syllable   Syllable

'Metrics' is the study of the structure of verse, that is a sequence of feet. Generally speaking, verse marks the difference between prose and poetry. As the linguist Roman Jakobson has stated, the basic principle of poetry is the 'parallelism', i.e. each verse is formally equal to all the other verses of the same type. A piece of poetry is usually made up of a number of parallel verses. Such a parallelism can be achieved cross-linguistically in different ways. There are syllable-counting verses, e.g. in Japanese, and tone-regulating verses, e.g. in Chinese. As for European poetry, two main types of versification are attested, i.e. accentual and quantitative verse.

In accentual-based verse systems, the recurring pattern which creates the parallelism is given by the occurrence of a given number of syllables and by stress placement. A very clear example of an accentual verse is the iambic pentameter, traditionally employed in English poetry. This type of verse consists of ten syllables, but its most salient feature is the occurrence of five iambic feet. An iambic foot consists of two syllables, where the first one occurs in the weak position and the second one in the strong position:

(5)   Iambic foot

          Weak syllable   Strong syllable

In English, the strong position is associated with the accent. In (6), for example, there are five accents which fall on the strong syllables of the five iambic feet:

(6)   *of hand, of foot, of lip, of eye, of brow* (Shakespeare)
            1   2   3   4   5

In a similar fashion, the Italian hendecasyllable verse consists of eleven syllables, where one accent obligatorily falls on the tenth syllable, and two other accents may occupy different positions, giving rise to iambic feet. In the eleven-syllable line in (7), for example, accents fall on the second, fourth, sixth, eighth, and tenth syllables:

(7)   *amòr e 'l còr gentìl son(o)ùna còsa* (Dante)
          1 2   3   4   5 6 7   8 9 10 11
       'Love and the gentle heart are one thing'

Also note in (7) an occurrence of the so-called 'synaloepha' (from the Greek 'fusion'), that is the fusion of the ending vowel of a word with the initial vowel of the following one, e.g. *sono una* becomes *son(o)una* by synaloepha.

In quantitative-based verse systems, in contrast, which are typical of Greek and Latin poetry, the recurring verse pattern is given by the regular sequence of long and short syllables. As a consequence, the iambic foot consists of a short syllable followed by a long one:

(8)   Iambic foot

          Short syllable   Long syllable

In quantitative-based verse systems the position of the accent is irrelevant and the number of the syllables may vary, given that it is often possible to replace a long syllable with two short ones and vice versa.

Greek grammarians used to identify another hierarchically higher unit, i.e. the 'metron'. An iambic metron, for example, consists of two iambic feet, while a trochaic metron consists of two trochaic feet:

(9)   a. iambic metron: ◡ — ◡ —

       b. trochaic metron: — ◡ — ◡

The Romans, in contrast, used to name the verse after the number of feet rather than of metra. For this reason, the main type of verse in ancient drama is called 'iambic trimeter' in Greece but 'iambic senarius' in Rome (note that three iambic metra correspond to six iambic feet). The structure of the trimeter differs slightly from the senarius, as in the Greek verse the feet are perceived as if they were grouped into pairs, while in the Latin version each foot stands on its own.

5.9 Hexameter and pentameter

The most important verse in classical poetry is the dactylic hexameter. As the Greek name itself suggests, a hexameter consists of six (*hex*) dactylic metra. In this case, the Greek 'metron' coincides with the Roman 'foot'. A dactylic metron (or foot) is a set consisting of one long syllable and two short syllables. In example (10), taken from Virgil's *Aeneid*, we have conventionally marked the six dactyls by placing an accent (the so-called *ictus*) on long syllables at the beginning of each foot (note that this traditional procedure has no scientific value, but is simply an attempt to translate the ancient quantitative verse into a modern accentual verse):

(10)   1   2   3   4   5   6
     quádrupedánte putrém sonitú quatit úngula cámpum (Verg. *Aen.* 8, 594)
     – ᴗᴗ – ᴗ ᴗ – ᴗᴗ – ᴗᴗ – ᴗᴗ – ᴗ

    'With a four-footed beat, the hoof shakes the crumbling ground'

Note that the last foot of the hexameter (the sixth one) is not a dactyl but rather a trochee. For this reason, the hexameter is said to be a 'catalectic' verse, precisely because in the structure of the last foot the last syllable is missing.

Example (10) contains five 'pure' dactylic feet, since each of them consists of one long syllable and two short ones. According to the above-mentioned principle, i.e. a long syllable may replace two short ones, each dactylic metron of the hexameter can be realized either by a pure dactyl, i.e. one long syllable and two short ones, or by a 'spondee', i.e. two long syllables. The verse in (11) is an example of a hexameter consisting entirely of spondees ('holospondaic'):

(11)   1   2   3   4   5   6
     ólli réspondít rex Álbái longái (Enn. *Ann.* 31 Sk.)
     – – – – – – – – – – – –

    'The king of Alba Longa answered him'

Both holodactylic and holospondaic verses are quite exceptional and highly expressive. In example (10), the fast rhythm of the holodactylic verse is employed to describe a ride, while in example (11) the slow rhythm of the holospondaic verse is exploited for the description of a king's solemn answer. On the whole, however, the harmony of the line is usually provided by a clever alternation between dactyls and spondees. As a consequence, the hexameter will usually have the structure shown in (12):

(12)   1 _   2 _   3 _   4 _   5   6 _
       ‒∪∪ ‒∪∪ ‒∪∪ ‒∪∪ ‒∪∪ ‒ ∪

Note also that the replacement of two short syllables with a long one is allowed
in every foot but the penultimate, i.e. the fifth, which is almost obligatorily a
dactyl. However, we know that the last foot, i.e. the sixth, is 'catalectic', that is
it lacks the last element, the second short element of the dactyl. Moreover, the
last syllable of the hexameter can be either short or long, in accordance with
the general principle which states that all syllables in a verse-final position are
equal.

One crucial issue regarding the internal structure of the hexameter has to do
with the relationship between the metrical foot and the word which realizes it.
It may be the case that the beginning and the end of the word coincide with the
foot or, in contrast, that the foot is 'cut' by the last part of the word. For
example:

(13)   *Tītyre, tú| patuláe |recubáns | sub tégmine fắgī* (Verg. ecl.1, 1)
       ‒∪∪ ‒ ∪∪‒ ∪∪‒   ‒ ‒ ∪∪‒‒

       'Tityrus, you, reclining beneath the cover of a broad beech-tree'

In the second (*tū| patu*), third (*lae| recu*), and fourth (*bans| sub*) feet, the
word ending cuts the foot. This cut is called *caesura*, lit. 'cutting'. In contrast,
in the first (*Tītyre*), fifth (*tegmine*), and sixth (*fāgī*) feet there is no caesura,
since the end of the word coincides with the end of the foot.

In each verse there may be more than one caesura, as in example (13), but
only one is particularly salient, i.e. the so-called 'central caesura', which divides
the verse into two half-lines, each of which is called a 'hemistich'. There are
three possible types of central caesura in the hexameter. The first type is called
'masculine caesura' or 'semi-quinary', i.e. it occurs after the fifth half-foot, as
shown in example (13):

(14)   1 2 3 4 5
       Tītyre, tú patuláe | recubáns sub tégmine fắgī
       ‒ ∪∪ ‒ ∪∪ ‒

The second type of caesura is called 'feminine caesura' or 'after the third
trochee', i.e. it breaks the fifth half-foot in the double short element, creating a
trochee, as shown in example (15):

(15)   *témpora cúnctantíque| natántia lúmina sólvit* (Verg. Aen. 5, 856)
       ‒ ∪∪ ‒ ‒ ‒ ∪

       '(he strikes) his temples and closes his wavering eyes while he tries to resist'

Finally, the third type is called 'hephthemimeral caesura' or 'semi-septenary',
i.e. after the seventh half-foot, as in example (16):

(16)   *Éumenidés quibus ánguīnō | redimíta capíllō* (Catull. *carm.* 64, 193)
         – ᴗᴗ – ᴗ ᴗ – ᴗ ᴗ –

'You, Eumenides, whose (forehead) is crowned with snaky hair'

The semi-septenary caesura is often accompanied by the semi-tercet, i.e. a caesura after the third half foot, as in *-des | quibus* in example (16).

The opposite phenomenon of the caesura is the 'diaeresis', which takes place when the end of the foot coincides with the end of the word. In each line there may be more than one diaeresis, but only one is particularly relevant, the so-called 'bucolic diaeresis', which was typical of bucolic poets and divides the last two feet, i.e. the fifth and the sixth, from the remainder of the line, as shown in example (17):

(17)   *Sí canimús silvás, silváe sint | cónsule dígnae* (Virg. *ecl.* 4, 3)
         – ᴗ ᴗ – – – – – –   – ᴗ ᴗ – –

'If we sing about woods, let them be woods worthy of a consul'

As already mentioned, the fifth foot is obligatorily a pure dactyl, so the bucolic diaeresis occurs at the end of a word before the fifth foot, which highlights the final part of the verse, consisting of a dactyl and a spondee or a trochee, called the 'clausula' of the verse (cf. *cōnsule dignae* in example (17)).

Finally, there is another important type of verse, which is strictly linked to the hexameter, called 'pentameter'. The poet Ovid gave a funny explanation of the origin of this verse, which he said was derived from the hexameter by subtracting one foot (Ov. *am.* 1, 1, 3–4):

(18)   a.   *Pár erat ínferiór versús: rīsísse Cupídō*   (hexameter)
               – ᴗ ᴗ – ᴗ ᴗ – – –   – – ᴗ ᴗ – –

        b.   *dīcitur átqu(e) ūnúm súrripuísse pedém*   (pentameter)
               – ᴗ ᴗ –   – –   – ᴗ ᴗ – ᴗ ᴗ –

               'The following line was equal to the previous one:
               it is said that Cupid laughed and stole away one foot'

With these two lines, Ovid is telling us everything we need to know about the pentameter. First of all, the pentameter is derived from the hexameter by catalexis of the third and sixth half-foot. Its scheme is as follows (note the central diaeresis):

(19) $\overset{1}{-}\underset{\smile}{\smile}\overset{2}{-}\underset{\smile}{\smile}\overset{3}{-} \quad \overset{4}{-}\smile\smile\overset{5}{-}\smile\smile\overset{6}{\smile}$

Secondly, the pentameter alternates the hexameter, forming a two-line couplet. The sequence of a hexameter followed by a pentameter is called an 'elegiac couplet'. While the hexameter is the typical verse of epic poetry, the elegiac couplet is typical of elegiac poetry.

Part II

Morphology

6

Words, roots, and stems

6.1 What is a word?

A word is a basic linguistic unit, whose existence is intuitively clear both to ancient and to modern speakers (e.g. Varro, *De lingua Latina* X 77: *verbum dico orationis partem quae sit indivisa et minima* 'I define the word as the smallest indivisible part of the discourse'). For this reason, we will not attempt to further define this concept, but will rather focus on the description of its properties.

Words express some semantic meaning: through words, speakers give expression to their thoughts. Words also have syntactic properties: by combining with each other, they form bigger units which constitute the object of study of syntax. From a morphological point of view, however, one of the most salient properties of words is their *internal structure*. Words consist of a number of sub-units. By combining these sub-units, in accordance with a number of rules, it is possible to create and understand new words. Morphology may be seen as a system which comprises basic units and combinatorial rules. The first task, therefore, is the identification of the basic units of this system.

6.2 Basic units

As a first approximation, we can postulate that the basic units of morphology are the words listed in the dictionary. This is, however, a rather unsatisfactory definition. There are a number of reasons why words in a mental lexicon differ from words in a dictionary, e.g. they are not alphabetically ordered, but are rather organized into complex neural nets of sounds and meanings, and they belong to an open class, i.e. it is always possible to create new words or forget obsolete ones. Latin raises one additional issue, which plays a crucial role in the theory of morphology. Within poorly inflected languages, such as English, the basic morphological units *largely* coincide with simple words. This is due to the fact that in such languages words are typically inflected by adding some elements to basic units, which are clearly simple words, e.g. given the noun *boy* or the verb *to want*, the basic units for inflection are the noun *boy-* and the verb *want-*, respectively.

On the other hand, within richly inflected languages, such as Latin or Italian, cases in which a simple inflection is added to a base form coinciding with a simple word are quite rare. For example, if we take a noun such as Lat. *cōnsul* 'consul', this is inflected in the following way: nom. *cōnsul*, gen. *cōnsul-is*, dat. *cōnsul-ī*, acc. *cōnsul-em*, etc. In this special case, therefore, the base form is the noun *cōnsul-*, which happens to coincide with the dictionary entry, i.e. nominative singular. However, the mechanism of inflection for Latin nouns is usually far more complex. Most of the time, the base form which underlies the paradigm does not emerge on surface strings on its own, but it is a more abstract entity, which belongs only to the level of linguistic analysis. If we take, for example, the noun *crux* 'cross', its declension is as follows: nom. *crux*, gen. *cruc-is*, dat. *cruc-ī*, acc. *cruc-em*, etc. The abstract form underlying this paradigm is **cruc-*, as shown by the linguistic analysis that some ancient grammarians have already proposed (Varro, *De lingua Latina* IX 44). The problem is that such an abstract form never emerges in the language, and therefore is not attested in Latin dictionaries. The natural question is: is such a form only a mere theoretical postulation or does it correspond to some entity in the mental lexicon?

6.3 Dictionary entries

The usefulness of morphological abstraction could be questioned by the common practice of employing a specific *dictionary entry* to identify words, as used both by ancient grammarians and by modern vocabularies, which is the nominative singular for nouns, e.g. *lupus* 'wolf', the nominative singular masculine for adjectives, e.g. *altus* 'tall', and the first person singular of the present indicative for verbs, e.g. *laudō* 'to praise'.

Ancient grammarians were already aware of the fact that some issues arise with this practice, i.e. it is not sufficient to know the nominative singular form of a noun or the first person singular of the present indicative of a verb to compute its complete paradigm. As correctly pointed out by Varro (*De lingua Latina* IX 91), it is not possible to discern the structural difference between two words such as *lupus* 'wolf' and *lepus* 'hare' simply on the basis of the nominative form, since they both have an *-us* nominative ending, but the underlying inflectional paradigms are different, i.e. the genitive of the former is *lupī*, and that of the latter is *leporis*. The same reasoning applies to verbs, i.e. the first person singular of the present indicative is not sufficient to decipher the morphological difference between *volō* meaning 'to want' and *volō* meaning 'to fly'. For this reason, Latin dictionaries are forced to add the genitive of nouns, e.g. *lupus, -ī* vs. *lepus, -oris* and the infinitive of verbs, e.g. *volō, velle* vs. *volō, -āre.*

However, this is a mere practical device, which is not telling us anything about the nature of the base units of morphology. For reasons of economy, it is inadequate to postulate *two* base forms, given that one abstract form is sufficient, as will be argued below.

6.4 Roots

In Section 6.3, we reached the conclusion that dictionary entries cannot be considered basic morphological units. The reason is that such entries are too 'concrete' to refer to the abstract word itself. In particular, the presence of inflectional endings obscures the features of the underlying abstract form.

An alternative may be represented by the use of 'roots', e.g. *lup-* or *vol-*. Roots are important linguistic units, both for the acquisition of single languages and for comparative analysis. In the present discussion, we define 'root' as the common unit shared by different words belonging to the same family and expressing the most general meaning. For example, the Latin words *gen-us* 'birth', *gen-erāre* 'to beget', *in-gen-ium* 'innate quality', and *gen-itor* 'parent' share the same root *gen-*, and the speaker knows that they are all semantically related. Note also that the very same roots *lup-* and *vol-*, cf. Lat. *lupus* and *volō*, are also exhibited by the Italian words *lupo* 'wolf' and *volere* 'to want'. Tracing the evolution of the same original Indo-European roots into different languages is one of the tasks of historical linguistics.

Nevertheless, roots do not represent a satisfying solution to our problem, i.e. the identification of the basic units of morphology, either. While vocabulary entries are too 'concrete' to identify the structure of a word, roots are too 'abstract'. In particular, it is not possible to infer the morphological behaviour of a word from its root. As a matter of fact, the same root can underlie verbs, nouns, and adjectives, e.g. **duc-* is the root of both the noun *dux* 'leader' and the verb *dūcō* 'to lead'; the root **cal-* is shared by the noun *calor* 'heat', the verb *caleō* 'to be warm', and the adjective *calidus* 'warm'. In other words, the underlying abstract concept of all the words sharing a root is the same, but its morphological expression, i.e. the lexical category (noun, adjective, verb), may vary.

The crucial point is that the inflectional paradigm of a word cannot be properly inferred from the features of its root, e.g. there is no reason why the root **laud-* (cf. the verb *laudō*) should be inflected *laud-ās* in the second person singular of the present indicative, with *-ā-* as thematic vowel and not *-ē-*, for example. For this reason, we are forced to conclude that the basic units of morphology are neither dictionary entries nor roots.

6.5 Stems

The solution to the problem is now pretty straightforward. First of all, it is necessary that the root is completed by a mark of its lexical category (noun, adjective, verb). In this way, we will be able to distinguish the nominal basic unit $[duc]_N$ from the verbal basic unit $[dūc]_V$. Secondly, it is necessary that the root is completed by a thematic vowel, if it has one, which allows us to predict the inflectional behaviour of the word. In this way, we will be able to distinguish the behaviour of the base unit $[lup\text{-}o]_N$, of *lupus*, whose thematic vowel is *-o-*, from the base unit $[lepos]_N$, of *lepus*, with no thematic vowel. For this reason, we will posit that the thematic vowel is intrinsically part of the inflectional base, along with the root. We will thus assume that the basic morphological unit is an abstract word which comprises the root and a thematic vowel. This kind of unit belongs to a specific lexical category but lacks any inflection. Following a long grammatical tradition, we will call this unit the 'stem'. Sometimes the stem can have a more complex internal structure, i.e. it may contain stem-formants other than zero and the thematic vowel. For example, the stem of *genus*, if compared with *lepus*, should be analysed as $[genos]_N$. But the root must in fact be *gen-*, as demonstrated above. Thus, in this case the stem also contains a stem-formant *-os-*.

In summary, the basic unit of Latin morphology is the stem, which is a more abstract form than a word, as it does not contain any inflectional endings, but at the same time it is more concrete than a root, as it contains not only a lexical meaning but also some grammatical information, i.e. the lexical category and the thematic vowel.

6.6 Properties of stems

A stem such as $[lupo]_N$ will be analysed as a morphological unit consisting of a lexical morpheme, i.e. the root *lup-*, expressing the general meaning of the word, and a grammatical morpheme, i.e. the thematic vowel *-o-*, expressing the fact that the word belongs to a specific lexical category (noun), and to a particular inflectional paradigm (second declension).

The grammatical morpheme is usually phonetically realized as a *thematic vowel*, e.g. in the above-mentioned example *-o-* in *lup-o-* 'wolf'; or *-a-* in *ros-a-* 'rose'; or *-i-* in *coll-i-* 'hill'. However, it may be the case that the morpheme is phonologically null, i.e. it is a 'zero morpheme'. For example, *crux* and *dux* are sometimes called 'root nouns' because their stems are directly derived from the roots *cruc-* and *duc-*, respectively, without a thematic vowel. Similarly, verbs such as *ferō, ferre* 'to carry', and *volō, velle* 'to want' are sometimes called 'athematic', as they lack any thematic vowel, but are formed directly from the root, as opposed to the most common 'thematic' verbs, which form their stems by combining the root with a thematic vowel. So, the third person singular of the present indicative is *fer-t* and *vul-t* for *ferō* and *volō*, respectively, but *reg-i-t* for a thematic verb like *regō, regere* 'to direct'.

Whether it is realized by a thematic vowel or not, the grammatical morpheme is always part of the abstract morphological structure of the stem, because it is the element which allows us to predict the inflectional behaviour of the word. This is because the way in which a word is inflected depends on the properties of the stem. On the basis of the properties of the stem, we can predict the inflectional patterns of a given word (cf. the traditional Latin declensions and conjugations), and no further information is required. If the stem of a noun contains the thematic vowel *-a-*, e.g. *ros-a-*, the noun belongs to the inflectional paradigm called 'first declension'. On the other hand, if the stem contains the thematic vowel *-o-*, e.g. *lup-o-*, the noun belongs to the inflectional paradigm called 'second declension'. At the same time, stems containing the thematic vowels *-u-* and *-ē-* belong to the fourth and fifth declensions, respectively, e.g. *fructu-* 'fruit' and *diē-* 'day'. The third declension is the most peculiar, as it includes different stems. Nouns belonging to the third declension behave differently, depending on whether their stem does not contain any thematic vowel, e.g. *duc-*, or contains the thematic vowel *-i-*, e.g. *coll-i-*. Nervertheless, these two types of noun are both grouped by the grammatical tradition within the same inflectional class, called the 'third declension'. It is precisely the interference between *i*-stems and stems with no thematic vowel which triggers the striking irregularity typical of the third declension, which is characterized by a great number of exceptions. In order to make the task easier, we will always start by considering the properties of the stem.

Similarly, different thematic vowels (*-ā-*, *-ē-*, *-e/i-*, *-ī-*) also determine the existence of four conjugations of 'regular' or 'thematic' verbs, e.g. *laudāre* 'to praise' (1st conjugation), *monēre* 'to warn' (2nd conjugation), *legere* 'to bring together', 'to read' (3rd conjugation), *audīre* 'to hear' (4th conjugation). The fact that the same thematic vowels can appear both in nominal and in verbal stems implies that the information contained in the stem must specify the lexical category (noun or verb) as well, in order to predict whether the inflection is going to be nominal or verbal.

6.7 Formal representation of stems

So far, we have seen that the stem contains all the relevant information which is necessary for the application of morphological rules. In particular, not only does the stem contain the information about the lexical category of a word, it also contains a given number of intrinsic features, defining relevant grammatical properties, such as the gender of nouns (masculine, feminine, or neuter) or the transitive or intransitive value of verbs.

Stems may be graphically represented by means of labelled brackets, where the lexical category is encoded, along with other relevant grammatical features one wishes to highlight. Some examples of verbal and nominal stems are shown in (1):

(1) a. [ambulā]$_{V[intransitive]}$ (stem of the verb *ambulō* 'to walk')
     b. [rapi]$_{V[transitive]}$ (stem of the verb *rapiō* 'to seize')
     c. [rosa]$_{N[feminine]}$ (stem of the noun *rosa* 'rose')
     d. [fīlio]$_{N[masculine]}$ (stem of the noun *fīlius* 'son')

The representation in (1a) indicates that [ambulā] is the stem of an intransitive verb, while [rapi] in (1b) is the stem of a transitive verb. Similarly, in (1c) and (1d) the gender of the nominal stems [rosa] and [fīlio] is indicated.

In conclusion, the crucial point of this discussion is that stems are 'abstract words', without any inflection, but still they bear something more than a bare root. The stem is not the minimal unit of semantics or syntax, but it is rather the minimal unit of morphology, as it represents the unit to which all inflectional, derivational, and compositional rules apply.

A note on methodology

From a methodological point of view, the notion of stem developed above is in sharp contrast with the way in which this word is used by some structural linguists, such as Guy Serbat in his excellent *Les structures du latin* (Paris, 1994). This latter use is largely applied in school grammars nowadays, where words such as *villam* 'farm' (accusative) and *laudāmus* 'we praise' are typically decomposed into *vill-/laud-*, which are considered stems, and *-am/-āmus*, which are considered inflections. However, this analysis is largely uneconomical, as it increases the number of inflectional endings. Take as an example the accusative singular. Under the standard approach, there are four different endings (*-am, -um, -em, -im*), rather than a single one (*-m*). Similarly, the standard approach postulates the existence of four different endings for the first person plural of the present indicative (*-āmus, -ēmus, -imus, -īmus*), rather than a single one (*-mus*).

The same issue arises with suffixes, cf. words such as *laudābilis, dēlēbilis, legibilis*, and *audībilis*. If we start our analysis from stems like *laud-, dēl-, leg-*, and *aud-*, we are forced to invoke four types of suffix, i.e. *-ābilis, -ēbilis, -ibilis, -ībilis*, where in fact the single suffix *-bilis*, added to the verbal stems *laudā-, dēlē-, legi-, audī-*, would be sufficient. In other words, in all the above-mentioned cases, an inadequate notion of stem without thematic vowel would force us to postulate four different forms to express the same meaning.

On the other hand, there are cases where the same inadequate notion of stem would force us to postulate two identical forms to express different meanings. An example is

given by two inflected words such as *suis* 'you sew' and *suis* 'of the pig': although these
two forms are superficially identical, they actually differ at a deeper level of analysis.
However, school grammars typically decompose both of them in the same manner, i.e.
su-is. Under such an analysis, the very same ending *-is* should be able to tell us that the
word is a verb in one case and a noun in the other. Similarly, the very same stem *su-*
should be able to convey the meaning of 'to sew' in one case and the meaning of 'pig' in
the other.

These examples all show that when speakers analyse speech in order to understand
the meaning of words, they must rely not only on mechanisms of segmentation, but
also on more abstract procedures. In order to obtain a correct analysis of a word, the
primary information required is the syntactic category. Nevertheless, in the above
examples, the syntactic label (verb or noun) cannot be inferred from the grammatical
morpheme *-is*, but must be conveyed by the stem. This in turn implies the need to
distinguish a nominal stem *sū-* from a verbal stem *sue-*, contra the traditional analysis,
which argues that lexical morphemes are not inherently specified as nouns or verbs,
given that such an indication is arguably contained in the endings.

A solution to this problem is provided by the approach proposed above. If we want
to analyse a word in a proper way, we need to go beyond the surface form, in order to
identify the abstract stem and then reconstruct all the morphological operations which
led to the surface form. Under such an approach, the analysis of the two underlying
forms of *suis* should be as follows:

(2)   a. $[[\text{sue}]_V + \text{s}]$
       b. $[[\text{sū}]_N + \text{is}]$

In (2a) and (2b), the two stems are distinct, i.e. in (2a) we observe the verbal stem
$[\text{sue}]_V$ of the verb *suō, suere* 'to sew', while in (2b) we observe the nominal stem $[\text{sū}]_N$
of the noun *sūs, suis* 'pig'. Note that the endings should also be kept distinct, i.e. on the
one hand we have a second person singular verbal ending *-s*, while on the other hand
we have a nominal genitive ending *-is*. Two adjustment rules, that we shall discuss
below (cf. Chapter 8), explain the change $[[\text{sue}]_V + \text{s}] \rightarrow$ *suis* (vowel weakening of *ĕ* → *ĭ*
in final closed syllable before *s*) and $[[\text{sū}]_N + \text{is}] \rightarrow$ *suis* (vowel shortening *ū* → *ŭ* before
another vowel).

Now, the point could be made that such an approach may help to understand the
way in which the two words are derived through inflectional rules, but it is of little help
when it comes to understanding how the listener derives a verbal (2a) or nominal (2b)
stem from the very same surface string. Such an observation highlights an important
aspect of grammar, which gives further support to our claim.

Firstly, note that if we take the word *suis* in isolation, both options are possible, and
it would be impossible for the speaker to decide. This is because the grammatical
meaning of words is expressed by the whole sentence, rather than by the single word.
A word acquires a meaning only if it is given a complete grammatical analysis, which
must be syntactic as well, and not only morphological. Therefore, it is the syntactic
context that tells us whether the word is a noun or a verb, according to its structural
position. Once the speaker has identified the category of the stem (either verb or

noun), *suis* will be morphologically decomposed as in (2a) or (2b), in accordance with the label on the brackets of each structure.

In sum, in order to understand the meaning of words, the speaker must be able to identify their deep abstract morphological structure. This, in turn, can be identified only within a syntactic sequence. Although such a procedure may sound too complex at the beginning, it is simply a formalization of the procedure employed by translators. A well-known rule of translation is that words cannot be translated on their own, as if they were in isolation. This is the reason why the best dictionaries are those which accompany each possible meaning of a word by an exhaustive range of examples and contexts where that particular meaning can occur. In conclusion, the vast majority of words taken in isolation have a number of potentially different meanings, and in some cases (such as *suis*) a number of potentially different morphological structures as well. Only within a specific context of occurrence it is possible to determine the exact morphological and semantic interpretation of words.

7

Parts of speech

7.1 A short history

In Chapter 6, we argued that the stem of each word carries a label indicating its specific syntactic category. Ancient grammarians used the expression 'parts of speech' in order to refer to such categories, although they never reached an agreement about their total number. Contrary to the multiplicity of opinions expressed by classical authors, during the late imperial period eight categories began to be standardly recognized, i.e. nouns, pronouns, verbs, adverbs, participles, prepositions, conjunctions, and interjections (Char. *gramm*. GLK I 193, 6; Don. *gramm*. 585, 4–5 H.). However, some changes to the traditional inventory have been introduced in modern linguistics.

On the one hand, the participle is no longer considered a category on its own, but is rather treated as an adjective placed within a verbal paradigm. On the other hand, the adjective has become an independent category since the Middle Ages, i.e. a distinction has been drawn between the genuine *nōmen* and the *nōmen adiectīvus*. More recently, an independent category has been invoked for numerals as well, although this is now limited only to cardinal numbers, which actually belong to a wider category called 'quantifiers', while ordinals are taken to be adjectives.

This traditional classification of the 'parts of speech' carries both advantages and disadvantages. The greatest advantage is the recognition that the words of the mental lexicon are not all the same, but certainly belong to different syntactic classes, contra those linguistic approaches which reduce morphological analysis to 'morphemes' and 'concepts'.

The disadvantage lies in the expression 'parts of speech', where the notion of 'speech' itself is not particularly clear. Intuitively, speech can be defined as a set of sentences, which implies that its sub-elements are whole sentences, rather than single words. For this reason, linguists now prefer to use the expression 'word classes', rather than 'parts of speech'. However, this is a minor terminological issue, and in the following discussion we will keep the traditional expression.

Some parts of speech are easily recognizable cross-linguistically. This is the case for nouns and verbs, the fundamental distinction between which had already been pointed out by ancient philosophers and can be found across all languages. According to some researchers, this may have a physiological motivation, as shown by the existence of varieties of aphasia which selectively affect either nouns or verbs or, more simply, by the fact that it is usually easier for speakers to forget nouns rather than verbs, which may suggest that the two categories are stored in different areas of our memory.

On the other hand, the existence of other parts of speech raises more issues. An example is the article, which exists in English and in Italian, for example, but not in Latin or in Russian. A possible solution is the postulation of a wider category, the so-called 'determiner', which includes two sub-categories, i.e. articles and demonstratives. From a diachronic point of view, it is clear that the Italian article is a new category, derived from the Latin demonstrative, e.g. Lat. *ille homō* 'that man' > It. *l'uomo* 'the man'. A similar evolutionary pattern can be found in modern Italian as well, i.e. the demonstrative *questo* 'this' (often reduced to *'sto*) tends to replace the article in the colloquial spoken language and, as a consequence, it must be reinforced by a deictic (*questo qui* 'this here'). The very same phenomenon took place in the evolution of the Germanic languages, in Finnish and in Ancient Greek (in Homer's works, for example, the article still retains a clear demonstrative value).

7.2 The inventory

The lexical categories that we must postulate for Latin are the following: nouns, adjectives, verbs, adverbs, prepositions, pronouns, demonstratives, quantifiers, complementizers (that is, particles which introduce embedded clauses; cf. Section 23.1), conjunctions, and interjections.

The first four categories constitute open word classes and contain a large number of elements, unlike the remaining categories, which constitute closed classes, consisting of an extremely reduced number of elements. Ancient grammarians had already tried to identify these main categories, as shown in this passage taken from Varro:

(1) Dividitur oratio secundum naturam in quattuor partis: in eam quae habet casus et quae habet tempora et quae habet neutrum et in qua est utrumque (Varro *ling.* VIII 44)
     'Speech is naturally divided into four parts: one has cases, one has tenses, one has neither and one in which both exist'

In other words, Varro suggests a classification of the main lexical categories in terms of two syntactic features, i.e. tense and case. This classification is

TABLE 7.1 Major lexical categories

	+ Case	− Case
+ Tense	Adjective	Verb
− Tense	Noun	Adverb

summarized in Table 7.1, where Varro's original category 'participle' has been replaced by the modern category 'adjective'.

As shown in Table 7.1, a verb can express tense but not case, a noun can express case but not tense, an adjective can express both tense (when it is a participle) and case, while an adverb cannot express either of them. We will come back to this topic in Section 23.1. Now we are ready to develop a theory of inflection.

8

A theory of inflection

8.1 Formal representation of morphological rules

In Latin, just as in other languages, inflection is the morphological phenomenon by means of which a given stem belonging to a given lexical category
acquires new syntactically relevant information. More precisely, verbal inflection expresses information about tense (plus mood, voice, person, and number), while a nominal inflection mainly expresses case (plus number for nouns,
and gender and number for adjectives). Therefore, inflection obligatorily
attaches to the abstract stems of nouns, adjectives and verbs, while adverbs
cannot be inflected.

Starting from the morphological stem, which we have already defined, we
will formally represent an inflection as in (1):

(1) $[[\text{Stem}]_X {}_{[+ \text{ intrinsic features}]} + \text{Infl} {}_{[+ \text{ inflectional information}]}]_X {}_{[+ \text{ intrinsic features + inflectional}}$
$_{\text{information}]}$

The stem is included within the internal brackets, which carry the label of its
lexical category X and its intrinsic features. Both the lexical category and the
features are then copied on the label of the external brackets. The external
brackets are used to introduce the inflectional ending (Infl), which expresses
some grammatical information. This is in turn added to the features which are
inherently expressed by the stem. Therefore, the label on the external brackets
indicates all the grammatical properties on the entire inflected word. Some
examples of analysis of an inflected noun, adjective, and verb, respectively, are
reported in (2a–c):

(2) a. *rosam:* $[[\text{rosa}]_N {}_{[\text{fem.}]} + m_{[\text{accus. sg.}]}]_N {}_{[\text{fem. accus. sg.}]}$
      'the rose'

     b. *pauperis:* $[[\text{pauper}]_A {}_{[\text{mas.}]} + is_{[\text{gen. sg.}]}]_A {}_{[\text{mas. gen. sg.}]}$
      'of the poor'

     c. *rapit:* $[[\text{rapi}]_V {}_{[\text{trans. pres. indic.}]} + t_{[\text{act. 3rd pers. sg.}]}]_V {}_{[\text{trans. pres. indic. act. 3rd pers. sg.}]}$
      'he snatches'

In (2), an ending is attached to the stem without any phonological change.
This is, however, quite a rare state of affairs in Latin. Most of the time, when an

ending is attached, the stem undergoes some phonological changes. This is the difference between 'synthetic' and 'agglutinating' languages, i.e. while in the latter each single morpheme is an easily identifiable segment expressing some unique information, in the former the morphemes attached to a word cannot be readily decomposed into segments and may convey various pieces of information.

8.2 Adjustment rules

Phonological changes determined by the morphological context, i.e. morpho-phonological phenomena, can be synchronically described by a specific set of rules, usually called 'adjustment rules'. The main difference between a phonological rule and an adjustment rule lies in the fact that while the former applies indiscriminately to any word exhibiting a given phonological context, the latter applies only if a morpheme boundary occurs in the context. Such a difference can be formalized as in (3):

(3)   a. $x \rightarrow y \, / \, \_\_ \, z$
      b. $x \rightarrow y \, / \, \_\_ + z$

The notation in (3a) shows that a phonological rule turns every x segment into a y segment if x occurs in the context z. On the other hand, the notation in (3b) shows that an adjustment rule requires a morpheme boundary, signalled by +, in the context of z, for the rule to apply. This implies that an adjustment rule depends on the morphological context and only applies to certain lexical components. As a matter of fact, most of the adjustment rules of Classical Latin morphology are the synchronic reflex of older phonological rules which took place in the pre-literary period.

Generally speaking, adjustment rules can be grouped into two main categories, i.e. deletion and allomorphy. We shall start with the former.

8.3 Vowel deletion

The most important deletion rule, which largely applies to Latin morphology, is called the 'vowel deletion rule', and can be represented as in (4):

(4) $\breve{V} \rightarrow \varnothing \, / \, \_\_ + V$ (where $\breve{V}$ is ă, ŏ, or ĕ)

The above notation says that a short vowel becomes zero if it occurs before a morpheme boundary and another vowel. The only vowels which are affected by deletion are ă, ŏ, and ĕ. This is the kind of rule which determines the passage from the abstract structure of [[rosă] + īs], made by a stem and an ending, to the surface form *rosīs* (dative and ablative plural of *rosa*).

The starting point of this rule is the difficulty of pronouncing two adjacent vowels which belong to different syllables. Ancient grammarians used to refer to this kind of 'accident' with the word *hiātus*, which literally means 'open mouth', when moving from one vowel to the other.

Many languages tend to avoid this kind of phenomenon. The Italian case is particularly telling. In this language, vowel deletion takes the form of a general phonological rule, called 'elision', which avoids the clash between vowels in adjacent words. Elision is graphically represented by means of an apostrophe, e.g. *l'eroe* 'the hero'; *bell'uomo* '(a) nice man'; *tutt'altro* 'everything else'. In addition to this, vowel deletion in Italian is particularly productive not only within processes of inflection, but also within processes of nominal derivation, e.g. [[vino] + aio] → *vinaio* 'wine merchant'.

In Latin, vowel deletion extensively applies to inflectional paradigms of nominal stems ending in *ă* and in *ŏ*, e.g. the plural nominative [[lupŏ]+ī] becomes *lupī* and the plural dative [[lupŏ]+īs] becomes *lupīs*. As we will see later on, adjustment rules are useful tools which allow us to derive the actual phonological structure from the underlying abstract morphological structure.

As for its origin, this rule can be considered the synchronic reflex of historical phenomena. Derivations such as **lupo-ī > lupī* and **lupo-īs > lupīs* can be easily reconstructed in the historical morphology of Latin. In conclusion, vowel deletion plays a crucial rule in the description of the nominal inflection of stems ending in a short vowel.

8.4 Vowel shortening

In Section 8.3, we argued that vowel deletion only affects short vowels. In contrast, a long vowel occuring in the same context of vowel deletion, i.e. before a morpheme boundary and another vowel, is not deleted but simply shortened. This rule of vowel shortening is also known with the formula *vōcālis ante vōcālem corripitur* 'a vowel before another vowel is shortened' and can be formulated as in (5):

(5) $\bar{V} \rightarrow \breve{V}/$ ___ + V

This is the kind of rule which determines the passage from the abstract morphological structures [[rē] + ī] and [[monē] + ō] to the surface forms *reī* (genitive singular of *rēs* 'thing'), and *moneō* (1st person singular ind. pres. act. of *monēre* 'to advise'), respectively.

Another rule of vowel shortening has the same input, i.e. a long vowel, and the same output, i.e. a short vowel, but a different triggering context, i.e. a final syllable before any consonants except *s*:

(6) $\tilde{V} \rightarrow \breve{V} / \_\_\_ + C \, \#$ (except if $C = s$)

The formula in (6) shows that, if a long vowel in a final syllable is followed by a consonant desinence different from s, the vowel is shortened. This explains the reason why the abstract structures [[rē] + m] and [[monē] + t], for example, become the surface forms *rem* (accusative singular of *rēs*) and *monet* (1st person singular ind. pres. act. of *monēre*), respectively. Conversely, a long vowel is preserved before -*s*, e.g. *rēs* (nominative singular) and *monēs* (2nd person singular ind. pres. act.).

Finally, note that a long vowel is generally shortened before a liquid or nasal followed by a stop consonant, e.g. *monent* (3rd person plural ind. pres. act.) and *monentur* (3rd person plural ind. pres. pass.) from the same stem [monē], as a consequence of the reflex of an old Indo-European sound law, i.e the so-called 'Osthoff's Law'. In contrast, a vowel is always lengthened before the consonant clusters -*nf*- and -*ns*-, e.g. *īnfēlīx* and *īnsānus* (Cic. *orat.* 159).

8.5 Vowel weakening

The last adjustment rule of Latin morphology affecting short vowels is called 'vowel weaking' (or sometimes 'Latin ablaut'). This rule affects the quality of the vowel, which tends to 'weaken', i.e. to become closer. In other words, an open (low) vowel tends to change into a close (higher) vowel. Two crucial distinctions must be drawn, i.e. between open and closed syllables on the one hand, and between medial and final syllables on the other, so that four possible contexts can be distinguished.

First of all, in medial open syllables, all short vowels change into *i*, as shown in (7), where σ stands for any syllable:

(7) $\breve{V} \rightarrow \breve{\iota} / \sigma \, (+) \_\_\_ (+) \, C \, (+) \, V$

The formula in (7) states that if a short vowel occurs in a medial syllable which is open, the vowel becomes *i*, if a morpheme boundary occurs before, within, or after the syllable, as shown by the examples in (8):

(8) a. [re + [faciō]] → *reficiō*
        'to restore'

    b. [[mīlet] + is] → *mīlitis*
        'soldier' (gen. sg.)

As a matter of fact, this rule mainly affects the vowels *ă* and *ĕ*, as in examples (8a–b), while the vowels *ŏ* and *ŭ* are more rarely affected. Some examples of this latter case are shown in (9):

(9) a.   [[novo] + tās] → *novitās*
          'novelty'

     b.   [[caput] + is] → *capitis*
          'head' (gen. sg.)

Note that, if the consonant following the open syllable is *r*, the short vowels *ă*
and *ĭ* change into *ĕ*, as shown by example (10):

(10) a.   [re + [pariō]] → *reperiō*
           'to find out'

      b.   [[capi] + re] → *capere*
           'to take hold of'

Secondly, in medial closed syllables only the short vowel *ă* changes into *ĕ*,
as stated in (11):

(11)   *ă → ĕ* / σ (+) ___ (+) CCV

This formula says that before or after a morpheme boundary the vowel *ă* in a
medial closed syllable becomes *ĕ*, as shown by example (12):

(12)   [con + [damnō]] → *condemnō*
       'to condemn'

As for final syllables, a distinction must again be drawn between open and
closed ones. On the one hand, in final open syllables, only the vowel *ĭ* changes
into *ĕ*, as shown in (13):

(13)   *ĭ → ĕ* / σ___ + ∅ #

Rule (13) states that, if the stem vowel is a short *ĭ*, it becomes *ĕ* before a zero
ending, as shown by example (14):

(14)   [[mari] + ø] → *mare*
       'sea'

On the other hand, in final closed syllables, three different phenomena are
attested, i.e. (i) *ă* changes into *ĕ*; (ii) *ĕ* changes into *ĭ* before *s* and *t*; and (iii) *ŏ*
changes into *ŭ* before *s* and *m*, as shown in (15):

(15)   a. *ă → ĕ* / σ___ C + C #
       b. *ĕ → ĭ* / σ___ + {s, t} #
       c. *ŏ → ŭ* / σ___ + {s, m} #

Rule (15a) states that *ă* becomes *ĕ* if it occurs in a final closed syllable before a
consonant ending, as shown by example (16):

(16)   [[arti] + [[fac] + s]] → *artifex*
       'master of an art'

Rule (15b) states that a stem vowel *ĕ* becomes *ĭ* if it precedes the endings *-s* or *-t*, as shown by example (17):

(17) [[lege] + t] → *legit*
      'he reads' (3rd pers. sg. ind. pres.)

Finally, rule (15c) states that a stem vowel *ŏ* becomes *ŭ* if it precedes the endings *-s* or *-m*, as shown by example (18):

(18) [[lupo] + s] → *lupus*
      'wolf'

To conclude, note that the combination of these rules will allow us to explain most of the irregularities that we shall find in the declension of nouns and conjugation of verbs in a very simple and systematic way.

8.6 Rhotacism

In the previous sections we mentioned two types of adjustment rule, i.e. vowel deletion (Section 8.3) and vowel allomorphy (shortening in Section 8.4 and weakening in Section 8.5). A very clear case of consonant allomorphy can be represented by 'rhotacism', i.e. the voicing of an intervocalic sibilant *s*. The origin of rhotacism lies in an old phonological rule of pre-literary Latin, which can be represented as in (19):

(19) *s* → *r* / V__V

The above rule reads: '*s* becomes *r* in an intervocalic context'. This means that Old Latin speakers pronounced *plūrima* as *plūsima*, *meliōrem* as *meliōsem*, and *harēnam* as *hasēnam*, as noted by Varro (*ling.* VII 26). The exact chronology of this phenomenon is reported by Cicero (*epist.* IX 21, 2), who claims that Lucius Papirius Crassus (consul in 339 BC) was the first one in his family to change his name from *Papīsius* to *Papīrius*. Through the *Digestus* (I 2, 2, 36), we also learn that the use of the grapheme *r* in the spelling of the names *Valeriī* and *Fūriī* (previously spelt *Valesiī* and *Fūsiī*) was introduced by Appius Claudius Caecus, who was consul in 312 BC.

This suggests that, from a diachronic point of view, rhotacism was a phenomenon which was completed over a brief period of time, coming into action during the fourth century BC. After that period the rule ceased to be productive, as shown by the fact that the Greek loanwords which entered Latin after that period are not affected by this rule, e.g. *basis* 'base'.

However, it is interesting to note that, along with diachronic rhotacism, there exists another type of rhotacism, that is, synchronic. As a matter of fact, rhotacism continued to operate in Classical Latin, in particular morphological contexts. A former phonological rule thus became an adjustment rule, which can be formalized as in (20):

(20) $s \rightarrow r / V \underline{\quad} + V$

Rule (20) reads: '*s* becomes *r* in an intervocalic context, before a morpheme boundary'.

This rule applies to the inflection of nouns whose stem ends in *s* preceded by a vowel, e.g. [aes], [flōs], [honōs]. These nouns have a consonant stem, so they belong to the third declension. In particular, their nominative and vocative singular bear a zero ending, that we shall call a pure stem, i.e. *aes* 'bronze', *flōs* 'flower', *honōs* 'honour'. However, the endings of the other cases all begin with a vowel. This leads to the creation of the morpho-phonological context formalized above in (20), which triggers the application of rhotacism. In (21), we report some examples of the application of the rule when the *-is* ending is added to the stem:

(21)   a. [[aes] + is]   →   *aeris*
        b. [[flōs] + is]   →   *flōris*
        c. [[honōs] + is] →   *honōris*

Synchronic rhotacism applies within the inflectional paradigm of the stem [flōs] like an allomorphic rule which specifies the distribution of the allomorphs *flōs-* and *flōr-*. The very same rule applies also to derivational paradigms, triggering the distribution of the allomorphs *flōs-*, before a consonant, and *flōr-*, before a vowel, e.g. *flōs-culus* 'little flower' and *flōr-idus* 'flowering', respectively.

Note that rhotacism is not specific to Latin, but takes place in other languages as well, including English, cf. the allomorphs *was* (no rhotacism) and *were* (rhotacism). Clearly, these are only separate but phonologically parallel independent innovations, with different conditioning environments, as the conditioning factor in Germanic was the position of stress, which is not relevant to Latin.

9

Noun declensions

9.1 Case, gender, and number

After considering some theoretical aspects, we are now ready to describe the behaviour of the Latin inflection. We shall first consider nouns, whose main feature is their ability to express case, gender, and number.

Since case has a syntactic nature, we will be able to fully understand this concept only after dealing with case theory (cf. Chapter 20). For the sake of the present discussion, therefore, it will be sufficient for us to go through an informal preliminary description.

Case encodes the syntactic role of a word (or group of words) within a given sentence. For example, in a sentence like *The boy has closed the door*, *the boy* bears an abstract case, called nominative, which signals its function as subject. Similarly, *the door* bears another abstract case, called accusative, which signals its function as direct object. The element which assigns abstract case to the subject and object is the verb.

Abstract case is thus a universal syntactic property and bears a crucial role within the sentence structure. If a verb like *close* were not able to assign case, the sentence would be ill-formed, because a sentence cannot lack a subject (cf. **has closed the door*) or—in this case—an object (cf. **the boy has closed*). This means that abstract case must be assigned to nominal groups, otherwise the resulting sentence will be ill-formed.

Morphological case is the concrete manifestation of abstract case, as in many languages words which belong to case-marked nominal groups exhibit some morphological change. Therefore, morphological case is nothing but modifications words undergo in order to overtly mark the presence of abstract case.

While abstract case is a universal property of the grammar of any language, the presence of morphological case is subject to cross-linguistic variation. Languages such as Latin, Ancient Greek, or German exhibit rich case systems, extensively described by grammars. In other languages, such as English or Italian, the morphological case system is very reduced, which explains why some grammars argue that case is absent from such languages. As a matter of fact, Italian and English still exhibit some relics of morphological case in the pronominal system. In Table 9.1, we can observe that third person singular pronouns exhibit three different morphological forms for three different cases in Italian.

TABLE 9.1 Italian third person singular pronouns

	mas.	fem.
nominative	*egli*	*ella*
dative	*gli*	*le*
accusative	*lo*	*la*

The same is true for English, which, in spite of its notorious inflectional poverty, still retains some morphological expression of case in the pronominal system, as shown in Table 9.2, which illustrates the different forms of the third person singular.

TABLE 9.2 English third person singular pronouns

	mas.	fem.	neut.
nominative	*he*	*she*	*it*
accusative/dative	*him*	*her*	*it*

The crucial point, however, is that both Italian and English possess an abstract case system which directly corresponds to the Latin one. We shall take Italian as an example. A well-known fact about this language is that during its evolution from Latin, nominal endings ceased to mark case, i.e. Italian adjectives and nouns only agree in gender and number. As a consequence, the presence of an article bearing morphological case is compulsory. In Latin, there are no articles: a nominal group can consist of a single noun, or a noun and a demonstrative. In the latter case, the demonstrative agrees with the noun without adding any new information about case:

(1) a. Marius librum(acc.) legit (Lat.)
        'M. reads the book'

     b. Marius illum(acc.) librum(acc.) legit (Lat.)
        'M. reads that book'

     c. Marius librō(abl.) contentus est (Lat.)
        'M. is happy about the book'

     d. Marius illō(abl.) librō(abl.) contentus est (Lat.)
        'M. is happy about that book'

In contrast, Italian typically requires the presence of an article as well, which is historically derived from the Latin demonstrative, as shown in the examples in (2) (ill-formed sentences are marked by a star):

(2) a. *Mario legge libro (It.)
         '*M. reads book'

     b. Mario legge il(acc.) libro (It.)
         'M. reads the book'

     c. *Mario è contento libro (It.)
         '*M. is happy about book'

     d. Mario è contento del(gen.) libro (It.)
         'M. is happy about the book'

This means that in Latin, case information is conveyed by the morphology on the noun, which is provided with case-marking endings, and the demonstrative, when present, simply agrees. In Italian, on the other hand, the very same information is conveyed by the morphology on the article, which is combined with case-marking prepositions (*di, a, con*). For this reason, the article must be present. The examples in (2) marked by a star are ill-formed precisely because they do not contain any case markers.

In other words, while in Italian case information is contained in the article, in Latin the very same information is conveyed by nominal endings. If we compare the structure of the two languages, we will find both a partial analogy and a partial difference: the syntactic information contained in each single element is different, but the overall information conveyed is the same, i.e. gender, number, and case. A further point in favour of this claim comes from the fact that in Ancient Greek the article, which was present in the language, was not obligatory, since the noun was provided with case-marking endings.

Similarly, the evolution of the article in Germanic languages, including English, is parallel to the evolution of this category in Romance languages. Neither the definite nor the indefinite articles have been reconstructed for proto-Germanic, and their emergence in the modern varieties is typically linked to the loss of case-marking endings and, more generally, to the weakening of inflectional morphology.

In conclusion, we can arguably claim that, while abstract case is a universal property of nominal groups of any language, its superficial morphological realization is subject to cross-linguistic variation.

Latin, in particular, exhibits six morphological cases, as shown in Table 9.3.

TABLE 9.3 The Latin case system

Case	Example	Translation
nominative	*rosa*	*the rose* (subject)
genitive	*rosae*	*of the rose*
dative	*rosae*	*to the rose*
accusative	*rosam*	*the rose* (object)
vocative	*rosa*	*rose!*
ablative	*rosā*	*with the rose, for the rose, from the rose*

The study of the functions played by each case constitutes one of the most important fields of Latin syntax, as we shall see in further detail in the relative section (cf. Chapter 21). Note that the order of cases given above and through-out the work adheres to the continental European and American tradition, as well as to the tradition of ancient grammars such as Donatus (cf. Don. *gramm.* 586, 16 H.), while the common British order is nominative – vocative – accusative – genitive – dative – ablative.

In addition to case, Latin nominal morphology also expresses gender (masculine, feminine, neuter) and number (singular, plural). This is another area which is subject to cross-linguistic variation. Some languages, e.g. Hungarian, have no grammatical gender at all. In contrast, the distinction between neuter vs. masculine/feminine gender can be found in German, but not in Italian. In this respect, it is important to stress the fact that gender is a mere grammatical property of words and should not be confused with the physical properties of objects denoted by words.

This is crucially shown by the fact that the very same objects can be denoted by masculine words in one language and feminine words in another. For example, in German the word 'sun' is feminine (*die Sonne*) and the word 'moon' is masculine (*der Mond*), while in Italian and Latin it is the other way round. Moreover, although Italian words typically exhibit the same gender as the corresponding Latin word, especially if the two are historically related, this is not necessarily always the case, e.g. Lat. *lapis* 'stone' (generally masculine) became It. *lapide* 'gravestone' (feminine). As a general rule, in Latin, names of rivers and winds are typically masculine, names of trees, plants, regions, islands, and cities are feminine, and names of fruits and metals are neuter.

Number too may be subject to cross-linguistic variation. While Slovene or Ancient Greek possess a 'dual' number, such a category does not exist in Latin or English (the only trace in Latin is the -ō ending in *ambō* and *duō* > *duo* because of iambic shortening). Moreover, the very same object can be denoted by a singular word in one language and a plural word in another, e.g. in English the word 'people' is plural (cf. *people say* vs. **people says*), but the corresponding word *populus* is singular in Latin; conversely, in Latin the word *dīvitiae* is plural, while the corresponding word in English, i.e. 'wealth', is singular (though the plural 'riches' is also attested).

For this reason, in the course of the following discussion of Latin declensions we will give indications not only about case, but also about gender and number, when relevant.

9.2 The five declensions

Latin distinguishes five declensions, corresponding to the five vowels of the language. More precisely, each stem belongs to a given declension depending on its thematic vowel:

- if the stem ends in *a*, the word belongs to the *first* declension;
- if the stem ends in *o*, the word belongs to the *second* declension;
- if the stem ends in *i*, the word belongs to the *third* declension;
- if the stem ends in *u*, the word belongs to the *fourth* declension;
- if the stem ends in *ē*, the word belongs to the *fifth* declension.

Note that if the stem ends in a consonant (cf. C-stem), we may expect the word to belong to another independent declension, but in fact traditional grammar places it within the third declension, given the fact that the inflection of C-stems partially overlaps with the inflection of *i*-stems, often causing confusion.

Stems are then combined with different endings expressing number and case, as shown in Table 9.4.

Table 9.4 does not include the neuters, which always exhibit the same ending in the nominative, accusative, and vocative, i.e. *-m* or a zero ending in the singular, and the characteristic *-a* ending in the plural.

We shall now look in turn at each of the declensions and at the peculiarities of each of the paradigms.

TABLE 9.4 Endings of the five declensions

	Singular		Plural	
	1st and 2nd decl.	3rd, 4th, 5th decl.	1st and 2nd decl.	3rd, 4th, 5th decl.
nom.	+ ø (+ s)		+ ī (+ j)	+ (ē)s
gen.	+ ī (+ j)	+ (i)s	+ $_{long}$ + rum	+ um
dat.	+ i (+ j)	+ ī	+ īs	+ (i)bus
acc.	+ m		+ $_{long}$ + s	+ (ē)s
voc.	+ ø (+ e)	= nominative	= nominative	
abl.	+ $_{long}$ (+ e)		+ īs	+ (i)bus

9.3 The first declension

The thematic vowel of first declension stems is a short *a*. From a diachronic point of view, this short vowel is actually derived from a long one, which has survived in the plural genitive and accusative only. From a synchronic, descriptive point of view, we will thus associate the stem with the short vowel.

As is the case for all inflectional paradigms, information about number and case must be added to the stem (which is already inherently specified for its gender), by means of a given set of endings, which are basically the same for the first and second declension on the one hand, and for the third, fourth, and fifth on the other.

Tables 9.5 to 9.22 are organized as follows. For each singular and plural case, the first column contains the abstract morphological stem, i.e. [rosa], to which the various endings are attached. In the second column, the actual surface form is reported in bold, which is the result of the application of adjustment rules.

TABLE 9.5 First declension (fem.): *rosa* 'rose'

	Singular		Plural	
nom.	[rosa] + ø	**rosa**	[rosa] + j	**rosae**
gen.	[rosa] + j	**rosae**	[rosa] + $_{long}$ + rum	**rosārum**
dat.	[rosa] + j	**rosae**	[rosa] + īs	**rosīs**
acc.	[rosa] + m	**rosam**	[rosa] + $_{long}$ + s	**rosās**
voc.	[rosa] + ø	**rosa**	[rosa] + j	**rosae**
abl.	[rosa] + $_{long}$	**rosā**	[rosa] + īs	**rosīs**

Notes

Singular

The nominative has a zero ending, i.e. the surface form coincides with the abstract stem. Prescriptive grammars usually call it 'asigmatic' nominative, i.e. 'without -*s*'. In fact, in all the five declensions, the nominative is either 'sigmatic', i.e. with an -*s* ending, or 'asigmatic', i.e. without the -*s* ending.

The ending of the genitive and dative singular is the semivowel [j], which is the result of the phonetic erosion of two archaic endings, i.e. a long -*ī* (in the genitive) and a short -*i* (in the dative), that appear in the second declension. A relic of the ancient genitive ending is found in archaic poetry, e.g. *longāī*. In Classical Latin, the outcome of the fusion between the thematic vowel [a] and the semivowel [j] is the diphthong *ae*.

The accusative ending is -*m*.

The vocative coincides with the nominative (this is the case for all declensions, except for the second one).

The ablative ending is a phonological feature of length which is added to the short stem vowel (cf. [+ long]). This is simply a synchronic rule. From a historical point of view, the vowel was originally long and was followed by an archaic -*d* ending, which left some traces in Archaic Latin inscriptions, e.g. *sententiād* 'by opinion'.

Plural

Nominative and vocative: the ancient ending was -*ī*, which became [j] (for its further evolution cf. genitive and dative singular).

The genitive ending -*rum* and the accusative ending -*s* are accompanied in synchrony by the lengthening of the thematic vowel. From a historical point of view, the vowel was long.

In the dative and ablative, the vocalic ending -*īs* creates the context for the application of the adjustment rule (4) described in Section 8.3, which deletes the thematic vowel (so the outcome is *rosīs* and not *rosaīs).

Other remarks

Gender. The vast majority of the nouns belonging to the first declension are feminine. There are few exceptions, such as *agricola* 'farmer', *nauta* 'sailor', and *poēta* 'poet', which are masculine. No neuter nouns are attested within this declension.

Number. Dīvitiae 'wealth', *īnsidiae* 'snare', and *reliquiae* 'remainder' are plural. Traditional school grammars call them *plūrālia tantum* 'plurals only'.

Archaisms. (a) *Familia* 'household' still retains an additional archaic -*s* genitive form, which is employed in legal expressions such as *pater familiās* 'father of the family'. (b) *filia* 'daughter', *dea* 'goddess', *mūla* 'she-mule', and *equa* 'mare' still retain an additional archaic -*bus* dative/ablative plural, which is employed in some legal expressions in order to distinguish them from the corresponding masculine forms, e.g. *filiīs et filiābus* 'to the sons and daughters'.

Grecisms. (a) Some words of Greek origin, such as *amphora* 'amphora (Greek vessel)' and *drachma* 'drachma (Greek coin)', exhibit an archaic genitive plural ending -*um*, i.e. *amphorum, drachmum*. This ending is also found in some compounds ending in -*cola* and -*gena*, e.g. *Grāiugena* 'a Grecian by birth', gen. pl. *Grāiugenum*. (b) Some proper nouns of Greek origin belong to the first declension, but they retain their original Greek nominative and accusative endings. In particular, male names have the nominative ending in -*ās* or -*ēs*, e.g. *Aenēās, Anchīsēs*, and the accusative ending in -*ān* or -*ēn*, e.g. *Aenēān, Anchīsēn* vs. the Latin forms *Aenēam, Anchīsem*; names for females end in -*ē* in the nominative, e.g. *Helenē, Niobē* vs. the Latin forms *Helena, Nioba*, and in -*ēn* in the accusative, e.g. *Helenēn, Niobēn* vs. the Latin forms *Helenam, Niobam*.

9.4 The second declension

The second declension stems end in -o-. If the o-stem is preceded by -r-, the thematic vowel is deleted in the nominative and vocative.

This declension also contains some neuter nouns, which have distinctive endings for the nominative, accusative, and vocative.

For these reasons, we will distinguish three paradigms, i.e. a general one which applies to masculine o-stems, a specific one which applies to masculine stems with -r- before the thematic vowel, and one for neuter stems.

9.4.1 Masculine

TABLE 9.6 Second declension (mas.): *lupus* 'wolf'

	Singular		Plural	
nom.	[lupo] + s (and vowel weakening)	lupus	[lupo] + ī	lupī
gen.	[lupo] + ī	lupī	[lupo] + long + rum	lupōrum
dat.	[lupo] + long	lupō	[lupo] + īs	lupīs
acc.	[lupo] + m (and vowel weakening)	lupum	[lupo] + long + s	lupōs
voc.	[lupo] + e	lupe	[lupo] + ī	lupī
abl.	[lupo] + long	lupō	[lupo] + īs	lupīs

Notes

Singular

The nominative is sigmatic, i.e. it ends in -s. The thematic vowel -o- becomes -u- because of vowel weakening in final closed syllable (cf. rule (15c) in Section 8.5). An archaic -os nominative is attested in some ancient inscriptions and archaisms, such as *servos* (in this case archaic writers have retained the -o- because it is preceded by the semivowel -v-).

The original ending of the genitive, i.e. -ī, has survived. For this reason, vowel deletion affects the thematic vowel -o- of the second declension (contra the survival of -a- in the first declension, where the ending -ī was reduced to the semivowel [j], which does not create the correct context for the application of vowel deletion).

The dative ending is synchronically a phonological feature, i.e. [+ long]. From a historical point of view, the original ending was -ī (that is the same ending which was reduced to [j] in the first declension).

The accusative has the same ending as the first declension, i.e. -m. The thematic vowel -o- becomes -u- for vowel weakening, just as in the nominative.

The vocative of o-stems is the only one which is different from the nominative. The ending is -e and it deletes the thematic vowel -o-. If *i* precedes the thematic vowel, the resulting vocative form is not -ie, but -ī, e.g. the vocative of *filius* is *filī*; the vocative of *Gāius* is *Gāī*.

The ablative ending is the phonological feature [+ long]. Originally, a -d ending was attested (cf. also the first declension).

Plural
Nominative and vocative: cf. genitive singular.

The genitive ending is -rum, which is accompanied by the lengthening of the thematic vowel (cf. the first declension).

The -īs ending of the dative and ablative creates the context for the application of the adjustment rule which deletes the thematic vowel (cf. the first declension).

The accusative ending is -s, and it is accompanied by the lengthening of the thematic vowel (cf. the first declension).

Other remarks
Gender. The vast majority of second declension nouns with the -us nominative are masculine. There are a few feminine nouns, such as *alvus* 'belly' and *humus* 'ground', and typically names of trees, cities, and islands, e.g. *cupressus* 'cypress', *fāgus* 'beech-tree', *Corinthus* 'Corinth', and *Rhodus* 'Rhodes'. Only three neuter nouns with the -us nominative are attested, i.e. *vīrus* 'poison', *vulgus* 'the great mass', and *pelagus* 'sea'.

Archaisms. As is the case for the first declension, there are a few nouns which exhibit an archaic -um genitive plural, which can be found in legal expressions, e.g. *praefectus fabrum* 'officer in charge of *fabrī*'; *collēgium Quindecemvirum* 'board of the Fifteen Men', and in particular in some coin names, e.g. *nummum* 'of sesterces', *talentum* 'of talents'.

Irregular noun. Deus 'god' is inflected irregularly. The vocative singular coincides with the nominative, i.e. *deus*. In the plural, there exist alternative and contracted forms, along with the regular ones, i.e. nominative *deī/diī/dī*; genitive *deōrum/deum*; dative and ablative *deīs/diīs/dīs*.

9.4.2 Masculine (stems in -r- before the thematic vowel)

TABLE 9.7 Second declension (mas., stems in -r- before the thematic vowel): *puer* 'boy'

	Singular		Plural	
nom.	[puero] + ø + vowel deletion	**puer**	[puero] + ī	**puerī**
gen.	[puero] + ī	**puerī**	[puero] + long + rum	**puerōrum**
dat.	[puero] + long	**puerō**	[puero] + īs	**puerīs**
acc.	[puero] + m (and vowel weakening)	**puerum**	[puero] + long + s	**puerōs**
voc.	[puero] + ø + vowel deletion	**puer**	[puero] + ī	**puerī**
abl.	[puero] + long	**puerō**	[puero] + īs	**puerīs**

Notes

The nominative singular is asigmatic and is characterized by the deletion of the thematic vowel, e.g. the stem [puero] becomes *puer*. This is often the case when a vowel precedes -*r*-, although there are some exceptions, e.g. *ferus, sincērus*. If a consonant precedes instead, -*r*- undergoes a process of vocalization and becomes -*er*, e.g. the stem [agro] first becomes **agr* (thematic vowel deletion) and then *ager* (vocalization of -*r*).

The accusative singular is the same as in *lupum*.

The vocative singular coincides with the nominative (*contra* the case of *lupe*), even if a vocative *puere* is well attested, at least in Plautus.

The ablative singular ending is synchronically a phonological feature, i.e. [+ long], which allows the thematic vowel to avoid deletion. The archaic ending was -*d* (cf. also the first and second declensions).

Other remarks
Number. The noun *liber* 'book', whose stem is [libro] and whose genitive is *librī*, should not be confused with the adjective *līber* 'free', whose stem is [lībero] and whose genitive is *līberī*. The adjective, in particular, is employed in the plural form with the function of a noun, as if it belonged to the category of *plūrālia tantum*, i.e. *līberī* 'children'.

9.4.3 Neuter

TABLE 9.8 Second declension (neut.): *dōnum* 'gift'

	Singular		Plural	
nom.	[dōno] + m (and vowel weakening)	**dōnum**	[dōno] + ă	**dōna**
gen.	[dōno] + ī	**dōnī**	[dōno] + $_{long}$ + rum	**dōnōrum**
dat.	[dōno] + $_{long}$	**dōnō**	[dōno] + īs	**dōnīs**
acc.	[dōno] + m (and vowel weakening)	**dōnum**	[dōno] + ă	**dōna**
voc.	[dōno] + m (and vowel weakening)	**dōnum**	[dōno] + ă	**dōna**
abl.	[dōno] + $_{long}$	**dōnō**	[dōno] + īs	**dōnīs**

Notes

Singular
The nominative ending is -*m*. The thematic vowel -*o*- becomes -*u*- for vowel weakening (cf. the nominative and accusative of masculine stems; also note the archaic form *dōnom*, which is still attested in inscriptions).

The genitive, dative, and ablative coincide with those of the masculine paradigm.

The accusative and vocative of neuter stems *always* coincide with the nominative, for all declensions.

Plural

The nominative ending is -*a*, which is typical of neuter plurals. We will find this again in the third declension.

The genitive, dative, and ablative coincide with those of the masculine paradigm.

The accusative and vocative of neuter stems *always* coincide with the nominative.

Other remarks

Gender. Second declension nouns with *um*-nominative are always neuter.

Number. Words such as *arma* 'weapons' are *plūrālia tantum*. Some plural words acquire a collective meaning which cannot be predicted on the basis of the singular form:

(3) a. auxilium
        'help'
     b. auxilia
        'auxiliary troops'

(4) a. castrum
        'castle'
     b. castra
        'encampment'

(5) a. vinculum
        'band'
     b. vincula
        'prison'

The masculine word *locus* 'place' also exhibits a neuter plural with a different meaning:

(6) a. locī
        'passages in literary works'
     b. loca
        'geographical places'

Grecisms. Some proper nouns sometimes retain the Greek ending in the nominative and accusative, e.g. *Dēlos, Dēlon*, vs. the Latin forms *Dēlus, Dēlum*, and the neuter *Īlion*, vs. *Īlium*.

9.5 The third declension

There are three different types of third declension stems, i.e. (1) C(onsonant)-stems; (2) *i*-stems; (3) a mixed class, which partially overlaps with (1) and (2). We shall now consider the first type, using the classification of consonants proposed in Section 3.3.

9.5.1 C-stems

9.5.1.1 Velar stops (voiceless *c* and voiced *g*)

TABLE 9.9 Third declension (mas./fem., velar stops): *rēx* 'king'

	Singular		Plural	
nom.	[rĕg] + s	rēx	[rĕg] + ēs	rēgēs
gen.	[rĕg] + is	rēgis	[rĕg] + um	rēgum
dat.	[rĕg] + ī	rēgī	[rĕg] + ibus	rēgibus
acc.	[rĕg] + em	rēgem	[rĕg] + ēs	rēgēs
voc.	[rĕg] + s	rēx	[rĕg] + ēs	rēgēs
abl.	[rĕg] + e	rēge	[rĕg] + ibus	rēgibus

Notes

The nominative and vocative singular of all the stems ending in a stop consonant is sigmatic. The sequences *c* + *s* and *g* + *s* are graphically rendered by a double consonant, i.e. *x*, whose phonetic value is [ks]. Therefore, in stems ending in a voiced [g], a process of devoicing takes place, whereby [g] becomes [k] when it immediately precedes a voiceless consonant. The underlying form [rēgs] is thus pronounced [rēks] and spelt *rēx*.

Other examples

(7) with -*c*-
   a. calix, calicis
      'goblet'
   b. rādīx, rādīcis
      'root'
   c. vōx, vōcis
      'voice'

(8) with -*g*-
   a. coniux, coniugis
      'consort'
   b. lēx, lēgis
      'law'
   c. grex, gregis
      'flock'

9.5.1.2 Bilabial stops (voiceless *p* and voiced *b*)

TABLE 9.10 Third declension (mas./fem., bilabial stops): *ops* 'power'

	Singular		Plural	
nom.	[op] + s	ops	[op] + ēs	opēs
gen.	[op] + is	opis	[op] + um	opum
dat.	[op] + ī	opī	[op] + ibus	opibus
acc.	[op] + em	opem	[op] + ēs	opēs
voc.	[op] + s	ops	[op] + ēs	opēs
abl.	[op] + e	ope	[op] + ibus	opibus

Notes

Only a few nouns belong to this class. In the nominative and vocative singular, the sequences *p+s* and *b+s* are not orthographically altered, according to Classical Latin spelling, but they are both pronounced [ps], as a consequence of devoicing (cf. the stems reported above ending in velar stops). Note, however, that the spelling *plēps* for *plēbs* 'people' is well attested in archaic authors and inscriptions.

Other examples

(9)   with -*p*-
      a. daps, dapis
         'feast'
      b. Cyclōps, Cyclōpis
         'Cyclops'

(10) with -*b*-
      a. caelebs, caelibis
         'celibate'
      b. trabs, trabis
         'beam'

9.5.1.3 Dental stops (voiceless *t* and voiced *d*)

TABLE 9.11 Third declension (mas./fem./neut., dental stops): *quiēs* 'rest'

	Singular		Plural	
nom.	[quiēt] + s	quiēs	[quiēt] + ēs	quiētēs
gen.	[quiēt] + is	quiētis	[quiēt] + um	quiētum
dat.	[quiēt] + ī	quiētī	[quiēt] + ibus	quiētibus
acc.	[quiēt] + em	quiētem	[quiēt] + ēs	quiētēs
voc.	[quiēt] + s	quiēs	[quiēt] + ēs	quiētēs
abl.	[quiēt] + e	quiēte	[quiēt] + ibus	quiētibus

Notes

In Latin, the sequences *t* + *s* and *d* + *s* are banned from word-final position. For this reason, the nominative and vocative singular trigger deletion of the stop, e.g. the abstract form [quiēts] becomes *quiēs*, and similarly [mercēds] becomes *mercēs*.

This class also includes some neuter stems, which retain their pure stem in the nominative, accusative, and vocative singular with a zero ending, e.g. *caput* 'head'. Note that the genitive and dative singular of *caput* are affected by vowel weakening, i.e. *capitis, capitī* (cf. rule (9b) in Section 8.5).

If the neuter stem ends with two consonants, the last one is deleted in the nominative, accusative, and vocative singular, e.g. *cor* (<*cord), *cordis* 'heart', *lac* (<*lact), *lactis* 'milk'.

The nominative, accusative, and vocative plural of neuters always have a regular -*a* ending, e.g. *capita, corda*.

Other examples

(11) with -*t*-
      a. aestās, aestātis
         'summer'
      b. cīvitās, cīvitātis
         'citizienship'
      c. virtūs, virtūtis
         'virtue'

(12) with -*d*-
      a. laus, laudis
         'praise'
      b. palūs, palūdis
         'marshland'
      c. pēs, pedis
         'foot'

On the weakening of -ĕ- preceding a stop in bisyllabic C-stems

In all the C-stems listed above, if the stem is bisyllabic and the stop is preceded by a short -*e*-, an alternance between -*e*- and -*i*- is typically attested, e.g. *iūdex, iūdicis* 'judge'; *princeps, principis* 'leader'; *mīles, mīlitis* 'soldier'.

A simple synchronic explanation of this alternation is that -*e*- changes into -*i*- in the genitive and other cases by virtue of vowel weakening in medial open syllables (cf. rule (8b) in Section 8.5). Note that this change does not occur in the nominative and vocative singular, because -*e*- is not in medial but in final position, thus escaping the context of application of the rule.

From a diachronic point of view, the issue is more complex. The structure of *iūdex* was originally *ious-dik-s and should have become **iūdix, iūdicis*, but the nominative/vocative was remade analogically on *princeps*. In turn, the vowel of *princeps* was originally -*a*- (cf. *capiō*), which became -*e*- in the closed syllable in the nominative/

vocative and -*i*- in the open syllable in the oblique cases. The original nominative/ vocative *mīlets > *mīless* survived in Old Latin (e.g. Plaut. *Aul.* 526), as opposed to the light syllable attested in Ovid (*Epistulae* 11.48).

9.5.1.4 Nasals (alveolar *n* and bilabial *m*)

TABLE 9.12 Third declension (mas./fem./neut., nasals): *regiō* 'region'

	Singular		Plural	
nom.	[regiōn] + ∅ (+ cons. deletion)	**regiō**	[regiōn] + ēs	**regiōnēs**
gen.	[regiōn] + is	**regiōnis**	[regiōn] + um	**regiōnum**
dat.	[regiōn] + ī	**regiōnī**	[regiōn] + ibus	**regiōnibus**
acc.	[regiōn] + em	**regiōnem**	[regiōn] + ēs	**regiōnēs**
voc.	[regiōn] + ∅ (+ cons. deletion)	**regiō**	[regiōn] + ēs	**regiōnēs**
abl.	[regiōn] + e	**regiōne**	[regiōn] + ibus	**regiōnibus**

Notes

The nominative and vocative singular are usually asigmatic and trigger the deletion of the nasal in masculine and feminine nouns. The vowel -*ō* in word-final position tends to shorten during the classical period, e.g. *leŏ*, *leōnis* 'lion'. There are also some exceptional sigmatic forms, e.g. *canis, canis* 'dog'; *sanguīs* (also *sanguen*), *sanguinis* 'blood'.

If the nasal stop is preceded by a short -*o*-, this latter undergoes vowel weakening (cf. rule (7) in Section 8.5), and becomes *ĭ* in the entire declension, except for the nominative and vocative singular, where the dropping of *n* + *s* triggered the lengthening of the vowel (compensatory lengthening), which has retained its timbre, e.g. *orīgō, orīginis* 'origin'; *imāgō, imāginis* 'image'.

The nasal is always retained in the nominative, accusative, and vocative singular of the neuter stems, e.g. *agmen, agminis* 'an army column'; *nōmen, nōminis* 'name'. In these examples, the genitive singular and the remaining cases show that -*ĭ*- is the result of vowel reduction from -*ĕ*-.

Other examples

(13) with -*ōn*-
   a. actiō, actiōnis
      'action'
   b. legiō, legiōnis
      'legion'
   c. sermō, sermōnis
      'speech'

(14) with -on-
a. homō, hominis
'man'
(an archaic accusative in -ōn- is also attested in Ennius, i.e. *homōnem*,
possibly analogical from the nominative)
b. cardō, cardinis
'hinge'
c. virgō, virginis
'young girl'

(15) with -em-
hiems, hiemis
'winter'
(this is the only stem with the nasal *m*)

Note the noun/adjective *senex, senis* 'old', whose nominative and vocative singular
exhibit a different stem from the remainder of the paradigm, due to its expansion by
means of a suffix, i.e. *-ec-*.

9.5.1.5 Liquids (lateral *l* and trill *r*)

TABLE 9.13 Third declension (mas./fem./neut., liquids): *cōnsul* 'consul'

	Singular		Plural	
nom.	[cōnsul] + ø	cōnsul	[cōnsul] + ēs	cōnsulēs
gen.	[cōnsul] + is	cōnsulis	[cōnsul] + um	cōnsulum
dat.	[cōnsul] + ī	cōnsulī	[cōnsul] + ibus	cōnsulibus
acc.	[cōnsul] + em	cōnsulem	[cōnsul] + ēs	cōnsulēs
voc.	[cōnsul] + ø	cōnsul	[cōnsul] + ēs	cōnsulēs
abl.	[cōnsul] + e	cōnsule	[cōnsul] + ibus	cōnsulibus

Notes

The nominative and vocative singular are asigmatic.

Neuter stems with two liquid consonants in final position exhibit deletion of one of
them in the nominative, accusative, and vocative singular, e.g. *far, farris* 'grain', *mel,
mellis* 'honey'.

Stop + r-stems. The stems of *pater, patris* 'father', *māter, mātris* 'mother', and *frāter,
frātris* 'brother' are [patr], [mātr], and [frātr], respectively. Synchronically, in the
nominative the sequence stop + r undergoes a process of vocalization, resulting in *-er*
(cf. also nouns such as *ager* in the second declension). The comparison with Greek,
however, suggests that, historically, *-ēr* was long, as in Old Latin.

r/n-stems.   Some neuter stems are highly irregular, as a consequence of an old alternance between *-r* and *-n*, e.g. *iter, itineris* 'journey'; *femur, feminis* 'thigh', *iecur, iecinoris* 'liver' (also nom. *iocur* and gen. *iecoris, iocineris*, and *iocinoris*).

Grecisms. Āēr 'air' and *aethēr* 'heaven', both of Greek origin, can sometimes exhibit the Greek accusative forms, i.e. *āera* (vs. the Latin form *āerem*) and *aethera*, respectively.

Other examples

(16)   with *l*
    a. exul, exulis
       'exile'
    b. sāl (< *sals), salis
       'salt'
    c. sōl, sōlis
       'sun'

(17)   with *r*
    a. agger, aggeris
       'earthwork'
    b. fūr, fūris
       'thief'
    c. ōrātor, ōrātōris
       'speaker'

9.5.1.6 Voiceless alveolar fricative (*s*)

TABLE 9.14 Third declension (mas./fem., voiceless alveolar fricative): *flōs* 'flower'

	Singular		Plural	
nom.	[flōs] + ∅	flōs	[flōs] + ēs	flōrēs
gen.	[flōs] + is	flōris	[flōs] + um	flōrum
dat.	[flōs] + ī	flōrī	[flōs] + ibus	flōribus
acc.	[flōs] + em	flōrem	[flōs] + ēs	flōrēs
voc.	[flōs] + ∅	flōs	[flōs] + ēs	flōrēs
abl.	[flōs] + e	flōre	[flōs] + ibus	flōribus

TABLE 9.15 Third declension (neut., voiceless alveolar fricative): *corpus* 'body'

	Singular		Plural	
nom.	[corpos] + ∅ (and vowel weakening)	**corpus**	[corpos] + a	**corpora**
gen.	[corpos] + is	**corporis**	[corpos] + um	**corporum**
dat.	[corpos] + ī	**corporī**	[corpos] + ibus	**corporibus**
acc.	[corpos] + ∅ (and vowel weakening)	**corpus**	[corpos] + a	**corpora**
voc.	[corpos] + ∅ (and vowel weakening)	**corpus**	[corpos] + a	**corpora**
abl.	[corpos] + e	**corpore**	[corpos] + ibus	**corporibus**

Notes

The nominative and vocative singular (and the accusative singular of neuter nouns) are asigmatic, thus the pure stem emerges. If the vowel preceding -*s*- is a short -*o*-, it becomes -*u*- for vowel weakening, as in the second declension, e.g. *corpus* from [corpos], parallel to *lupus* from [lupos], cf. *tempus, temporis* 'time'.

Since the endings for the remaining cases all begin with a vowel, the correct context emerges for the application of rhotacism (cf. rule (20) in Section 8.6), i.e. intervocalic [s] becomes [r]. Sometimes -*r* is analogically extended to the nominative, and the final vowel is regularly shortened, e.g. *labōs/labor, labōris* 'work'.

Rhotacism does not apply to stems ending in double [ss], cf. *os* (<*oss), *ossis* 'bone', as opposed to *ōs, ōris* 'mouth'.

The stem of *cinis, cineris* 'ashes' is [cinis]. The nominative and vocative singular exhibit the pure stem. In the remainder of the cases, two adjustment rules apply, since the endings begin with a vowel. First of all, the -*s*- of the stem becomes -*r*- for the application of rhotacism: [[cinis] + is] → [ciniris]). Secondly, -*i*- becomes -*e*- before -*r*- in an open syllable from the application of rule (10b) in Section 8.5: [ciniris] → *cineris*.

os/es-**stem**. The neuter *genus, generis* 'birth' shows stem alternance between -*os*- and -*es*-, i.e. nominative, accusative, and vocative singular are formed from the stem [genos], while the remaining cases are derived from the stem [genes], cf. *scelus, sceleris* 'crime'; *fūnus, fūneris* 'funeral'.

Other examples

(18) masculine/feminine
   a. arbōs/arbor, arboris
      'tree'
   b. honōs/honor, honōris
      'honour'
   c. mōs, mōris
      'habit'

(19) neuter
       a. aes, aeris
          'copper'
       b. iūs, iūris
          'law'
       c. vās, vāsis
          'vessel'

9.5.2 i-stems

9.5.2.1 Feminine

TABLE 9.16 Third declension (fem., *i*-stems): *sitis* 'thirst'

	Singular		Plural	
nom.	[siti] + s	sitis	[siti] + ēs	sitēs
gen.	[siti] + s	sitis	[siti] + um	sitium
dat.	[siti] + long	sitī	[siti] + bus	sitibus
acc.	[siti] + m	sitim	[siti] + ēs	sitēs
voc.	[siti] + s	sitis	[siti] + ēs	sitēs
abl.	[siti] + long	sitī	[siti] + bus	sitibus

Notes

In the nominative, accusative, and vocative plural, the thematic vowel -*i*- before the ending -*ēs* is exceptionally deleted, from the analogical influence of the C-stems.

An archaic accusative plural in -*īs* is sometimes attested in poetry.

Other examples

(20) a. febris
          'fever'
       b. puppis
          'poop'
       c. turris
          'tower'
       d. tussis
          'cough'

Note that *vīs* 'strength' is a defective noun in the singular, because it only has the accusative *vim* and the ablative *vī*, and lacks the genitive and dative forms, which are replaced by the forms of a synonym, i.e. *rōbur* (gen. *rōboris*, dat. *rōborī*), whose proper meaning is 'oak'. The plural instead is formed from the stem [vīri] (nom./acc./voc. *vīrēs*, gen. *vīrium*, dat./abl. *vīribus*).

9.5.2.2 Neuter

TABLE 9.17 Third declension (neut., *i*-stems): *animal* 'animal'

	Singular		Plural	
nom.	[animāli] + ø (+ vowel delet.)	**animal**	[animāli] + a	**animālia**
gen.	[animāli] + s	**animālis**	[animāli] + um	**animālium**
dat.	[animāli] + long	**animālī**	[animāli] + bus	**animālibus**
acc.	[animāli] + ø (+ vowel delet.)	**animal**	[animāli] + a	**animālia**
voc.	[animāli] + ø (+ vowel delet.)	**animal**	[animāli] + a	**animālia**
abl.	[animāli] + long	**animālī**	[animāli] + bus	**animālibus**

Notes

The nominative, accusative, and vocative singular are asigmatic and exhibit optional stem vowel deletion in the final syllable. More precisely, vowel deletion creates words whose nominative ends in -*al* and in -*ar*, e.g. [animāli] + ø → *animal*, with vowel shortening of *ā* in the final syllable (cf. rule (6) in Section 8.4). In the absence of vowel deletion, -*ī* becomes -*ĕ*, by virtue of a general adjustment rule (cf. rule (14) in Section 8.5), e.g. [mari] + ø → *mare*.

Other examples

(21) words in -*al*
       a. capital, capitālis
          'capital offence'
       b. tribūnal, tribūnālis
          'tribunal'
       c. vectīgal, vectīgālis
          'tax'

(22) words in -*ar*
       a. calcar, calcāris
          'spur'
       b. exemplar, exemplāris
          'model'
       c. lacūnar, lacūnāris
          'ceiling'

(23) words in -*e*
       a. cubīle, cubīlis
          'bed'
       b. mare, maris
          'sea'
       c. rēte, rētis
          'net'

9.5.3 *Mixed class*

9.5.3.1 *i*-stems with the influence of C-stems

TABLE 9.18 Third declension (mas./fem., *i*-stems with the influence of C-stems): *nāvis* 'ship'

	Singular		Plural	
nom.	[nāvi] + s	**nāvis**	[nāvi] + ēs	**nāvēs**
gen.	[nāvi] + s	**nāvis**	[nāvi] + um	**nāvium**
dat.	[nāvi] + long	**nāvī**	[nāvi] + bus	**nāvibus**
acc.	[nāvi] + em	**nāvem**	[nāvi] + ēs	**nāvēs**
voc.	[nāvi] + s	**nāvis**	[nāvi] + ēs	**nāvēs**
abl.	[nāvi] + e	**nāve**	[nāvi] + bus	**nāvibus**

Notes

In the accusative and ablative singular, the stems of this class take the inflections of C-stems, i.e. *-em* and *-e*. The endings of the *i*-stems, i.e. *-im* and *-ī*, are rarely attested in this case.

Some stems also show a nominative and vocative singular in *-ēs*.

The plural coincides with that of *i*-stems.

Other examples

(24) nominative in *-is*
   a. cīvis
       'citizien'
   b. classis
       'fleet'
   c. ignis
       'fire'

(25) nominative in *-ēs*
   a. caedēs
       'massacre'
   b. clādēs
       'disaster'
   c. nūbēs
       'cloud'

Irregularities. (a) *Iuppiter, Iovis* 'Jupiter': the nominative and vocative derive from the contraction of the old vocative **Iou-pater*. (b) *bōs, bovis* 'ox': the nominative and vocative singular, as well as the genitive plural and the dative-ablative, are usually contracted forms, i.e. *bōs, boum,* and *bōbus* (or *būbus*), respectively. (c) *sūs, suis* 'pig' and *grūs, gruis* 'crane' are originally *ū*-stems. The dative-ablative plural of *sūs* is either *suibus* or *sūbus*. (d) *nix, nivis* 'snow', which exhibits *g/vi* alternance, is originally a labiovelar stem (**snigu-*). (e) *carō* (also *carnis*), *carnis* 'flesh' alternates between *n*-stem and *i*-stem.

9.5.3.2 Stems with syncope

TABLE 9.19 Third declension (mas./fem., stems with syncope): *falx* 'sickle'

	Singular		Plural	
nom.	[falci] + s + syncope	falx	[falci] + ēs	falcēs
gen.	[falci] + s	falcis	[falci] + um	falcium
dat.	[falci] + long	falcī	[falci] + bus	falcibus
acc.	[falci] + em	falcem	[falci] + ēs	falcēs
voc.	[falci] + s + syncope	falx	[falci] + ēs	falcēs
abl.	[falci] + e	falce	[falci] + bus	falcibus

Notes

In the nominative and vocative singular the thematic vowel is exceptionally deleted through a process called 'syncope'. This process preferably takes place if the stem is bisyllabic and the stem vowel is preceded by a consonant cluster formed by a liquid or nasal and a stop. Thus, when the *-s* ending is added, the result of the syncope is the formation of a monosyllable ending in the sequence stop + *s*. The evolution of this group coincides with the one we have already described for C-stems, (cf. Section 9.5.1), that is:

(26) velar + *s* → *x*
    a. arx, arcis
        'stronghold'
    b. merx, mercis
        'goods'

(27) bilabial + *s* → *ps, bs*
    a. stirps, stirpis
        'stock'
    b. urbs, urbis
        'city'

(28) dental + *s* → deletion of the dental
    a. līs, lītis
        'quarrel'
    b. mons, montis
        'mountain'

In those few cases where the nominative is disyllabic or trisyllabic, the stress falls on the last syllable, that is the position it occupied before the syncope, e.g. *Arpīnás* from [Arpīnātis] 'of Arpinum'; *optimás* from [optimātis] 'aristocratic'; *Samnís* from [Samnītis] 'of Samnium'.

A note on the traditional distinction between parisyllabic and imparisyllabic words

In order to describe the third declension, many school grammars refer to the following clue, as stated by the Latin grammarian Priscian. The starting observation is that, statistically, the genitive of C-stems typically contains one syllable more than the nominative, e.g. *rēx, rēgis*, whereas this is not true for *i*-stems, whose nominative and genitive typically contain the same number of syllables, e.g. *cīvis, cīvis*. Accordingly, the third declension is said to include two inflectional paradigms, i.e. one for the *parisyllabic* (e.g. *cīvis*) and one for the *imparisyllabic* (e.g. *rēx*) words.

Such a view, however, lacks any empirical foundation, as there is strong cross-linguistic evidence that the grammar of natural languages seldom counts the number of syllables to predict the inflection of words. To make matters worse, this prescriptive rule implies a clear contradiction, i.e. imparisyllabic words with two consonants before the singular genitive ending, e.g. *urbs, urbis*, are taken to be parisyllabic. Even if we ignore this contradiction, such a rule would force the learner to acquire a long list of exceptions, which become unnecessary if the declension is predicted from the properties of the stem, instead. For these reasons, we have not taken into account such a complex and unjustified approach in our grammar.

9.6 The fourth declension

The vast majority of Latin nouns belong to the first three declensions. The last two declensions in contrast contain an extremely reduced number of elements. In particular, the fourth declension includes a small number of *u*-stems. Also note that some nouns which belong to the fourth declension also exhibit corresponding second declension forms, e.g. *domus* and *fructus*. As for their gender, the vast majority of stems belonging to the fourth declension are masculine or neuter.

TABLE 9.20 Fourth declension (mas./fem.): *exercitus* 'army'

	Singular		Plural	
nom.	[exercitu] + s	**exercitus**	[exercitu] + $_{long}$ + s	**exercitūs**
gen.	[exercitu] + $_{long}$ + s	**exercitūs**	[exercitu] + um	**exercituum**
dat.	[exercitu] + ī	**exercituī**	[exercitu] + ibus	**exercitibus**
acc.	[exercitu] + m	**exercitum**	[exercitu] + $_{long}$ + s	**exercitūs**
voc.	[exercitu] + s	**exercitus**	[exercitu] + $_{long}$ + s	**exercitūs**
abl.	[exercitu] + $_{long}$	**exercitū**	[exercitu] + ibus	**exercitibus**

TABLE 9.21 Fourth declension (neut.): *cornū* 'horn'

	Singular		Plural	
nom.	[cornū] + ø	**cornū**	[cornū] + a	**cornua**
gen.	[cornū] + s	**cornūs**	[cornū] + um	**cornuum**
dat.	[cornū] + ø	**cornū**	[cornū] + ibus	**cornibus**
acc.	[cornū] + ø	**cornū**	[cornū] + a	**cornua**
voc.	[cornū] + ø	**cornū**	[cornū] + a	**cornua**
abl.	[cornū] + _{long}	**cornū**	[cornū] + ibus	**cornibus**

Notes

The nominative masculine and feminine are sigmatic, the nominative neuter is asigmatic.

According to rule (4) in Section 8.3, vowel deletion does not apply to -*u*-. For this reason, vowel deletion does not apply to dative singular masculine and to genitive plural. In the dative singular neuter, the original ending has disappeared.

In the plural neuter declension, the thematic vowel is shortened if it precedes another vowel, in accordance with the rule *vōcālis ante vōcālem corripitur* (cf. rule (5) in Section 8.4).

An archaic or perhaps analogical ending -*ubus* for the dative and ablative plural is rarely attested. In Classical Latin, the -*ibus* form was generalized.

Other examples

(29) masculine
    a. āctus
       'act'
    b. aestus
       'heat'
    c. cōnsulātus
       'consulate'
    d. frūctus
       'fruit'

(30) feminine
    a. anus
       'old woman'
    b. manus
       'hand'
    c. nurus
       'daughter-in-law'

(31) neuter
    a. genū
       'knee'
    b. pecū
       'cattle'
    c. verū
       'spit'
    d. gelū/gelus (alternating)
       'frost'

Note that *domus* was predominantly an *o*-stem in Old Latin and, consequently, it fluctuates between the second and fourth declension, cf. sg. nom. *domus*, gen. *domī/ domūs*, dat. *domuī/domō*, acc. *domum*, abl. *domō*; pl. nom. *domūs*, gen. *domuum/ domōrum*, dat./abl. *domibus*, acc. *domōs/domūs*.

It may be also useful to note that *Iēsus*, which is not a classical noun, becomes *Iēsum* in the accusative and *Iēsū* in all other cases.

9.7 The fifth declension

The fifth declension includes a small number of *ē*-stems. Similarly to the the fourth declension, there are some nouns which exhibit corresponding forms belonging to another declension, in this case the first one, e.g. *canitiēs/canitia* 'white hair'; *māteriēs/māteria* 'material'; or the third one, e.g. *plēbēs/plēbs* 'people'.

TABLE 9.22 Fifth declension (fem.): *rēs* 'thing'

	Singular		Plural	
nom.	[rē] + s	**rēs**	[rē] + s	**rēs**
gen.	[rē] + ī	**reī**	[rē] + rum	**rērum**
dat.	[rē] + ī	**reī**	[rē] + bus	**rēbus**
acc.	[rē] + m	**rem**	[rē] + s	**rēs**
voc.	[rē] + s	**rēs**	[rē] + s	**rēs**
abl.	[rē]	**rē**	[rē] + bus	**rēbus**

Notes

In the genitive and dative singular, the thematic vowel is shortened before the vowel ending, in accordance with the adjustment rule *vōcālis ante vōcālem corripitur* (cf. rule (5) in Section 8.4). There are, however, some exceptions. In Plautus and Terence, the original long vowel *rēī* or the diphthong *rei* are attested, beside the shortened form *rĕī*. In Classical Latin, the nouns *diēs, diēī* 'day', *aciēs, aciēī* 'troops', and *faciēs, faciēī* 'face' usually preserve the long vowel.

In the accusative singular, the thematic vowel is shortened in a final syllable before *-m*, following rule (6) in Section 8.4.

Note that *diēs* retains its feminine gender when it is used to denote a specific day, e.g. *diēs dicta* 'the agreed day', otherwise it tends to acquire masculine gender, e.g. *tertius diēs* 'the third day'.

Other examples

(32) a. fidēs, fideī
         'faith'
     b. speciēs, speciēī
         'species'
     c. spēs, speī
         'hope'

10

Adjective declensions

Adjectives largely follow the same inflectional patterns as nouns. There are two classes of inflection. The first one (Table 10.1) includes stems ending in the vowels -o-/-a-, which follow the first and second declension. The second class (Tables 10.2 and 10.3) includes C-stems and i-stems, which follow the third declension.

10.1 First class

TABLE 10.1 First class (o/a-stems): bonus 'good'

	Singular			Plural		
	mas.	fem.	neut.	mas.	fem.	neut.
nom.	bonus	bona	bonum	bonī	bonae	bona
gen.	bonī	bonae	bonī	bonōrum	bonārum	bonōrum
dat.	bonō	bonae	bonō	bonīs	bonīs	bonīs
acc.	bonum	bonam	bonum	bonōs	bonās	bona
voc.	bone	bona	bonum	bonī	bonae	bona
abl.	bonō	bonā	bonō	bonīs	bonīs	bonīs

Notes
As is also the case for the second declension, if -r- precedes the stem vowel, the nominative singular masculine is asigmatic (with optional -r- vocalization), e.g. *miser, misera, miserum* from the stem [misero/a] and *pulcher, pulchra, pulchrum* from the stem [pulchro/a].

10.2 Second class

10.2.1 C-stems

TABLE 10.2 Second class (C-stems): *vetus* 'old'

	Singular			Plural		
	mas.	fem.	neut.	mas.	fem.	neut.
nom.	vetus	vetus	vetus	veterēs	veterēs	vetera
gen.	veteris	veteris	veteris	veterum	veterum	veterum
dat.	veterī	veterī	veterī	veteribus	veteribus	veteribus
acc.	veterem	veterem	vetus	veterēs	veterēs	vetera
voc.	vetus	vetus	vetus	veterēs	veterēs	vetera
abl.	vetere	vetere	vetere	veteribus	veteribus	veteribus

Notes

The nominative and vocative singular are the same for all the three genders. In the above example, the stem of nom. and voc. is [vetos] (*vetus* by vowel weakening), while the remaining cases are derived from the stem [vetes] (*veter-* by rhotacism). The stem alternation -*os*-/-*es*- is the same as in the noun *genus, generis*.

Consistent with the behaviour of C-stems, the ablative ending is -*e*, the genitive plural ending is -*um*, and the nominative/accusative/ablative plural neuter ending is -*a*.

The ablative ending of some of the adjectives belonging to this class is -*i*, because of the influence of stems ending in a vowel, which constitute the vast majority of the second class adjectives.

Other examples

(1) a. compos, compotis
        'self-controlled'
     b. dīves, dīvitis
        'rich'
     c. pauper, pauperis
        'poor'

10.2.2 i-stems

TABLE 10.3 Second class (*i*-stems): *ācer* 'sharp'

	Singular			Plural		
	mas.	fem.	neut.	mas.	fem.	neut.
nom.	ācer	ācris	ācre	ācrēs	ācrēs	ācria
gen.	ācris	ācris	ācris	ācrium	ācrium	ācrium
dat.	ācrī	ācrī	ācrī	ācribus	ācribus	ācribus
acc.	ācrem	ācrem	ācre	ācrēs	ācrēs	ācria
voc.	ācer	ācris	ācre	ācrēs	ācrēs	ācria
abl.	ācrī	ācrī	ācrī	ācribus	ācribus	ācribus

Notes

In the above example, i.e. a -*ri*- stem [ācri], the nominative and vocative singular have three different forms for the three genders, i.e. (i) a zero ending accompanied by the deletion of the thematic vowel and vocalization of -*r* into -*er* for the masculine; (ii) an -*s* ending for the feminine; (iii) a zero ending with the adjustment rule $i \rightarrow e$ in the final syllable for the neuter. Adjectives of this type have therefore three endings for the nominative singular, i.e. -*er*, -*is*, -*e*. Note, however, that most adjectives with the stem vowel -*i*- can have either two endings (-*is*, -*e*), e.g. *brevis* (masculine/feminine) and *breve* (neuter), or just one, e.g. *fēlīx* for all three genders.

Consistent with the behaviour of *i*-stems, the ablative ending is -*ī*, the genitive plural ending is -*ium*, and the nominative/accusative/ablative plural neuter is -*ia*. Conversely, the accusative singular masculine and feminine is -*em* from the influence of the C-stems.

In the accusative plural masculine and feminine, an archaic ending -*īs* is also attested, e.g. *ācrīs*.

Other examples

(2)   a. *celer, celeris, celere*
            'quick'
       b. *facilis, facile*
            'easy'
       c. *prūdens*
            'wise'

10.3 Comparative and superlative

Adjectives decline in three possible degrees, i.e. positive, e.g. *happy, beautiful*, comparative, e.g. *happier, more beautiful*, and superlative, e.g. *happiest, most beautiful, very beautiful*.

In Latin, the comparative is formed by adding the suffix *-ior* (masculine and feminine) / *-ius* (neuter) to the adjectival stem, with the deletion of the thematic vowel. The comparative follows the same inflectional paradigm as second class adjectives with a C-stem. We report some examples in (3) for the masculine/feminine:

(3) a. *clārus, -a, -um*   [[clāro]$_A$ + ior]$_A$ *clārior*   'more famous'
   b. *pulcher, -ra, -rum*   [[pulchro]$_A$ + ior]$_A$ *pulchrior*   'more beautiful'
   c. *ācer, -is, e*   [[ācri]$_A$ + ior]$_A$ *ācrior*   'sharper'
   d. *fortis, -e*   [[forti]$_A$ + ior]$_A$ *fortior*   'stronger'
   e. *audāx*   [[audāci]$_A$ + ior]$_A$ *audācior*   'bolder'

The superlative is derived by adding the suffix *-issimus, -a, -um*, plus the usual deletion of the thematic vowel. It follows the same inflectional paradigm as first class adjectives. We report some examples in (4) for the masculine:

(4) a. *clārus, -a,-um*   [[clāro]$_A$ + issimus]$_A$ *clārissimus*   'most famous'
   b. *fortis, -e*   [[forti]$_A$ + issimus]$_A$ *fortissimus*   'strongest'
   c. *audāx*   [[audāci]$_A$ + issimus]$_A$ *audācissimus*   'boldest'

If the nominative ends in *-er* or *-ilis*, the suffix is not *-issimus* but rather *-simus*, where *-is-* has been dropped. Some examples are reported in (5) (note the assimilation between *-s-* and the liquid):

(5) a. *pulcher, -ra, -rum*   *pulcher-simus   >   *pulcherrimus*   'most beautiful'
   b. *pauper*   *pauper-simus   >   *pauperrimus*   'poorest'
   c. *ācer, -is, -e*   *ācer-simus   >   *ācerrimus*   'sharpest'
   d. *facilis, -e*   *facil-simus   >   *facillimus*   'easiest'

Some frequently attested adjectives exhibit an irregular inflectional paradigm, characterized by changes in the stem (the same is true for English):

(6) a. *bonus*   'good'   *melior*   'better'   *optimus*   'best'
   b. *malus*   'bad'   *pēior*   'worse'   *pessimus*   'worst'
   c. *māgnus*   'big'   *māior*   'bigger'   *māximus*   'biggest'
   d. *parvus*   'small'   *minor*   'smaller'   *minimus*   'smallest'
   e. *multus*   'much'   *plūs*   'more'   *plūrimus*   'most'

Finally, some adjectives do not form the comparative and superlative by means of inflections, but they simply add *magis* 'more' and *māximē* 'most', e.g. *idōneus* 'fit', *magis idōneus* 'fitter', *māximē idōneus* 'fittest'.

As for their meaning, it is important to determine whether the comparative and superlative are accompanied by a term of comparison or if they are used on their own. The former type is called 'relative', whereas the second one is called 'absolute'. For example, the comparative *pulchrior* means 'more beautiful' (than somebody else) when it is relative, and 'a little bit too beautiful' when it is absolute. Similarly, the superlative *pulcherrimus* means 'the most beautiful' (of some group) when it is relative, but 'very beautiful' when it is absolute.

11

Adverbs

Adverbs cannot be inflected, so there is little to say about their morphology. Usually the dictionary entry coincides with the adverb itself, e.g. *mox* 'soon', *saepe* 'often'. However, it is useful to note that, in Latin, similarly to English, it is also possible to derive adverbs from adjectives by adding a suffix, e.g. *quick* → *quickly*. In this way, it possible to infer the meaning of many adverbs from the meaning of the adjectives from which they are derived, without consulting a dictionary.

11.1 Formation and comparison

Usually, adverbs are derived from adjectives by adding the suffix *-ē* (first class adjectives) and *-iter* (second class adjectives) to the stem.

Similarly to the corresponding adjectives, adverbs have degrees of comparison, i.e. a comparative form (suffix *-ius*) and a superlative one (suffix *-issimē*), as shown in Table 11.1.

Adverbs derived from the irregular adjectives *bonus* 'good' and *malus* 'bad' are irregular themselves, i.e. *bene* 'well' and *male* 'ill'. From *māgnus* 'big' and

TABLE 11.1 Adverbs: formation and comparison

Adjective	Adverb	Comparative	Superlative
molestus 'troublesome'	*molestē* 'with trouble'	*molestius* 'with more trouble'	*molestissimē* 'with most trouble'
pulcher 'beautiful'	*pulchrē* 'beautifully'	*pulchrius* 'more beautifully'	*pulcherrimē* 'very beautifully'
celer 'quick'	*celeriter* 'quickly'	*celerius* 'more quickly'	*celerrimē* 'most quickly'
gravis 'heavy'	*graviter* 'heavily'	*gravius* 'more heavily'	*gravissimē* 'most heavily'

parvus 'small' no positive adverb can be derived, but only the comparative and the superlative, i.e. *magis* 'more', *minus* 'less' and *māximē* 'most', *minimē* 'least', respectively.

Adverbs can also be derived from adjectives by adding the ablative or accusative singular neuter endings -*ō* or -*um*, albeit less frequently, e.g. *falsus* 'liar' → *falsō* (but also *falsē*) 'falsely'; *multus* 'great' → *multum* 'much'.

Finally, some adverbs are derived from nouns by adding the suffix -*im*, e.g. *fūrtum* 'theft' → *fūrtim* 'furtively'; *pars* 'part' → *partim* 'partly'.

12

Pronouns

Traditional grammars place different elements under the category of pronouns. For this reason, they tend to be rather confusing in their treatment of this category. To make the task easier, we will identify different subgroups and describe their features separately.

12.1 Personal and reflexive

Personal pronouns represent the only sub-category which properly fulfils the function of a 'pro-noun', i.e. they stand *prō nōmine* 'in the place of a noun', e.g. a pronoun like 'he' can occupy the same position as the full noun 'John'.

The label 'personal' comes from the word 'person'. This latter originally belonged to theatre jargon, where it was used to indicate the character of a play. A sentence can be compared to a small play with a few actors, i.e. there is an 'I' who is talking to a 'you' about 'him/her/it'. Human language is designed to allow communication between three grammatical 'persons'.

For this reason, there are three personal pronouns, i.e. 'I' (first person), 'you' (second person), and 'he/she/it' (third person), with the corresponding plural forms, i.e. 'we', 'you', and 'they'.

From a morphological point of view, the declension of personal pronouns is highly irregular, as it is often the case for high-frequency words. This is because the declension of unknown words must be inferred on the basis of a certain set of rules, while the declension of very common words can be simply memorized.

For this reason, although the declension of personal pronouns does contain stems and endings, it is advisable to memorize the single forms, without applying any inflectional rules, due to the strong irregularity of their paradigm (see Tables 12.1 and 12.2).

12.1.1 First and second person

TABLE 12.1 Personal pronouns: first and second person

| | Singular | | Plural | |
	1st pers.	2nd pers.	1st pers.	2nd pers.
nom.	ego 'I'	tū 'you'	nōs 'we'	vōs 'you'
gen.	meī	tuī	nostrī/nostrum	vestrī/vestrum
dat.	mihi	tibi	nōbīs	vōbīs
acc.	mē	tē	nōs	vōs
abl.	mē	tē	nōbīs	vōbīs

Notes

The first person vocative is never used (because it is very unlikely that speakers address themselves by saying 'o me/us'). The second person vocative coincides with the nominative (cf. *heus, tū* 'hey, you').

The second form of the genitive plural has a partitive value, i.e. *nostrum* means 'among us', *vestrum* means 'between you'. For example, *nēmō nostrum* means 'none of us', that is 'none among us', as opposed to *memor sīs nostrī* 'be mindful of us'.

Ego, mihi, and *tibi* are pyrrhic in the classical period, but they are still frequently iambic in Plautus (*egō, mihī, tibī*). This is clearly a case of iambic shortening.

12.1.2 Third person

TABLE 12.2 Personal pronouns: third person

| | Singular | | | Plural | | |
	mas.	fem.	neut.	mas.	fem.	neut.
nom.	is 'he'	ea 'she'	id 'it'	iī (eī, ī) 'they'	eae	ea
gen.	eius	eius	eius	eōrum	eārum	eōrum
dat.	eī	eī	eī	iīs (eīs, īs)	iīs (eīs, īs)	iīs (eīs, īs)
acc.	eum	eam	id	eōs	eās	ea
abl.	eō	eā	eō	iīs (eīs, īs)	iīs (eīs, īs)	iīs (eīs, īs)

Notes

From a historical point of view, Latin lacks a proper form of non-reflexive personal pronoun for the third person. Its function is supplied by the original determinative *is* 'that/he'.

There is an alternation in the stem between *i-* and *e-*.

The endings of the genitive and dative singular are *-ius* and *-ī*, respectively, which are typical of the pronominal declension. As for the genitive, the spelling EIIVS of inscriptions suggests a pronunciation with a diphthong *ei-* and a short syllable beginning with a semivowel, *-jus*, which is confirmed by the disyllabic scansion, trochaic or pyrrhic (*e-jus*), of classical poetry. In Plautus, *eius* may also be frequently reduced to a monosyllable by a phenomenon of contraction called synizesis. As for the dative, two archaic scansions are commonly found in Plautus, i.e. a spondaic *ēī* and a monosyllabic *ei*, while the iambic *eī* spread in classical poetry.

The nominative plural masculine is *iī* or *ii* in Classical Latin, while in Plautus it is commonly a monosyllabic *ei* or *ī*, but only rarely *eī*. The Plautine forms survived as archaisms in later times.

The dative/ablative plural is *īīs* or *iis* in Classical Latin, while the archaic Plautine forms are *eis*, *īs*, and *eīs*.

12.1.3 Reflexive

Reflexive pronouns are used in order to refer to oneself. For the first and second persons, the same forms of the personal pronouns are used. For the third persons, the special forms of the reflexive pronoun are used for all genders and numbers, i.e. gen. *suī* 'of himself/herself/itself/themselves'; dat. *sibi*; acc. *sē*; abl. *sē*. The last two forms may be also reinforced by reduplication, i.e. *sēsē*.

As a rule, third person reflexive pronouns always refer to the subject of the sentence, otherwise the personal pronoun *is*, correctly inflected, is employed.

According to modern linguistic theories, this is due to the fact that reflexive pronouns are *anaphoric* elements, that is elements which lack an autonomous referent and must refer to an antecedent, as shown by the examples in (1):

(1)   a. Caesar$_i$ sē$_i$ ad nēminem adiunxit (Cic. *Phil.* V 44)
          'Caesar did not join anyone'
          (lit. Caesar$_i$ did not join himself$_i$ to anyone)

      b. Phaethō$_i$ lībertus eum$_j$ nōn vīdit (Cic. *Att.* III 8, 2)
          'Phaeto$_i$ the freedman did not see him$_j$'

In (1a), the anaphor *sē* is co-indexed with the antecedent *Caesar* to which it refers. In contrast, the pronoun *eum* in (1b) has an independent referent, which is different from *Phaethō*.

The behaviour of anaphors is governed by the so-called 'Binding Theory', which states that anaphors must be bound in their domain. A prototypical example of domain is the one delimited by the subject, which dominates the entire clause. This explains why the anaphor *sē* must be bound by the subject. Binding Theory also states that pronouns must be free in their domain. Consequently, the referent of the pronoun *is* must be different from the referent of the subject.

12.2 Possessive

Possessive pronouns are not proper pronouns, but they belong rather to the category of nominal 'modifiers', strictly speaking, similarly to adjectives (for this reason, they also inflect like adjectives).

In contrast to personal pronouns, the pronominal use of this category always presupposes the underlying presence of a noun. This is also the case in English, e.g. when we say *mine* or *yours*, an implicit noun is always understood.

There are three possessive pronouns (see Table 12.3), referring to the three grammatical persons, i.e. *meus* 'my', which refers to the 'I' dimension, *tuus* 'your', which refers to the 'you' dimension and *suus* 'his/her/its/their', which refers to the third person dimension.

TABLE 12.3 Possessive pronouns

	Singular	Plural
1st pers.	**meus, -a, -um** 'my'	**noster, -tra, -trum** 'our'
2nd pers.	**tuus, -a, -um** 'your'	**vester, -tra, -trum** 'your'
3rd pers.	**suus, -a, -um** 'his/her/its'	**suus, -a, -um** 'their'

Notes
The declension of possessive pronouns coincides with the one of first class adjectives.

The vocative is employed only for the first person. The two forms are: sg. *mī* and pl. *noster*.

The possessive pronoun *suus* is an anaphor and it usually refers to the subject, otherwise the pronoun *eius* is employed, as shown by example (2):

(2) Tīmocharēs$_i$ Fabriciō cōnsulī pollicitus est sē$_i$ Pyrrhum$_j$ venēnō per filium suum$_i$, quī pōtiōnibus eius$_j$ praeerat, necātūrum (Val. Max. 6, 5, 1)
     'Timocharcs$_i$ promised the consul Fabricius that he$_i$ would kill Pyrrhus$_j$ with the poison, by means of his$_i$ son, who was in charge of his$_j$ drinks'

While the anaphors *sē* and *suus* must be bound by their antecedent, i.e. they must be co-indexed with the subject *Tīmocharēs*, the pronoun *eius* must be free, i.e. its referent must be different from the subject *Tīmocharēs* (cf. its actual referent, *Pyrrhus*).

12.3 Demonstrative

Similarly to possessive pronouns, demonstrative pronouns actually belong to the category of nominal 'modifiers', that is, they are more similar to adjectives than to pronouns. This is because their function is not to replace nouns, but rather to modify them, in order to express their demonstrative value. The latter term comes from Lat. *dēmonstrāre*, meaning 'to indicate something'. This is also the case in English, e.g. when we use the demonstrative *that*, optionally accompanied by one pointing finger, we always mean 'that person' or 'that thing'.

There are three demonstrative pronouns (see Tables 12.4–12.6), referring to the three grammatical persons, i.e. *hic* 'this' refers to the dimension which is near to 'I', *iste* 'that (of yours)' refers to the dimension which is near to 'you', and *ille* 'that (one)' refers to the dimension which is near to 'him/her/it'.

Demonstratives can also be employed in order to refer to an element which has already been mentioned in the course of the discussion (this is the so-called 'anaphoric' use). In that case, *hic* indicates an element mentioned in the nearest context, while *ille* indicates an element mentioned in an earlier context.

Finally, *iste* can sometimes acquire a negative meaning of scorn or contempt, e.g. 'that damned', while *ille* can acquire an emphatic value, meaning 'that famous'.

12.3.1 Hic 'this'

TABLE 12.4 Demonstrative pronouns: *hic*

	Singular			Plural		
	mas.	fem.	neut.	mas.	fem.	neut.
nom.	hic	haec	hoc	hī	hae	haec
gen.	huius	huius	huius	hōrum	hārum	hōrum
dat.	huic	huic	huic	hīs	hīs	hīs
acc.	hunc	hanc	hoc	hōs	hās	haec
abl.	hōc	hāc	hōc	hīs	hīs	hīs

Notes

All singular cases (with the exception of the genitive), and the nominative/accusative plural neuter, exhibit the suffix -*c*, which entails a 'deictic value' (from the Greek *déiknymi* 'to demonstrate'). This suffix originally derives from an ancient particle, i.e. *ce*, which was employed to reinforce the demonstrative.

The vowel of the nominative is etymologically short in the masculine and neuter, but the metrical scansion of the syllable is usually long in the neuter *hōc* < *hŏcc* < *hŏd-c*. On the other hand, *hǐc* is always short in Plautus and Terence, but tends to be analogically lengthened after neuters in later poets.

The genitive *huius* is generally disyllabic, i.e. with initial diphthong *ui-* and a short syllable -*us*. In Plautus it may be reduced to a monosyllable by synizesis. The dative *huic* is generally monosyllabic in Classical Latin.

12.3.2 Iste 'that (of yours)'

TABLE 12.5 Demonstrative pronouns: *iste*

	Singular			Plural		
	mas.	fem.	neut.	mas.	fem.	neut.
nom.	iste	ista	istud	istī	istae	ista
gen.	istīus	istīus	istīus	istōrum	istārum	istōrum
dat.	istī	istī	istī	istīs	istīs	istīs
acc.	istum	istam	istud	istōs	istās	ista
abl.	istō	istā	istō	istīs	istīs	istīs

Notes

The only forms to memorize are those of the nominative singular, as this paradigm exhibits the usual pronominal endings -*ius* and -*ī* for the genitive and dative, while the rest of the forms regularly follow the first class of adjectives.

The deictic suffix -*c* survives only in some archaic forms, especially in Plautus, cf. nom. sg. *istic, istaec, istuc*; acc. *istunc, istanc, istuc*; abl. *istōc, istāc, istōc*; nom. pl. feminine and neuter *istaec*.

12.3.3 Ille 'that (one)'

TABLE 12.6 Demonstrative pronouns: *ille*

	Singular			Plural		
	mas.	fem.	neut.	mas.	fem.	neut.
nom.	ille	illa	illud	illī	illae	illa
gen.	illīus	illīus	illīus	illōrum	illārum	illōrum
dat.	illī	illī	illī	illīs	illīs	illīs
acc.	illum	illam	illud	illōs	illās	illa
abl.	illō	illā	illō	illīs	illīs	illīs

Notes

The inflectional paradigm is similar to that of *iste*.

A few traces of the archaic form *olle* are preserved in Cicero (*ollōs* and *olla*) and Virgil (*ollī*). The deictic suffix *-c* is largely used in Plautus, cf. nom. sg. *illic, illaec, illuc*; acc. *illunc, illanc, illuc*; abl. *illōc, illāc, illōc*; nom. pl. feminine and neuter *illaec*.

12.4 Determinative

The so-called determinative pronouns are similar to the demonstratives. Similarly to the latter, they fulfil an anaphoric function, as they refer to an element which is already known in the context.

The original determinative *is* has supplied the function of the third person personal pronoun. From its stem, two determinative pronouns are derived, i.e. *īdem* 'the same' (see Table 12.7) and *ipse* 'self' (see Table 12.8). From a semantic point of view, the former expresses a relationship of identity with a person/thing which is already given in the context, while the latter highlights the most important person/thing, in contrast to some other entity.

12.4.1 Īdem 'the same'

TABLE 12.7 Determinative pronouns: *īdem*

	Singular			Plural		
	mas.	fem.	neut.	mas.	fem.	neut.
nom.	īdem	eadem	idem	iīdem	eaedem	eadem
gen.	eiusdem	eiusdem	eiusdem	eorundem	earundem	eorundem
dat.	eīdem	eīdem	eīdem	iīsdem	iīsdem	iīsdem
acc.	eundem	eandem	idem	eōsdem	eāsdem	eadem
abl.	eōdem	eādem	eōdem	iīsdem	iīsdem	iīsdem

Notes

This declension is derived from the third person pronoun *is, ea, id*, with the addition of the suffix *-dem*.

The nominative singular masculine *īdem* is derived from *ĭs-dem*.

All the alternative archaic forms that we noted in the declension of *is* are also attested in the declension of *īdem*, e.g. dative singular *eīdem* and *eidem*; nominative plural masculine *īdem* and *eīdem*; dative/ablative plural *īsdem* and *eisdem*.

12.4.2 Ipse 'self'

TABLE 12.8 Determinative pronouns: *ipse*

	Singular			Plural		
	mas.	fem.	neut.	mas.	fem.	neut.
nom.	ipse	ipsa	ipsum	ipsī	ipsae	ipsa
gen.	ipsīus	ipsīus	ipsīus	ipsōrum	ipsārum	ipsōrum
dat.	ipsī	ipsī	ipsī	ipsīs	ipsīs	ipsīs
acc.	ipsum	ipsam	ipsum	ipsōs	ipsās	ipsōs
abl.	ipsō	ipsā	ipsō	ipsīs	ipsīs	ipsīs

Notes

This pronoun was originally derived from *is, ea, id* through the addition of the suffix *-pse*. Some traces can be found in Plautus, e.g. *eumpse, eampse, eōpse, eāpse*. In Classical Latin, *ipse* lost the original morphology of *is* and a new stem *ipso-/ipsa-* emerged, with its own regular pronominal declension, unlike *īdem*, which is still transparently composed by *is* and *-dem*.

12.5 Interrogative

The so-called interrogative pronouns belong to a category which is completely different from those considered so far, i.e. pronouns and nominal modifiers. Interrogative elements rather resemble those particles which introduce embedded clauses, that we called 'complementizers' (cf. Section 7.2). This is also the case in English, where an interrogative pronoun such as *who* in *I wonder who saw Mary* fulfils a similar function to the complementizer *if* in *I wonder if she has left*.

Interrogatives are used to replace an element which is unknown to the speaker and are placed in a clause-initial position, e.g. *quid is fēcit?* 'what did he do?' This is an instance of so-called 'wh-movement', that we shall discuss in further detail later on (cf. Section 24.3). This name derives from the fact that, in Indo-European languages, interrogative constituents typically comprise an interrogative word (either a pronoun, an adjective, or an adverb) whose stem includes a labiovelar stop, cf. Lat. *qu-* (*quis, quī, quālis, quantus*), or the result of the evolution of an original Indo-European labiovelar stop, cf. En. *wh-* (*who, which*, from which the expression 'wh-words' is derived), Ger. *w-* (*wer, was*), It. *ch-* (*chi, che cosa*).

Here we will simply describe the inflectional patterns of Latin interrogative pronouns. There are four main groups (cf. Sections 12.5.1 - 12.5.4).

12.5.1 quis? 'who'; quid? 'what'

TABLE 12.9 Interrogative pronouns: *quis, quid*

	Singular		Plural	
	mas./fem.	neut.	mas./fem.	neut.
nom.	quis	quid	quī	quae
gen.	cuius	cuius	quōrum	quōrum
dat.	cuī	cuī	quibus	quibus
acc.	quem	quid	quōs	quae
abl.	quō	quō	quibus	quibus

Notes

The masculine forms can also be used to refer to females, e.g. *quis tū es, mulier?* 'who are you, woman?'

Cuius corresponds to En. *whose*, and *quem* to *whom* (note that English has preserved traces of inflection in the interrogative pronoun series).

The archaic forms of the genitive and dative are *quoius* and *quoi(ī)*, respectively; the scansion is either disyllabic or monosyllabic, by virtue of synizesis.

From *quis*, *quid* three other interrogative pronouns are derived, i.e. *quis-nam* 'who in the world?', *ec-quis*, and *num-quis* 'any(one/thing)?'

12.5.2 quī?, quae?, quod? 'which/what kind of?'

TABLE 12.10 Interrogative pronouns: *quī, quae, quod*

	Singular			Plural		
	mas.	fem.	neut.	mas.	fem.	neut.
nom.	quī	quae	quod	quī	quae	quae
gen.	cuius	cuius	cuius	quōrum	quārum	quōrum
dat.	cuī	cuī	cuī	quibus	quibus	quibus
acc.	quem	quem	quod	quōs	quās	quae
abl.	quō	quā	quō	quibus	quibus	quibus

12.5.3 uter?, utra?, utrum? 'which of the two?'

Its declension coincides with first class adjectives, except for the genitive *-īus* (*utrīus*) and the dative *-ī* (*utrī*).

12.5.4 quālis?, quāle? 'of what kind?'; quantus?, -a?, -um? 'how much?'; quot? 'how many?'

These are inflected like adjectives, except for *quot*, which is invariant.

12.6 Relative

Relative pronouns are similar to interrogatives, in terms of both inflection and syntactic function. As for their morphology, some essential information is reported in Sections 12.6.1 and 12.6.2.

12.6.1 quī *'who' (mas.)*, quae *'who' (fem.)*, quod *'which' (neut.)*

The inflection of the relative pronoun coincides with *quī?*, *quae?*, *quod?* (cf. Table 12.10).

12.6.2 quisquis *'whoever'*; quīcumque *'whoever'*, *'whatever'*

Quisquis 'whoever', *quidquid* 'whatever', and *quīcumque, quaecumque, quod-cumque* 'whoever', 'whatever' are traditionally called 'relative-indefinite' pronouns and are derived from the relative pronoun *quī, quae, quod*.

Similarly to interrogatives, relative pronouns replace a constituent and occupy a clause-initial position. The main difference is that a relative clause is always embedded, and that relative pronouns function as a link with the main clause.

The internal structure of relative clauses will be considered in further detail in Chapter 25. For the purposes of the present discussion, it is sufficient to note that a relative embedded clause occupies the position of a nominal adjunct, e.g.:

(3)   The bridge, which had been damaged by the storm, was repaired.

Note that the relative clause, i.e. *which had been damaged by the storm*, modifies its antecedent, i.e. *the bridge*, just like an adjective modifies a noun. The mechanism is the same in Latin, as shown in example (4):

(4)   Pons, quī fuerat tempestāte interruptus, paene erat refectus (Caes. *civ.* I 41, 1)
      'The bridge, which had been broken down by the storm, was almost repaired'

There are many possibilities for the relative pronoun to replace an element of the embedded clause. It can be used to replace the object of the embedded clause, as shown in example (5):

(5)   Dum mīlitēs, quos imperāverat, convenīrent (Caes. *civ.* I 7, 6)
      'Until the soldiers, whom he had ordered, should assemble'

Otherwise, it can be used to replace an indirect object, as in example (6):

(6)   Ad nostras nāvēs prōcēdunt, quibus praeerat D. Brūtus (Caes. *civ.* I 56, 4)
      'They are approaching our ships, of which Decimus Brutus was the master'

Note that the antecedent of the relative pronoun is not necessarily the subject of the main clause, but may well be another complement, similarly to *ad nostras nāvēs* in example (6), or *ex Lepontiis* in the example (7):

(7)   Rhēnus autem oritur ex Lepontiis, quī Alpēs incolunt (Caes. *civ.* IV 10, 3)
      'But the Rhine springs among the Lepontii, who inhabit the Alps'

Also note that in Latin the relative pronoun always overtly agrees in gender and number with the antecedent, whereas its case depends on its original base position within the embedded clause.

12.7 Indefinite

The so-called indefinite pronouns actually belong to a different category, i.e. that of 'quantifiers', along with numerals. They are used to denote a quantity and can either modify a noun, just like adjectives, or they can stand on their own in a pronominal function.

We report below a list of quantifiers which inflect like adjectives:

nōnnulli 'some' (cf. *nūllus* in Table 12.11)
multus 'much'
paucus 'few'
omnis 'every', 'all' (the whole set divided into parts)
cunctus 'all' (all together, all in a body)
ūniversus 'all' (the entire)

The following pronouns, in contrast, exhibit a 'pronominal declension', i.e. *-īus* for the genitive and *-ī* for the dative:

alter 'the other one (between two)'
alius 'another one (among many)'
tōtus 'all' (the whole set)
sōlus 'alone'

Other indefinite pronouns are derived from an interrogative pronoun by adding a prefix or a suffix, and inflect like interrogatives. A complete list is given below:

aliquis, aliquid 'someone' (pron.)
aliquī, aliqua, aliquod 'some' (adj.)
quis, quid 'someone' (after *si, nisi, num, ne, an,* instead of *aliquis*; it refers to a hypothetical non-existent person or thing)
quisquam, quaequam, quicquam 'anyone' (pronoun and adjective; it is used after the negation *nec*; *nec quisquam* means 'nor anyone')
quīdam, quaedam, quiddam (pron.), and *quoddam* (adj.) 'a certain one' (it refers to a real person or thing the speaker knows but is unwilling to mention; it can also be used to blur a concept; it should not be confused with the particle *quidem* 'at least')
quisque, quidque (pron.); *quisque, quaeque, quodque* (adj.) 'each one' (it has distributive value and must always rely on a preceding term)
quīvīs, quidvīs (pron.); *quīvīs, quaevīs, quodvīs* (adj.) 'whom you please'

quīlibet, quidlibet (pron.); quīlibet, quaelibet, quodlibet (adj.) 'whatever you like'

uter, utra, utrum (pron. and adj.) 'either (of the two)'

neuter, neutra, neutrum (pron. and adj.) 'neither the one nor the other'

Finally, the pronoun/adjective nēmō/nūllus 'nobody' exhibits a special paradigm (see Table 12.11).

TABLE 12.11 Indefinite pronouns/adjectives: nēmō/nūllus

	Pronoun		Adjective		
	mas./fem.	neut.	mas.	fem.	neut.
nom.	nēmō	nihil (nīl)	nūllus	nūlla	nūllum
gen.	nūllīus	nūllīus reī	nūllīus	nūllīus	nūllīus
dat.	nēminī	nūllī reī	nūllī	nūllī	nūllī
acc.	nēminem	nihil (nīl)	nūllum	nūllam	nūllum
abl.	nullō	nūllā rē	nūllō	nūllā	nūllō

In negative clauses it is replaced by the form ūllus, ūlla, ūllum 'any one', which is inflected in the same way.

13

Numerals

13.1 Cardinals and ordinals

According to traditional grammars, the category of numeral pronouns includes two sets of elements, i.e. the so-called 'cardinal' numerals, which are treated as 'quantifiers' by modern linguists, and the so-called 'ordinal' numerals, which are adjectives. Both types are summarized in Table 13.1.

TABLE 13.1 Numerals: cardinals and ordinals

Arabic numerals	Roman numerals	Cardinals	Ordinals
1	I	ūnus, -a, -um	prīmus, -a, -um
2	II	duo, -ae, -o	secundus, -a, -um
3	III	trēs, -ia	tertius, -a, -um
4	IV	quattuor	quartus, -a, -um
5	V	quīnque	quīntus, -a, -um
6	VI	sex	sextus, -a, -um
7	VII	septem	septimus, -a, -um
8	VIII	octō	octāvus, -a, -um
9	IX	novem	nōnus, -a, -um
10	X	decem	decimus, -a, -um
11	XI	ūndecim	ūndecimus, -a, -um
12	XII	duodecim	duodecimus, -a, -um
13	XIII	tredecim	tertius decimus
14	XIV	quattuordecim	quartus decimus
15	XV	quīndecim	quīntus decimus
16	XVI	sēdecim	sextus decimus
17	XVII	septendecim	septimus decimus

(continued)

Table 13.1 Continued

Arabic numerals	Roman numerals	Cardinals	Ordinals
18	XVIII	duodēvīgintī	duodēvīcēsimus
19	XIX	ūndēvīgintī	ūndēvīcēsimus
20	XX	vīgintī	vīcēsimus
21	XXI	ūnus et vīgintī (vīgintī ūnus)	ūnus et vīcēsimus (vīcēsimus prīmus)
22	XXII	duo et vīgintī (vīgintī duo)	alter et vīcēsimus (vīcēsimus secundus)
28	XXVIII	duodētrīgintā	duodētrīcēsimus
29	XXIX	ūndētrīgintā	ūndētrīcēsimus
30	XXX	trīgintā	trīcēsimus
40	XL	quadrāgintā	quadrāgēsimus
50	L	quīnquāgintā	quīnquāgēsimus
60	LX	sexāgintā	sexāgēsimus
70	LXX	septuāgintā	septuāgēsimus
80	LXXX	octōgintā	octōgēsimus
90	XC	nōnāgintā	nōnāgēsimus
100	C	centum	centēsimus
200	CC	ducentī, -ae, -a	ducentēsimus
300	CCC	trecentī, -ae, -a	trecentēsimus
400	CD	quadringentī, -ae, -a	quadringentēsimus
500	D	quīngentī, -ae, -a	quīngentēsimus
600	DC	sescentī, -ae, -a	sescentēsimus
700	DCC	septingentī, -ae, -a	septingentēsimus
800	DCCC	octingentī, -ae, -a	octingentēsimus
900	CM	nōngentī, -ae, -a	nōngentēsimus
1000	M	mīlle	mīllēsimus

Notes

As for cardinals, only the numbers *ūnus*, *duo*, and *trēs* have their own declension (see Tables 13.2 and 13.3). In particular, *ūnus* exhibits the typical pronominal endings, i.e. *-īus* and *-ī* in the genitive and dative, respectively, while *duo* employs the 'dual' ending in *-ō* in the nominative (and occasionally in the accusative masculine), which is affected by iambic shortening in Classical Latin. *Ambō* 'both' is inflected in the same way that *duo* is. *Trēs* behaves like an *i*-stem.

TABLE 13.2 Numerals: *ūnus*, *duo*

	ūnus			*duo*		
	mas.	fem.	neut.	mas.	fem.	neut.
nom.	ūnus	ūna	ūnum	duo	duae	duo
gen.	ūnīus	ūnīus	ūnīus	duōrum	duārum	duōrum
dat.	ūnī	ūnī	ūnī	duōbus	duābus	duōbus
acc.	ūnum	ūnam	ūnum	duōs	duās	duo
abl.	ūnō	ūnā	ūnō	duōbus	duābus	duōbus

TABLE 13.3 Numerals: *trēs*

	trēs		
	mas.	fem.	neut.
nom.	trēs	trēs	tria
gen.	trium	trium	trium
dat.	tribus	tribus	tribus
acc.	trēs	trēs	tria
abl.	tribus	tribus	tribus

Numbers between *quattuor* and *centum* cannot be inflected, while those between *ducentī* (200) and *nōngentī* (900) follow the same declension as first class adjectives.

Mīlle cannot be inflected, although a parallel form is attested, i.e. *mīlia* 'thousands', which is inflected as a third declension neuter noun. All numbers above 1,000 are derived from *mīlia*, i.e. *duo mīlia*, *decem mīlia*, *centum mīlia*, *deciēs centēna mīlia* 'one million'.

13.2 Distributives and numeral adverbs

In addition to cardinals and ordinals, Latin also exhibits some numeral adjectives with a distributive value, meaning 'many at a time', i.e. *singulī* 'one at a time', i.e. 'one each', 'one by one', *bīnī* 'two at a time', *ternī* 'three at a time', and so on, e.g. *quaternī, quīnī, sēnī, septēnī, octōnī, novēnī, dēnī, vīcēnī, trīcēnī, quadrāgēnī*, etc. They are inflected as first class adjectives.

Finally, numerals are used to derive a set of adverbs meaning 'many times'. The first ones have a special form, i.e. *semel* 'once', *bis* 'twice', *ter* 'three times', *quater* 'four times'. Conversely, from *quīnquiēs* 'five times' on, they are formed by adding the suffix *-iēs* to the corresponding cardinal, e.g. *sexiēs, septiēs, octiēs, noviēs, deciēs, vīciē(n)s, trīciēs, quadrāgiēs*, etc.

14

Verbal inflection

14.1 The three stems of the verb

The inflection of Latin verbs is particularly rich. This is because the inflectional information is expressed jointly by the stem, the tense suffix, and the inflectional ending. The stem codifies a preliminary piece of information. Each verb, except for defective ones, possesses three different stems, for present, past, and nominal forms. Traditional grammars and vocabularies codify this information by means of the so-called verbal 'paradigm', e.g. *laudō, -ās, laudāvī, laudātum, -āre* 'to praise', as in the Italian and American tradition, or *laudō, laudāre, laudāvī, laudātum*, as in the British one. Both notations, however, are somewhat redundant, as the very same stem of the present is identified by three inflected forms, i.e. *laudō, laudās, laudāre*, although the single infinitival form, i.e. *laudā-re*, would be sufficient.

Therefore, the morphological base from which all the verbal forms are derived can be represented by the following set of three stems:

(1)   a. [laudā]_V (stem of *īnfectum* 'imperfective')
      b. [laudāv]_V (stem of *perfectum* 'perfective')
      c. [laudāt]_N (stem of *supīnum* 'supine')

As shown by the categorial labels (V and N), each verb is provided with two verbal stems, e.g. *laudā-* and *laudāv-*, and a nominal one, e.g. *laudāt-*. In the traditional terminology of Latin grammar, which goes back to Varro, the two verbal stems are called, respectively, the 'stem of the *īnfectum*', from which the present, the imperfect, and the future are derived, and the 'stem of the *perfectum*', from which the perfect, the pluperfect (i.e. past perfect), and the future perfect are derived. The third stem is traditionally called the 'stem of the *supīnum*', from which some nominal and adjectival forms are derived, including the supine and the perfect and future participle. It is advisable to memorize these paradigms, since the three stems cannot be predicted from fixed rules but must be recorded in our mental lexicon, or looked up in the dictionary.

The fact that each verb is associated with three different stems, rather than a single one as with the nouns, is not exclusive to Latin. In English, for example, irregular verbs are typically associated with different stems, e.g. *go, went, gone*. As for regular verbs, a diachronic distinction can be made between 'weak' and 'strong' forms. The former derive from original weak Germanic verbs which formed the preterite and the participle by means of a dental suffix, cf. Modern En. *work, work-ed, work-ed*. Strong verbs, in contrast, are derived from original strong Germanic verbs which formed the preterite and the participle by changing the quality of the stem vowel (this is known as *ablaut variation* in comparative and Germanic linguistics), giving rise to surface forms which are no longer predictable and must be memorized instead, cf. Modern En. *sing, sang, sung*. Diachronically, the strategy of derivation of weak verbs became the winning one, so that today weak verbs derived via a dental suffix are called 'regular', while strong verbs derived via ablaut are improperly called 'irregular'. Latin exhibits a similar pattern. On the one hand, it exhibits 'regular verbs'. In this case, the stems of the *perfectum* and of the *supīnum* are derived from the stem of the *īnfectum* by means of the suffixes -*v*- and -*t*-, respectively, as shown in (2) with the verb *audiō* 'to hear':

(2)   a. [audī]$_V$ (stem of *īnfectum*: *audiō*)
      b. [audī+v]$_V$ (stem of *perfectum*: *audīvī*)
      c. [audī+t]$_N$ (stem of *supīnum*: *audītum*)

On the other hand, the stems of the *perfectum* and of the *supīnum* of 'irregular' verbs are affected by various phenomena, each of which should be memorized.

As for the stem of the *perfectum*, there may be cases of ablaut variation, mainly of the quantitative type, e.g. *legō, lēgī*, and more rarely of the qualitative type, e.g. *agō, ēgī*, or zero variation, e.g. *vertō, vertī*. Other common phenomena include: addition of the suffixes -*u*- or -*s*-, e.g. *moneō, mon-u-ī; rēpō, rēp-s-ī*; reduplication, e.g. *tendō, te-tendī*; and more rarely deletion of the suffix, e.g. *crē-sc-ō, crē-vī*, or of the nasal infix, e.g. *ru-m-pō, rū-pī*.

As for the stem of the *supīnum*, the most common phenomena are vowel weakening, e.g. *moneō, monitum*, vs. the regular forms *dēleō, dēlētum*, and variations in the suffix, such as -*s* instead of -*t* if the stem vowel is followed by a dental, e.g. *lūdō, lūsum* from [lūd+s]. Another interesting phenomenon is the so-called 'Lachmann's Law', whereby a verbal stem ending in a voiced consonant lengthens its vowel in the formation of the *supīnum*, e.g. *agō, āctum*, vs. *facio, factum*, as a compensation for the devoicing of the stem consonant before the voiceless -*t* of the suffix: [ag+t] → [āc+t].

14.2 Tense suffixes

Once we have the stem of the *īnfectum* and of the *perfectum*, all remaining information about mood and tense for the indicative and the subjunctive is expressed by inflectional suffixes, called 'tense suffixes'.

In Table 14.1, we report as an example the verb *laudō*. The prototypical Latin verb system is based on three tenses for the indicative and two tenses for the subjunctive, both for the stem of the *īnfectum* [laudā] and for the stem of the *perfectum* [laudāv].

TABLE 14.1 Tense suffixes

Suffix	Stem	Mood and Tense	Example (1st pers. pl.)
Ø	[laudā]	Indicative present	*laudā-mus*
-bā-	[laudā+bā]	Indicative imperfect	*laudā-bā-mus*
-be-	[laudā+be]	Indicative future	*laudā-bi-mus*
Ø	[laudāv]	Indicative perfect	*laudāv-imus*
-erā-	[laudāv+erā]	Indicative pluperfect	*laudāv-erā-mus*
-eri-	[laudāv+eri]	Indicative future perfect	*laudāv-eri-mus*
-ē-	[laudā+ē]	Subjunctive present	*laud-ē-mus*
-rē-	[laudā+rē]	Subjunctive imperfect	*laudā-rē-mus*
-eri-	[laudāv+eri]	Subjunctive perfect	*laudāv-eri-mus*
-issē-	[laudāv+issē]	Subjunctive pluperfect	*laudāv-issē-mus*

Note that the information about mood and tense is expressed jointly by the stem and the suffix. Similarly to nominal inflections, different adjustment rules apply to verbal inflections whenever the relevant context emerges, e.g. the underlying structure of the future indicative is [[laudā+be]+mus], where vowel weakening applies, giving rise to the surface form *laudābimus*. In a similar way, vowel deletion applies to the present subjunctive [[laudā+ē] +mus], giving rise to the surface form *laudēmus*.

14.3 Inflectional endings

The union of the stem and the tense suffix, which expresses mood and tense, is combined with the inflectional endings, which express agreement information, i.e. person, number, and voice, and which always occupy a word-final position.

In Table 14.2, we report the two types of endings employed by Latin, one for active and one for passive verbs.

TABLE 14.2 Active and passive endings

Active ending	Information	Passive ending	Information
-ō/-m	1st pers. singular active	*-or/-r*	1st pers. singular passive
-s	2nd pers. singular active	*-ris* (archaic *-re*)	2nd pers. singular passive
-t	3rd pers. singular active	*-tur*	3rd pers. singular passive
-mus	1st pers. plural active	*-mur*	1st pers. plural passive
-tis	2nd pers. plural active	*-minī*	2nd pers. plural passive
-nt	3rd pers. plural active	*-ntur*	3rd pers. plural passive

The perfect indicative active is characterized by a dedicated set of inflectional endings (Table 14.3).

TABLE 14.3 Perfect indicative active: inflectional endings

-ī	1st pers. singular active
-istī	2nd pers. singular active
-it	3rd pers. singular active
-imus	1st pers. plural active
-istis	2nd pers. plural active
-ērunt (archaic *-ēre*)	3rd pers. plural active

Having so many distinctive endings for a single tense is quite redundant, as they all express not only the same person and number information as conveyed by the active endings, but also the same tense information as conveyed by the stem of the *perfectum*. However, such redundancy is necessary, since the stem of the *perfectum* of some irregular verbs coincides with that of the *īnfectum* (cf. *vertī* from *vertō* mentioned above). In this sense, different endings are required in order to supply a piece of information that the stem may not always convey.

14.4 Inflectional information: mood and tense

'Mood' (from Lat. *modus* 'manner', 'way') is a word previously employed by ancient grammars to indicate the speakers' attitude towards their utterance.

The Latin moods are the indicative, the subjunctive, the imperative, the infinitive, the supine, the participle, the gerund, and the gerundive. In the Latin verb system, the fundamental opposition is between the indicative, i.e. the objective mood, and the subjunctive, i.e. the subjective mood.

14.4.1 Tenses of the indicative

The indicative is used to express an action seen in its pure *objectivity*. For this reason, the indicative is the most precise mood to express the temporal collocation of the action with respect to the speech time. We report below the value of each of the tenses of the indicative:

> *present*: expresses an action occurring at the time of the utterance. It can be either punctual or durative, e.g. *scribō* 'I write' or 'I am writing'. The Latin present indicative can also be used to connote more nuanced aspectual values, such as the *conative*, e.g. 'I strive to write'; the so-called *historical present*, that is the use of the present instead of the perfect in order to emphasize immediacy and liveliness to the narration, e.g. *Cicerō scrībit* 'Cicero writes', even though Cicero is dead and obviously no longer writing; and the *gnomic* present, from the Greek *gnōmē* 'maxim' (a proverb is always valid).

> *imperfect*: expresses an ongoing action in the past, e.g. *scrībēbam* 'I was writing', 'I used to write'. The imperfect can also convey a conative value, i.e. 'I was striving to write', or an iterative value, i.e. 'I was repeatedly writing'. Note that these aspectual values are sometimes not relevant in English, so that the Latin imperfect can also be translated as the past simple: 'I wrote'.

> *perfect*: in contrast to English, Latin does not morphologically distinguish the present perfect, e.g. 'I have written', from the past simple, e.g. 'I wrote'. The Latin perfect *scrīpsī* indicates a past action without any specification about its present relevance.

> *pluperfect*: expresses a punctual past action which took place before another past action, e.g. *scrīpseram* 'I had written'.

> *future*: expresses a durative action in the future. Note that Latin does not distinguish between volitional and predictive future, e.g. *scrībam* 'I shall/will write', 'I shall/will be writing'.

> *future perfect*: expresses a future action taking place before another future action, e.g. *scrīpserō* 'I shall have written'. It can sometimes be used to express the certain future accomplishment of an action.

14.4.2 Tenses of the subjunctive

The subjunctive (from Latin *subiungō*, lit. 'to subjugate', i.e. 'to subjoin', 'to subordinate') is the standard mood of subordinate clauses. When it is used in independent clauses, it expresses the *subjectivity* of an action, with an emphasis on will and possibility. In turn, the category of will can be divided into three sub-types:

i. *exhortative*: replaces the imperative mood in the third person singular and in the first and third person plural. It is used in the present tense, e.g. *faciat!* 'let him do it!'. The exhortative subjunctive can also be used to express the negative imperative instead of the common periphrasis *nolī*+infinitive, e.g. *nolī facere* 'don't do it!'. For this use, the perfect subjunctive, e.g. *nē fēceris*, is more peremptory than the present, e.g. *nē faciās*.

ii. *optative*: is used to express a desire, cf. Lat. *optāre* 'to desire'. It is often accompanied by the adverb *utinam* 'if only!', 'would that!'. The distinction between an attainable or unattainable desire determines the tense, as shown in Table 14.4.

TABLE 14.4 Tenses of the subjunctive: attainable vs. unattainable desire

	Attainable desire 'if only he did that!'	Unattainable desire 'if only he had done that!'
In the present	**present** subj. *utinam faciat*	**imperfect** subj. *utinam faceret*
In the past	**perfect** subj. *utinam fēcerit*	**pluperfect** subj. *utinam fēcisset*

Since there is no handy idiomatic translation of these forms into English, we simply report a possible approximation, that is 'if only he did / had done that'. The context usually determines the exact meaning and allows the reader to formulate a suitable translation.

iii. *concessive*: indicates something that is conceded ('granted that…', 'let…'). It is often accompanied by the adverb *sānē* 'certainly'. Since a concession implies feasibility, only the present and the perfect are employed, e.g. *faciat sānē*, lit. 'certainly, let him do that' and *fēcerit sānē*, lit. 'certainly, let him have done that', respectively.

The category of possibility is also divided into three sub-types:

i. *potential*: indicates an action which may happen. It is often accompanied by adverbs such as *fortasse* or *forsitan* 'perhaps'. The subject is
typically an indefinite pronoun, e.g. *aliquis* or *quis* 'someone'.
A possibility in the present is equally expressed by the present or perfect,
e.g. *faciat quis* or *fēcerit quis*, both meaning 'someone may do that'. The
imperfect, or less frequently the pluperfect, is used to express a possibility in the past, e.g. *faceret quis* or *fēcisset quis* 'someone may have
done that'. Note that the potential subjunctive is often employed in the
main clause of conditional sentences, e.g. *si hoc dicas, erres* 'if you were
to say this, you would be mistaken' (cf. Section 28.6).

ii. *deliberative* or *dubitative*: is used in questions to express a doubt about
what one is about to do. It is usually accompanied by a first person
subject. The tenses employed are the present for present reference, e.g.
quid agam? 'what I am to do?' or 'what shall I do?', and the imperfect for
past reference, e.g. *quid agerem?* 'what should I have done?'

iii. *hypothetical* and *irrealis*: these two traditional categories constitute a
single system to express an hypothesis. Through the selection of tenses,
it is possible to distinguish an achievable hypothesis, i.e. hypothetical
subjunctive (present and perfect), from an unachievable one, i.e. irrealis
subjunctive (imperfect and pluperfect). The system is summarized in
Table 14.5.

TABLE 14.5 Tenses of the subjunctive: possibility vs. irreality

	Possibility	Irreality
In the present	**present** subj.	**imperfect** subj.
	faciat 'let's suppose that he does that'	*faceret* 'he would do that (but he doesn't)'
In the past	**perfect** subj.	**pluperfect** subj.
	fēcerit 'let's suppose that he did that'	*fēcisset* 'he would have done that (but he didn't)'

14.5 The four conjugations

Latin verbs are traditionally divided into four classes or conjugations. The final
vowel of the stem of the *īnfectum* determines the conjugation to which each
verb belongs:

- if the stem ends in *ā*, the verb belongs to the first conjugation;
- if the stem ends in *ē*, the verb belongs to the second conjugation;
- if the stem ends in *e*, the verb belongs to the third conjugation;
- if the stem ends in *i*, the verb belongs to the third conjugation (sub-category of verbs in -io);
- if the stem ends in *ī*, the verb belongs to the fourth conjugation.

Note that, similarly to the third declension, the third conjugation is the most complex, as it includes two different kinds of stem, i.e. stems ending in short *-e* and stems ending in short *-i*.

The four conjugations are based on the stem of the *īnfectum* only. However, the stems of the *perfectum* and of the *supīnum* are not predictable from the conjugation class, but must be stored in the lexicon for each verb. Below, we report some examples of verbal paradigms:

First conjugation: *amō, -ās, -āvī, -ātum, -āre* 'to love'; *iuvō, -ās, iūvī, iūtum, -āre* 'to help'; *parō, -ās, -āvī, -ātum, -āre* 'to supply'; *stō, -ās, stetī, statum, -āre* 'to stand'; *vocō, -ās, -āvī, -ātum, -āre* 'to call'. Note that the verb *dō, -ās, dedī, datum, -are* 'to give' has a short *-a-* in all forms except for *dās* and *dā*.

Second conjugation: *caveō, -ēs, cāvī, cautum, -ēre* 'to beware'; *habeō, -ēs, habuī, habitum, -ēre* 'to have'; *sedeō, -ēs, sēdī, sessum, -ēre* 'to sit'; *spondeō, -ēs, spopondī, sponsum, -ēre* 'to promise'; *videō, -ēs, vīdī, vīsum, -ēre* 'to see'.

Third conjugation: *agō, -is, ēgī, āctum, -ere* 'to lead'; *cadō, -is, cecidī, cāsum, -ere* 'to fall'; *dīcō, -is, dīxī, dictum, -ere* 'to say'; *petō, -is, -ī(v)ī, -ītum, -ere* 'to strive for'; *vincō, -is, vīcī, victum, -ere* 'to win'.

Third conjugation (verbs in -iō): *cupiō, -is, -ī(v)ī, -ītum, -ere* 'to desire'; *fugiō, -is, fūgī, (fugitūrus), -ere* 'to run away'; *iaciō, -is, iēcī, iactum, -ere* 'to throw'; *rapiō, -is, -uī, -tum, -ere* 'to seize'; *sapiō, -is, -i(v)ī, -ere* 'to taste of' (but also 'to be acquainted with the value of things', 'wise').

Fourth conjugation: *aperiō, -īs, -uī, -tum, -īre* 'to open'; *dormio, -īs, -ī(v)ī, -ītum, -īre* 'to sleep'; *sentiō, -īs, sensī, sensum, -īre* 'to feel'; *sciō, -īs, -ī(v)ī, -ītum, -īre* 'to know'; *veniō, -īs, vēnī, ventum, -īre* 'to come'.

We shall now describe the forms derived from the stem of the *īnfectum* for each conjugation (see Tables 14.6–14.10).

14.6 Active voice

14.6.1 First conjugation

TABLE 14.6 Active voice: first conjugation

Tense	Person	Mood: **Indicative**		Mood: **Subjunctive**	
Present		'I praise', 'I am praising'		'I praise', 'I may praise', 'I would praise'	
	1st sg.	[laudā]+ō	laudō	[[laudā]+ē]+m	laudem
	2nd sg.	[laudā]+s	laudās	[[laudā]+ē]+s	laudēs
	3rd sg.	[laudā]+t	laudat	[[laudā]+ē]+t	laudet
	1st pl.	[laudā]+mus	laudāmus	[[laudā]+ē]+mus	laudēmus
	2nd pl.	[laudā]+tis	laudātis	[[laudā]+ē]+tis	laudētis
	3rd pl.	[laudā]+nt	laudant	[[laudā]+ē]+nt	laudent
Imperfect		'I was praising', 'I used to praise'		'I was praising', 'I might praise', 'I would praise'	
	1st sg.	[[laudā]+bā]+m	laudābam	[[laudā]+rē]+m	laudārem
	2nd sg.	[[laudā]+bā]+s	laudābās	[[laudā]+rē]+s	laudārēs
	3rd sg.	[[laudā]+bā]+t	laudābat	[[laudā]+rē]+t	laudāret
	1st pl.	[[laudā]+bā]+mus	laudābāmus	[[laudā]+rē]+mus	laudārēmus
	2nd pl.	[[laudā]+bā]+tis	laudābātis	[[laudā]+rē]+tis	laudārētis
	3rd pl.	[[laudā]+bā]+nt	laudābant	[[laudā]+rē]+nt	laudārent
Future		'I shall/will praise'			
	1st sg.	[[laudā]+be]+ō	laudābō		
	2nd sg.	[[laudā]+be]+s	laudābis		
	3rd sg.	[[laudā]+be]+t	laudābit		
	1st pl.	[[laudā]+be]+mus	laudābimus		
	2nd pl.	[[laudā]+be]+tis	laudābitis		
	3rd pl.	[[laudā]+be]+unt	laudābunt		

Notes

Present indicative: in the first person singular, the thematic vowel -*ā*- is deleted before the ending -*ō*. However, the adjustment rule for long vowels before other vowels would predict shortening and not deletion (cf. rule (5) in Section 8.4). The reason for this exceptional behaviour is that shortening would produce a clash of vowels (cf. **aō*), which is not admitted in Latin phonology. The ending is a long -*ō* in Old and Classical Latin and tended to become short in later stages of the language. As for the remaining persons, the thematic vowel -*ā*- becomes short before a consonant (except -*s*) in syllable-final position (cf. rule (6) in Section 8.4), but remains long in syllable-internal position.

Future indicative: in the first person singular and third person plural (with the latter exceptionally exhibiting the ending -*unt* instead of -*nt*) the vowel of the suffix -*be*- is deleted. As for the remaining persons, the vowel of the suffix -*be*- becomes *i* because of the adjustment rules of vowel weakening (cf. rules (7) and (15b) in Section 8.5).

Present subjunctive: the thematic vowel -*ā*- is always deleted before the tense suffix -*ē*- for the same reasons as in the present indicative (**aē* is not admitted).

14.6.2 Second conjugation

TABLE 14.7 Active voice: second conjugation

Tense	Person	Mood: **Indicative**		Mood: **Subjunctive**	
Present		'I warn', 'I am warning'		'I warn', 'I may warn', 'I would warn'	
	1ˢᵗ sg.	[monē]+ō	**moneō**	[[monē]+ā]+m	**moneam**
	2ⁿᵈ sg.	[monē]+s	**monēs**	[[monē]+ā]+s	**moneās**
	3ʳᵈ sg.	[monē]+t	**monet**	[[monē]+ā]+t	**moneat**
	1ˢᵗ pl.	[monē]+mus	**monēmus**	[[monē]+ā]+mus	**moneāmus**
	2ⁿᵈ pl.	[monē]+tis	**monētis**	[[monē]+ā]+tis	**moneātis**
	3ʳᵈ pl.	[monē]+nt	**monent**	[[monē]+ā]+nt	**moneant**

Imperfect		'I was warning', 'I used to warn'		'I was warning', 'I might warn', 'I would warn'
1st sg.	[[monē]+bā]+m	monēbam	[[monē]+rē]+m	monērem
2nd sg.	[[monē]+bā]+s	monēbās	[[monē]+rē]+s	monērēs
3rd sg.	[[monē]+bā]+t	monēbat	[[monē]+rē]+t	monēret
1st pl.	[[monē]+bā]+mus	monēbāmus	[[monē]+rē]+mus	monērēmus
2nd pl.	[[monē]+bā]+tis	monēbātis	[[monē]+rē]+tis	monērētis
3rd pl.	[[monē]+bā]+nt	monēbant	[[monē]+rē]+nt	monērent

Future		'I shall/will warn'	
1st sg.	[[monē]+be]+ō	monēbō
2nd sg.	[monē]+be]+s	monēbis
3rd sg.	[monē]+be]+t	monēbit
1st pl.	[monē]+be]+mus	monēbimus
2nd pl.	[monē]+be]+tis	monēbitis
3rd pl.	[monē]+be]+unt	monēbunt

Notes

Present indicative: the thematic vowel -ē- is not deleted in the first singular person before the ending, but is simply shortened, i.e. -eō, as predicted by rule (5) in Section 8.4 (cf. *vōcālis ante vōcālem corripitur*). The reason for the different treatement of the thematic vowel of the first and second conjugation is that, in contrast to *aō in the first conjugation, the cluster eō is regularly admitted in Latin phonology, e.g. eō can be the first person singular of the present indicative of the verb *īre* 'to go', or the ablative singular masculine and neuter of the pronoun *is* 'he'. As for the remaining persons, the thematic vowel -ē- becomes short before a consonant (except for -s) in syllable-final position; it remains long in syllable-internal position, cf. the first conjugation.

Future indicative: cf. the first conjugation.

Present subjunctive: the thematic vowel -ē- preceding the tense suffix -ā- is not deleted, as in the first conjugation, but regularly shortened, i.e. *moneās*.

14.6.3 Third conjugation

Table 14.8 Active voice: third conjugation

Tense	Person	Mood: **Indicative**		Mood: **Subjunctive**	
Present		'I read', 'I am reading'		'I read', 'I may read', 'I would read'	
	1st sg.	[lege]+ō	legō	[[lege]+ā]+m	legam
	2nd sg.	[lege]+s	legis	[[lege]+ā]+s	legās
	3rd sg.	[lege]+t	legit	[[lege]+ā]+t	legat
	1st pl.	[lege]+mus	legimus	[[lege]+ā]+mus	legāmus
	2nd pl.	[lege]+tis	legitis	[[lege]+ā]+tis	legātis
	3rd pl.	[lege]+unt	legunt	[[lege]+ā]+nt	legant
Imperfect		'I was reading', 'I used to read'		'I was reading', 'I might read', 'I would read'	
	1st sg.	[[lege]+ēbā]+m	legēbam	[[lege]+rē]+m	legerem
	2nd sg.	[[lege]+ēbā]+s	legēbās	[[lege]+rē]+s	legerēs
	3rd sg.	[[lege]+ēbā]+t	legēbat	[[lege]+rē]+t	legeret
	1st pl.	[[lege]+ēbā]+mus	legēbāmus	[[lege]+rē]+mus	legerēmus
	2nd pl.	[[lege]+ēbā]+tis	legēbātis	[[lege]+rē]+tis	legerētis
	3rd pl.	[[lege]+ēbā]+nt	legēbant	[[lege]+rē]+nt	legerent
Future		'I shall/will read'			
	1st sg.	[[lege]+ā]+m	legam		
	2nd sg.	[lege]+ē]+s	legēs		
	3rd sg.	[lege]+ē]+t	leget		
	1st pl.	[lege]+ē]+mus	legēmus		
	2nd pl.	[lege]+ē]+tis	legētis		
	3rd pl.	[lege]+ē]+nt	legent		

Notes

Present indicative: the short thematic vowel -*e*- is regularly deleted before vowel in the first person singular and third person plural (with the latter exceptionally exhibiting the ending -*unt* instead of -*nt*). In the remaining persons, -*e*- becomes -*i*- because of vowel weakening.

Imperfect indicative: in contrast to the first two conjugations, the tense suffix is -*ēbā*- and not -*bā*-.

Future indicative: the tense suffix is -*ā*- (first person singular) and -*ē*- (all other persons). Deletion of the thematic vowel and shortening of the vowel before a consonant (except for -*s*) in syllable-final position always take place.

Present subjunctive: the thematic vowel is always deleted before the tense suffix -*ā*-.

14.6.4 Third conjugation (verbs in -iō)

TABLE 14.9 Active voice: third conjugation (verbs in -*iō*)

Tense	Person	Mood: **Indicative**		Mood: **Subjunctive**	
Present		'I take', 'I am taking'		'I take', 'I may take', 'I would take'	
	1st sg.	[capi]+ō	**capiō**	[[capi]+ā]+m	**capiam**
	2nd sg.	[capi]+s	**capis**	[[capi]+ā]+s	**capiās**
	3rd sg.	[capi]+t	**capit**	[[capi]+ā]+t	**capiat**
	1st pl.	[capi]+mus	**capimus**	[[capi]+ā]+mus	**capiāmus**
	2nd pl.	[capi]+tis	**capitis**	[[capi]+ā]+tis	**capiātis**
	3rd pl.	[capi]+unt	**capiunt**	[[capi]+ā]+nt	**capiant**
Imperfect		'I was taking', 'I used to take'		'I was taking', 'I might take', 'I would take'	
	1st sg.	[[capi]+ēbā]+m	**capiēbam**	[[capi]+rē]+m	**caperem**
	2nd sg.	[[capi]+ēbā]+s	**capiēbās**	[[capi]+rē]+s	**caperēs**
	3rd sg.	[[capi]+ēbā]+t	**capiēbat**	[[capi]+rē]+t	**caperet**
	1st pl.	[[capi]+ēbā]+mus	**capiēbāmus**	[[capi]+rē]+mus	**caperēmus**
	2nd pl.	[[capi]+ēbā]+tis	**capiēbātis**	[[capi]+rē]+tis	**caperētis**
	3rd pl.	[[capi]+ēbā]+nt	**capiēbant**	[[capi]+rē]+nt	**caperent**

(continued)

TABLE 14.9 Continued

Tense	Person	Mood: **Indicative**		Mood: **Subjunctive**
Future		'I shall/will take'		
	1st sg.	[[capi]+ā]+m	**capiam**	
	2nd sg.	[capi]+ē]+s	**capiēs**	
	3rd sg.	[capi]+ē]+t	**capiet**	
	1st pl.	[capi]+ē]+mus	**capiēmus**	
	2nd pl.	[capi]+ē]+tis	**capiētis**	
	3rd pl.	[capi]+ē]+nt	**capient**	

Notes

The thematic vowel is a short -*i*-, and as such it is never deleted. This is correctly predicted by the adjustment rule of vowel deletion, which states that only short *a*, *o*, and *e* are deleted before another vowel (cf. rule (4) in Section 8.3). Tense suffixes and inflectional endings coincide with those of the third conjugation.

Imperfect subjunctive: the thematic vowel -*i*- regularly becomes -*e*- before -*r*-, as predicted by the adjustment rule affecting short vowels in an open medial syllable before -*r*- (cf. rule (10b) in Section 8.5).

Some sigmatic forms are attested in Archaic Latin for the future indicative, e.g. *capsō*, *faxō*, and the present subjunctive, e.g. *capsim*, *faxim*.

14.6.5 Fourth conjugation

TABLE 14.10 Active voice: fourth conjugation

Tense	Person	Mood: **Indicative**		Mood: **Subjunctive**	
Present		'I hear', 'I am hearing'		'I hear', 'I may hear', 'I would hear'	
	1st sg.	[audī]+ō	**audiō**	[[audī]+ā]+m	**audiam**
	2nd sg.	[audī]+s	**audīs**	[[audī]+ā]+s	**audiās**
	3rd sg.	[audī]+t	**audit**	[[audī]+ā]+t	**audiat**
	1st pl.	[audī]+mus	**audīmus**	[[audī]+ā]+mus	**audiāmus**
	2nd pl.	[audī]+tis	**audītis**	[[audī]+ā]+tis	**audiātis**
	3rd pl.	[audī]+unt	**audiunt**	[[audī]+ā]+nt	**audiant**

Imperfect			'I was hearing', 'I used to hear'		'I was hearing', 'I might hear', 'I would hear'
	1st sg.	[[audī]+ēbā]+m	**audiēbam**	[[audī]+rē]+m	**audīrem**
	2nd sg.	[[audī]+ēbā]+s	**audiēbās**	[[audī]+rē]+s	**audīrēs**
	3rd sg.	[[audī]+ēbā]+t	**audiēbat**	[[audī]+rē]+t	**audīret**
	1st pl.	[[audī]+ēbā]+mus	**audiēbāmus**	[[audī]+rē]+mus	**audīrēmus**
	2nd pl.	[[audī]+ēbā]+tis	**audiēbātis**	[[audī]+rē]+tis	**audīrētis**
	3rd pl.	[[audī]+ēbā]+nt	**audiēbant**	[[audī]+rē]+nt	**audīrent**
Future			'I shall/will hear'		
	1st sg.	[[audī]+ā]+m	**audiam**		
	2nd sg.	[audī]+ē]+s	**audiēs**		
	3rd sg.	[audī]+ē]+t	**audiet**		
	1st pl.	[audī]+ē]+mus	**audiēmus**		
	2nd pl.	[audī]+ē]+tis	**audiētis**		
	3rd pl.	[audī]+ē]+nt	**audient**		

Notes

The thematic vowel is a long -ī-, and as such it is never deleted, but simply shortened before another vowel and in final position before a consonant, except -s (cf. the vowel shortening rules (5) and (6) in Section 8.4). In all other contexts it remains long.

The perfect indicative form *audībam* and the future *audībō* are attested in Archaic Latin.

14.6.6 The imperative

The imperative is the mood of orders, e.g. En. 'read!' In addition to the present, which only employs the second person, e.g. Lat. *lege!*, *legite!*, Latin also has the future imperative, which is employed to express a moral duty. In this case, the third person also has its own distinctive ending, e.g. *legitō* 'he shall read'; *leguntō* 'they shall read'.

Table 14.11 shows the complete paradigm of the four conjugations.

TABLE 14.11 The imperative

Tense	Pers.	1st conjug.	2nd conjug.	3rd conjug.	3rd conjug. (verbs in -iō)	4th conjug.
Present		'praise!'	'warn!'	'read!'	'take!'	'listen!'
	2nd sg.	laudā	monē	lege	cape	audī
	2nd pl.	laudāte	monēte	legite	capite	audīte
Future		'you shall praise'	'you shall warn'	'you shall read'	'you shall take'	'you shall listen'
	2nd sg.	laudātō	monētō	legitō	capitō	audītō
	3rd sg.	laudātō	monētō	legitō	capitō	audītō
	2nd pl.	laudātōte	monētōte	legitōte	capitōte	audītōte
	3rd pl.	laudāntō	monēntō	leguntō	capiuntō	audiuntō

Notes

The second person singular of the present imperative coincides with the pure stem.

In the third conjugation, the thematic vowel -e- becomes -i- in syllable-internal position, while the thematic vowel -i- becomes -e- in word-final position (cf. rules (7) and (13) in Section 8.5).

In the third and fourth conjugations, the third person plural of the future imperative ends in -untō rather than -ntō (cf. the first two conjugations).

The verbs dīcō, dūcō, and faciō usually have a truncated form for the second person singular of the present imperative, i.e. dīc, dūc, and fac.

14.6.7 Tenses derived from the perfectum

The four conjugations differ only in terms of forms derived from the stem of the īnfectum, whereas all the forms derived from the stem of the perfectum coincide.

Similarly to the tripartition of tenses of the īnfectum into present, imperfect, and future, the tenses of the perfectum indicative are divided into perfect, pluperfect, and future perfect. As for the subjunctive, the bipartition of the īnfectum into present and imperfect corresponds to that of the perfectum into perfect and pluperfect.

We report in Table 14.12 a summary of moods and tenses. Note that proper translation of the subjunctive depends on the clause in which it is

TABLE 14.12 Moods and tenses of the *infectum* and *perfectum*

Tense	Mood: **Indicative**	Mood: **Subjunctive**
Present	**laudō** 'I praise'	**laudem** 'I praise', 'I may praise', 'I would praise'
Imperfect	**laudābam** 'I was praising'	**laudārem** 'I was praising', 'I might praise', 'I would praise'
Future	**laudābō** 'I shall praise', 'I will praise'	
Perfect	**laudāvī** 'I praised', 'I have praised'	**laudāverim** 'I praised', 'I have praised', 'I may have praised'
Pluperfect	**laudāveram** 'I had praised'	**laudāvissem** 'I had praised', 'I would have praised', 'I might have praised'
Future perfect	**laudāverō** 'I shall have praised'	

used. For this reason, translations of single forms given throughout the chapter are mainly indicative.

The inflection of tenses derived from the stem of the *perfectum* is completely regular and does not raise any specific issues. Table 14.13 shows as an example the paradigm of the verb *dīcere* 'to say' (stem of the perfect: [dīx]).

TABLE 14.13 Tenses derived from the *perfectum*: endings for all conjugations (active voice)

Tense	Pers.	Mood: **Indicative**		Mood: **Subjunctive**	
Perfect		'I said', 'I have said'		'I said', 'I have said', 'I may have said'	
	1st sg.	[dīx]+ī	dīxī	[[dīx]+eri]+m	dīxerim
	2nd sg.	[dīx]+istī	dīxistī	[[dīx]+eri]+s	dīxeris
	3rd sg.	[dīx]+it	dīxit	[[dīx]+eri]+t	dīxerit
	1st pl.	[dīx]+imus	dīximus	[[dīx]+eri]+mus	dīxerimus
	2nd pl.	[dīx]+istis	dīxistis	[[dīx]+eri]+tis	dīxeritis
	3rd pl.	[dīx]+ērunt	dīxērunt	[[dīx]+eri]+nt	dīxerint

(continued)

TABLE 14.13 Continued

Tense	Pers.	Mood: **Indicative**		Mood: **Subjunctive**	
Pluperfect		'I had said'		'I had said', 'I would have said', 'I might have said'	
	1st sg.	[[dīx]+erā]+m	dīxeram	[[dīx]+issē]+m	dīxissem
	2nd sg.	[[dīx]+erā]+s	dīxerās	[[dīx]+issē]+s	dīxissēs
	3rd sg.	[[dīx]+erā]+t	dīxerat	[[dīx]+issē]+t	dīxisset
	1st pl.	[[dīx]+erā]+mus	dīxerāmus	[[dīx]+issē]+mus	dīxissēmus
	2nd pl.	[[dīx]+erā]+tis	dīxerātis	[[dīx]+issē]+tis	dīxissētis
	3rd pl.	[[dīx]+erā]+nt	dīxerant	[[dīx]+issē]+nt	dīxissent
Future perfect		'I shall have said'			
	1st sg.	[[dīx]+eri]+ō	dīxerō		
	2nd sg.	[[dīx]+eri]+s	dīxeris		
	3rd sg.	[[dīx]+eri]+t	dīxerit		
	1st pl.	[[dīx]+eri]+mus	dīxerimus		
	2nd pl.	[[dīx]+eri]+tis	dīxeritis		
	3rd pl.	[[dīx]+eri]+nt	dīxerint		

Notes

The perfect indicative has its own distinctive endings (cf. Table 14.3). For the third person plural, the archaic endings *-ēre* and more rarely *-ĕrunt* are also attested, especially in poetry.

In Archaic Latin it is possible to find haplological forms for the second person singular of the perfect indicative, e.g. *dīxtī, nōstī* for *dīxistī, nōvistī*.

Both in Archaic and Vulgar Latin, the so-called 'syncopated' perfects are frequently attested, i.e. perfects in *-āvī, -ēvī, -īvī* can drop the *-v-* and the following vowel, e.g. *amārunt, amāram < amāvērunt, amāveram*. In this way, we can give a principled explanation of the origin of forms such as Fr. *aima* from Lat. *amát < amāvit*, and It. *udì* from Lat. *audít < audīvit*.

14.6.8 Nominal and adjectival forms of the verb

The verbal conjugation also contains some forms which are in fact nominal or adjectival. This phenomenon is halfway between inflection and derivation, since these forms switch the category of the stem from Verb to Noun or Adjective, as regularly happens when a word is derived by means of a derivational suffix (cf. Section 15.4). The nominal or adjectival forms of the active verb are the infinitive, the participle, the gerund, and the supine. Some forms are derived from the stem of the *īnfectum*, i.e. the present infinitive *laudā-re*, the present participle *laudā-ns*, and the gerund *laudandī*; one form is derived from the stem of the *perfectum*, i.e. the perfect infinitive *laudāv-isse*; and the remaining forms are derived from the stem of the *supīnum*, i.e. the future infinitive *laudāt-ūrum*, the future participle *laudāt-ūrus,* and the supine *laudāt-ūm*. Table 14.14 shows the active paradigm of the four conjugations.

Notes

The present infinitive, e.g. *laudāre*, is derived by adding the suffix *-re* to the stem of the *īnfectum*. As usual, the thematic vowel *-i-* of third conjugation verbs in *-iō* becomes *-e-* before *-r* (cf. rule (10b) in Section 8.5).

The perfect infinitive, e.g. *laudāvisse*, is derived by adding the suffix *-isse* to the stem of the *perfectum*. Some syncopated forms are also attested, e.g. *laudāsse.*

The future infinitive denotes an upcoming event, e.g. *laudātūrum esse*. It is derived by combining the infinitive of *esse* with the future participle, in the singular and plural accusative case, in the masculine, feminine, and neuter gender.

The present participle, e.g. *laudāns*, is derived by adding the suffix *-nt-* (first and second conjugation) and *-ent-* (third and fourth conjugation) to the stem of the *īnfectum*. It is inflected like a second class adjective. The thematic vowel is shortened in *laudantis*, etc. because of Osthoff's Law (cf. the final paragraph of Section 8.4).

The future participle, e.g. *laudātūrus*, is derived by adding the suffix *-ūr-* to the stem of the supine. It is inflected like a first class adjective.

The gerund, e.g. *laudandī*, is derived by adding the suffix *-nd-* (first and second conjugation) and *-end-* (third and fourth conjugation) to the stem of the *īnfectum*. The gerund is a verbal noun which can be inflected in the genitive, dative, accusative (only when it is preceded by a preposition), and ablative. For the nominative and accusative without a preposition, the infinitive is used instead.

The supine, e.g. *laudātum*, is a noun denoting an action and is derived by adding the suffix *-um* to the stem of the *supīnum*. It indicates purpose and is used on few occasions, but especially after verbs of motion, e.g. *cubitum īre* 'to go to sleep'. Note that there is a vowel quantity opposition between *lēctum* and *captum*, because of Lachmann's Law (cf. the final paragraph of Section 14.1).

TABLE 14.14 Nominal and adjectival forms of the verb (active voice)

Mood	Tense		1st conjug.	2nd conjug.	3rd conjug.	3rd conjug. (verbs in -io)	4th conjug.
Infinitive	Present		laudāre 'to praise'	monēre 'to warn'	legere 'to read'	capere 'to take'	audīre 'to hear'
	Perfect		laudāvisse 'to have praised'	monuisse 'to have warned'	lēgisse 'to have read'	cēpisse 'to have taken'	audīvisse 'to have heard'
	Future		laudātūrum, -am, -um esse 'to be about to praise'	monitūrum, -am, -um esse 'to be about to warn'	lēctūrum, -am, -um esse 'to be about to read'	captūrum, -am, -um esse 'to be about to take'	audītūrum, -am, -um esse 'to be about to hear'
Participle	Present		laudāns, -ntis 'praising'	monēns, -ntis 'warning'	legēns, -ntis 'reading'	capiēns, -ntis 'taking'	audiēns, -ntis 'hearing'
	Future		laudātūrus, -a, -um 'about to praise'	monitūrus, -a, -um 'about to warn'	lēctūrus, -a, -um 'about to read'	captūrus, -a, -um 'about to take'	audītūrus, -a, -um 'about to hear'
Gerund	gen.		laudandī	monendī	legendī	capiendī	audiendī
	dat.		laudandō	monendō	legendō	capiendō	audiendō
	acc.		laudandum	monendum	legendum	capiendum	audiendum
	abl.		laudandō '(the act of) praising'	monendō '(the act of) warning'	legendō '(the act of) reading'	capiendō '(the act of) taking'	audiendō '(the act of) hearing'
Supine			laudātum 'to praise'	monitum 'to warn'	lēctum 'to read'	captum 'to take'	audītum 'to hear'

14.7 Passive voice

We shall now describe the forms of the passive voice for each conjugation (see Tables 14.15–14.19).

14.7.1 First conjugation

TABLE 14.15 Passive voice: first conjugation

Tense	Person	Mood: **Indicative**		Mood: **Subjunctive**	
Present		'I am (being) praised'		'I am praised', 'I may be praised', 'I would be praised'	
	1ˢᵗ sg.	[laudā]+or	**laudor**	[[laudā]+ē]+r	**lauder**
	2ⁿᵈ sg.	[laudā]+ris	**laudāris**	[[laudā]+ē]+ris	**laudēris**
	3ʳᵈ sg.	[laudā]+tur	**laudātur**	[[laudā]+ē]+tur	**laudētur**
	1ˢᵗ pl.	[laudā]+mur	**laudāmur**	[[laudā]+ē]+mur	**laudēmur**
	2ⁿᵈ pl.	[laudā]+minī	**laudāminī**	[[laudā]+ē]+minī	**laudēminī**
	3ʳᵈ pl.	[laudā]+ntur	**laudantur**	[[laudā]+ē]+ntur	**laudentur**
Imperfect		'I was (being) praised'		'I was being praised', 'I might be praised', 'I would be praised'	
	1ˢᵗ sg.	[[laudā]+bā]+r	**laudābar**	[[laudā]+rē]+r	**laudārer**
	2ⁿᵈ sg.	[[laudā]+bā]+ris	**laudābāris**	[[laudā]+rē]+ris	**laudārēris**
	3ʳᵈ sg.	[[laudā]+bā]+tur	**laudābātur**	[[laudā]+rē]+tur	**laudārētur**
	1ˢᵗ pl.	[[laudā]+bā]+mur	**laudābāmur**	[[laudā]+rē]+mur	**laudārēmur**
	2ⁿᵈ pl.	[[laudā]+bā]+minī	**laudābāminī**	[[laudā]+rē]+minī	**laudārēminī**
	3ʳᵈ pl.	[[laudā]+bā]+ntur	**laudābantur**	[[laudā]+rē]+ntur	**laudārentur**
Future		'I shall be praised'			
	1ˢᵗ sg.	[[laudā]+be]+or	**laudābor**		
	2ⁿᵈ sg.	[[laudā]+be]+ris	**laudāberis**		
	3ʳᵈ sg.	[[laudā]+be]+tur	**laudābitur**		
	1ˢᵗ pl.	[[laudā]+be]+mur	**laudābimur**		
	2ⁿᵈ pl.	[[laudā]+be]+minī	**laudābiminī**		
	3ʳᵈ pl.	[[laudā]+be]+untur	**laudābuntur**		

Notes

Present indicative: in the first person singular, the thematic vowel *-ā-* is deleted before the ending *-or*, for the same reasons as those discussed in the active voice (cf. Section 14.6.1).

In the second person singular, an alternative form *-re* is also attested in archaic and poetic texts.

In the third person plural, the vowel before *-nt-* is short, because of Osthoff's Law (cf. the final paragraph of Section 8.4). Note that the vowel is short, but the syllable is long, so the stress is *laudántur*.

Future indicative: in the first person singular, the vowel of the suffix *-be-* is deleted before the ending *-or*. As for the other persons, the vowel of the suffix *-be-* becomes *i* because of vowel weakening, with the exception of the second person singular, which is followed by *-r* (cf. rules (7) and (10) in Section 8.5). In the third person plural, the vowel of the suffix *-be-* is deleted before the ending *-untur*.

Present subjunctive: the thematic vowel *-ā-* is always deleted before the tense suffix *-ē-* (cf. Section 14.6.1).

14.7.2 Second conjugation

TABLE 14.16 Passive voice: second conjugation

Tense	Person	Mood: **Indicative**		Mood: **Subjunctive**	
Present		'I am (being) warned'		'I am warned', 'I may be warned', 'I would be warned'	
	1st sg.	[monē]+or	**moneor**	[[monē]+ā]+r	**monear**
	2nd sg.	[monē]+ris	**monēris**	[[monē]+ā]+ris	**moneāris**
	3rd sg.	[monē]+tur	**monētur**	[[monē]+ā]+tur	**moneātur**
	1st pl.	[monē]+mur	**monēmur**	[[monē]+ā]+mur	**moneāmur**
	2nd pl.	[monē]+minī	**monēminī**	[[monē]+ā]+minī	**moneāminī**
	3rd pl.	[monē]+ntur	**monentur**	[[monē]+ā]+ntur	**moneantur**
Imperfect		'I was (being) warned'		'I was being warned', 'I might be warned', 'I would be warned'	
	1st sg.	[[monē]+bā]+r	**monēbar**	[[monē]+rē]+r	**monērer**
	2nd sg.	[[monē]+bā]+ris	**monēbāris**	[[monē]+rē]+ris	**monērēris**
	3rd sg.	[[monē]+bā]+tur	**monēbātur**	[[monē]+rē]+tur	**monēretur**
	1st pl.	[[monē]+bā]+mur	**monēbāmur**	[[monē]+rē]+mur	**monērēmur**
	2nd pl.	[[monē]+bā]+minī	**monēbāminī**	[[monē]+rē]+minī	**monērēminī**
	3rd pl.	[[monē]+bā]+ntur	**monēbantur**	[[monē]+rē]+ntur	**monērentur**

Future		'I shall be warned'
1st sg.	[[monē]+be]+or	**monēbor**
2nd sg.	[[monē]+be]+ris	**monēberis**
3rd sg.	[[monē]+be]+tur	**monēbitur**
1st pl.	[[monē]+be]+mur	**monēbimur**
2nd pl.	[[monē]+be]+ minī	**monēbiminī**
3rd pl.	[[monē]+be]+untur	**monēbuntur**

Notes

Present indicative: in the first person singular, the thematic vowel -ē- is not deleted, but is simply shortened, for the same reasons as those discussed in the active voice (cf. Section 14.6.2).

Future indicative: cf. first conjugation (Section 14.7.1).

Present subjunctive: the tense suffix is -ā-; the thematic vowel -ē- is not deleted, but is simply shortened, for the same reasons as those discussed in the active voice (cf. Section 14.6.2).

14.7.3 Third conjugation

TABLE 14.17 Passive voice: third conjugation

Tense	Person	Mood: **Indicative**		Mood: **Subjunctive**	
Present		'I am (being) read'		'I am read', 'I may be read', 'I would be read'	
	1st sg.	[lege]+or	**legor**	[[lege]+ā]+r	**legar**
	2nd sg.	[lege]+ris	**legeris**	[[lege]+ā]+ris	**legāris**
	3rd sg.	[lege]+tur	**legitur**	[[lege]+ā]+tur	**legātur**
	1st pl.	[lege]+mur	**legimur**	[[lege]+ā]+mur	**legāmur**
	2nd pl.	[lege]+minī	**legiminī**	[[lege]+ā]+minī	**legāminī**
	3rd pl.	[lege]+untur	**leguntur**	[[lege]+ā]+ntur	**legantur**

(continued)

TABLE 14.17 Continued

Tense	Person	Mood: **Indicative**		Mood: **Subjunctive**	
Imperfect		'I was (being) read'		'I was being read', 'I might be read', 'I would be read'	
	1st sg.	[[lege]+ēbā]+r	**legēbar**	[[lege]+rē]+r	**legerer**
	2nd sg.	[[lege]+ēbā]+ris	**legēbāris**	[[lege]+rē]+ris	**legerēris**
	3rd sg.	[[lege]+ēbā]+tur	**legēbātur**	[[lege]+rē]+tur	**legerētur**
	1st pl.	[[lege]+ēbā]+mur	**legēbāmur**	[[lege]+rē]+mur	**legerēmur**
	2nd pl.	[[lege]+ēbā]+minī	**legēbāminī**	[[lege]+rē]+minī	**legerēminī**
	3rd pl.	[[lege]+ēbā]+ntur	**legēbantur**	[[lege]+rē]+ntur	**legerentur**
Future		'I shall be read'			
	1st sg.	[[lege]+ā]+r	**legar**		
	2nd sg.	[[lege]+ē]+ris	**legēris**		
	3rd sg.	[[lege]+ē]+tur	**legētur**		
	1st pl.	[[lege]+ē]+mur	**legēmur**		
	2nd pl.	[[lege]+ē]+minī	**legēminī**		
	3rd pl.	[[lege]+ē]+ntur	**legentur**		

Notes

Present indicative: in the first person singular and third person plural, the thematic vowel -*e*- is deleted before the endings -*or* and -*untur*. As for the remaining persons, the thematic vowel -*e*- regularly becomes -*i*- because of vowel weakening, with the exception of the second person singular, where it precedes -*r*- (cf. rules (7) and (10) in Section 8.5).

Imperfect indicative: the tense suffix is -*ēbā*-, as in the active voice (cf. Section 14.6.3).

Future indicative: the tense suffix is -*ā*- (first person singular) and -*ē*- (other persons). The thematic vowel is always deleted.

Present subjunctive: the thematic vowel is regularly deleted before the tense suffix -*ā*-.

14.7.4 Third conjugation (verbs in -iō)

TABLE 14.18 Passive voice: third conjugation (verbs in -iō)

Tense	Person	Mood: **Indicative**		Mood: **Subjunctive**	
Present		'I am (being) taken'		'I am taken', 'I may be taken', 'I would be taken'	
	1st sg.	[capi]+or	**capior**	[[capi]+ā]+r	**capiar**
	2nd sg.	[capi]+ris	**caperis**	[[capi]+ā]+ris	**capiāris**
	3rd sg.	[capi]+tur	**capitur**	[[capi]+ā]+tur	**capiātur**
	1st pl.	[capi]+mur	**capimur**	[[capi]+ā]+mur	**capiāmur**
	2nd pl.	[capi]+minī	**capiminī**	[[capi]+ā]+minī	**capiāminī**
	3rd pl.	[capi]+untur	**capiuntur**	[[capi]+ā]+ntur	**capiantur**
Imperfect		'I was (being) taken'		'I was being taken', 'I might be taken', 'I would be taken'	
	1st sg.	[[capi]+ēbā]+r	**capiēbar**	[[capi]+rē]+r	**caperer**
	2nd sg.	[[capi]+ēbā]+ris	**capiēbāris**	[[capi]+rē]+ris	**caperēris**
	3rd sg.	[[capi]+ēbā]+tur	**capiēbātur**	[[capi]+rē]+tur	**caperētur**
	1st pl.	[[capi]+ēbā]+mur	**capiēbāmur**	[[capi]+rē]+mur	**caperēmur**
	2nd pl.	[[capi]+ēbā]+minī	**capiēbāminī**	[[capi]+rē]+minī	**caperēminī**
	3rd pl.	[[capi]+ēbā]+ntur	**capiēbantur**	[[capi]+rē]+ntur	**caperentur**
Future		'I shall be taken'			
	1st sg.	[[capi]+ā]+r	**capiar**		
	2nd sg.	[[capi]+ē]+ris	**capiēris**		
	3rd sg.	[[capi]+ē]+tur	**capiētur**		
	1st pl.	[[capi]+ē]+mur	**capiēmur**		
	2nd pl.	[[capi]+ē]+minī	**capiēminī**		
	3rd pl.	[[capi]+ē]+ntur	**capientur**		

Notes

The thematic vowel is never deleted. The tense suffixes and the endings are the same as the third conjugation (cf. Section 14.6.4).

Present indicative: in the second person singular the thematic vowel *-i-* regularly becomes *-e-* before *-r-* (cf. rule (10b) in Section 8.5).

Imperfect subjunctive: the thematic vowel *-i-* always becomes *-e-* before *-r-*.

14.7.5 Fourth conjugation

TABLE 14.19 Passive voice: fourth conjugation

Tense	Person	Mood: **Indicative**		Mood: **Subjunctive**	
Present		'I am (being) heard'		'I am heard', 'I may be heard', 'I would be heard'	
	1st sg.	[audī]+or	audior	[[audī]+ā]+r	audiar
	2nd sg.	[audī]+ris	audīris	[[audī]+ā]+ris	audiāris
	3rd sg.	[audī]+tur	audītur	[[audī]+ā]+tur	audiātur
	1st pl.	[audī]+mur	audīmur	[[audī]+ā]+mur	audiāmur
	2nd pl.	[audī]+minī	audīminī	[[audī]+ā]+minī	audiāminī
	3rd pl.	[audī]+untur	audiuntur	[[audī]+ā]+ntur	audiantur
Imperfect		'I was (being) heard'		'I was being heard', 'I might be heard', 'I would be heard'	
	1st sg.	[[audī]+ēbā]+r	audiēbar	[[audī]+rē]+r	audīrer
	2nd sg.	[[audī]+ēbā]+ris	audiēbāris	[[audī]+rē]+ris	audīrēris
	3rd sg.	[[audī]+ēbā]+tur	audiēbātur	[[audī]+rē]+tur	audīrētur
	1st pl.	[[audī]+ēbā]+mur	audiēbāmur	[[audī]+rē]+mur	audīrēmur
	2nd pl.	[[audī]+ēbā]+minī	audiēbāminī	[[audī]+rē]+minī	audīrēminī
	3rd pl.	[[audī]+ēbā]+ntur	audiēbantur	[[audī]+rē]+ntur	audīrentur

Future   'I shall be heard'

1st sg.	[[audī]+ā]+r	**audiar**
2nd sg.	[[audī]+ē]+ris	**audiēris**
3rd sg.	[[audī]+ē]+tur	**audiētur**
1st pl.	[[audī]+ē]+mur	**audiēmur**
2nd pl.	[[audī]+ē]+minī	**audiēminī**
3rd pl.	[[audī]+ē]+ntur	**audientur**

Notes

The thematic vowel *-ī-* is never deleted, but is simply shortened before another vowel.

14.7.6 Tenses derived from the perfectum

In the passive voice, the forms of the tenses that in the active voice are derived from the stem of the *perfectum* are obtained by combining the perfect participle with the auxiliary *sum* 'to be' (cf. Table 14.23). In particular, the auxiliary is inflected for the present, imperfect, and future and it is combined with the participle to form the perfect, pluperfect, and the future perfect. A summary of moods and tenses is given in Table 14.20.

TABLE 14.20 Tenses derived from the *perfectum*: endings for all conjugations (passive voice)

Tense	Pers.	Mood: **Indicative**		Mood: **Subjunctive**	
Perfect		'I was praised', 'I have been praised'		'I was praised', 'I have been praised', 'I may have been praised'	
	1st sg.	laudātus, -a, -um	sum	laudātus, -a, -um	sim
	2nd sg.		es		sīs
	3rd sg.		est		sit
	1st pl.	laudātī, -ae, -a	sumus	laudātī, -ae, -a	sīmus
	2nd pl.		estis		sītis
	3rd pl.		sunt		sint

(continued)

TABLE 14.20 Continued

Tense	Pers.	Mood: **Indicative**		Mood: **Subjunctive**	
Pluperfect		'I had been praised'		'I had been praised', 'I would have been praised', 'I might have been praised'	
	1st sg.	laudātus, -a, -um eram		laudātus, -a, -um essem	
	2nd sg.		erās		essēs
	3rd sg.		erat		esset
	1st pl.	laudātī, -ae, -a	erāmus	laudātī, -ae, -a essēmus	
	2nd pl.		erātis		essētis
	3rd pl.		erant		essent
Future Perfect		'I shall have been praised'			
	1st sg.	laudātus, -a, -um erō			
	2nd sg.		eris		
	3rd sg.		erit		
	1st pl.	laudātī, -ae, -a	erimus		
	2nd pl.		eritis		
	3rd pl.		erunt		

14.7.7 Nominal and adjectival forms of the verb

The nominal forms of the passive verb are the infinitive, the participle, the gerundive, and the supine. Some forms are derived from the stem of the *īnfectum*, i.e. the present infinitive *laudā-rī* and the gerundive *laudā-ndus*, while the remaining forms are derived from the stem of the *supīnum*, i.e the periphrastic forms of the perfect infinitive *laudāt-um esse* and of the future infinitive *laudāt-um īrī*, the supine *laudāt-ū*, and the perfect participle *laudāt-us* (which is also employed in the periphrastic conjugation of the *perfectum*, e.g. *laudātus sum, eram*, etc., cf. in Table 14.20). Table 14.21 shows the paradigm of the four conjugations.

Notes
The present infinitive, e.g. *laudārī*, is derived by combining the suffix -*rī* (first, second, and fourth conjugation) and -*ī* (third conjugation) with the stem of the *īnfectum*.

The perfect infinitive, e.g. *laudātum esse*, is formed by combining the accusative case of the perfect participle with the infinitive *esse*.

TABLE 14.21 Nominal and adjectival forms of the verb (passive voice)

Mood	Tense	1st conjug.	2nd conjug.	3rd conjug.	3rd conjug. (verbs in -io)	4th conjug.
Infinitive	Pres.	laudārī 'to be praised'	monērī 'to be warned'	legī 'to be read'	capī 'to be taken'	audīrī 'to be heard'
	Perf.	laudātum, -am, -um esse 'to have been praised'	monitum, -am, -um esse 'to have been warned'	lectum, -am, -um esse 'to have been read'	captum, -am, -um esse 'to have been taken'	audītum, -am, -um esse 'to have been heard'
	Fut.	laudātum īrī 'to be about to be praised'	monitum īrī 'to be about to be warned'	lectum īrī 'to be about to be read'	captum īrī 'to be about to be taken'	audītum īrī 'to be about to be heard'
Participle	Perf.	laudātus, -a, -um 'having been praised'	monitus, -a, -um 'having been warned'	lectus, -a, -um 'having been read'	captus, -a, -um 'having been taken'	audītus, -a, -um 'having been heard'
Gerundive		laudandus, -a, -um 'that should be praised', 'to be praised'	monendus, -a, -um 'that should be warned', 'to be warned'	legendus, -a, -um 'that should be read', 'to be read'	capiendus, -a, -um 'that should be taken', 'to be taken'	audiendus, -a, -um 'that should be heard', 'to be heard'
Supine		laudātū 'to (be) praised'	monitū 'to (be) warned'	lectū 'to (be) read'	captū 'to (be) taken'	audītū 'to (be) heard'

The future infinitive, e.g. *laudātum īrī*, is formed by combining the supine active with the present infinitive passive of the verb *īre* 'to go'.

The perfect participle, e.g. *laudātus*, is a first class adjective derived from the stem of the supine.

The gerundive, e.g. *laudandus*, is derived by adding the suffix -*nd*- (first and second conjugation) and -*end*- (third and fourth conjugation) to the stem of the *īnfectum*. It is inflected in the same way as first class adjectives.

The supine, e.g. *laudātū*, is a verbal noun derived by adding the suffix -*ū* to the stem of the supine. It indicates purpose and is used on only a few occasions, especially in conjunction with adjectives, e.g. *mīrābile dictū* 'wondrous to say', lit. 'wondrous to be said'.

14.8 Active and passive periphrastic conjugations

Traditional grammars employ the label 'periphrastic conjugations' to refer to two verbal systems consisting of the combination of a nominal form of the verb, i.e. the future participle or the gerundive, and various forms of the verb *sum* 'to be'.

14.8.1 Active periphrastic conjugation

The active periphrastic conjugation is formed by combining the future participle with the verb *sum* and is employed to express something which is either imminent, intended, or bound to happen. It can be translated by expressions such as 'I am about to', 'I am going to', etc., as shown in examples (3) to (5):

(3) Nisi forte hospites *ventūri sunt* (Plaut. *Stich.* 356)
     'Unless guests *are about to come*'

(4) Bellum *scrīptūrus sum*, quod populus Rōmānus cum Iugurthā rege Numidārum
         gessit (Sall. *Iug.* 5, 1)
     '*I am going to write* about the war which the people of Rome waged with
         Jugurtha, king of the Numidians'

(5) Quā nocte *peritūrus fuit*, lēgit (Sen. *epist.* 71, 11)
     'He spent in reading the night wherein *he intended to die*'

14.8.2 Passive periphrastic conjugation

The passive periphrastic conjugation is formed by combining the gerundive with the verb *sum*, and is employed to express something which is either necessary, or convenient, or advisable. The person for whom it is necessary, convenient, or advisable to do something is assigned dative case (cf. dative of agency in Section 21.4). It can be translated using expressions such as 'I have to', 'it is necessary/advisable that I', 'I must' etc., as shown in examples (6) to (8):

(6)   *Expurgandus est* sermō (Cic. *Brut.* 258)
      'The language *must be purged*'

(7)   *Moriendum est* enim omnibus (Cic. *Tusc.* I 9)
      'For all *have to die*'

(8)   *Laudandus est* adulescens (Quint. *decl. min.* 260, 3)
      'The young man *has to be praised*'

14.9 Deponent verbs

Ancient grammars used the word 'deponent' in order to indicate a verb which has 'dropped' its active morphology (cf. Lat. *dēpōnō* 'to put down') and only retains the passive, albeit with an active meaning. However, this label refers only to the morphological properties of deponent verbs, and does not reveal anything else about their nature. To make this explanation easier, we will identify two groups of verbs, i.e. transitive deponents and intransitive deponents.

A transitive deponent verb such as *hortor* 'to exhort' is a verb that, by virtue of its meaning, implies a strong involvement between the subject and the action. For this reason, such verbs originally employed a specific type of Indo-European morphology, called 'middle', which has survived in some languages, e.g. Ancient Greek. From a syntactic point of view, these verbs are able to assign accusative case to their objects, similarly to a common transitive active verb, e.g. *mīlites hortārī* 'to exhort the soldiers', although some of them can also be used intransitively, e.g. *pauca loquī* 'to say a few words', but more commonly *loquī* 'to speak'.

In contrast, some special deponent verbs such as *morior* 'to die' are inherently intransitive. In linguistics, these 'special' intransitive verbs are called 'unaccusative', with reference to the fact that they are not able to assign accusative case to their underlying object. In other words, they differ form regular intransitive verbs in that they do have an object, which is nevertheless raised to the subject position to receive case. This concept will become clearer in Section 27.5. For the sake of the present discussion, it is sufficient for us to remember that the subject of these verbs is always somebody or something which is affected by the action, as is usually the case for objects. Unaccusative verbs are not unique to Latin, but can be found in English and Italian as well, among many other languages. In Italian, in particular, they can be easily recognized because they select the auxiliary 'be' instead of the auxiliary 'have', e.g. *è morto* 'he died' vs. *ha esortato* 'he exhorted'. In English, it is possible to promote the object to the subject position by suppressing the role of the subject, e.g. *This book translates easily.*

As for their inflection, all the forms of deponent verbs coincide with the forms of passive verbs in the indicative and subjunctive moods. The only dedicated paradigm is the imperative, and in particular the present forms in *-re, -minī*, simply because passive verbs do not have an imperative. In addition to this, deponent verbs have integrated within their paradigm the other nominal forms which do not exist for the passive, i.e. present and future participle and gerund, that have been shaped on the model of active verbs. The form of the future infinitive is active, e.g. *hortātūrum esse* instead of **hortātum īrī*. Finally, both the supine active and passive may be formed, e.g. *grātulātum venīre* 'to come to congratulate' or *maior nātū* 'older by birth', though these are very rare (cf. Table 14.22).

14.10 Semi-deponent verbs

Semi-deponent verbs are so-called because they inflect like active verbs in the tenses derived from the stem of the *īnfectum* and like deponent verbs in the tenses derived from the stem of the *perfectum*. We give below a list of the most common examples:

soleō, solēs, solitus sum, solēre 'to be accustomed'
audeō, audēs, ausus sum, audēre 'to dare'
gaudeō, gaudēs, gāvīsus sum, gaudēre 'to rejoice'
cōnfīdō, cōnfīdis, cōnfīsus sum, cōnfīdere 'to trust'

The perfect participle of both deponent and semi-deponent verbs typically has past meaning and active sense, e.g. *hortātus* 'having exhorted'; *gāvīsus* 'having rejoiced'. However, the participles of some verbs can have present meaning:

arbitror: *arbitrātus* 'thinking'
audeō: *ausus* 'daring'
cōnfīdō: *cōnfīsus* 'confiding'
reor: *ratus* 'thinking'
vereor: *veritus* 'fearing'

Finally, some perfect participles of deponent verbs can exceptionally have passive meaning:

adipiscor: *adeptus* 'having gained' or 'having *been* gained'
comitor: *comitātus* 'having accompanied' or 'having *been* accompanied'
meditor: *meditātus* 'having reflected' or 'having *been* reflected'
populor: *populātus* 'having destroyed' or 'having *been* destroyed'

TABLE 14.22 Deponent verbs

Mood/Tense	1st conjug.	2nd conjug.	3rd conjug.	3rd conjug. (verbs in -iō)	4th conjug.
	'to rejoice'	'to fear'	'to follow'	'to suffer'	'to bestow'
Ind. Pres.	laetor	vereor	sequor	patior	largior
Impf.	laetābar	verēbar	sequēbar	patiēbar	largiēbar
Fut.	laetābor	verēbor	sequar	patiar	largiēbor
Perf.	laetātus sum	veritus sum	secūtus sum	passus sum	largītus sum
Pluperf.	laetātus eram	veritus eram	secūtus eram	passus eram	largītus eram
Fut.Perf.	laetātus ero	veritus ero	secūtus ero	passus ero	largītus ero
Subj. Pres.	laeter	verear	sequar	patiar	largiar
Impf.	laetārer	verērer	sequerer	paterer	largīrer
Perf.	laetātus sim	veritus sim	secūtus sim	passus sim	largītus sim
Pluperf.	laetātus essem	veritus essem	secūtus essem	passus essem	largītus essem
Imper. Pres.					
sg.	laetāre	verēre	sequere	patere	largīre
pl.	laetāminī	verēminī	sequiminī	patiminī	largīminī
Imper. Fut.					
sg.	laetātor	verētor	sequitor	patitor	largītor
pl.	laetāntor	verēntor	sequuntor	patiuntor	largiuntor
Inf. Pres.	laetārī	verērī	sequī	patī	largīrī

(continued)

TABLE 14.22 Continued

Mood/ Tense	1st conjug.	2nd conjug.	3rd conjug.	3rd conjug. (verbs in -iō)	4th conjug.
Perf.	laetātum esse	veritum esse	secūtum esse	passum esse	largitum esse
Fut.	laetātūrum esse	veritūrum esse	secūtūrum esse	passūrum esse	largitūrum esse
Part. Pres.	laetāns	verēns	sequēns	patiēns	largiēns
Perf.	laetātus	veritus	secūtus	passus	largitus
Fut.	laetātūrus	veritūrus	secūtūrus	passūrus	largitūrus
Gerund	laetandī	verendī	sequendī	patiendī	largiendī
Gerundive	laetandus	verendus	sequendus	patiendus	largiendus
Supine	laetātum	veritum	secūtum	passum	largitum
	laetātū	veritū	secūtū	passū	largitū

14.11 Irregular verbs

In addition to regular verbs, which are divided into four conjugations, in accordance with their thematic vowel, there exist some irregular verbs. These are typically high-frequency words and it is thus advisable to memorize their paradigms (cf. Tables 14.23 to 14.27). They are characterized by the ablaut variation between different stems, e.g. *su-/es-*; *vol-/vel-*, and by the frequent lack of thematic vowel (for this reason, they are sometimes called 'athematic verbs').

TABLE 14.23 *Sum* 'to be'

	Indicative	Subjunctive	Imperative	Infinitive	Participle
Present	'I am'	'I may be', 'I would be'	'be!'	'to be'	
	sum	sim		esse	
	es	sīs	es		
	est	sit			
	sumus	sīmus			
	estis	sītis	este		
	sunt	sint			
Imperfect	'I was'	'I might be', 'I would be'			
	eram	essem			
	erās	essēs			
	erat	esset			
	erāmus	essēmus			
	erātis	essētis			
	erant	essent			
Future	'I shall be'		'you shall be'	'to be about to be'	'about to be'
	erō			futūrum,	futūrus,
	eris		estō	-am, -um	-a, -um
	erit		estō	esse	
	erimus			or	
	eritis		estōte	fore	
	erunt		suntō		

(continued)

TABLE 14.23 Continued

	Indicative	Subjunctive	Imperative	Infinitive	Participle
Perfect	'I was', 'I have been'	'I may have been'		'to have been'	
	fuī	fuerim		fuisse	
	fuistī	fueris			
	fuit	fuerit			
	fuimus	fuerimus			
	fuistis	fueritis			
	fuērunt	fuerint			
Pluperfect	'I had been'	'I would have been', 'I might have been'			
	fueram	fuissem			
	fuerās	fuissēs			
	fuerat	fuisset			
	fuerāmus	fuissēmus			
	fuerātis	fuissētis			
	fuerant	fuissent			
Future perfect	'I shall have been'				
	fuerō				
	fueris				
	fuerit				
	fuerimus				
	fueritis				
	fuerint				

Notes

Similarly to colloquial English, where *is* can be reduced to *'s*, in the archaic spoken Latin of Plautus and Terence *es* and *est* are also attested in a reduced form, e.g. *amatust* (from *amatus 'st*); *iratas* (from *irata 's*); *numquamst* (from *numquam 'st*).

The archaic form for the third person plural of the perfect indicative *fuērunt* is *fuēre*.

In archaic and poetic Latin it is possible to find other forms for the present subjunctive, i.e. *siem, siēs, siet, sient*, and also *fuam, fuas*, etc.; for the imperfect subjunctive: *forem, fores*, etc.

The present participle *ēns is attested only in some prefixed forms, e.g. absēns 'absent' and praesēns 'present'.

TABLE 14.24 Volō 'to be willing', 'to want'; nōlō 'to be unwilling', 'to not wish'; mālō 'to prefer'

		Indicative	
Present	volō	nōlō	mālō
	vīs	nōn vīs	māvīs
	vult	nōn vult	māvult
	volumus	nōlumus	mālumus
	vultis	nōn vultis	māvultis
	volunt	nōlunt	mālunt
Imperfect	volēbam	nōlēbam	mālēbam
	volēbās	nōlēbās	mālēbās
	etc.	etc.	etc.
Future	volam	nōlam	mālam
	volēs	nōlēs	mālēs
	etc.	etc.	etc.
		Subjunctive	
Present	velim	nōlim	mālim
	velīs	nōlīs	mālīs
	velit	nōlit	mālit
	velīmus	nōlīmus	mālīmus
	velītis	nōlītis	mālītis
	velint	nōlint	mālint
Imperfect	vellem	nōllem	māllem
	vellēs	nōllēs	māllēs
	etc.	etc.	etc.
		Imperative	
Present		nōlī	
		nōlīte	
Future		nōlītō	
		nōlītōte	
		nōluntō	

(continued)

TABLE 14.24 Continued

	Infinitive		
		Infinitive	
Present	**velle**	**nōlle**	**mālle**
		Participle	
Present	**volēns**	**nōlēns**	

Notes

Tenses derived from the stem of the *perfectum* are regular (*voluī, nōluī, māluī*).

TABLE 14.25 *Ferō* 'to bear'

	Indicative		Subjunctive	
	Active	Passive	Active	Passive
Present	ferō	feror	feram	ferar
	fers	**ferris**	ferās	ferāris
	fert	**fertur**	ferat	ferātur
	ferimus	ferimur	ferāmus	ferāmur
	fertis	ferimini	ferātis	ferāmini
	ferunt	feruntur	ferant	ferantur
Imperfect	ferēbam	ferēbar	**ferrem**	**ferrer**
	ferēbās	ferēbāris	**ferrēs**	**ferrēris**
	ferēbat	ferēbātur	ferret	ferretur
	ferēbāmus	ferēbāmus	**ferrēmus**	**ferrēmur**
	ferēbātis	ferēbāmini	**ferrētis**	**ferrēmini**
	ferēbānt	ferēbāntur	**ferrēnt**	**ferrēntur**
Future	feram	ferar		
	ferēs	ferēris		
	etc.	etc.		

Notes

The imperative is 'athematic': present **fer, ferte**; future **fertō, fertō, fertōte, feruntō**.

Tenses derived from the stem of the *perfectum* (*tulī*) and the stem of the supine (*lātum*) are regular.

TABLE 14.26 *Eō* 'to go'

	Indicative			Subjunctive	
Present	Imperfect	Future	Present	Imperfect
eō	ībam	ībō	eam	īrem
īs	ībās	ībis	eās	īrēs
it	ībat	ībit	eat	īret
īmus	ībāmus	ībimus	eāmus	īrēmus
ītis	ībātis	ībitis	eātis	īrētis
eunt	ībant	ībunt	eant	īrent

Notes

Present imperative: ī, īte.

Future imperative: ītō, ītō; ītōte, euntō.

Present infinitive: īre.

Future infinitive: ītūrum, -a, -um esse.

Present participle: iēns, euntis.

Gerund: eundī, etc.

Gerundive: eundum (est).

As for tenses derived from the stem of the perfect, the forms are *iī, iistī, iit*, etc., sometimes contracted before *-s*, i.e. *īsti, īstis, īsse*. The analogic forms *īvī, īvistī* are rarely attested.

TABLE 14.27 *Fiō* 'to become', 'to happen', 'to be made', 'to be done' (passive of *faciō*)

	Indicative			Subjunctive	
Present	Imperfect	Future	Present	Imperfect
fīō	fīēbam	fīam	fīam	fierem
fīs	fīēbās	fīēs	fīās	fierēs
fit	fīēbat	fiet	fīat	fieret
fīmus	fīēbāmus	fīēmus	fīāmus	fierēmus
fītis	fīēbātis	fīētis	fīātis	fierētis
fiunt	fīēbant	fient	fīant	fierent

Notes

Present imperative: **fī, fīte.**

Future imperative: **fītō, fītō; fītōte.**

Present infinitive: **fierī.**

Perfect infinitive: **factum, -am, -um esse.**

Future infinitive: **futūrum, -a, -um esse** or **fore.**

Perfect participle: **factus, -a, -um.**

Future participle: **futūrus, -a, -um.**

Gerundive: **faciendus, -a, -um.**

Tenses derived from the stem of the perfect are regular: *factus sum, es, est,* etc.

Finally, we shall consider the verb *edō, -is, ēdī, ēsum, edere* 'to eat', which belongs to the third conjugation. Along with the regular forms, it also exhibits some short forms, which nearly coincide with those of *esse* (the only difference is the long *e-*, e.g. *es* 'you are' vs. *ēs* 'you eat'). For this reason, it is important to pay attention to the difference between the inflected forms of *esse* and the inflected forms of *edere*.

The most common short forms are:

Present indicative: **ēs, ēst, ēstis.**
Present subjunctive: **edim** in Plautus.
Imperfect subjunctive: **ēssem, ēsses, ēsset, ēssēmus, ēssētis, ēssent.**
Present imperative: **ēs, ēste.**
Future imperative: **ēstō.**
Present infinitive: **ēsse.**
Present indicative passive: **ēstur.**

14.12 Defective verbs

Defective verbs are so called because they lack a complete conjugation, i.e. some forms are missing. The importance of this category was particularly emphasized by prescriptive grammars devoted to the translation *into* Latin. Indeed, it was important for a translator not to use forms which did not exist. On the other hand, this category of verbs does not raise any particular issue for those who are interested in the translation *from* Latin, as, if a form does not exist, it will not appear in any texts. However, a short list is given here, for the sake of completeness:

Three archaic verbs of saying: *aiō, inquam,* and *for.* With these verbs, only the third person singular of the present and perfect indicative is usually employed in Classical Latin, i.e. *ait* and *inquit* (the present and the perfect coincide), *fātur* and *fātus est*. Note that *aiō* had an archaic spelling *aiiō*, also attested in Cicero, according to *Quint.* I 4, 11. Its attested forms are the second person singular and third person plural of the present indicative, i.e. *ais* and *aiunt*, respectively, as well as all the persons of the imperfect (*aiēbam, aiēbas*, etc.) and the present participle (*aiens*). Note that *inquam* and *inquis* are also well attested.

Queō 'to be able' and *nequeo* 'not to be able' are almost exclusively inflected for the present indicative and subjunctive. For the remaining forms, the verb *possum* is preferred.

The polite phrases *cedo* 'give me' and *quaeso* 'please', and the greetings *ave* and *salve* 'hail' and *vale* 'farewell' are isolated verbal forms.

The verb *coepī* 'I have begun', 'I began', has only the forms derived from the perfect stem. For the present, the prefixed verb *incīpiō* is used instead.

The only class of defective verbs which may also raise some issues for those who are interested in translation from Latin are the so-called 'resultative' perfect verbs, i.e. verbs which are inflected only for the tenses derived from the *perfectum*, in order to express a result. Therefore, it is important to identify and translate them as present and not past forms:

meminī 'I recalled to my memory', thus 'I remember', not 'I remembered'
ōdī 'I took a strong dislike to', thus 'I hate', not 'I hated'.

This resultative meaning is also found in a verb with a complete paradigm, i.e. pres. *noscō* 'I become acquainted with' and perf. *nōvī* 'I became acquainted with', thus 'I know'.

15

Derivation

15.1 Formal representation

Derivation is a morphological device which creates a new word by adding an affix to another word. An affix is an element which can be added at the beginning (prefix), inside (infix), or at the end (suffix) of a word. While prefixes and suffixes are very common in word formation, infixes are rarely employed. The only example in Latin is the so-called 'nasal infix', which can be used to emphasize the dynamic aspect of an action, e.g. the derived word *accu-m-bō* 'to lay oneself down' vs. the base form *accubō* 'to lie'.

The base for the derivation is the lexical stem, to which an affix is attached, similarly to what happens for inflection, whereby an ending is attached to the stem. However, note that while the inflection *adds* some syntactic information to the stem, e.g. number and case for nouns, the derivation *changes* some features of the stem and creates the stem of a new word, e.g. the adjective *rosāceus* 'made of roses', derived from the noun *rosa*.

For this reason, the formal representation of a derivational rule must specify not only the affix which gets attached, but also the 'base', i.e. the set of words which can be affected by that rule, and the 'output', i.e. the set of words produced by that rule. Leaving aside infixes, we will identify two classes of derivational rules, i.e. prefixation and suffixation, with different morphological structures:

(1) a. $[\text{Pre} + [a]_X]_X$ e.g. $[pr\bar{o} + [c\bar{o}nsul]_N]_N$
     b. $[[a]_X + \text{Suf}]_Y$ e.g. $[[am\bar{a}]_V + bilis]_A$

In both cases, the base is a stem [a] which belongs to a given lexical category X. Starting from the stem, a new complex morphological unit is created, with its own internal structure which includes a prefix or a suffix. When the word is derived by means of a prefix, it typically retains the same category as the base, e.g. *prōcōnsul* is a noun, just like its base *cōnsul*. We list in (2) some examples of derivation of verbs from verbs, adjectives from adjectives, and nouns from nouns:

(2) a. V → V   trahere → abs-trahere   'to drag away'
     b. A → A   fēlīx   → īn-fēlīx   'un-happy'
     c. N → N   custōs   → sub-custōs   'deputy-keeper'

In contrast, when a word is derived by means of a suffix, there is a change of category, e.g. *amāre* is a verb, but *amābilis* is an adjective. We list in (3) some examples of denominal, deadjectival, and deverbal forms:

(3) a. N → A   fāma   → fām-ōsus   'notorious'
     b. N → V   dōnum → dōn-āre   'to give'
     c. A → N   audāx   → audāc-ia   'boldness'
     d. A → V   acerbus → acerb-āre   'to aggravate'
     e. V → N   fluere   → flū-men   'river'
     f. V → A   bibere   → bib-āx   'given to drink'

In both cases, i.e. prefixation and suffixation, the morphological process always involves a semantic change, i.e. the affix always changes the meaning of the base, e.g. the prefix *abs-* in *abs-trahō* 'to drag away' modifies the meaning of the verb *trahō* 'to drag'; similarly, the suffix *-ōsus* in *fāmōsus* 'notorious' modifies the meaning of the noun *fāma* 'rumor'.

Prefixes and suffixes are employed to enrich the lexical inventory of a language with new words. For this reason, it is important to know the morphological rules of word formation and to learn the semantic value of the most important affixes. Knowledge of these facts, which is traditionally overlooked in the classroom, is necessary if one wishes to master the lexicon of a language. By knowing the meaning of base words and affixes, it is possible, at least to a certain extent, to understand new words. For this reason, derivational rules represent an important tool of linguistic creativity and, more generally, of acquisition of the lexicon. We report in Sections 15.2 to 15.5 a small inventory of the most productive prefixes and suffixes in Latin.

15.2 Prefixes

The vast majority of prefixes are those which get attached to a verbal stem and which are traditionally called 'preverbs'. They are used to derive new verbs in order to express wider semantic and aspectual variations of the action, e.g. *ad-veniō* 'to come to', *con-veniō* 'to come together', *per-veniō* 'to arrive at', *re-veniō* 'to come back', *sub-veniō* 'to come up to', etc. In this sense, Latin prefixed verbs typically correspond to English particle verbs, where the same aspectual information is conveyed by a postposed particle. Preverbs in Latin can be either independent prepositions, e.g. *ab, ad, cum* (prefix *con-*), or prefixes which cannot appear in isolation, e.g. *amb-, dis-, re-, sē-*. We report in Table 15.1 a list of the most common.

TABLE 15.1 Latin preverbs

Prefix	Examples
ab(s) 'away from'	*abs-cīdō* 'to cut off' *ab-dūcō* 'to lead away'
ad 'to'	*ad-dūcō* 'to bring to' *ad-dō* 'to add'
am(b)- 'around'	*amb-ūrō* 'to burn up' *am-plector* 'to embrace'
ante 'before'	*ante-cēdō* 'to go before' *ante-pōnō* 'to set before'
con- '(together) with'	*con-currō* 'to run together' *com-mittō* 'to bring together'
dē 'down'	*dē-currō* 'to run down' *dē-pōnō* 'to set down'
dis- 'apart'	*dis-cernō* 'to set apart', i.e. 'to separate' *dis-pōnō* 'to put apart', i.e. 'to distribute'
ē / ex 'out'	*ex-pellō* 'to drive out' *ē-rumpō* 'to make break out'
in 'in'	*in-cidō* 'to fall in' *im-mittō* 'to let in'
ne- 'not'	*ne-queō* 'not to be able' *ne-sciō* 'not to know'
ob 'in front of'	*ob-dūcō* 'to draw before' *oc-currō* 'to run up to'
per 'through'	*per-vādō* 'to pass through' *per-lūceō* 'to shine through'
prae 'before'	*prae-moneō* 'to forewarn' *prae-scrībō* 'to write before'
praeter 'past'	*praeter-eō* 'to go past' *praeter-mittō* 'to let pass'
prō 'in front of'	*prō-nuntiō* 'to make publicly known' *prō-tendō* 'to stretch forth'
re(d)- 'backward'	*red-dō* 'to give back' *re-scrībō* 'to write back'
sē- 'apart from'	*sē-cēdō* 'to go apart' *sē-parō* 'to separate'

sub	*sub-mittō* 'to put down'
'under, below'	*suc-currō* 'to run under', 'to assist'
super	*super-sum* 'to be over', 'to survive'
'over'	*super-pōnō* 'to place over'
trā(ns)	*trāns-vehō* 'to carry across'
'across'	*trāns-nō* or *tra-nō* 'to swim across'

Notes

If the final consonant of a prefix meets the initial consonant of the verb, various phenomena of assimilation take place, i.e. the consonant of the prefix tends to become similar or identical to the consonant of the verb, e.g. [ad+cēdō] → *accēdō*; [ad+loquor] → *alloquor*; [ad+petō] → *appetō*; [dis+fīdō] → *diffīdō*; [con+mittō] → *committō*; etc.

If the verbal root contains a short *-ă-* or *-ĕ-*, they undergo vowel weakening in the derived verb, i.e. they become *-ĭ-* in an open syllable and *-ĕ-* in a closed syllable, e.g. [con+canō] → *concinō*; [ad+emō] → *adimō*; [con+damnō] → *condemnō* (cf. adjustment rules (7) and (11) in Section 8.5).

The original spatial meaning of the prefix is often weakened in order to express only the aspectual value of a 'punctual' event, e.g. *con-ficiō* does not mean 'to do together' but 'to complete'; also the English counterpart of *ex-clāmō* means 'to call out', not in the sense of 'to invite to go out', but rather in the sense of 'to exclaim'.

In many traditional grammars some sets of prefixed verbs are inadequately called 'compounds', e.g. 'compounds of *sum*', 'compounds of *eō*', and 'compounds of *ferō*'. In fact, these are not compounds but common aspectual verbs, which are derived by means of the prefixes listed above. The paradigms of these verbs are reported in Tables 15.2–15.4.

15.3 Prefixed verbs with *sum*, *eō*, and *ferō*

TABLE 15.2 Prefixed verbs with *sum*

Paradigm			Translation
ab-sum, -es	*āfuī*	*abesse*	'to be away', 'to be absent'
ad-sum, -es	*adfuī*	*adesse*	'to be present'
dē-sum, -es	*dēfuī*	*deesse*	'to fail', 'to be missing'
īn-sum, -es	*īnfuī*	*inesse*	'to be in'
inter-sum, -es	*interfuī*	*interesse*	'to be between', 'to take part'
ob-sum, -es	*obfuī*	*obesse*	'to be against', 'to hurt'
pos-sum, potes	*potuī*	*posse*	'to be able'
prae-sum, -es	*praefuī*	*praeesse*	'to be set over', 'to preside over'

(continued)

TABLE 15.2 Continued

	Paradigm		Translation
prō-sum, prōdes	*prōfuī*	*prōdesse*	'to do for', 'to benefit'
sub-sum, -es	*fuī sub*	*subesse*	'to be under'
super-sum, -es	*superfuī*	*superesse*	'to remain over', 'to survive'

TABLE 15.3 Prefixed verbs with *eō*

	Paradigm			Translation
ab-eō, -īs	*abiī*	*abitum*	*abīre*	'to go away'
ad-eō, -īs	*adiī*	*aditum*	*adīre*	'to go to', 'to visit'
ante-eō, -īs	*anteiī*	*anteitum*	*anteīre*	'to go before', 'to precede'
circum-eō, -īs	*circumiī*	*circumitum*	*circumīre*	'to go around'
co-eō, -īs	*coiī*	*coitum*	*coīre*	'to go together'
ex-eō, -īs	*exiī*	*exitum*	*exīre*	'to go out'
in-eō, -īs	*iniī*	*initum*	*inīre*	'to go into', 'to begin'
inter-eō, -īs	*interiī*	*interitum*	*interīre*	'to go among', 'to go to ruin'
ob-eō, -īs	*obiī*	*obitum*	*obīre*	'to go towards', 'to die'
per-eō, -īs	*periī*	*periturus*	*perīre*	'to pass through', 'to die'
prae-eō, -īs	*praeiī*	*praeitum*	*praeīre*	'to go before', 'to precede'
praeter-eō, -īs	*praeteriī*	*praeteritum*	*praeterīre*	'to go by'
prō-d-eō, -īs	*prōdiī*	*prōditum*	*prōdīre*	'to go forth'
red-eō, -īs	*rediī*	*reditum*	*redīre*	'to go back'
sub-eō, -īs	*subiī*	*subitum*	*subīre*	'to go under', 'undergo'
trāns-eō, -īs	*transiī*	*transitum*	*transīre*	'to go across'
vēn-eō, -īs	*vēniī*	—	*vēnīre*	'to be sold'

TABLE 15.4 Prefixed verbs with *ferō*

	Paradigm			Translation
(ab) au-ferō, -fers	*abstulī*	*ablātum*	*auferre*	'to take away'
(ad) af-ferō, -fers	*attulī*	*allātum*	*afferre*	'to bring to'
ante-ferō, -fers	*antetulī*	*antelātum*	*anteferre*	'to set before'
circum-ferō, -fers	*cirumtulī*	*circumlātum*	*circumferre*	'to carry around'
cōn-ferō, -fers	*contulī*	*collātum*	*cōnferre*	'to bring together'
dē-ferō, -fers	*dētulī*	*dēlātum*	*dēferre*	'to take down'

dif-ferō, -fers	*distulī*	*dilātum*	*differre*	'to put off', 'to postpone'
ef-ferō, -fers	*extulī*	*elātum*	*efferre*	'to take out'
in-ferō, -fers	*intulī*	*illātum*	*inferre*	'to bring forth'
of-ferō, -fers	*obtulī*	*oblātum*	*offerre*	'to bring in front', 'to offer'
per-ferō, -fers	*pertulī*	*perlātum*	*perferre*	'to bear (through)'
prae-ferō, -fers	*praetulī*	*praelātum*	*praeferre*	'to set before', 'to prefer'
prō-ferō, -fers	*prōtulī*	*prōlātum*	*prōferre*	'to carry out'
re-ferō, -fers	*rettulī*	*relātum*	*referre*	'to bring back'
suf-ferō, -fers	*sustinuī*	*sustentum*	*sufferre*	'to carry under', 'to endure'
trans-ferō, -fers	*transtulī*	*translātum*	*transferre*	'to transport'

Notes

Possum contains a special prefix, i.e. *pot-*, whose *-t-* is retained before the forms of *sum* beginning with a vowel, e.g. *pot-es*, but is assimilated to *-s-* before *-s-*, e.g. *pos-sum* from **pot-sum*. The imperfect subjunctive and the present infinitive are irregular, since they are shortened, i.e. *possem* instead of **potessem* and *posse* instead of **potesse*, respectively. The stem of the perfect is *potu-*; its inflection is regular.

In *prōsum* a euphonic *-d-* is inserted between the suffix *prō-* and the forms of *sum* beginning with a vowel, e.g. *prō-d-es*, *prō-d-esse*.

In the paradigm of *sufferō*, the perfect *sustinuī* and the supine *sustentum* are borrowed from the synonym *sustineō*, because the forms *sustulī* and *sublātum* supply the perfect and the supine of the verb *tollō* 'to remove'. Consequently, *sustulī* usually means 'I removed', not 'I endured'.

15.4 Suffixes

Suffixes are very productive in word formation, not only in Latin, but also in English, which has inherited from Latin suffixes which are still employed today to form new words. In a few cases, the productivity of the original Latin suffixes has even increased in Modern English, as is the case for *-ion* or *-ment*.

In Latin, just as in Italian, if the suffix begins with a vowel, the base is affected by the rule of vowel deletion, e.g. from the Latin stem *fāma* 'rumor' we obtain *fām-ōsus* 'notorious' (cf. It. *fama* 'fame' and *fam-oso* 'famous').

In contrast to prefixes, suffixes usually change the lexical category of the base, e.g. the suffix *-bilis* is attached to verbs to form adjectives, such as *amā-bilis* 'lovely', *dēlē-bilis* 'that may be destroyed', *condūci-bilis* 'profitable', *audī-bilis* 'audible', etc. There are a few exceptions, mainly collective nouns, in which the lexical category of the base is retained and only the grammatical features are modified, e.g. the abstract feminine nouns *client-ēla* 'clientship' and *mīlit-ia* 'military service' are derived from the animate masculine nouns *cliens* 'client' and *mīles* 'soldier', respectively. For this reason, it is useful to group the suffixes into different classes (see Tables 15.5 to 15.9), in accordance with the lexical category of the base and of the derived word.

TABLE 15.5 Deverbal nouns (V → N)

Action nouns	
Suffix	Examples
-ium	*gaud-ium* 'joy' (from *gaudeō* 'to rejoice')
	imper-ium 'command' (from *imperō* 'to command')
-mentum	*fundā-mentum* 'foundation' (from *fundō* 'to found')
	vesti-mentum 'clothing' (from *vestiō* 'to clothe')
-ōr	*dol-or* 'pain' (from *doleō* 'to be in pain')
	tim-or 'fear' (from *timeō* 'to fear')
-tiō	*expedī-tiō* 'expedition' (from *expediō* 'to prepare')
	ōrā-tiō 'speech' (from *ōrō* 'to speak')

Agent nouns	
-tōr	*amā-tor* 'lover' (from *amō* 'to love')
	audī-tor 'hearer' (from *audiō* 'to hear')
-trix	*creā-trix* 'she who produces' (from *creō* 'to create')
	liberā-trix 'she who releases' (from *liberō* 'to set free')

Instrument nouns	
-bulum	*vocā-bulum* 'word' (from *vocō* 'to call')
	vēnā-bulum 'hunting-spear' (from *vēnor* 'to hunt')
-trum	*arā-trum* 'plough' (from *arō* 'to plough')
	fere-trum 'bier' (from *ferō* 'to carry')

TABLE 15.6 Deverbal adjectives (V → A)

Suffix	Examples
-āx	*ed-āx* 'greedy' (from *edō* 'to eat')
	rap-āx 'rapacious' (from *rapiō* 'to snatch')
-bilis	*accūsā-bilis* 'that may be prosecuted' (from *accūsō* 'to accuse')
	vīsi-bilis 'that may be seen' (from *videō* 'to see')
-bundus	*errā-bundus* 'wandering about' (from *errō* 'to wander')
	mori-bundus 'moribund' (from *morior* 'to die')
-idus	*cal-idus* 'warm' (from *caleō* 'to be warm')
	tim-idus 'fearful' (from *timeō* 'to fear')

TABLE 15.7 Denominal adjectives (N → A)

Suffix	Examples
-ālis	*autumn-ālis* 'autumnal' (from *autumnus* 'autumn')
	nāv-ālis 'naval' (from *nāvis* 'ship')
-ānus	*mont-ānus* 'of mountains' (from *mons* 'mountain')
	Rōm-ānus 'Roman' (from *Rōma* 'Rome')
-ārius	*argent-ārius* 'of money' (from *argentum* 'money')
	greg-ārius 'of the herd' (from *grex* 'herd')
-ātus	*barb-ātus* 'bearded' (from *barba* 'beard')
	hast-ātus 'armed with a spear' (from *hasta* 'spear')
-ensis	*circ-ensis* 'of the circus' (from *circus* 'circus')
	for-ensis 'public' (from *forum* 'town square')
-eus	*aur-eus* 'golden' (from *aurum* 'gold')
	corpor-eus 'of the body' (from *corpus* 'body')
-icius	*aedīl-icius* 'of an aedile' (from *aedīlis* 'aedile')
	tribūn-icius 'of a tribune' (from *tribūnus* 'tribune')
-icus	*cīv-icus* 'of citizens' (from *cīvis* 'citizen')
	domin-icus 'of the master' (from *dominus* 'master')
-īnus	*equ-īnus* 'of a horse' (from *equus* 'horse')
	fēmin-īnus 'feminine' (from *fēmina* 'woman')
-ius	*patr-ius* 'fatherly' (from *pater* 'father')
	Mart-ius 'of Mars' (from *Mars* 'Mars')
-ōsus	*anim-ōsus* 'full of courage' (from *animus* 'courage')
	morb-ōsus 'sick' (from *morbus* 'sickness')
-ticus	*aquā-ticus* 'growing in water' (from *aqua* 'water')
	rūs-ticus 'rural' (from *rūs* 'country')
-ulentus	*lut-ulentus* 'muddy' (from *lutum* 'mud')
	op-ulentus 'rich' (from *ops* 'wealth')

TABLE 15.8 Deadjectival nouns (A → N)

Suffix	Examples
-ia	*audāc-ia* 'boldness' (from *audāx* 'bold')
	superb-ia 'loftiness' (from *superbus* 'haughty')
-itia	*laet-itia* 'joy' (from *laetus* 'joyful')
	mal-itia 'ill-will' (from *malus* 'bad')
-itās	*dign-itās* 'dignity' (from *dignus* 'worthy')
	nov-itās 'novelty' (from *novus* 'new')
-tūdō	*forti-tūdō* 'strength' (from *fortis* 'strong')
	sōli-tūdō 'loneliness' (from *solus* 'alone')

TABLE 15.9 Denominal and deadjectival verbs (N → V; A → V)

Suffix	Examples
-ā-	*damn-ā-re* 'to condemn' (from *damnum* 'damage')
	laud-ā-re 'to praise' (from *laus* 'praise')
	līber-ā-re 'to set free' (from *līber* 'free')
	nov-ā-re 'to renew' (from *novus* 'new')

15.5 Evaluative suffixes

The so-called 'evaluative' suffixes represent a special class of suffixes which can be added to nouns, adjectives, and verbs without affecting either the category or the features of the base, but simply adding a semantic nuance. A prototypical example is represented by diminutives, which can be either nouns, e.g. *fīliolus* 'little son', from the noun *fīlius* 'son', adjectives, e.g. *tenellus* 'somewhat tender', from the adjective *tener* 'tender', or verbs *sorbillō* 'to sip', from the verb *sorbeō* 'to drink'.

This very same category also includes suffixes which express variations in the intensity of the action, such as frequentatives, e.g. *rog-itō* 'to ask persistently', from *rogō* 'to ask'; inchoatives, e.g. *fervē-scō* 'to begin to boil', from *ferveō* 'to boil'; and volitionals, e.g. *cap-essō* 'to seize eagerly', from *capiō* 'to take'.

A list of the most important evaluative suffixes is reported in Tables 15.10 to 15.14.

TABLE 15.10 Diminutive nouns and adjectives

Suffix	Category	Examples
-ulus	N	*foc-ulus* 'stove' (from *focus* 'fireplace')
		rēg-ulus 'petty king' (from *rēx* 'king')
	A	*pallid-ulus* 'palish' (from *pallidus* 'pale')
		parv-ulus 'very small' (from *parvus* 'small')
-ellus	N	*ag-ellus* 'little field' (from *ager* 'field')
		lib-ellus 'small book' (from *liber* 'book')
	A	*mis-ellus* 'poor little' (from *miser* 'wretched')
		nov-ellus 'somewhat new' (from *novus* 'new')

TABLE 15.11 Pejorative nouns and adjectives

Suffix	Category	Examples
-aster	N	*fīli-aster* 'stepson' (from *fīlius* 'son')
		parasīt-aster 'sorry parasite' (from *parasītus* 'parasite')
	A	*surd-aster* 'rather deaf' (from *surdus* 'deaf')

TABLE 15.12 Frequentative verbs

Suffix	Examples
-ito	*clām-itō* 'to bawl' (from *clāmō* 'to shout')
	curs-itō 'to run about' (from *currō* 'to run')

TABLE 15.13 Inchoative verbs

Suffix	Examples
-sco	*pallē-scō* 'to turn pale' (from *palleō* 'to be pale')
	rubē-scō 'to turn red' (from *rubeō* 'to be red')

TABLE 15.14 Volitional verbs

Suffix	Examples
-essō	*lac-essō* 'to provoke' (from *laciō* 'to entice')
	fac-essō 'to carry out' (from *faciō* 'to do')
-uriō	*ēs-uriō* 'to desire to eat' (from *edō* 'to eat')
	part-uriō 'to be in labor' (from *pariō* 'to bear')

15.6 The concept of morphological structure

Prefixes and suffixes create complex words which are characterized by a specific hierarchical structure. This approach to the analysis of derived words differs from the approach adopted by traditional grammars, which typically analyse the internal structure of words by means of a linear segmentation. However, such an innovation is necessary, as a mere linear segmentation is not sufficient to express the difference between two words which exhibit the same sequence 'prefix+stem+suffix', as shown in the examples in (4):

(4) a. īn-fructu-ōsus
         'unfruitful'

     b. in-citā-tor
         'instigator'

Despite the superficial similarity in (4a) and (4b), there is a difference in the hierarchical organization of the internal constituents of the two words. In (4a), the noun *fructus* 'fruit' is the base, to which the suffix *-ōsus* is first attached (forming the derived adjective *fructu-ōsus* 'fruitful'), and then the negative prefix *in-* (forming the prefixed adjective *in-fructuōsus*). In other words, the morphological structure of this word requires that suffixation precedes prefixation. The reverse is not possible, i.e. it is not possible to add the prefix *in-* before the suffix is added, forming something like **īn-fructus*. The same is true for English **unfruit*, which does not exist.

In contrast, the base of example (4b) is the verb *citāre* 'to set in motion', to which the prefix *in-* is first attached (forming the prefixed verb *in-citāre* 'to instigate'), followed by the suffix *-tor* (forming the derived noun *incitā-tor*). In this case too, the reverse order is impossible, i.e. it is not possible to add the suffix before the prefix is added (**citā-tor* does not exist in Latin).

In other words, the morphology of *īn-fructu-ōsus* and *in-citā-tor* is characterized by a different hierarchical organization of the internal structure. This can be graphically represented as in (5):

(5) a. [in+ [[fructu]$_N$+ōso]$_A$]$_A$
     b. [[in+ [citā]$_V$]$_V$ +tōr]$_N$

In (5a) the negative prefix *in-* is added to the adjective *fructuōsus*, whose morphological structure [[fructu]$_N$ +ōso]$_A$ signals its previous derivation through suffixation from the noun *fructus*. In the overall morphological structure of *īnfructuōsus*, the suffix belongs to a more embedded level of derivation than the prefix.

In contrast, the suffix *-tōr* in (5b) is added to the verb *incitāre*, whose morphological structure [in+ [citā]$_V$]$_V$ signals its previous derivation through prefixation from the verb *citāre*. In this case, therefore, the element which belongs to the most embedded level of derivation is the prefix.

The concept of morphological structure is also useful to explain sequences of derivation. In order to represent the sequence of application of two prefixes or suffixes to the same base, we will resort again to a system of embedded brackets, as shown in (6) (*dēpereō* 'to be completely destroyed'; *festīvitas* 'festivity'):

(6)   a. [dē+ [per+ [eō]]]
      b. [[[fest] +īv] +itās]

In (6a) the derivational sequence is the following: *eō* 'to go' → *per-eō* 'to go to ruin' → *dē-per-eō* 'to go completely to ruin'. In (4b), in contrast, the sequence is the following: *festum* 'holiday' → *fest-īvus* 'festive' → *fest-īv-itās* 'festivity'.

The application of sequences of prefixes and suffixes is subject to cross-linguistic variation. While Romance languages exhibit a vast number of long derived words, e.g. It. *precipit-evol-issim-evol-mente* 'very precipitously', German languages prefer long compounds, e.g. Ger. *Donau-dampf-schif-fahrts-gesellschaft* 'Danube Steamboat Shipping Company'. Literary Latin preferably avoids very long derived or compound words. Nevertheless, in Latin, and later on in Romance, derivation is far more productive than composition. Indeed, it is often the case that the very same word is affected by a process of derivation three times, e.g. $e\bar{o}_V$ 'to go' → $ambi\bar{o}_V$ 'to go round' → $ambiti\bar{o}_N$ 'canvassing for votes' → $ambiti\bar{o}sus_A$ 'ambitious', or even four times, e.g. the word *in-ex-pugn-ā-bilis* 'impregnable' is formed by combining a base, i.e. *pugna*, with two prefixes and two suffixes, as shown in (7), which summarizes the derivational sequence of the word: $pugna_N$ 'battle' → $pugnāre_V$ 'to fight' → $expugnāre_V$ 'to take by assault' → $expugnābilis_A$ 'assailable' → $inexpugnābilis_A$ 'impregnable':

(7)

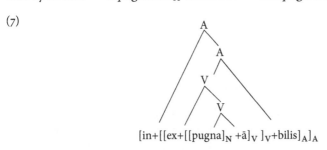

$[in+[[ex+[[pugna]_N +\bar{a}]_V]_V+bilis]_A]_A$

In (7), the usual representation of the morphological structure by means of labelled brackets is accompanied by a tree. From a conceptual point of view, these two types of representation, i.e. labelled brackets and trees, are equivalent, and in the following chapters we will freely alternate them in the representation of syntactic structures. The choice between one or the other depends simply on a graphic preference, i.e. labels are usually preferred for small structures, while trees are employed with more complex ones. In both cases, the important empirical observation which is captured by these representations is the existence of some units which get attached to the 'head' of the structure in accordance with a specific hierarchical order.

Finally, also note that derivational rules do not necessarily apply to any stems of simple words, e.g. it is not necessarily the case that any simple noun constitutes the base from which to derive a denominal verb in *-āre*, nor is it possible to derive an agentive noun in *-tor* or an abstract noun in *-tiō* from any verb. This is the crucial difference between derivation, which is optional, and inflection, which is obligatory.

15.7 Parasynthetic verbs

Some denominal and deadjectival verbs are derived by adding a prefix and a suffix simultaneously. These are the so-called 'parasynthetic' verbs, shown in (8):

(8) (a) *ager* 'field'   → *per-agr-āre* 'to wander through fields' *agr-āre* *per-ager*
    (b) *rēte* 'net'   → *ir-rēt-īre*   'to catch in a net'   *rēt-īre* *ir-rēte*
    (c) *fortis* 'strong' → *cōn-fort-āre* 'to strengthen'   *fort-āre* *cōn-fortis*

As is clear from the examples in (8), parasynthetic verbs are derived from their base (either a noun or an adjective) by adding a prefix and a suffix, but the intermediate forms consisting of the base and the suffix or the base and the prefix do not exist.

A possible account for this special type of derivation is suggested by the structure of another class of verbs, which are almost identical to parasynthetic verbs, notwithstanding the fact that they are formed through two derivational steps:

(9) (a) *hiems* 'winter' →*hiem-āre* 'to pass the winter'→*per-hiemāre* 'to pass all winter'
    (b) *laqueus* 'noose'→*laque-āre* 'to noose'   →*il-laqueāre* 'to take in a noose'
    (c) *firmus* 'firm' →*firm-āre* 'to make firm'   → *con-firmāre* 'to confirm'

These verbs are derived simply by applying two common rules of derivation in sequence, i.e. first of all, a suffix is added to a noun, in order to form a verb. Then, a prefix is added to the verb. We have already described this type of derivation when we analysed words such as *īnfructuōsus* in Section 15.6. The morphological structure of *perhiemāre* can be thus represented as in (10):

(10)   [per+ [[hiem]$_N$+āre]$_V$]$_V$

The very same structural analysis can also be applied by analogy to all parasynthetic verbs, such as *peragrāre* [per+[agr+āre]], and so on, provided that the intermediate stage of the derivation is a possible but not an existing word, e.g. **agr-āre*. Note that parasynthetic verbs also exist in other languages, e.g. It. *ab-bell-ire* 'to make beautiful', 'to embellish', En. *befriend* and Ger. *be-freund-en* 'to become friends with'.

16

Composition

16.1 Formal representation

Composition (or 'compounding') is a morphological operation which creates a new word by combining two simple words. For this reason, composition is an important device for linguistic creativity. With respect to derivation, composition allows greater freedom: while the former creates new words by means of a limited number of affixes, the latter can resort to the entire set of words of a language and combine them.

Despite this freedom, the process of composition is constrained by some rules, i.e. the random combination of two words is not sufficient to create a well-formed compound. When speakers create new words, they are forced to follow rules which are part of the linguistic system and are thus shared by their interlocutors. These latter, in turn, will be able to understand the meaning of the new word exactly by virtue of those shared rules.

In Latin, a compound is formed by combining two stems, which belong to a given lexical category. We propose in (1) a possible way to formalize the general structure of a compound:

(1) $[[a]_X + [b]_Y]_Z$

The notation in (1) shows that the two stems, i.e. [a] and [b], which belong to the lexical categories X and Y, respectively, are combined into a complex stem, which belongs to the category Z and which contains a morpheme boundary (+). For example, the adjective *noctivagus* 'night-wandering', i.e. 'that wanders about by night', is formed by combining the stem $[nocti]_N$ of the noun *nox* 'night' (first member) with the stem $[vago]_A$ of the adjective *vagus* 'wandering' (second member).

An adjustment rule which also applies to inflected and derived words is vowel deletion (cf. rule (4) in Section 8.3). Note that, in compounding, all vowels are affected by vowel deletion. For example, the *i*-stem of the noun *fūnis* 'rope' undergoes vowel deletion before the initial vowel of the second member of the compound *fūn-ambulus* 'tightrope walker'.

The morphology of compounds includes two additional specific adjustment rules. The first is the changing of the thematic vowel of the first member into *ĭ* if the second member begins with a consonant:

(2) $\breve{V} \rightarrow \breve{\imath} \, / \, \underline{\quad} + C$

This is a particular application of the general rule (7) in Section 8.5. For example, the thematic vowel *-o-* of the stem of the first member *bellum* 'war' of the compound *belli-potens* 'mighty in battle' becomes *ĭ*, since the second member begins with a consonant.

The second adjustment rule of compounds is the addition of *ĭ* between the two stems of the compound, if the first one ends in a consonant and the second one begins with a consonant:

(3) $\emptyset \rightarrow \breve{\imath} \, / \, C \, \underline{\quad} + C$

An example is represented by the compound *lēg-i-fer* 'lawgiver', where an *ĭ* is added between the first stem, which ends in a consonant, and the second one, which also begins with a consonant. As a result of the convergence of the two rules in (2) and (3), the vowel which occurs before a second member of a compound beginning with a consonant is always *-ĭ-*, or sometimes the phonologically conditioned variant *-ŭ-* before labials, e.g. *locu-plēs* 'rich in lands', *stellu-micans* 'shining with stars'.

16.2 Composition and juxtaposition

Latin compounds can be divided into two main groups, according to the degree of strength of the internal boundary of the components. We shall call them 'proper compounds' and 'juxtapositions'. Proper compounds contain a morpheme boundary, e.g. *caeli+cola* 'inhabitant of the sky'. The two stems of a proper compound are strictly linked and cannot be separated.

In contrast, 'juxtapositions' contain a word boundary, e.g. *iūs#iūrāndum* 'oath' (lit. 'the legal formula to be taken as an oath'), and the union between the two members is weaker, as shown by the fact that they can be freely used either in combination or separately. In other words, a juxtaposition is nothing but the combination of two morphologically independent words expressing a single concept.

There are two very common types of juxtaposition. The first is the combination of a noun and a determinative adjective or a genitive noun, e.g. *rēs#pūblica* 'commonwealth' or *terrae#mōtus* 'earthquake'. The second is the combination of a perfect participle of a verb and a manner adverb, e.g. *bene#dictum* 'good word'.

From a diachronic point of view, there is a tendency for internal boundaries to become weaker, with a switch from a word boundary to a morpheme boundary (# > +). In other words, juxtapositions tend to become proper compounds. An example of this tendency is provided by a grammar of the late period, called the *Appendix Probi*, which lists *aquae ductus* 'aqueduct' and *terrae mōtus* as the correct forms in Classical Latin, contrary to the popular spoken language, where the forms *aquiductus* and *terrimotium* gradually spread. This means that while classical forms were juxtapositions, with a genitive word as the first member, i.e. *aquae*, *terrae*, the forms of the late period became proper compounds, with the reduction into *-i-* of the thematic vowel of the first member. Such an evolution from juxtaposition to compound is completed in the Romance languages, e.g. Italian, where we find the forms *acquedotto* 'aqueduct' and *terremoto* 'earthquake' (and also Lat. *rēs pūblica* > It. *repubblica* 'republic'; Lat. *rōs marīnus* > It. *rosmarino* 'rosemary', etc.).

16.3 The so-called compounds of *faciō*

The notion of juxtaposition is useful in order to understand the nature of those verbs that traditional grammars inadequately call 'compounds' of *faciō* 'to make', 'to do'. Starting from the stem of *faciō*, two main types of verb can be formed, i.e. aspectual verbs derived by means of a prefix, on the one hand, and juxtapositions, on the other.

Verbs like *cōn+ficiō* 'to accomplish' are not compounds, but rather prefixed verbs. Their stem is affected by vowel weakening in medial open syllables after a morpheme boundary (cf. rule (7) in Section 8.5: *+faciō* → *+ficiō*), as is usually the case for verbs derived by adding a prefix. In addition to this, verbs like *cōnficiō* can be passivized, i.e. *cōnficiōr*, contrary to *faciō*, which is substituted by *fīō* in the passive. We report in (4) some examples of prefixed verbs with a passive ending in *-ficior*:

(4)   a. *ad+ficiō*   passive: *adficior*
         'to produce'

      b. *ef+ficiō*   *efficior*
         'to accomplish'

      c. *per+ficiō*   *perficior*
         'to complete'

      d. *prae+ficiō*   *praeficior*
         'to place at the head'

      e. *re+ficiō*   *reficior*
         'to reconstruct'

As for juxtapositions, the first member is either a verbal stem or an adverb, e.g. *cale#faciō* or *satis#faciō*. The second member coincides with *faciō*, both phonologically and inflectionally, as shown in (5):

(5) a. *āre#faciō*   passive: *ārefīō*
       'to dry up'

     b. *assuē#faciō*   *assuēfīō*
        'to accustom to'

     c. *cale#faciō*   *calefīō*
        'to make warm'

     d. *expergē#faciō*   *expergēfīō*
        'to awaken'

     e. *lique#faciō*   *liquefīō*
        'to liquefy'

     f. *pate#faciō*   *patefīō*
        'to lay open'

     g. *satis#faciō*   *satisfīō*
        'to satisfy'

Note that the stem vowel *-ē-* of the verb in the first member is generally shortened, probably starting from the iambic shortening in *cale-*, *lique-*, *pate-*. However, it does not become *-i-*, as these verbs are juxtapositions and not proper compounds, as confirmed by the fact that they can be exceptionally separated by tmesis, e.g. *facit āre* (Lucr. VI 962).

16.4 The typology of Latin compounds

Latin compounds are peculiar in that, in the vast majority of cases, the second member is not a simple stem, but rather a suffixed word, e.g. the second member of the compound *agri-cola* (which literally means 'cultivator of the land') is derived from the verb *colere* 'to cultivate'. The morphological structure of the second member, which means 'cultivator', can be represented as in (6):

(6) $[[\text{cole}]_V + a]_N$

Therefore, Latin compounds are classified not only in terms of the categories of the first and second member, but also in terms of the suffix which may be present on the second member.

16.4.1 Synthetic compounds (agent nouns)

The typology of Latin compounds includes four main groups. The first group, which is the most common, contains the so-called 'synthetic' compounds. The first type of these compounds is characterized by the presence, in the second member, of an element derived from a verbal stem with an agentive meaning (as in the *-cola* example in (6)). In other words, there is a morphological process of double 'synthesis', which involves both composition and derivation. The semantics is determined by the agent noun contained in the second member. The first member acts as a complement of the second member. Some examples are reported in (7)–(10):

(7)   suf. *-a-*
    a. *agri-col-a*
      'farmer'

    b. *lucri-fug-a*
      'that avoids gain', 'spendthrift'

(8)   suf. *-o-*
    a. *magni-fic-us*
      'that makes great things', 'eminent'

    b. *urbi-cap-us*
      'that takes cities', 'conqueror'

(9)   suf. *-Ø-*
    a. *arti-fex*
      'that creates art', 'artist'

    b. *tubi-cen*
      'that plays the *tuba*', 'trumpeter'

(10)   suf. *-nt-*
    a. *arqui-tene-ns*
      'that holds a bow', 'archer'

    b. *omni-pote-ns*
      'that can do anything', 'almighty'

16.4.2 Synthetic compounds (action nouns and abstract nouns)

The second type of synthetic compound is represented by compounds whose second member is an action noun derived from a verbal stem or an abstract noun derived from a nominal stem. The suffix is always *-ium*, and the meaning of the compound is determined by the second member, to which the first one is subordinated. We report some examples in (11) and (12):

(11)   action nouns
    a. *armi-lustr-ium*
      'purification of weapons' (name of a festival)

    b. *nau-frag-ium*
      'breaking of the ship', 'shipwreck'

(12)   abstract nouns

    a. *aequi-noct-ium*
       'identical (to the day) night', 'equinox'

    b. *vēri-verb-ium*
       'true word', 'etymology'

16.4.3 Possessive compounds

The third group is represented by the so-called 'possessive' compounds, also known by the Sanskrit example *bahuvrīhi*, meaning 'possessing a lot of rice'. The most salient feature of this type of compound is the fact that the second member was originally nominal but has been converted into an adjective. The first member, in contrast, can be nominal or adjectival. From a semantic point of view, it expresses a relationship of possession, along the following lines: 'possessing the second member, which is qualified by the first'. We list some examples in (13) and (14):

(13)   suf. -Ø-

    a. *albi-capillus*
       'grey-haired'

    b. *angui-pēs*
       'snake-footed'

(14)   suf. -*i*-

    a. *citi-rēm-is*
       'with swift oars'

    b. *tauri-form-is*
       'bull-shaped'

16.4.4 Determinative compounds

The last type of compound includes the so-called 'determinative' or *tatpuruṣa* (another Sanskrit example, meaning 'his son'). This is the only type of compound which does not include any suffixes, but simply two nominal or adjectival stems, where the first one is subordinated to the second one. Some examples are reported in (15):

(15)   a. *perenni-servus*
       'permanent slave'

    b. *capri-ficus*
       'wild fig tree'

    c. *multi-cupidus*
       'much-desiring'

    d. *nuci-prūnum*
       'nut-plum'

Note that the four types of compound that we have identified so far are characterized by some relevant stylistic differences. Poetry usually prefers agent nouns, e.g. *nāviger* 'ship-carrying', *frondifer* 'leaf-bearing', and *frūgiferens* 'fruit-bearing', which appear in the first twenty lines of Lucretius' *De Rerum Natura*, while prose prefers abstract nouns, e.g. technical terms of astronomy, such as *aequinoctium*, lit. 'equal night', i.e. 'equinox', and *solstitium*, lit. 'a standing still of the sun', i.e. 'solstice'. Possessive compounds are highly poetical, cf. epic epithets such as *magnanimus* 'great-souled' (for a hero), and *sonipes* 'noisy-footed' (for a horse), while determinatives are very rare and are found mainly in works of prose. Juxtapositions such as *pignoriscapiō* 'seizing as a pledge' and *senātūs-cōnsultum* 'senate decree' are also typical of prose.

We will now conclude this section with a final observation about the syntactic typology of compounds, i.e. why is it the case that combinations of a noun and an adjective and verb-initial combinations are rarely attested? This is due to the fact that, in Archaic Latin, adjectives typically precede nouns, and verbs are placed in final position. This implies that verb-initial compounds and adjective+noun compounds are structurally incoherent according to the parameters of early Latin syntax. Also note that while in Latin compounds the object usually precedes the verb (similarly to most English compounds), Italian exhibits a spreading of the reverse order, as shown in the following examples, where an OV Latin compound typically corresponds to a VO Italian compound and mostly to an OV English compound (Table 16.1).

The few exceptions to this tendency can be found mostly in Vulgar Latin, e.g. VO in *fulcipedia* 'footrest' (Petr. 75, 6). Only after the transition from Latin to Romance, with the syntactic shift from OV to VO as the base word order, did the internal order of compounds change accordingly. In Italian, for example, the most productive types of compound exhibit the order NA and VN, e.g. *cassaforte* 'safe', lit. 'box-strong', and *lavapiatti* 'dishwasher', lit. 'washer-dishes', although some cases of reverse orders are still attested, e.g. *multisala* 'multiplex', lit. 'many rooms', and *pestifero* 'scamp', lit. 'plague-

TABLE 16.1 Word order of compounds

Latin: OV	Italian: VO	English: OV	English: VO
candēli-fer	porta-candele	candle-holder	
flucti-fragus	frangi-flutti		break-water
pedi-sequus	tira-piedi	under-strapper	
silvi-cola	guarda-boschi	forest-keeper	

bringer', as a consequence of the influence of relic Latin forms. On the other hand, Germanic languages exhibit a stronger conservative tendency in the morphology of compounds. Although most of them, including English, have shifted from OV to VO as the base word order, compounds still retain a head-final order, e.g. *braveheart* and *taxi driver*.

Part III

Syntax

17

Preliminary notions: valency and theta-roles

17.1 Valency

Inflected words are the maximal units of morphology and the minimal units of syntax at the same time, since morphology is concerned with structure within words, while syntax is concerned with structure between words. From a morphological point of view, words belong to syntactic categories, e.g. nouns, adjectives, verbs, etc., and express some inflectional information, e.g. gender, number, case, etc. From a syntactic point of view, in contrast, the relevant information is the way in which words interact. In this respect, traditional grammars often employ expressions such as 'construction', as if they were independent structures, rather than the product of the interaction between single words with different properties, which determine the way in which words can combine. Modern linguistics has adopted the opposite view, i.e. words are claimed to have an external structure and syntax is viewed as the projection of the properties of words.

One of the first attempts to develop this perspective is captured by the theory of 'valency', which was elaborated in the middle of the twentieth century by the French linguist Lucien Tesnière. Valency is a metaphor borrowed from chemistry: in the same way that atoms have a valency, i.e. they can bind a given number of different atoms, verbs too have a valency, i.e. they act as the gravitational centre of a given number of grammatical elements.

In particular, verbs can be classified according to the number of elements they obligatorily select in order to form a sentence:

i. Zero-valent or avalent verbs: these are traditionally called 'impersonal verbs' and do not select any elements, including the subject, e.g. *pluit* 'it rains'; *fulminat* 'there is lightning'; *tonat* 'it is thundering'.

ii. Monovalent verbs: this class includes intransitive verbs, which obligatorily select one and only one element, i.e. the subject, e.g. *Terentius ambulat* 'Terence is walking'; *Sallustius quiescit* 'Sallust is resting'; *Aristoteles disputat* 'Aristotle is discussing'.

iii. Bivalent verbs: this class includes transitive or intransitive verbs which obligatorily select a subject and an object (either direct or of a different kind), e.g. *Caesar vincit Pompeium* 'Caesar wins over Pompey'; *pater indulget filio* 'the father indulges his son'; *Dominus miseretur nostri* 'Lord has mercy on us'.

iv. Trivalent verbs: this class includes ditransitive verbs, which obligatorily select a subject, a direct object, and an indirect object, e.g. *ego dono praeceptorem auro* 'I give some gold to the teacher'; *tempero me vino* 'I abstain (myself) from wine'; *fraudo creditorem pecuniis* 'I steal money from the creditor'.

The notion of valency is very useful. It is part of the intrinsic grammatical information of each verb and cannot be inferred from other semantic elements, but must be stored in the speaker's mental lexicon. In dictionary entries, valency is informally recorded by means of labels such as 'transitive' or 'intransitive'.

Note that two lexical entries which have roughly the same meaning in two languages can differ in terms of their valency, as is the case for some verbs which are transitive in English and intransitive in Latin, e.g. En. *to envy someone* / Lat. *alicui invidere,* or the other way round, e.g. En. *to despair of something* / Lat. *aliquid desperare.*

However, it may also be the case that different meanings of the same verb are associated with different valency values within the very same language, as is the case for Lat. *dicere* 'to say', which can be either monovalent, e.g. *Cicero ornate dicit* 'Cicero speaks well', or bivalent *Cicero aliquid dicit* 'Cicero says something'.

For this reason, when looking up the meaning of a verb in a dictionary, we must always take into account its valency values (cf. what traditional grammars call 'constructions' of the verb). This means that the study of the words of a language must include not only their generic semantics, but also their ability to become the centre of syntactic constructions.

17.2 Theta-roles

The theory of valency has been re-elaborated by the so-called 'thematic theory', or theta theory, in the tradition of generative grammar. The most important innovation is the abandonment of the calculation of the number of arguments. We have already mentioned the idea that a sentence can be compared to a small play (cf. Section 12.1). However, it is not sufficient to list the *number* of actors in order to put on a play, but their *role* must also be specified. This means that, for each sentence, it is necessary to specify not only the number of arguments, but also the semantic value that the verb assigns to each of them.

Therefore, for each lexical entry, our mental lexicon must specify both the *quantity*, i.e. the valency number, and the *quality*, i.e. the semantic value of arguments. Each verb will then select as many arguments as its valency specifies, and it will also assign them some specific semantic values, called 'thematic roles' or 'theta-roles'.

For example, a trivalent verb such as En. *to tell* is associated with three empty slots, which we shall call 'argument positions', which must be filled in to form a sentence, as shown in (1):

(1)   *The mum*   told   *a story*   *to the kids*
           1   2   3

In addition to these three argument positions, the lexical entry of *tell* specifies three theta-roles, i.e. (1) an Agent for the subject; (2) a Theme, that is the person or thing involved in the event, for the object; (3) a Benefactive for the indirect object:

(2)   *The mum*   told   *a story*   *to the kids*
           1   2   3
        Agent   Theme   Benefactive

In a parallel fashion, a verb such as Lat. *neco* 'to kill' is specified not only as bivalent, but more specifically as having an Agent subject and a Patient object. This piece of information is particularly relevant in that not all verbs assign an Agent theta-role to their subject: there are some verbs which assign the role of Experiencer to their subject, e.g. *timeo* 'to fear' and *video* 'to see', while some others assign the role of Patient, e.g. *vapulo* 'to be flogged'.

The distinction between syntactic values, i.e. argument positions, and semantic values, i.e. theta-roles, is fundamental in resolving some apparent paradoxes which arise in traditional grammatical analyses. For example, if we take three sentences with a monovalent verb, such as *servus clamat* 'the slave is shouting', *servus timet* 'the slave is afraid', and *servus vapulat* 'the slave is being flogged', we can reasonably claim that in all the three sentences *servus* is the syntactic subject, but its theta-role varies, in accordance with the verb, i.e. Agent (assigned by *clamo*), Experiencer (assigned by *timeo*), or Patient (assigned by *vapulo*).

In addition to this, it is possible to find Latin trivalent verbs, such as *do* 'to give' and *accipio* 'to receive', the thematic structure of the two being opposite. From a logical point of view, they both express the same action, i.e. there is 'somebody' who is giving 'something' to 'somebody else'. However, the theta-roles assigned to the subject, the direct object, and the indirect object are the reverse, i.e. the theta-roles assigned by *do* are Agent, Theme, and Benefactive, respectively, e.g. *Marius dat librum filio* 'Marius gives a book to his son', while the theta-roles assigned by *accipio* are the opposite, i.e. Benefactive, Theme, and Source, respectively, e.g. *filius accipit librum a Mario* 'the son receives a book from Marius'.

Theta-roles are typically assigned by the verb to nouns or nominal constituents, as shown by the above examples. However, there are some cases in which theta-roles can be assigned to embedded clauses. This is the case for *narro* 'to tell', which can assign its second theta-role (Theme) either to a nominal constituent, e.g. *narra rem*, lit. 'tell the thing', or to an embedded sentence, e.g. *narra quid agas*, lit. 'tell what you are doing'.

To sum up, each verb must be specified for the theta-roles it assigns. This is the 'thematic structure' or 'theta grid' of the lexical entry. The thematic structure can be graphically represented as in (3) and (4), where each verb is accompanied by the specification of its set of theta-roles:

(3)   Thematic structure

    a. do $_{<Agent, Theme, Benefactive>}$
       'to give'

    b. accipio $_{<Benefactive, Theme, Source>}$
       'to receive'

    c. ferio$_{<Agent, Patient, Instrument>}$
       'to strike'

    d. neco $_{<Agent, Patient>}$
       'to kill'

    e. lego $_{<Agent, Theme>}$
       'to bring together', 'to read'

    f. timeo $_{<Experiencer, Theme>}$
       'to fear'

    g. eo $_{<Agent, Goal>}$
       'to go'

    h. vapulo $_{<Patient>}$
       'to be flogged'

    i. cresco $_{<Theme>}$
       'to come into being'

    j. curro $_{<Agent>}$
       'to run'

    k. pluit $_{<Theme>}$
       'to rain'

(4)   Theta-roles

    a. Agent: the participant which intentionally initiates the action.
    b. Benefactive: the entity that benefits from the action.

    c. Experiencer: the entity that experiences some psychological state.

    d. Goal: the entity towards which the action is directed.

    e. Instrument: the entity which unintentionally starts the action.

    f. Patient: the person or thing undergoing the action.

    g. Source: the entity from which something is moved as a consequence of the action.

    h. Theme: the person or thing involved in the action.

If compared to the traditional theory of valency, thematic theory provides a better description of many syntactic phenomena and is able to express more semantic nuances.

One of the clearest examples of this is the expression of possession. In the past, grammarians had already noted the fact that Latin preferably expresses the possessor as a Benefactive, e.g. *est mihi nata*, literally 'there is to me a daughter', rather than as an Agent, e.g. *possideo natam* 'I have a daughter'. Similarly, in Russian possession is expressed by means of a locative relationship between the possessor and the possessed, e.g. у меня есть дочь 'at me there is a daughter'.

The expressive power which derives from the various uses of theta-roles is manifold, as shown by the two sentences in (5), written by the same author:

(5)   a. Chrysis vapulat (Petr. *Sat.* 132, 5)
       'Chrysis is being flogged'

     b. Servus accipiet plagas (Petr. *Sat.* 28, 7)
       'The slave will be flogged'
       (lit. 'The slave will receive some lashes')

Vapulare in (5a) and *accipere plagas* in (5b) convey almost the same meaning, since they both refer to the very same action, i.e. 'to be flogged'. However, while in sentence (5a) the subject, i.e. *Chrysis*, is the Patient, in sentence (5b) the subject, i.e. *servus*, is the Benefactive. Note that the notions 'Patient' and 'Benefactive' must not be confused with the notion of subject, i.e. while the former two are theta-roles, the last is a syntactic position.

For this reason, the traditional analysis, which defines the subject as 'the one who performs the action', would lead us to a specious analysis, since there exist active sentences whose subject is rather affected by the action, as in *Chrysis vapulat*. A language in which all the subjects are Agents and all the objects are Patients is logically plausible, but far less flexible. In fact, natural languages do not consist of logical operators and concepts, but rather of words with specific properties. According to the thematic theory, it is possible to claim that a verb not only expresses an abstract action, but it also possesses an external semantic grid, that is a sort of 'logical template' which specifies the way in which this word will interact with the other elements in the sentence.

Another common definition of the subject is the following: 'the subject is that which the sentence is about'. This definition is quite controversial as well. Sentence (5b), for example, is about a slave, indeed, but it is also about lashes. A solution to this problem will be offered in Chapter 18, when we consider the difference between theta-roles, e.g. Agent and Patient, and syntactic positions, e.g. Subject and Object, in further detail.

We shall now conclude this section with a final remark about a second major difference between valency theory and thematic theory. According to the latter, all major lexical categories, that is, not only verbs but also nouns, adjectives, and prepositions, can have a thematic structure. If it is true that the assignment of theta-roles is a peculiar feature of verbs, which are the centre of complex structures, it is also true that there are other word classes which can perform a similar function and may be the centre of equally complex structures.

Firstly, prepositions typically assign some peculiar theta-roles, such as Goal, e.g. *ad Romam* 'to Rome', Time, e.g. *post urbem conditam* 'after the foundation of Rome', or Cause, e.g. *ab hoste* 'by the enemy'.

Moreover, adjectives are able to form nominal predicates, similarly to verbal predicates, as shown by the examples in (6) (broadly speaking, the predicate is the part of the sentence which combines with the subject to form a sentence, cf. Sections 19.2 and 19.5 for a formal discussion of verbal and nominal predicates):

(6)   a. Nunc tu mihi places (Plaut. *Capt.* 870)
          'Now I like you'
          (lit. 'now you like to me')

      b. Nunc tu mihi amicus es (Plaut. *Cas.* 615)
          'Now you are a friend to me'
          (lit. 'now you are friendly to me')

The adjective *amicus* in (6b) behaves like a bivalent predicate, just like the verb *placeo* in (6a). In fact, we can also push the comparison further and argue that the adjective *amicus* has the same thematic structure as the verb *placeo*, since the two arguments *tu* and *mihi* are assigned the same theta-roles by the verbal predicate in (6a) and by the nominal predicate in (6b), i.e. Theme and Benefactive, respectively.

Finally, nouns also have their own thematic structure, which can be as complex as the thematic structure of verbs. In this respect, an important distinction must be drawn between 'object nouns' and 'event nouns'. Object nouns, e.g. *scutum* 'shield', only assign a generic Possessor theta-role, e.g. *scutum militis* 'the soldier's shield'. Event nouns, on the other hand, are derived from verbs, e.g. *adventus* 'coming' from *advenio* 'to come', and therefore are able to assign the same theta-roles as verbs, as shown in the examples in (7):

(7)   a. Hostes adveniunt
          'Enemies are coming'

      b. Adventus hostium
          'The coming of the enemies'

The verb *advenio* in (7a) and the derived noun *adventus* in (7b) have the same thematic structure, which specifies the assignment of a single Agent theta-role to the subject of the verb and to the genitive of the event noun, respectively.

18

Phrases

18.1 Phrase analysis

Syntax is mainly concerned with the combination of words into hierarchically ordered units, e.g. words combine into simple sentences, and simple sentences combine into compound sentences. The minimal units of syntax are words, which are associated with specific properties, and structure building is the essential operation carried out by syntax. However, as we have seen in morphology, it is not always the case that minimal units coincide with the basic units of a grammatical component. In Latin morphology, for example, morphemes are the minimal units which can express meaning, but the basic units for the application of morphological rules are the stems, which represent an intermediate stage between a morpheme and a word. This is true also for syntax, whose basic units are intermediate elements, halfway between a single word and an entire sentence.

Therefore, the first task we are faced with in the study of formal syntax is again the identification of the basic units. At present, all scholars agree that the basic unit of syntax is the phrase. The notion of phrase is pretty intuitive, if we think about the fact that it is possible to move groups of words within the sentence in any language, e.g. in English both [*I will leave*] [*tomorrow morning*] and [*tomorrow morning*] [*I will leave*] are equally possible.

In the following, we will try to give a more formal definition of such groups of words or, more technically, 'phrases'. This is possible through a method of structural analysis called 'immediate constituent analysis', elaborated by the American linguist Leonard Bloomfield in the first half of the twentieth century.

According to this method, it is possible to identify the basic units of a sentence, i.e. the phrases, by using two empirical procedures, i.e. segmentation and substitution. In this respect, note that it is possible to identify a phrase simply by looking at the distributional properties of words, as shown by the examples in (1):

(1)   a. Caesar exercitum reduxit (Caes. *Gall.* III 29, 3)
         'Caesar led back the army'

b. Locorum asperitas hominum ingenia duraverat (Curt. VII 3,6)
   'The roughness of their climate had hardened the nature of the inhabitants'

In sentences like (1a) and (1b), traditional grammars typically identify two units, i.e. a subject and a predicate. In this way, however, they inadequately merge two different conceptual issues into one discourse, i.e. a syntactic one (the subject) and a logical one (the predicate). In fact, on a logical level we should rather say that there are two arguments and one predicate. In sentence (1a) the predicate is *reduxit* and the arguments are *Caesar* and *exercitum*, while in sentence (1b) the predicate is *duraverat* and the arguments are *locorum asperitas* and *hominum ingenia*. But this analysis already comes 'for free' from the thematic theory, which defines the logical template of words, e.g. *reduco* and *duro* are bivalent verbs. What is still missing, rather, is the description of the syntactic functions of subject and object.

The analysis based on immediate constituents is a strategy to define such functions and to identify the basic units of a sentence by exploiting the distributional properties of words. Starting from a given sentence, the first step is the identification of the point at which the sentence can be split into two meaningful parts, that is two phrases. Firstly, a mechanical approach can be attempted, by placing the segmentation point after the first word. In the examples in (1), we would obtain the segmentation in (2):

(2)   a. Caesar | exercitum reduxit
      b. Locorum | asperitas hominum ingenia duraverat

In order to check that the segmentation is correct, one can substitute each of the two segments with a segment of the same type, taken from another sentence, and check whether the new sentence is still well-formed. For example, if we combine the first segment of (2a) with the second segment of (2b) and then the other way round, i.e. the first segment of (2b) with the second segment of (2a), we obtain the two new sentences in (3):

(3)   a. *Caesar | asperitas hominum ingenia duraverat
      b. *Locorum | exercitum reduxit

Both sentences are ungrammatical, as indicated by the asterisk. That is, they are ill-formed because they violate some language principles. This means that our first attempt at segmentation and combination has failed.

As a second attempt, we keep the same segmentation of sentence (1a) as above in (2a), repeated in (4a), but we place the segmentation point in (1b) immediately after the second word, as in (4b):

(4)   a. Caesar | exercitum reduxit
      b. Locorum asperitas | hominum ingenia duraverat

Now we try again to combine the first segment in (4a) with the second segment in (4b), and then the first segment in (4b) with the second segment in (4a), and we obtain the result shown in (5):

(5)　a. Caesar | hominum ingenia duraverat
　　　b. Locorum asperitas | exercitum reduxit

This new attempt at segmentation and combination is successful, since both the resulting sentences in (5) are grammatical, i.e. well-formed, given that they do not violate any basic syntactic rules, even if they do not make much sense in terms of semantics (cf. Chomsky's famous example *colorless green ideas sleep furiously*).

We could easily multiply the examples, but we would always find that a sentence can be divided into two segments, which can be combined with other segments of the same type taken from different sentences. For example, if we take two sentences such as *consuetudo | concinnat amorem* 'custom harmonizes love' (Lucr. IV 1283) and *veritas | odium parit* 'truth breeds hatred' (Ter. Andr. 68), we can divide them into segments and recombine these into new well-formed sentences, such as *consuetudo | odium parit* and *veritas | concinnat amorem*. Needless to say, the same procedure can be applied to any other language, in that this phenomenon is a universal feature of human language.

In contrast to traditional grammars, in modern linguistics these segments are known as 'noun phrase' and 'verb phrase', respectively. This terminology avoids any false allusion to logic, i.e. a phrase is nothing but a sub-set of the sentence. More precisely, a phrase is a syntactic unit which is named after its main constituent, i.e. the noun and the verb, respectively.

The main constituent of a phrase is called its 'head' and it is the only element which can replace the whole phrase. The head of a phrase can be easily identified by means of the two procedures described above, i.e. segmentation and substitution.

For example, the main constituent of the noun phrase *locorum asperitas* is the noun *asperitas*, since *asperitas* but not *locorum* can be placed alone before a verb phrase:

(6)　a. Asperitas [hominum ingenia duraverat]
　　　b. *Locorum [hominum ingenia duraverat]
　　　c. Asperitas [exercitum reduxit]
　　　d. *Locorum [exercitum reduxit]

In a parallel fashion, the main constituent of the verb phrase *hominum ingenia duraverat* is the verb *duraverat*, since the single verb can be combined with a noun phrase, e.g. *Caesar* or *locorum asperitas*, to form grammatical sentences, as shown in (7a) and (7c):

(7) a. [Caesar] duraverat
     b. *[Caesar] hominum ingenia
     c. [Locorum asperitas] duraverat
     d. *[Locorum asperitas] hominum ingenia

On the other hand, a single noun phrase, such as *hominum ingenia*, cannot be combined with another noun phrase, e.g. *Caesar* or *locorum asperitas*, as shown by the ungrammaticality of (7b) and (7d).

Now that we have identified the basic syntactic units, i.e. phrases, we can try to define the notion of 'subject' and 'object'. The subject is the noun phrase immediately contained by the sentence, e.g. *Caesar* and *locorum asperitas* in example (1). Note that it is necessary to specify that the subject is 'immediately' contained by the sentence, because the same sentence may contain other noun phrases which are not subjects. For example, a sentence with a transitive verb typically contains an additional noun phrase, i.e. its object. In example (1) *exercitum* and *hominum ingenia* are the objects of the verbs *reduxit* and *duraverat*, respectively. Both *exercitum* and *hominum ingenia* are noun phrases not immediately contained by the sentence; they are instead immediately contained by their verb phrases, i.e. *exercitum reduxit* and *hominum ingenia duraverat*, respectively. In other words, immediate constituent analysis shows that the object is more closely related to the verb than to the subject, a fact that will be captured by the formal representations described below, where subjects and objects are represented on distinct levels, i.e. as specifiers and complements, respectively.

18.2 Phrase structure

Phrases, e.g. *locorum asperitas* in (1b), are not linear sequences of words, but rather exhibit an internal hierarchical organization. We have already identified their main constituent, that is the so-called head. Now we will describe their internal hierarchical structure, called 'phrase structure', in further detail.

We shall start from the head of the phrase, that is a word which belongs to a given category. For example, if we take a phrase such as *Helvetiorum iniuriae populi Romani* 'the outrages of the Helvetii to the Roman people' (Caes. *Gall.* I 30, 2), its head is the Noun *iniuriae*. In other words, the category of the lexical head of the phrase is N.

The first step in the formation of a phrase is the combination of the head with its most closely linked element, i.e. its 'complement'. This can be graphically represented as in (8):

(8)

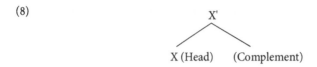

$$X'$$

X (Head)   (Complement)

In the tree in (8), X is a variable for a lexical head, which stands for N, A, V, or P. The combination of the head and its complement is called an 'X' phrase', which reads as 'X-bar phrase'.

   For example, if the head is the noun *iniuriae* and the complement is the noun phrase *populi Romani*, then *iniuriae populi Romani* is a noun phrase of the X' level, as shown in (9) (NP stands for 'noun phrase'):

(9)

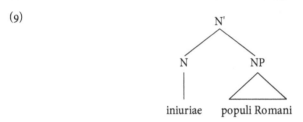

N'

N   NP

iniuriae   populi Romani

The second step is the expansion of the phrase, in order to combine the head and its complement with the less closely related element, i.e. the 'specifier', as shown in (10):

(10)

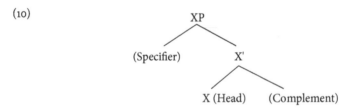

XP

(Specifier)   X'

X (Head)   (Complement)

The combination of the head, the complement, and the specifier is called XP, that is, the phrase of X, which is the 'maximal' projection of the phrase structure. Alternatively, the label X" (X 'double bar') is used, to underlie its relation with X' (X 'bar'). The two notations are equivalent. The complete structure of (10) is shown in (11):

(11)

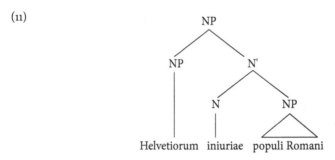

NP

NP   N'

N   NP

Helvetiorum iniuriae populi Romani

The phrase formed by the head *iniuriae*, the complement *populi Romani*, and the specifier *Helvetiorum* is called NP, that is noun phrase. Note that *Helvetiorum* is less closely related to the head, hence is analysed as the specifier of the head, rather than a complement, as it behaves like the subject of the nominal expression, whose structure mirrors the structure of verbal expressions (cf. the discussion in Section 18.1 about the relation between the subject and the object with respect to the verb).

The syntactic tree (or 'phrase marker') graphically represents the fact that the relations among the internal constituents of a phrase are not only linear (horizontal), but also hierarchical (vertical). In order to understand a sentence, the speaker must be able to infer the complex hierarchical relations established by words, instead of simply recording the meaning of their linear sequence.

In sum, the asymmetric structure connecting the head, the specifier, and the complement represents the universal core of the phrase. This very same structure is shared by all phrases, regardless of the specific value of X. As a consequence, this universal phrase structure XP will be extended to all phrases in the following discussion, i.e. not only the NP (noun phrase), but also the VP (verb phrase), the AP (adjective phrase), the PP (prepositional phrase), and finally the entire syntax of the sentence.

18.3 Adjuncts

We have already seen that every phrase has a nucleus, i.e. a head, a specifier, and a complement. In addition to this, a phrase can exhibit some optional elements, typically adjectives and adverbs, called 'adjuncts'. Adjuncts are less closely linked to the head of the phrase than any of the other elements. For example, the phrase *Helvetiorum iniuriae populi Romani* can be expanded by adding one or more adjectival adjuncts, such as *magnae*, *veteres*, etc. In Caesar's work, this phrase is accompanied by the adjective *veteres*:

(12)

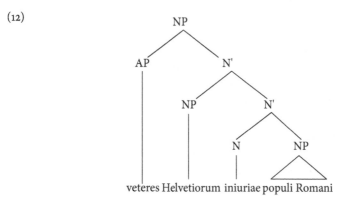

veteres Helvetiorum iniuriae populi Romani

By adding one or more adjuncts, such as adjectives or prepositional phrases specifying the time or the place, we expand the NP. This wider structure, which comprises the nucleus of the phrase and its adjuncts, is still called a noun phrase or, more accurately, a 'nominal expression'.

18.4 Syntactic movement

Another key concept in understanding Latin phrase structure is the notion of 'syntactic movement'. First of all, consider the relation between the head and the complement of a phrase. We have already seen that the head is hierarchically higher than the complement. As a consequence, the head precedes the complement in the surface string, as is the case for English, e.g. *the spoiling of the fields*, vs. **of the fields the spoiling*. However, Latin admits both the head–complement order, e.g. *populatio agrorum*, that is the most frequently attested (cf. Livy: 3, 63, 4; 3, 70, 13; 4, 10, 1; etc.), and the complement–head one, e.g. *agrorum populatio* (cf. Livy's only attestation in 23, 14, 7). The current hypothesis is that the latter order is derived from the former via syntactic movement, as shown in (13):

(13)

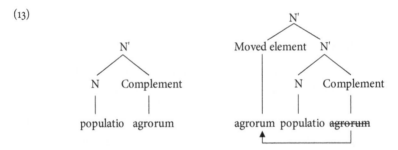

In other circumstances, both orders are allowed, albeit with different syntactic configurations, e.g. En. *the arrival of Caesar* or *Caesar's arrival*. In other words, the different cross-linguistic orders of the head and its complement simply reflect a surface phenomenon. The deep structure of the phrase, in contrast, is not determined by the linear order of elements but by their hierarchical organization. Although the relative order of the head and its complement can vary cross-linguistically, the hierarchical organization of the internal constituents of a phrase is universal.

To sum up, when the head of a phrase is accompanied by other dependent elements, these are all hierarchically ordered. This hierarchy corresponds to a canonical linearization, which includes the following elements, in this order: specifier, head, and complement. The canonical order of the internal constituents of a phrase can be modified by some instances of movement. In Latin, for example, both *animus hominis* and *hominis animus* are grammatical, and correspond to It. 'l'animo dell'uomo' and En. 'the soul of man' and 'man's soul', respectively. Similarly, *liber Ciceronis* and *Ciceronis liber* correspond to It. 'il libro di Cicerone' and En. 'the book of Cicero' and 'Cicero's book', respectively.

18.5 Pragmatic movement

Latin is a 'discourse configurational' language, i.e. its phrase structure encodes not only a basic morphosyntactic meaning, but also a wide range of pragmatic values. Pragmatics refers to the strategy used by the speakers to present information to their interlocutors, e.g. a typical pragmatic division is between old and new information. Therefore, another possible instance of movement is the displacement of a constituent from its base position to achieve a particular pragmatic meaning. Consider the noun phrase in (14):

(14)   caerula caeli templa (Enn. *ann.* 54 Sk.)
       'the blue spaces of the sky'

From a pragmatic point of view, the relative order of the adjectival adjunct *caerula* and the nucleus of the noun phrase *caeli templa* is identical to the English translation 'the blue spaces of the sky': that is the unmarked linear order. The only difference is that *caeli templa* is derived from *templa caeli* via syntactic movement (cf. *agrorum populatio* from *populatio agrorum* described in (13)). However, the position of the adjective is the same as in the canonical structure of *veteres iniuriae populi Romani* described in (12). Nevertheless, in Latin the following order is also attested:

(15)   caeli caerula templa (Enn. *ann.* 48 Sk.)

In (15), *caeli* has left its canonical position inside the NP and has moved to the so-called 'left periphery' of the phrase. This movement can be represented as in (16):

(16)

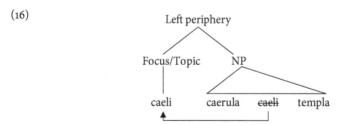

In (16), the constituent *caeli* has been moved to the left periphery of the phrase, commonly known as Focus or Topic. The 'focus' is the element the speaker wants to emphasize or contrast, while the 'topic' is what is being talked about, the known information, as opposed to the 'comment', which is what is being said about the Topic. Elements can be displaced for emphasis (Focus), or to make reference to an element which is already known to the interlocutor (Topic). Sometimes this distinction is not clear-cut, as a topic can also be focused.

In any case, the essential point of the present discussion is that in Latin all phrases have a core syntactic strucuture, as described in the previous paragraphs, and a pragmatic left periphery, which is presented in (16). Note that any elements of the phrase can be displaced to the Topic/Focus position. For example, the phrase *militaris illa virtus* 'that military virtue' (Cic. *leg. Manil.* 64) should be analysed as in (17):

(17)   militaris illa ~~militaris~~ virtus

In this case, the displaced element is the adjectival adjunct *militaris*. The movement of an element to the left periphery of the phrase is also called 'left edge fronting'.

We shall now conclude this section with a short note about translation from Latin to English. The first step is the recognition of the organization of phrases in the Latin text, whose canonical phrase order may have been disrupted by various instances of syntactic and pragmatic movement. Once the components of each phrase have been identified, one can proceed with the translation, bearing in mind that in English the head must be placed after the specifier but before the complement (if this is not the possessor, e.g. *Caesar*, in which case the head follows, e.g. *Caesar's book*), and that all adjectival and adverbial adjuncts must be placed before the head.

This is also the traditional method of translation, whereby all the components of the phrase are reordered according to the syntax of the target language. All in all, it is a rather useful technique, provided that the procedure is not too mechanical and that the translator is always aware of the fact that all the attested dislocations are not random choices of a weird language but rather convey a precise meaning in the information structure of Latin. The order *militaris illa virtus* in example (17), instead of *illa virtus militaris*, is meant to emphasize that the virtue we are talking about is the military one, rather than the civil or any other kind of virtue. By the same token, *caeli caerula templa* in (16) is more poetic than *caerula templa caeli*, since it emphasizes the image of the sky and creates a stylistic figure called alliteration, which consists of the repetition of the initial phoneme of two adjacent words, e.g. *caeli caerula*. All these phenomena must be recognized by classical philologists, bearing in mind also that pragmatics in English is expressed mainly by stress and intonation, not by movement. Consequently, the difference among the various pragmatically driven orders of Latin will be inevitably lost in the written English translation.

18.6 The noun phrase

All phrases share a common underlying structure, despite the surface differences. Now we shall consider each of them in turn, starting with noun phrases, which have largely been exemplified in the Section 18.5.

In the simplest case, a noun phrase consists of a single noun, e.g. *descriptio* 'description', since the only essential constituent of a phrase is its head. In this case, the minimal and the maximal projections coincide:

(18)
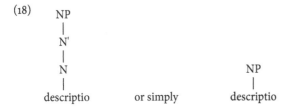

The structure in (18) can be expanded by adding a complement, a specifier, and one or more adjuncts, in accordance with specific structural rules described in the previous paragraph. Some simplified structures are shown in (19)–(22):

(19)
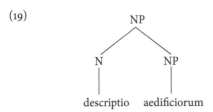

'the description of the buildings' (Cic. *leg. agr.* 40): head and complement

(20)
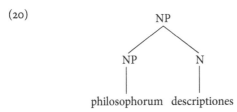

'the philosophers' description' (Cic. *de orat.* I 221): specifier and head

(21)

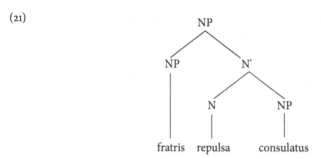

'the defeat of his brother for the consulship' (Cic. *Tusc.* IV 40): specifier, head, and complement

(22)

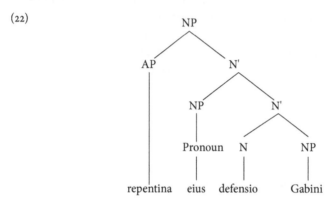

'his sudden defense of Gabinius' (Cic. *fam.* I 9, 20): adjunct, specifier, head, and complement

We shall now consider more complex structures, such as the one exemplified by *illa subtilis descriptio partium* 'that precise disposition of the parts' (Cic. *nat. deor.* II 121). In addition to the head (*descriptio*), the complement (*partium*), and an adjunct (*subtilis*), this phrase contains the demonstrative *illa*. The Latin demonstrative belongs to the universal category of determiners (D). D projects a phrase, called DP, which dominates the NP. The phrase marker of the above example is shown in (23):

(23)

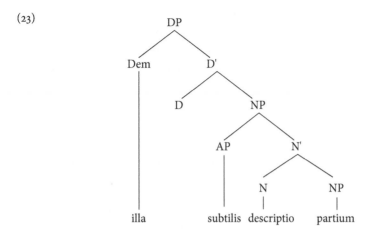

Note that the above phrase structure is universal, which implies that different languages can 'exploit' or 'activate' different positions, in accordance with language-specific parameters and the elements exhibited by each phrase. In the Latin example in (23), the position of D is empty, and the demonstrative occupies the specifier of D, as Latin does not have any articles. English, on the other hand, has both demonstratives and articles, which means that the position of D can also be activated.

Interestingly, it is not possible to 'doubly fill' the DP, either in English, with a demonstrative and an article, e.g. *this the precise description of the parts*, or in Latin, with two demonstratives, e.g. *illa ista subtilis descriptio partium*. This shows that the Latin demonstrative is not a mere adjunct, unlike adjectives, whose occurrences can be freely augmented, e.g. *sollers subtilisque descriptio partium*. Conversely, the demonstrative is a specifier, hence only one occurrence per phrase is permitted.

Finally, note that the DP can be dominated by a higher phrase, called 'quantifier phrase' (QP). Consider example (24):

(24)   omne id medium tempus (Gell. III 2, 4)
       'all this intervening time'

In addition to the head (*tempus*), this phrase exhibits an adjectival adjunct (*medium*), a demonstrative (*id*), and a quantifier (*omne*). The quantifier occupies the head of the QP, as shown in (25):

(25)

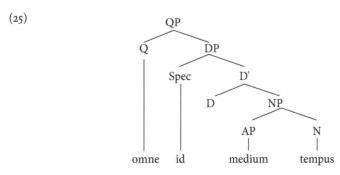

The phrase marker in (25) shows the hierarchy of the components of the nominal expression. In the unmarked order, the quantifier precedes the demonstrative, the demonstrative precedes all adjectives, and all adjectives precede the noun, which occupies the bottom position, that is the head of the proper noun phrase.

We know that the linear order of elements in a noun phrase can be altered via various instances of movement. In (26), we shall give an overview of the effects of the optional movement of the head of the NP, i.e. the noun:

(26)   a. No movement of the Noun with respect to the genitive specifier:

AP	Gen NP	N	
nocturna	mulierum	sacrificia	(Cic. *leg.* II 21)
publica	miserorum	causa	(Caes. *civ.* III 18, 3)
varii	urbium	situs	(Sen. *dial.* VI 18, 4)

   b. Movement of the Noun to the left of the genitive:

AP	N	Gen NP	~~N~~	
nocturna	sacrificia	mulierum	~~sacrificia~~	(Cic. *leg.* II 35)
peregrina	facies	hominis	~~facies~~	(Plaut. *Pseud.* 964)
superior	pars	arborum	~~pars~~	(Cato *agr.* 18, 4)

   c. Movement of the Noun to the left of the genitive and of the Adjective:

N	AP	Gen NP	~~N~~	
admiratio	magna	vulgi	~~admiratio~~	(Cic. *fam.* VII 1, 3)
status	pristinus	rerum	~~status~~	(Liv. V 37, 2)
vis	incredibilis	animi	~~vis~~	(Curt. X 5, 27)

   d. No movement of the Noun with respect to Adjuncts:

AP	AP	N	
parvulis	equestribus	proeliis	(Caes. *Gall.* V 50, 1)
summus	Romanus	eques	(Liv. XXIV 8, 3)
virides	pineas	nuces	(Colum. VII 8)

   e. Movement of the Noun to the left of the first Adjunct before the Noun:

AP	N	AP	~~N~~	
magnus	miles	Rhodius	~~miles~~	(Plaut. *Epid.* 300)
novos	hostes	Labicanos	~~hostes~~	(Liv. IV 45, 3)
veteres	cives	Romanos	~~cives~~	(Liv. VIII 8, 14)

   f. Movement of the Noun to the left of two Adjuncts:

N	AP	AP	~~N~~	
res	veteres	religiosas	~~res~~	(Gell. II 10, 4)
vocabulum	antiquum	Graecum	~~vocabulum~~	(Gell. I 18, 2)
aedibus	modicis	Hortensianis	~~aedibus~~	(Suet. *Aug.* 72, 1)

Moreover, we also know that any components of the phrase can be left-dislocated to the positions of Focus or Topic:

(27) Left-dislocation to Top/Foc:

Top/Foc	QP	AP	NP	N	
verbum	aliquod	ardens		~~verbum~~	(Cic. *orat.* 27)
Silurum		colorati	~~Silurum~~	vultus	(Tac. *Agr.* 11, 2)
Graeco	aliquo	~~Graeco~~		doctore	(Cic. *de orat* II 75)

Although many other examples could be added, we would always end up with the same hierarchical structure and an infinite number of surface variations. In this respect, it is important to bear in mind that that although word order in Latin can be extremely free, the translation into English always requires that the head precede its complement, while the position of adjuncts should be independently established according to the specific context.

18.7 The verb phrase

Similarly to noun phrases in their simplest form, verb phrases can consist of the single lexical head, i.e. a verb. This is the case for impersonal verbs that are zero-valent, i.e. verbs which do not select any arguments. The corresponding phrase marker is in (28):

(28)

This very same structure applies to monovalent verbs as well, that is intransitive verbs, which only select a subject, e.g. *stella micat* 'the star is shining'. We already know from the immediate constituent analysis that the subject of a sentence is not contained within the verb phrase, but is rather an autonomous noun phrase. However, evidence will be given which shows that the subject is actually placed within the verb phrase, at least at the initial stage, and is only later displaced to its surface autonomous position. For the time being, it is sufficient for us to consider only the final stage, in which the verb phrase does not contain its subject. Therefore, a verb phrase whose head is *micat* has the same structure as *pluit* in (28).

As for transitive verbs, these select a subject and another noun phrase, which is placed within the verb phrase. In example (1), i.e. *Caesar exercitum reduxit*, the verb phrase comprises its verbal head and its complement, i.e. a noun phrase, traditionally called 'direct object'. Accordingly, the phrase

marker of the verb phrase comprises the head and its complement, as represented in (29):

(29)

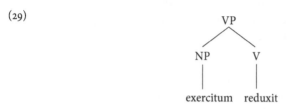

Note that, when comparing Latin and English, the issue of linear order
immediately arises. In English, the head typically precedes its complement,
as shown by the translation of example (1)/(29) '(Caesar) led back the army'. In
Latin, on the other hand, the hierarchical structure head+complement mainly
corresponds to a linear order in which the complement precedes the head, as
in example (29) *exercitum reduxit*, although the reverse order is also attested,
e.g. *reduxit exercitum* (Tac. *ann.* XV 8, 2). In other words, the intermediate
node formed by the head and its complement can correspond to two linear
orders in Latin. Similarly to the analysis proposed for noun phrases, one could
argue that these different linear orders are the result of the movement of a
constituent, starting from the same underlying hierarchical structure. In
particular, it can be argued that the object noun phrase is able to leave its
complement position, which is placed after V, to move to a higher position,
which we shall call the position of 'object agreement'. In other words, the
object is able to move across the verb, causing a shift from VO to OV order. As
a first approximation, we can represent this movement as in (30):

(30)

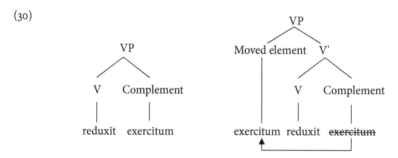

If we assume that such a movement is allowed in Latin but not in English, we
obtain a satisfying account of the different behaviour of the two languages, and
also of the internal shifting characteristic of Latin. The reasons for this
movement will be better investigated when we analyse the whole sentence
structure. For the time being, it is sufficient for us to keep the analysis at a

descriptive level and proceed with the exploration of the other possible structural configurations of verb phrases.

We shall now consider the structure of a verb phrase whose head is a trivalent, or ditransitive, verb. These verbs select a subject, a direct object, and an indirect object, as in *Hannibal ab exercitu accepit imperium* 'Hannibal received the power from the army' (Nep. *Hamilc.* 3, 3). The head of the phrase is the verb *accepit*, the complement is the direct object *imperium*, and the adjunct is the indirect object *ab exercitu*. These internal layers can be represented as in (31):

(31)

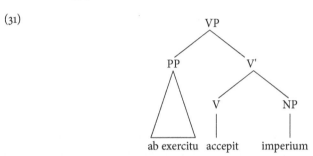

ab exercitu accepit   imperium

The representation in (31) shows that the direct object is more closely linked to the head (V) than the indirect object is. Other adjuncts of manner, place, time, cause, etc., e.g. *maxime, tarde*, etc., can be added to further levels of projection.

We should now add some further remarks about the linear order of elements. One of the most striking features of Latin is the extreme freedom of its word order, which, nevertheless, is not random. In particular, the most frequently attested linear order in the verb phrase is as in (32):

(32)   Direct Object – Indirect Object – Verb

However, any other orders are possible. How can we explain this empirical observation? One possibility is to argue that the underlying order does not coincide with the most frequently attested surface order. In the example *ab exercitu accepit imperium*, the order is as in (33):

(33)   Indirect Object – Verb – Direct Object

The order in (33) reflects the canonical hierarchical structure of phrases, whereby the adjunct precedes the head and the head precedes the complement. As a matter of fact, this order is very uncommon, since the object in Latin needs to move from the complement position to the object agreement position, as mentioned above. This means that, on its way to the landing site, the object can move across the verb, and also across the indirect object, giving rise to the most frequently attested word order in Latin. In other words, the movement of the object can affect word order as in (34):

(34)

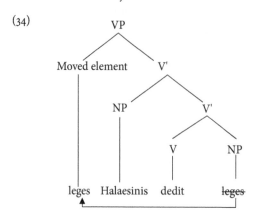

'He gave regulations to the inhabitants of Halaesa' (Cic. *II Verr.* 2, 122)

This specific instance of movement also allows us to explain why in the most frequently attested order the indirect object is nearer to the verb than the direct object, contrary to what we might expect from the hierarchy of the internal constituents of the phrase.

Finally, in order to explain any other possible orders, we must posit the existence of a left periphery in the verb phrase as well, where any elements can be displaced, for reasons of discourse structure, i.e. topicalization or focalization. In this way, we can account for those cases in which the verb precedes all the other elements of the phrase, as in (35):

(35)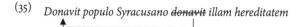

'He gave that inheritance to the citiziens of Syracuse' (Cic. *II Verr.* 2, 45)

Although many other examples could be provided, our conceptual tools, i.e. canonical verb phrase structure and movement, are sufficient to explain any word order alterations that we might encounter. The analysis of phrase structure has thus shown that the very same underlying linguistic structure can generate a variety of possible orders, which provide the speaker with greater expressive power.

From a practical point of view, the first step of a Latin-to-English translation is the identification of the hierarchical organization of the internal constituents of phrases as they appear in the Latin text, and the reorganization of these elements in accordance with English linear order rules.

In (36), we give an overview of the effects of some of the optional movements that may take place within the Latin VP, giving origin to different linear
combinations of V, direct object (DO) and indirect object (IO):

(36)   a. No movement (very marked order):

IO	V	DO	
regioni	dedit	nomen	(Curt. VII 41, 31)
telis	accipit	ictus	(Lucr. IV 1052)
Hectori	donavit	balteum	(Hyg. *fab.* 112, 2)

   b. Movement of the Direct Object to the left of the Verb and the Indirect Object
       (canonical order):

DO	IO	V	~~DO~~	
arma	Satricanis	ademit	~~arma~~	(Caes. *civ.* III 18, 3)
mancipia	Sallustio	redditit	~~mancipia~~	(Cic. *Att.* XI 20, 2)
nomen	flumini	dedit	~~nomen~~	(Liv. I 3, 9)

   c. Movement of the Indirect Object to the left periphery (marked order):

Top/Foc	DO	~~IO~~	V	~~DO~~	
civitate	multos	~~civitate~~	donavit	~~multos~~	(Cic. *pro Arch.* 26)
Scribonio	negotium	~~Scribonio~~	dedit	~~negotium~~	(Liv. XXXV 6, 5)
ad Scipionem	nuntios	~~ad Scipionem~~	mittit	~~nuntios~~	(Sen. *dial.* VI 18, 4)

   d. Movement of the Verb to the left periphery (marked order):

Top/Foc	(DO)	IO	~~V~~	(DO)	
mittit	Vatinium	ad ripam	~~mittit~~ Vatinium		(Caes. *civ.* III 19, 2)
mittit		in Sardiniam	~~mittit~~ Valerium		(Caes. *civ.* I 30, 2)
mittit		homini	~~mittit~~ munera		(Cic. *II Verr.* 4, 62)

To conclude, we shall now consider the last position which can be filled
within a phrase, i.e. the specifier. In the verb phrase this is typically occupied
by the subject. In this way, we get to the maximal projection of the verb, i.e. the
VP. In a sentence like *novi praetores ambo in hiberna exercitus deduxerunt*
'both new praetors brought down their armies to winter quarters' (Liv. XXXIX
21, 10), the verb phrase can be analysed as in (37):

(37)

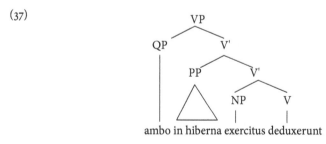

In Chapter 19, we will see that the subject, or a sub-part of it, is actually
displaced from its base position in the specifier of the VP to some higher

position. On the whole, the verb phrase has a hierarchical structure which perfectly corresponds to the structure of the noun phrase, i.e. they both comprise a lexical head, a complement, some adjuncts, and a specifier. In the verb phrase, in particular, the presence of a direct or indirect object is determined by the thematic structure of the verb. The number of adjuncts, in contrast, can freely vary, e.g. in example (37) we can delete *in hiberna* and obtain *ambo exercitus deduxerunt*, or we can add another adjunct and obtain *ambo tarde in hiberna exercitus deduxerunt*. In any case, the hierarchical layering of the internal constituents remains the same.

18.8 The adjective phrase

In its simplest form, the adjective phrase consists of the bare lexical head. In Section 18.6, we came across many examples of adjective phrases consisting of a bare adjective, which is added to a nominal head, e.g. *subtilis* (*descriptio*), *medium* (*tempus*), etc.

On the other hand, there are some adjectives which select for a complement. For example, in *nimis cupidus cognoscendi* 'very eager to know' (Apul. *met.* II 1), the head is the adjective *cupidus*, which assigns the role of Theme to its complement, while its specifier is an intensifier adverb:

(38)

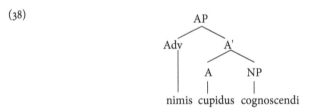

As for the linear order, the head precedes the complement in example (38), as in English. However, in Latin adjective phrases, just as in noun and verb phrases, the neutral order is the reverse one, whereby the complement precedes the head, e.g. *valde spectandi cupidus* 'very eager to see' (Cic. *de orat.* II 161):

(39)

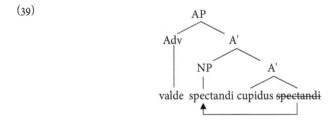

Moreover, adjective phrases possess a left periphery to host displaced focalized/topicalized elements as well, e.g. *gloriae nimis cupidus* 'very desirous of glory' (Aur. Vict. *Caes.* 43, 1):

(40)   gloriae nimis cupidus ~~gloriae~~

As with noun and verb phrases, we can suppose that the base order of adjective phrases is head–complement, and that all the other linear orders are derived via movement.

18.9 The prepositional phrase

We shall now complete our overview of phrases by reviewing the structure of the prepositional phrase. Contrary to other types of phrase, a prepositional phrase cannot consist of the head alone. In fact, only a few prepositions can stand on their own, but when this happens, they are typically classified as adverbs, e.g. *ante* 'before' and *post* 'after'.

In all other cases, prepositions take a nominal complement and sometimes a specifier. For example, the very common expression *usque ad portas* 'up to the city-gates' (Cic. *Catil.* 1, 21) consists of the head, i.e. a preposition, a complement, i.e. a noun phrase, and a specifier, i.e. an intensifier adverb:

(41)

```
                    PP
                   /  \
                 Adv    P'
                  |    /  \
                  |   P    NP
                  |   |    |
               usque  ad  portas
```

Similarly to adjective phrases, prepositional phrases do not allow any optional positions for adjuncts. Unlike noun, verb, and adjective phrases, the linear order of prepositional phrases is quite rigid in Latin, where the head typically precedes the complement, e.g. a prepositional phrase like **portas ad* is never attested in Latin and would probably have been considered ungrammatical by native speakers.

As a matter of fact, some prepositional phrases of the complement–head type are attested in Latin, cf. the so-called 'postpositions'. The only common ones are a few fixed expressions in which the head and the complement are merged, forming a single word, e.g. *quo-ad* 'as far as'; *vobis-cum* 'with you'; *parum-per* 'for a little while'. Otherwise, a small number of rarely attested forms are found in the works of some archaic authors, such as Plautus, e.g.

Merc. 821 *virum clam* 'behind her husband's back'; *Cist.* 677 *loca haec circiter* 'around these places'; *Stich.* 71 *gratiam per* 'as a favour', and Ennius, e.g. *ann.* 482 Sk. *quibus ex* 'among which'.

In Classical Latin, it is possible to focalize in the left periphery a constituent of the complement of a prepositional phrase, but only with poetic licence, cf. Catullus' famous line *multas per gentes et multas per aequora vectus* 'carried through many nations and over many seas' (*carm.* 101, 1).

In sum, all the phrase types reviewed so far, i.e. NP, VP, AP, and PP, clearly share some structural features. The number of the internal elements of each phrase varies, depending on the thematic properties of the corresponding head, i.e. N, V, A, and P. However, their hierarchical organization around the head is always fixed, i.e. specifier – adjunct(s) – head – complement. This salient feature of phrases is fundamental for language acquisition, since it significantly simplifies the speaker's task of coding and decoding linguistic structures.

In conclusion, we can argue for the existence of a universal principle of language and of a parameter subject to cross-linguistic variation. The former is represented by the cross-linguistic existence of the same hierarchical phrase structure. The latter concerns instead the linear order of the single elements within the phrases, which can be affected by various instances of movement.

19

The simple sentence

19.1 The inflection phrase

In Chapter 18 we reached a fundamental generalization concerning phrase structure, i.e. all phrases are built in the same way. Now we can extend our analysis to the structure of the simple sentence, which can be viewed as a sort of super-constituent, containing all the phrases reviewed so far. In particular, the same analysis that we implemented for single phrases will now be applied to the overall structure of a complete sentence, i.e. we will see that the sentence is organized as a complex phrase, with a structure that is parallel to the one of any other phrase.

The starting point of our analysis is the information expressed by the inflectional morphology of the verb, which includes mood, tense, person, number, and voice. This abstract element, that we shall label I, from 'inflection', plays a crucial role in the structural analysis of a sentence. The verbal inflection provides the predicate with the necessary instructions to form a sentence. In other words, the translation into 'tense' and 'person' is the process which turns an abstract verbal idea with a generic potentiality, expressed by the verb, into a concrete sentence. Accordingly, we will argue that I, the inflectional information of the verb, is the functional head of a simple sentence, i.e. a sentence is nothing but the projection of the verbal inflection.

Following the usual mechanism of phrase building, the head I combines with its complement, i.e. VP, to form the intermediate projection I'. This latter is what traditional grammars call 'predicate'. This intermediate phrase, in turn, takes an NP as its specifier, which is the subject. In this way, we get to the maximal projection of I, that is the whole sentence, labelled I" or IP, which stands for 'inflection phrase'. The phrase marker of a simple sentence like *Terentius ambulat* 'Terence is walking' is shown in (1):

(1)

IP

NP   I'

VP   I

N   V

Terentius ambula- t

In example (1), the verbal inflection is an abstract element I, meaning: 'active present indicative, third person singular', and is considered to be the head of the sentence. In order to understand the details of the above structure, we will now briefly recapitulate the way in which the verbal inflection is built. We have already seen that Latin verbs express their inflectional features in a cumulative way. A first piece of inflectional information is conveyed by the stem, e.g. the stem *ambula-* (stem of the present) of the verb *ambulare*. The remaining inflectional information is expressed via tense and person suffixes. It is reasonable to argue that these are all placed in I, where they get attached to the verbal stem hosted by V.

A piece of evidence in favour of the claim that suffixes and endings are placed in I is provided by analytic types of inflection, such as the perfect of deponent verbs, e.g. *adulescens locutus est* 'the young man spoke' (Liv. XLV 13, 13), where a first piece of inflectional information is provided by the stem of the perfect participle, i.e. *locutus*, while the remainder is expressed by the auxiliary *esse*, which lexicalizes I:

(2)

In this case the verbal stem and the inflection are not attached, but simply placed aside, but the phrase structure that we have called IP remains the same.

In the examples mentioned so far, the head of the phrase, i.e. I, has been placed in final position. Nevertheless, we know that the surface word order of Latin is never rigid, e.g. *locutus est* is as frequently attested as *est locutus* (cf. Liv. XLV 34, 13).

Consider now the behaviour of English instead. In compound tenses, the head obligatorily precedes the complement:

(3)

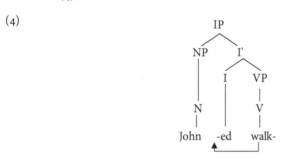

The very same order can also be found in Italian (*Gianni ha parlato*), while in German embedded clauses the order is the reverse (*dass Johann gesprochen hat*).

Now the question is: how do we analyse sentences with no auxiliaries in languages such as English, e.g. *John walked*? The most common analysis is shown in (4):

(4)

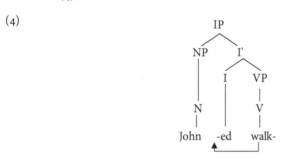

In particular, the assumption is that in English the functional head I always precedes the complement, and that V is raised to I (or I is lowered down onto V) to be attached to its endings. Therefore, it is reasonable to assume that a similar structure is shared by Latin.

Note that the functional head I tends to be conceived in a more abstract way in recent linguistic theories. In particular, I is no longer considered to be the position hosting the affixes that will be attached to V, but is rather seen as the place where the inflectional structure of the verb, which has already been generated by morphological rules, is simply 'checked'. This checking operation can be achieved either by V-to-I movement or by I-to-V movement. For this reason, a phrase structure in which the head I regularly precedes the complement VP may also be admitted in Latin.

We shall now leave aside the problem of word order in Latin and English, which is described in greater detail below, and move on to the analysis of the content of I, i.e. the inflectional content of the verb.

19.2 The verbal predicate

After describing the structure of the IP, we can now analyse the structure of simple sentences consisting of a subject, a verbal predicate, and a direct object in further detail. For example, the sentence *Tyrii Africam incolunt* 'Tyrians inhabit Africa' (Sen. *cons. Helv. 7*, 2) consists of two noun phrases and one verb phrase, as we already know from the immediate constituent analysis:

(5)

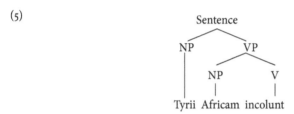

Consider now a more detailed analysis. First of all, it is necessary to indicate the presence of the functional head I, which represents the inflectional information of the verb. Given the assumption that the head I precedes its complement, we can propose the structure in (6), which shows that the sentence is made up of a subject NP and a verbal predicate I':

(6)

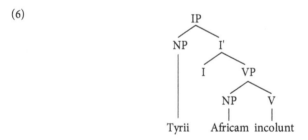

Secondly, we need to revise the internal structure of the VP. We know that the verb *incolunt* selects the complement *Africam* (NP) as its direct object. On the basis of the general principles of phrase structure, the node consisting of the head V and its complement NP has to be labelled 'intermediate projection' (V'). In example (6), the node V' coincides with the phrase *Africam incolunt*. We can thus propose the expansion of the phrase marker in (7):

(7)

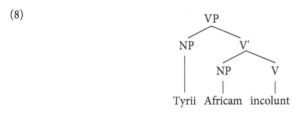

In this way, the position of the complement of the verb within the verb phrase is correctly formalized. We may now try to solve the problem of the specifier that we left open in Section 18.7, when we discussed the general structure of the verb phrase. Note that in the phrase marker in (7) the VP is a non-branching node; this means that its specifier is empty. This is not a problem per se, as the noun phrases *Tyrii* and *Africam* also have no specifier.

The problem is that by leaving the position of the specifier of the VP empty, we imply that there is no relation between the verb and its subject. On the one hand, this is correct, in that the subject is placed out of the VP, in the specifier of the IP. However, the verb assigns a theta-role to its subject and it would be preferable to claim that this assignment is internal to the VP. As a tentative solution, we could fill the position of the specifier of the VP with the subject, as represented in (8):

(8)

This structure solves the problem of the theta-marking of the subject, but does raise another issue. According to the structure in (8), the verb phrase contains all the arguments selected by the verb, i.e. not only the object but the subject as well. In this way, the verb phrase ends up coinciding with the entire sentence, contrary to its nature, i.e. the verb phrase is a constituent of the sentence, not the sentence itself. In other words, the subject should be placed in the specifier of the IP, rather than in the specifier of the VP. Thus, we need to come back to the previous phrase marker.

A possible way to solve this problem is to claim that the sentence structure is built in two different stages, which correspond to two different areas of the phrase marker:

(a) an internal area, that is the verb phrase, where all the thematic information is projected first. This is the reason why all the arguments of the verb must be placed within the VP, including the subject. It this way, the assignment of theta-roles can be internal to the VP.
(b) a proper sentential area, that we called inflection phrase (IP), where the mood and tense features of the verb are projected and where the person features of the verb and the subject agree.

According to this hypothesis, on which there is now general agreement among scholars, both phrase markers we proposed above in (7) and (8) are correct, as it is assumed that an instance of movement takes place in the passage from one stage to the other. More precisely, the subject NP is originally generated in the specifier of the VP and is later moved to the specifier of the IP, as shown in (9):

(9)

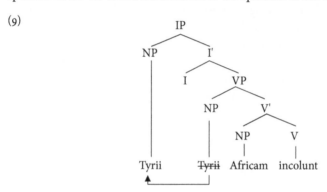

We will discuss the trigger of this movement when we introduce case theory in Chapter 20. For the time being, it is sufficient to note that although the operation of movement is purely conceptual and does not produce effects on the surface string in example (9), its effects can be visible in other examples. Subject movement is at the base of the so-called 'floating quantifiers' phenomenon. Consider again one of the examples mentioned in Section 18.7:

(10)   Novi praetores ambo in hiberna exercitus deduxerunt
       'Both new praetors brought down their armies to winter quarters'

We shall now assume that the specifier of the VP is initially filled not by the quantifier *ambo* alone, as we claimed in example (37) of Section 18.7, but rather by the entire subject noun phrase, i.e. *ambo novi praetores*. We have just assumed that the phrase *ambo novi praetores* moves from the specifier of the

VP to the specifier of the IP. Now, it is possible that, during its movement, the phrase drops one of its segments, in this case the quantifier *ambo*, which is thus 'stranded' in its base position:

(11) | Novi praetores | [ambo ~~novi praetores~~] in hiberna exercitus deduxerunt.

In conclusion, the representation of the phrase marker of a sentence can be more or less complex, in accordance with the formal properties one wishes to emphasize. Consider another example:

(12) Caesar haec genera munitionum instituit (Caes. *Gall.* VII 72, 1)
      'Caesar built these types of fortification'

We will represent the subject in its landing position, i.e. the specifier of the IP, while its base position, i.e. the specifier of the VP, will remain empty or marked by a dash co-indexed with the moved element, as shown in (13):

(13)

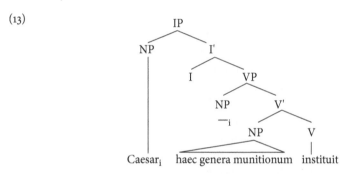

In this sense, it is not always necessary to give a complete analysis, e.g. if we do not need to emphasize the base position of the subject, we can leave out the indication of the specifier of the VP, as was done at the beginning of this chapter for the first analysis of the sentence *Tyrii Africam incolunt* in (6). Every time we draw a phrase marker, we should always opt for a more or less complex representation, in accordance with the need to emphasize and understand the exact behaviour of some elements of the sentence, and we should never claim that this phrase marker is the complete and final analysis of the sentence.

19.3 Subject and object

There are two canonical positions for noun phrases in the phrase marker of a simple sentence, i.e. the complement of the V and the specifier of the IP. By exploiting these two positions, we can achieve a better formal definition of two fundamental concepts we have already mentioned.

In the previous paragraphs, we defined the subject as the noun phrase immediately contained by the sentence node. More technically, we can now define the subject as the phrase placed in the specifier of the IP:

(14)

```
              IP
            /    \
          NP      I'
       (Subject)
```

On the other hand, we can define the object as the noun phrase placed in the complement of V:

(15)

```
              V'
            /    \
          V       NP
              (Object)
```

Therefore, we must posit that the subject and object positions are always present in the structure of a simple sentence headed by a transitive verb. There is, however, one problem with this assumption, i.e. sometimes both the subject and the object seem to be missing. We shall start with the subject.

Although the subject position must always be filled in English, cf. *I speak* vs. *speak*, there are languages, such as Italian, where both *io parlo* and *parlo* are grammatical, and the same is true in Latin, e.g. both *ego loquor* and *loquor* are admitted, the latter more frequently than the former.

This phenomenon can be explained by means of the so-called 'null-subject parameter', which differentiates the surface form of the sentence cross-linguistically. The examples in (16) show that while some languages, such as Latin, Italian, and Spanish, admit sentences which apparently lack a subject, the same is not possible in other languages, such as English, French, or German:

(16)   a. loquor (Lat.)
       b. parlo (It.)
       c. hablo (Sp.)
       d. *speak (En.)
       e. *parle (Fr.)
       f. *spreche (Ger.)
          'I speak'

As a matter of fact, there is evidence suggesting that an implicit subject is also present in apparently subjectless sentences. Indeed, all the above sentences lacking an explicit subject are synonymous with the following sentences, where an explicit pronominal subject has been inserted for each language:

(17)   a. ego loquor (Lat.)
       b. io parlo (It.)
       c. yo hablo (Sp.)
       d. I speak (En.)
       e. je parle (Fr.)
       f. ich spreche (Ger.)
           'I speak'

Traditional grammars correctly state that the personal pronoun is not expressed in Latin, unless it is emphatic. This phenomenon is simply labelled 'subject omission'. In contrast, in modern linguistics, the existence of a null pronoun has been suggested, which is not phonetically realized but is present in the logical form of the sentence, represented by the label 'pro' (to be read as 'little pro', cf. discussion in Chapter 26). We report below the formal representation of the above examples with a null subject:

(18)   a. pro *loquor*
       b. pro *parlo*
       c. pro *hablo*

The possibility of omitting the subject pronoun is a good example of a linguistic 'parameter', i.e. a property that is subject to cross-linguistic variation, as opposed to a universal 'principle'. The grammar of each language consists of a number of principles and parameters, such as hierarchical phrase structure and linear order, respectively. In this case, the specific parameter is the possibility, in some languages but not in others, to fill the subject position with the null pronoun, i.e. pro. The universal principle concerns instead the obligatory presence of a subject, either explicit or pro, in the specifier of the IP.

The notion of parameter thus allows us to distinguish the features of some groups of languages as opposed to others. As for the null-subject parameter, in particular, it is interesting to note that only languages which admit a null subject can also have impersonal verbs. Impersonal verbs typically disallow explicit subjects, as shown in the examples in (19):

(19)   a. (*id) pluit (Lat.)
       b. (*esso) piove (It.)
       c. (*el) llueve (Sp.)
       d. it is raining (En.)
       e. il pleut (Fr.)
       f. es regnet (Ger.)
           'It is raining'

Therefore, we can reasonably claim that there are some verbs which obliga-torily require a null subject in null-subject languages. In contrast, languages which do not admit null subjects do not admit impersonal verbs either.

Following this reasoning, we can conclude that there are no zero-valent verbs, strictly speaking. Contrary to what Tesnière argued, zero-valent verbs have a subject as well, just like monovalent verbs, albeit a null one. This explains why there are some special cases in which even impersonal verbs, such as Lat. *pluo* or It. *piovere*, can have an explicit subject, e.g. Verg. *georg.* IV 81 *nec de concussa tantum pluit ilice glandis* 'nor so many acorns hail from the shaken oak'.

The null-subject parameter must be distinguished from the null-object parameter. If, on the one hand, Latin patterns with null-subject languages such as Italian and Spanish, it differs from these latter since it extensively admits null objects too, which are very infrequent in Italian (cf. *un buon medico visita nudi*, lit. 'a good doctor examines (his patients) naked', where *nudi* 'naked' refers to the implicit object *i pazienti* 'the patients'). At the same time, while in Italian null objects are grammatical, albeit quite infrequent, in English they are completely banned. Although there are some cases in which a direct object seems to have been omitted, e.g. *this leads people to the following conclusion* or *this leads ~~people~~ to the following conclusion*, a number of syntactic tests, that we will not mention in this discussion, seem to suggest that the few English implicit objects should not be equated with Italian or Latin proper null objects, since the former but not the latter are 'syntactically inert'. For the sake of the present discussion, we will conclude that in Italian null objects are grammatical but infrequent, while in English they are ungrammatical.

In contrast, the use of null objects is very common in Latin, especially during the earliest stages of the language. In technical terms, this means that the object as well can be a null pronoun in Latin.

Consider the beginning of the well-known Law of the Twelve Tables reported in (20), where the two null pronouns, the subject and the object, respectively, take two different referents, i.e. the accuser (i) and the accused (j). Only this latter is also expressed by an explicit pronoun (*eum*) at the end:

(20)   Si *pro*$_i$ in ius *pro*$_j$ vocat, *pro*$_j$ ito. Ni *pro*$_j$ it, *pro*$_i$ antestamino. Igitur *pro*$_i$ eum$_j$ capito (*Lex XII Tab.* 1, 1)
'If (the accuser)$_i$ takes (the accused)$_j$ to court, (the accused)$_j$ shall go. If (the accused)$_j$ does not go, (the accuser)$_i$ shall call a witness. Only then (the accuser)$_i$ shall take him$_j$ by force'

This is of course an extreme case, but in Classical Latin null objects were also quite frequent. In the passage in (21), a trial concerning an exasperated man who killed his father after telling him that he was hoping to put an end to his reproaches in this way is being discussed:

(21)   *Nec hic, quia sic erat locutus, occidit* pro, *sed quia erat occisurus* pro, *sic locutus est* (Quint. *inst.* V 10, 47)
       'In fact, he did not kill (his father) for having said that, but he said that because he intended to kill (him)'

In the English translation, the explicit object must be added within brackets, not only in the first occurrence, i.e. *occidit* 'killed (his father)', but also in the second one, i.e. *occisurus* 'intended to kill (him)'. Note that the Latin implicit object is peculiar even among other null-object languages, i.e. while in Italian a null object can only have a generic interpretation, e.g. *aveva intenzione di uccidere* (pro) 'he intended to kill (someone)', in Latin it can also be used to refer to a specific person, as in the above example 'to kill (him)'.

19.4 Small clauses

So far we have discussed the structure of simple sentences with a verbal predicate, that is, sentences consisting of a verb phrase and two noun phrases, i.e. the subject and the object. However, there also exist smaller predicative structures, lacking the verbal predicate, which used to be called 'nominal sentences' by traditional grammars and are now known as 'small clauses'. Verbs such as En. *consider* and It. *ritenere* are typically employed in these constructions:

(22)   a. John considers [Mary stupid] (En.)
       b. Gianni ritiene [Maria stupida] (It.)

As a first approximation, expressions such as En. *Mary stupid* and It. *Maria stupida* can be analysed as reduced forms of embedded clauses with a nominal predicate, such as En. *that Mary is stupid* and It. *che Maria sia stupida*. Nevertheless, these structures are most commonly used as appositions, e.g. *Philip, king of the Macedonians*, and as predicative 'subject complements', e.g. *this song sounds good*, and 'object complements', e.g. *they painted the door red*. Some examples from Latin are reported in (23):

(23)   a. Philippus, rex Macedonum, decessit (Liv. XL 54, 1)
          'Philip, king of the Macedonians, died'

       b. Ego vivo miserrimus (Cic. *Att.* III 5, 2)
          'I live unhappily'
          (lit. 'I live unhappy')

       c. Dolorem summum malum iudicans (Cic. *off.* I 2, 5)
          'Considering pain the supreme evil'

Traditional grammars give the same analysis, both for the apposition (23a) and for the subject (23b) and object (23c) complement, i.e. in all cases, we are dealing with the reduced form of an embedded sentence with a nominal predicate. The Latin grammarian Priscian proposed the analysis in (24):

(24) 'Filius Pelei Achilles multos interfecit Troianos': [...] pro quo possumus 'qui est' vel 'qui fuit Pelei filius' dicere vel subaudire. Similiter [...] 'celer pedibus currit homo': subauditur 'qui est' (Prisc. *inst.* GLK III 212, 7–15).
'Achilles, son of Peleus, killed many Trojans': [...] instead of this expression, we can say or imply 'who is' or 'who was son of Peleus'. Similarly, [...] 'the man speedy of foot runs': it implies 'who is'.

This analysis correctly identifies the existence of small clauses in the examples *filius Pelei Achilles* and *celer pedibus homo*, instead of simple noun phrases with a head and an adjunct. However, this interpretation needs to be improved. There is evidence suggesting that small clauses are not simple nominal predicates without the copula, but rather autonomous structures which constitute the base for the formation of nominal predicates, as will be argued below.

In other words, a small clause is a pure autonomous predicative nucleus, which can be analysed as in (25) (SC stands for 'small clause'):

(25)

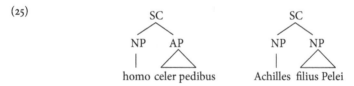

These structures combine a noun phrase with an adjective phrase, or a noun phrase with another noun phrase, in a predicative relationship which is similar to the one which holds between a subject and a nominal predicate. These structures are different from the ones reviewed so far, but they are extremely important because they are very common.

19.5 The nominal predicate

After describing small clauses, we can now analyse the structure of simple sentences with a nominal predicate in further detail. Consider the examples in (26):

(26) a. Ipse dux, fugae auctor, in proximos colles evasit (Liv. XXVIII 16, 6)
'The general, himself approving their flight, escaped to the nearest hills'

b. Piso auctor est (Liv. II 58, 1)
'Piso is the author'

We have already analysed the apposition *ipse dux, fugae auctor* in sentence (26a) as a small clause, as in (25). This means that (26b), a sentence with a nominal predicate, can also be analysed on the basis of the structure of the small clause *Piso auctor*. The crucial difference between the apposition in (26a) and the nominal predicate in (26b) is the presence, or lack thereof, of the copula *est*. If we added a copula to the small clause in (26a), we would obtain a sentence with a nominal predicate, i.e. *ipse dux fugae auctor fuit*.

This explains the recent proposal that sentences with a nominal predicate should be treated as 'expanded' small clauses. In particular, it is argued that the copula of a sentence with a nominal predicate is placed under the inflection head I, similarly to what we argued for sentences with a verbal predicate, such as *adulescens locutus est*. According to this proposal, the structure of a sentence with a nominal predicate is as in (27), where—for the moment—we place the head in final position:

(27)

In (27), the inflection head I, which hosts the copula, takes the entire small clause as a complement to form the intermediate projection I'. As we shall see later, the movement of the subject to the specifier of the IP, i.e. the canonical subject position, completes the phrase, giving rise to the maximal projection IP.

The notion of expanded small clause is particularly useful to catch the difference between the phrase structure of a sentence with a nominal predicate, such as *Piso auctor est*, and the phrase structure of a sentence with a verbal predicate, such as *Tyrii Africam incolunt*. Such a difference was not captured by old structuralist and generativist models in a satisfactory way, in that they simply noted the presence of two noun phrases and one verb phrase in both cases. The analysis proposed here instead claims that there are two autonomous noun phrases in a sentence with a verbal predicate, i.e. the subject and the object, while in a sentence with a nominal predicate the two phrases are nothing but the sub-components of the same small clause. Moreover, the structure of the verb phrase is present in sentences with a verbal predicate but not in sentences with a nominal predicate, where the verb *esse* is not a full verb, but rather a 'copula' which simply expresses the inflectional features of the verb without conveying any autonomous semantic meaning.

A further issue needs to be considered. While a simple sentence with a verbal predicate is labelled IP, we have used the label I' to indicate small clauses with a nominal predicate. This notation is useful to represent the reduced nature of this type of sentence in a structural way. However, one may reasonably wonder whether small clauses have a maximal projection too, i.e. an IP node. In fact this is correct, and its consequences are quite interesting. However, we need a theory of case and related syntactic movement before we can consider this issue. For this reason, we now leave the question aside in order to consider some further extension of the phrase structure of simple sentences in Section 19.6, and we will return to this issue in Chapter 20.

19.6 Indirect complements

We shall now conclude our analysis of the structure of simple sentences with a short discussion of two different types of adjunct. In example (31) of Section 18.7 we have already identified a first type of adjuncts, i.e. those which are placed within the VP, traditionally called 'indirect objects'. An additional example is provided below:

(28)   Decima legio per tribunos militum [VP ei gratias egit] (Caes. *Gall.* I 41, 2)
       'The tenth legion gave him thanks through its tribunes'

The thematic structure of the ditransitive verb *egit* requires a direct object, i.e. *gratias*, and an indirect object, i.e. *ei*. They are both placed within the verb phrase but they are distinct, in that the direct object is more closely linked to the verb than is the indirect object.

A second type of adjunct is represented by the so-called 'indirect complements', e.g. *per tribunos militum*, that is, elements which are less closely linked to the verb. From a structural point of view, these complements belong to the sentence (IP), but are external to the VP.

Indirect complements are also called 'circumstantials', since they add some extra information about place, time, cause, or manner. From a structural point of view, they modify the entire sentence and can occur with any kind of verb, regardless of their thematic structure, precisely because they are not verb arguments. Consider example (29):

(29)   Miles segniter arma capit, segniter e castris egreditur (Liv. X 35, 17)
       'The soldier slowly picks up the weapons and slowly emerges from the encampment'

Note that the very same adverb of manner, i.e. *segniter*, can modify both a sentence with a transitive verb, i.e. *arma capit*, and a sentence with an intransitive one, i.e. *e castris egreditur*. This provides evidence for the claim that the adverb *segniter* does not interact with the thematic structure of the verb and must therefore be placed outside the VP. The phrase marker of the sentence *miles segniter e castris egreditur* is shown in (30):

(30)

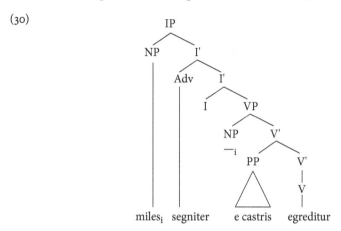

This structure represents the two different positions that adjuncts can occupy. The adjunct which is more closely linked to the verb, in that it is required by its thematic structure, is placed within the verb phrase, e.g. in (30) the prepositional phrase *e castris* is attached to V, in a higher structural position than the direct object. On the other hand, the adjunct which is less closely linked to the verb, in that it is not required by its thematic structure, like the adverb *segniter*, occupies the sentence adjunct position, i.e. it is placed out of the VP, but inside the IP.

19.7 SOV and SVO languages

Having completed an overview of the basic syntactic structure of simple sentences, we can now resume our observations about word order in a more systematic way. Word order in Latin is extremely free. Generally speaking, the most frequently attested order is Subject–Object–Verb. For this reason, Latin is said to be a predominantly SOV language. This is not a rigid ordering, in that SVO sentences are frequently attested as well, along with other less frequent orders, such as VOS, OVS, etc. Languages such as English and Italian are rigidly SVO. Some of the most recent research in generative grammar has tried to provide an explanation of this state of affairs, as follows.

The starting assumption is that SVO is the universal order and that all other attested orders are derived via movement. This is possible because the number of functional categories of the sentence that linguists postulate has been recently enriched. In particular, the functional head I has been split into three distinct categories, i.e. tense (T), subject agreement (AgrS), and object agreement (AgrO). The structure of the 'expanded' IP is shown in (31):

(31)

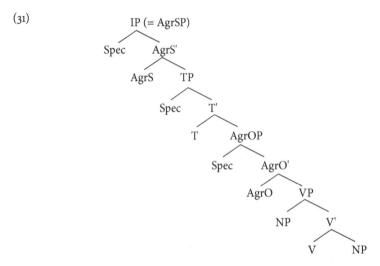

In (31), the IP has been split into three new phrases, projected by three functional heads, i.e. AgrO, T, and AgrS, which replace the former I. This implies that new specifier positions (Spec) are now available which can host the various components of the VP, i.e. the verb and the subject/object noun phrases. Starting from a base SVO order within the verb phrase, we can thus derive various word order variations via movement to these new Spec positions.

Note that it is not necessary to expand the structure of the IP every time we analyse a new sentence. We have already seen that the complexity of phrase markers that one can draw for each sentence depends on the linguistic features one wishes to emphasize. For the sake of the present discussion, it is important to underline the fact that the expanded IP allows us to move all the three elements which are base-generated within the VP, i.e. the subject, the object, and the verb, in order to account for all the attested surface orders.

In example (9) of Section 19.2, we have mentioned the first of these three movements, i.e. the movement of the subject noun phrase from the specifier of the VP to the specifier of the IP, that we shall now call specifier of AgrSP.

In example (30) of Section 18.7, we have encountered the second movement as well, when we analysed the structure of the verb phrase and we mentioned the possibility of the object moving before the verb. We can now be more precise: the object moves from the complement of V to the specifier of AgrO, causing a shift from SVO to SOV order.

We can also infer a hypothesis about the reason why this movement takes place in Latin but not in English. The crucial difference is related to the presence of a rich case morphology in Latin, which needs to be 'checked' by moving the object to the specifier of the related functional head, i.e. AgrO. The erosion of the case morphology of nouns could be a possible explanation for the shift from SOV to SVO which characterizes the history of many languages, including the Romance and the Germanic family. In other words, a strong case morphology requires the movement of the object, giving rise to an SOV order, while a weak case morphology does not require such a movement and—as a consequence—the base SVO order is not altered. One peculiarity of Classical Latin is that the movement of the object is optional, so both SOV and SVO orders are possible, with an increasing shift towards the latter order in Late and Vulgar Latin.

19.8 The periphery of the sentence

The discussion in Section 19.7 has left one issue unsolved. Although it is true that the two opposite chronological poles of Latin were typologically rigid, i.e. SOV in the pre-literary period and SVO in the pre-Romance period, during the classical period the language underwent a change which is not linear and progressive but rather extremely complex and varied. Saying that the verb-final order is more 'archaic' and 'literary', while the object-final order is 'later' and 'colloquial' is only an approximation. In fact, two counter-examples will suffice to undermine this statement:

(32)   Superbiter contemptim conterit legiones (Naev. *Poen.* 5 M.)
       'With arrogance and contempt he wastes the legions'

(33)   Aqua dentes habet (Petr. *Sat.* 42, 2)
       'The water has teeth'

Example (32) shows that Naevius, who was one of the most archaic Latin poets, may already have exploited the SVO order, which is identical to the Italian and English orders. On the other hand, the SOV order survived in the mouths of freedmen during the banquet of Trimalchio in Petronius, although some clearly pre-Romance features are already attested in the text.

There is one additional issue with Latin word order. Even if we split the IP into three functional heads, i.e. tense, subject agreement, and object agreement, there are not enough positions to account for all the word order related phenomena of Latin and other languages, including English and Italian. For example, both in Latin and in Italian subjects are frequently postverbal, cf. Lat. *natant pueri*, It. *nuotano i ragazzi* 'the boys are swimming'; both in Italian and in English the direct object can be placed in a sentence-initial position, where it is accompanied by a marked intonation to contrast it with a previously mentioned referent, cf. En. *MARK I have seen, not Mary*, It. *MARCO ho visto, non Maria*.

For this reason, a further expansion of the sentence structure is necessary, i.e. two additional functional heads have to be added, which express the so-called 'pragmatic structure' of the sentence. Pragmatics is a notion referring to the speaker's specific use of the information contained in a sentence. We have already mentioned these pragmatic functions, i.e. Topic (what is being talked about, the known information) and Focus (what is being emphasized or contrasted with other elements) when we described the structure of nominal expressions (cf. Section 18.5).

This time, the sentence phrase marker will be expanded above the IP level, in the so-called left periphery of the sentence. Similarly to nominal expressions, the sentence also has its own 'centre', that is the IP, and also a 'periphery'. We will see in Section 23.1 that this outermost layer above the IP may be called the CP (complementizer phrase), because it typically hosts the Complementizers, and in general it is related to the speaker's attitude and to information structure. By expanding the phrase marker in this way, we obtain two peripheral specifiers, which belong to the functional categories of Topic and Focus, respectively. These positions can host various elements which are displaced from their base position within the IP. For example, the sentence *transit Melitam Romanus* 'The Roman passes (over to) Malta' (lit. 'passes Malta the Roman') (Naev. *Poen.* 39 M.) is derived from the base order within the IP, i.e. *Romanus Melitam transit*, via two operations of displacement from the centre to the periphery as shown in (34) where the surface VOS order is derived from a deep SOV order:

(34)

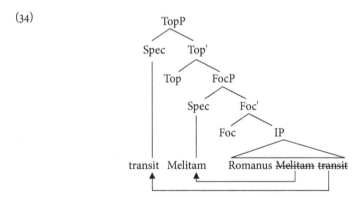

This analysis is sufficient to explain many other word order related phenom- ena. Firstly, all orders diverging from SOV and SVO are statistically less frequent. This follows from the fact that while SOV and SVO orders are produced within the IP, the remainder are the product of specific information structure devices *above* the IP, which require the displacement of some element to the left periphery to be topicalized or focalized. Secondly, the occurrence of sentences with marked orders is not unique to Latin but also affects other languages, including Italian and English, to various degrees. It is reasonable to suggest that in Latin, but also in Italian or English, all the orders diverging from SOV and SVO are derived via movement of certain constitu- ents to the left periphery. We shall now consider some examples taken from Latin.

The OSV order is the result of the topicalization of the object. In the unmarked order, the object occupies the *comment,* not the *topic,* position. This means that when the object occupies this latter position, which is sentence initial, it acquires a special emphasis:

(35)   Reliquos omnes, consecuti, equites nostri interfecerunt (Caes. *Gall.* I 53, 3)
       '(As for) all the others, our cavalry caught and murdered them'

The VSO order, in contrast, puts the *focus* on the verb because of the displacement of this latter to the left periphery of the sentence:

(36)   Miserat enim ei Pharnaces coronam auream (*Bell. Alex.* 70, 8)
       'For he, Pharnaces, had sent him a golden crown'
       (lit. 'had sent to him Pharnaces a golden crown')

Finally, the dislocation of both the verb and the object to the left periphery gives rise to the VOS and OVS orders. In this way the subject, which is unusually in final position, is emphasized.

(37)   Transit Melitam Romanus (Naev. *Poen.* 39 M.)
       'The Roman passes (over to) Malta'
       (lit. 'Passes Malta the Roman')

(38)   Idem facit Caesar (Caes. *Gall.* I 15, 1)
       'Caesar does likewise'
       (lit. 'the same does Caesar')

On the whole, it seems that it is possible to derive all the attested orders via movement to the left periphery. This is a very satisfactory state of affairs, in that it allows us to abandon a common view according to which Classical Latin is a non-configurational language, in that the ordering of S, O, and V can be freely arranged. This view is typically supported by artificial examples such as (39)–(44):

(39) a. Catullus amat Lesbiam (Lat.)
      b. Catullo ama Lesbia (It.)

(40) a. Catullus Lesbiam amat (Lat.)
      b. Catullo, Lesbia, *la* ama (It.)

(41) a. Amat Catullus Lesbiam (Lat.)
      b. *L'*ama Catullo, Lesbia (It.)

(42) a. Amat Lesbiam Catullus (Lat.)
      b. Ama Lesbia, Catullo (It.)

(43) a. Lesbiam Catullus amat (Lat.)
      b. Lesbia, Catullo *la* ama (It.)

(44) a. Lesbiam amat Catullus (Lat.)
      b. Lesbia, *la* ama Catullo (It.)

The English translation of examples (39)–(44) is always 'Catullus loves Lesbia'. Conversely, the very same six order alternations of Latin are possible in Italian as well, where they are rendered by means of the appropriate resumptive pronouns. The key point is that in Latin and in Italian, examples (39)–(44) do not convey the same meaning. More precisely, although they convey the same *logical* meaning, their *pragmatic* value, i.e. the way in which the information is presented to the listener, differs, as different emphasis is given to different constituents.

This means that a free word order does not imply that a language is non-configurational. An Italian speaker knows that the pragmatically unmarked order is SVO (cf. (39)). On the other hand, all the other orders are derived via movement of different elements to the left periphery of the sentence, i.e. via topicalization or focalization. In the Italian sentences (40) to (44), the commas mark the boundaries between the elements which have been displaced for pragmatic reasons and the remainder of the sentence.

There is no reason why the same mechanisms of focalization and topicalization should not apply to Latin. In fact, there are some cases in which the application of these pragmatically motivated movements is quite evident, cf. the dislocation of an element to the contrastive Focus in example (45):

(45) Alium illa amat, non illum (Plaut. *Bacch.* 593)
      'She loves another, not him'
      (lit. 'another she loves, not him')

Sometimes it is difficult to understand the author's communicative purpose and to discriminate a focalized element from a topicalized one, given that no native speaker judgements are now available. In any case, it is clear that, although word order is more flexible in Latin than in other languages such as English or Italian, it is not at all random. Latin also has an unmarked base order, i.e. SOV, an alternative order produced by an ongoing grammatical change, i.e. SVO, and a wide range of pragmatic variants derived via movement. For this reason, the placement of phrases within the sentence can be extremely complex and the different orderings are never equivalent.

This view is confirmed by the analysis previously made by ancient grammarians, such as Quintilian, who stated the following:

(46) Illa nimia quorundam fuit observatio, ut vocabula verbis, verba rursus adverbiis, nomina adpositis et pronominibus essent priora: nam fit contra quoque frequenter non indecore (Quint. *inst.* IX 4, 24).
      'The rule which some have sought to enforce that nouns should precede verbs, and verbs adverbs, while epithets and pronouns should follow their substantives, is excessive: for the contrary is often attested, not indecently'

This passage underlines the impossibility of establishing a fixed order, contrary to what has been suggested by some grammarians, who turned the tendency to place objects before verbs, and adverbial and adjectival adjuncts after nouns and verbs, into a rule. This is not, however, to say that anything goes:

(47) Felicissimum tamen sermo est cui et rectus ordo et apta iunctura et cum his numerus opportune cadens contigit. [...] Haec arbitror, ut in brevi, de ordine fuisse dicenda: qui si vitiosus est, licet et vincta ac sit apte cadens, tamen merito incomposita dicatur (Quint. *inst.* IX 4, 27–32)
      'The best speech is the one with the natural order, apt connection and appropriate rhythm [...]. This I think is, in brief, what had to be said on word order: if the order is faulty, our language will be deservedly charged of being disarranged, however compact and rhythmical it may be'

In this passage, Quintilian correctly acknowledges the importance of some factors, such as *apta iunctura*, that is the 'apt connection' of words, and *numerus*, that is 'rhythm' (whose importance had been stressed by Cicero's *Orator*, 149), which can affect word order. Nevertheless, he still follows the ancient rhetorical tradition, according to which there exists a *rectus ordo*, that is, a natural, correct order, as opposed to the *vitiosus* 'faulty' one (this concept had already been expressed in *Rhetorica ad Herennium*, IV 32, 44).

The most common term employed in ancient rhetoric to indicate a word order violation is *hyperbaton*. In example (48), Quintilian discusses an example of hyperbaton taken from one of Cicero's orations, and recognizes the expressive value of this rhetoric technique:

(48)   At cum decoris gratia traicitur longius verbum, proprie 'hyperbati' est nomen: 'animadverti, iudices, omnem accusatoris orationem in duas divisam esse partes' [Cic. *Cluent.* 1]. Nam 'in duas partes divisam esse' rectum erat, sed durum et incomptum (Quint. *inst.* VIII 6, 65)

'When a word is moved to some distance from its original place, for the sake of elegance, that is strictly called *hyperbaton*: 'I noted, gentlemen, that the speech of the accuser was divided into two parts (*in duas divisam esse partes*)'. The correct order would be *in duas partes divisam esse*, but this would have been harsh and ugly'

The 'correct order' mentioned by Quintilian coincides with the one we have already mentioned, that is subject – indirect object – verb, cf. *omnem accusatoris orationem – in duas partes – divisam esse*. In the stylistically marked order in contrast, i.e. in the hyperbaton, the indirect object is disrupted, i.e. *in duas | divisam esse | partes*. More precisely, one piece of the phrase, i.e. *in duas*, is separated from *partes* and receives a particular emphasis.

In more technical terms, the 'hyperbaton' is nothing but a discontinuous constituent. In Latin, there are some clear examples of the artistic elaboration which lies behind this procedure. One of the most famous examples is the so-called 'inlay' of attributive groups, which was particularly appreciated by poets. Sentence (49) will provide an example:

(49)   Amissos longo [~~amissos~~ socios] [~~longo~~ sermone] requirunt (Verg. *Aen.* I 217)

In example (49) the first constituent of each of the two noun phrases, i.e. *amissos socios* and *longo sermone*, has been separated from its head and moved to the left periphery of the sentence, in the Topic and Focus positions, respectively. The surface string, i.e. *amissos longo socios sermone*, exhibits an artificial word order, where the two phrases seem to overlap one another.

In fact, there is no need to refer to the expressive virtuosity of poetry to explain discontinuous phrases in Latin, in that these are common to all stylistic registers, i.e. for almost each sentence there is a phrase which is disrupted by elements belonging to another one. For example, a simple sentence such as *nostram scilicet de more ridebant invidiam* (Petr. *Sat.* 14, 7) is stylistically enriched by the focalization of *nostram*, which is extracted from the noun phrase *nostram invidiam*. Nevertheless, the structure of some types of phrases imposes a number of limits to the freedom of word order. With the exception of some archaisms and poetic expressions, it is not possible to separate a noun from its preposition, e.g. **ad pervenio urbem*. In prepositional phrases, it is only possible to separate the adjective from its noun and to insert the preposition within the discontinuous phrase, e.g. *magna cum laude* (cf. Section 18.9).

In conclusion, the first step of a correct translation from Latin to English is the reconstruction of the integrity of the phrases in order to understand the overall meaning of the sentence. Afterwards, it is possible to proceed with the analysis of the pragmatic and stylistic interpretation of the displaced elements, as they appear in the Latin surface string, in order to convey the same interpretative effects of the original sentence.

20

Case theory

20.1 Abstract case and morphological case

Case theory deals with the conditions which license the presence of noun phrases in a sentence. The basic principle is the so-called 'Case Filter':

(1) Case Filter: all overt noun phrases must be assigned abstract case.

The idea behind this principle is that grammar contains a mechanism which filters out all overt noun phrases lacking case. This means that if a sentence contains a noun phrase which has not been assigned abstract case, the sentence will be ill-formed.

   The existence of a Case Filter may sound trivial in Latin, where the stem of a noun or adjective lacking any case mark is just a morphological abstraction, in that all the words which appear in surface strings are inflected for case. On the other hand, languages such as English and Italian seem to behave differently, in that the vast majority of words apparently lack any inflection for case. Nevertheless, Case Filter is active in these languages as well. In order to understand this point, it is necessary to introduce the difference between abstract case and morphological case.

(2) a. Abstract case is a necessary property of noun phrases.
     b. Morphological case is the concrete realization of abstract case.

Morphological case is the set of modifications that words undergo in order to mark the presence of abstract case. While abstract case is a universal property of languages, its morphological realization, i.e. morphological case, is subject to cross-linguistic variation. Languages such as Latin, Greek, Russian, and German have a rich system of morphological cases, extensively described by grammars. Other languages such as English and Italian, on the other hand, have an impoverished morphological system. For this reason, traditional grammars usually claim that these languages lack case.

   As a matter of fact, there are some relics of morphological case both in English and in Italian, as shown in Section 9.1, where we observed that the third person singular pronouns still retain case and gender inflection, to varying degrees.

In sum, traditional grammars usually state that case is the indication of the logical function of a single word into the sentence. As a matter of fact, case is a property of a whole noun phrase rather than of a single word. Moreover, its function is primarily syntactic, and only secondarily logical. This concept will become clearer once we have introduced another fundamental distinction, i.e. structural vs. inherent case.

20.2 Structural and inherent case

The distinction between structural and inherent case is rooted in the traditional opposition between 'direct case' and 'oblique case', which is problematic, in that it is based on a non-immediately decipherable metaphor. The term *casus* (πτῶσις) itself is rather obscure, in that it is derived from the verb *cado* 'to fall' (πίπτω), although it is not clear what element should be 'falling'. It may be the pure stem of the word, which stays in the speaker's mind until it 'falls' into the concreteness of inflected forms. Otherwise, the idea might be that, in a hypothetical tree, there is a line starting from the top, the nominative, and reaching 'directly' to the accusative, while 'oblique' cases are derived from lateral branches which originate from the nominative.

Either way, the distinction between structural case and inherent case is more intuitive. As the word itself suggests, structural case crucially depends on the structural properties of phrases, i.e. on the position these phrases occupy within the phrase marker. The structural cases are the nominative and the accusative, which correspond to the structural positions of subject and object in a simple sentence with a transitive verb, as shown by example (3):

(3)

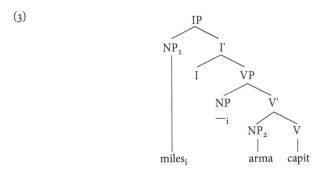

In Section 19.3, we defined NP_1 as the structural subject position, that is the specifier of the IP, where the subject is displaced from its base position, i.e. the specifier of the VP. We have also already introduced NP_2, that is, the object structural position, i.e. the complement of V, which in Latin is mostly raised to the position of AgrO before the verb (cf. Section 19.7).

We can now simply state that the noun phrase in the subject position is assigned structural nominative case. In a parallel fashion, the noun phrase in the object position is assigned structural accusative case.

It is important to stress the fact that syntactic position is a necessary but not sufficient condition for the assignment of structural case. For example, if in (3) the verb were an infinitive, the subject could not be assigned nominative case. Moreover, if the same verb were intransitive or passive, the object could not be assigned accusative case. Therefore, we have to revise our previous statement and say that, in the above-specified structural positions, the subject is assigned nominative case by the finite verbal inflection, while the object is assigned accusative case by the active voice of a transitive verb.

These claims have an interesting consequence. By positing that the structural position of the subject is a necessary condition for the nominative to be assigned, we can outline a common analysis of the overall structure of nominal and verbal predicates.

We shall start with verbal predicates. We have already seen that the subject is base-generated within the specifier of the VP and is later displaced to the specifier of the IP. We can now understand the reason for this obligatory displacement. The specifier of the VP is a position where a theta-role but not case can be assigned. Therefore, the Case Filter forces the subject noun phrase to move from the specifier of the VP to the specifier of the IP, where it can be assigned nominative case if the inflection of the verb is finite. We described this type of movement in Section 19.2, example (9), and it is exemplified again below:

(4)

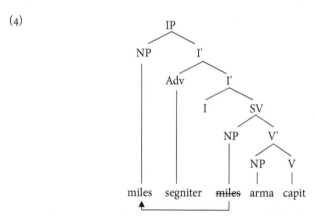

We shall now consider nominal predicates. In Section 19.5, example (27) we have represented sentences such as *Piso auctor est* up until the I' node.

However, it is reasonable to wonder whether sentences with a nominal predicate project the IP node as well. The question is legitimate not only for reasons of economy, i.e. it is desirable that all sentences project an IP, but also for a specific reason. The base position of the subject of a nominal predicate cannot be case-marked. As a consequence, the subject is forced to move to the specifier of the IP, just like the subject of a verbal predicate. This movement is evident in a sentence such as *sententia aperte falsa est* 'the opinion is clearly wrong' (Gaius *inst*. III 64), where one of the two constituents of the small clause *sententia falsa* moves to the subject position, i.e. the specifier of the IP, to receive nominative case. The complete structure of a sentence with a nominal predicate is shown in (5), where, for the sake of simplicity, we have sketched a head-final structure of IP, which, of course, could be derived from a head-initial one if we adopted the expanded IP hypothesis presented in Section 19.7:

(5)

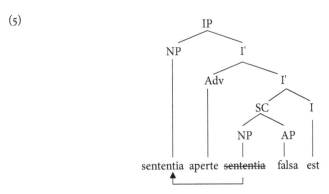

One interesting generalization emerges from this analysis, i.e. the subjects of both verbal and nominal predicates are assigned structural nominative case in the same structural position, i.e. the specifier of the IP.

The last point in this section concerns the other necessary condition to case-assignment, i.e. the presence of a case-assigner. For the sake of the present discussion, we shall assume that heads with specific features are case-markers. In particular, nominative case is assigned by a finite head I (either indicative or subjunctive), in a head–specifier configuration, while accusative case is assigned by an active head V, in a head–complement configuration.

Note that the head P can assign accusative case as well, in the same head–complement configuration, within a prepositional phrase, e.g. *ad urbem*.

This analysis represents the formalization of an intuition that ancient grammarians had already made about accusative case. The following dialogue between a master and his pupil about the first line of Virgil's Aeneid, i.e. *arma virumque cano*, is exemplary in this respect. The problem discussed concerns the abstract case expressed by *arma*, since in the neuter plural the very same morphological case can express both the nominative and the accusative:

(6)   Cuius est casus in hoc loco? Accusativi. Unde hoc certum est? A structura, id est ordinatione et coniunctione sequentium: 'cano' enim verbum accusativo iungitur (Prisc. *part.*, GLK III 462, 10)
'What is the case in this place? Accusative. How can we be sure about that? From the structure, that is from the organization and combination of the following words: for the verb "cano" is joined with the accusative'

In other words, the assignment of accusative case requires both the correct structural position and a case-assigner.

In sum, the assignment of structural cases, i.e. nominative and accusative, chiefly depends on the configurational properties of the elements contained in the phrase marker, i.e. it is mainly based on syntactic properties, and is only secondarily related to the logical or semantic properties of such elements. In fact, both the subject and the object can perform different thematic roles, depending on the verb which heads the sentence, e.g. the subject is often an Agent, but it may also be an Experiencer or a Patient, and the same is true for objects. The nominative case lacks any semantic information per se, and the same is true for the accusative, which is a mere mark of structural dependency. In conclusion, nominative and accusative are the only cases which can be assigned on purely structural grounds, simply because a given element is placed in a given structural position, and their assignment does not necessarily imply the assignment of a specific theta-role.

20.3 Agreement

When two syntactic elements agree, they share the same person, number, and gender features, and, in some circumstances, case as well.

In Latin, just as in English or Italian, the subject and the predicate agree. The subject has gender and number features, in addition to nominative case. When it is realized by a personal pronoun, it has person features as well. The predicate, either verbal or nominal, in addition to mood and tense, has a number of features shared with the subject, i.e. the same number and person features and, if it is a nominal predicate or a participle, gender and case as well. In other words, the subject and the verb agree in the expression of some information, as shown by examples (7)–(10):

(7)   a. ego$_{(1\ pers.\ sg.)}$ laudo$_{(1\ pers.\ sg.)}$ (Lat.)
b. I$_{(1\ pers.\ sg.)}$ praise$_{(1\ pers.\ sg.)}$ (En.)

(8)   a. is$_{(3\ pers.\ sg.)}$ laudat$_{(3\ pers.\ sg.)}$ (Lat.)
      b. he$_{(3\ pers.\ sg.)}$ praises$_{(3\ pers.\ sg.)}$ (En.)

(9)   a. puer$_{(nom.\ sg.\ mas.)}$ laudatus$_{(nom.\ sg.\ mas.)}$ est (Lat.)
      b. the boy$_{(sg.)}$ was praised$_{(sg.)}$ (En.)

(10) a. pueri$_{(nom.\ pl.\ mas.)}$ laudāti $_{(nom.\ pl.\ mas.)}$ sunt (Lat.)
      b. the boys$_{(pl.)}$ were praised$_{(pl.)}$ (En.)

From a syntactic perspective, the crucial point is that the agreement relation is established in a specifier–head or in a head–adjunct configuration.

In particular, the subject and the predicate agree in a specifier–head configuration, as shown in (11) (bear in mind that the subject is the specifier of the IP):

(11)

Although the verb agrees with its subject, there is no agreement with its object, since this latter occupies the position of complement rather than of specifier. Therefore, the relationship between the verb and its object is limited to case-assignment (accusative), without agreement.

Finally, recall that another kind of agreement is established within the noun phrase as well, as shown by examples (12)–(15):

(12) a. hic$_{(nom.\ sg.\ mas.)}$ puer$_{(nom.\ sg.\ mas.)}$ (Lat.)
      b. this$_{(sg.)}$ boy$_{(sg.)}$ (En.)

(13) a. hi$_{(nom.\ pl.\ mas.)}$ pueri$_{(nom.\ pl.\ mas.)}$ (Lat.)
      b. these$_{(pl.)}$ boys$_{(pl.)}$ (En.)

(14) a. bonus$_{(nom.\ sg.\ mas.)}$ puer$_{(nom.\ sg.\ mas.)}$ (Lat.)
      b. good$_{(sg.)}$ boy$_{(sg.)}$ (En.)

(15) a. boni $_{(nom.\ pl.\ mas.)}$ pueri $_{(nom.\ pl.\ mas.)}$ (Lat.)
      b. good$_{(pl.)}$ boys$_{(pl.)}$ (En.)

Note that demonstrative and possessive pronouns, as well as adjectival adjuncts, agree with the head of the noun phrase in gender, number, and case.

20.4 The passive construction

When we talked about structural case, we linked the movement of the subject NP to its need to receive nominative case. Generally speaking, movement establishes a relationship between two levels of syntactic representation.

In this case, the former is the level at which theta-roles are assigned, while the latter is the level at which cases are assigned. These two levels used to be called 'deep structure' and 'surface structure', respectively, while in recent theories the simple opposition between these two types of structure has been largely abandoned, since the instances of syntactic movements can be various. Instead, it now claimed that the construction of the syntactic structure is achieved through different 'stages'.

Bearing this distinction in mind, we can now proceed with the analysis of passive constructions. From a descriptive point of view, what we observe is that simple sentences with an active verb can be passivized. In this case, the verb acquires passive endings and the whole sentence structure is modified, especially in the relationship between the verb and its object.

The peculiar feature of a passive verb is that it has lost both the ability to assign accusative case to its object, and the ability to assign a theta-role to its subject. In other words, it is as if its passive morphology had 'absorbed' these two properties of verb assignment. As a consequence of this, a passive verb retains only its ability to assign a theta-role to its object.

We shall now proceed with an analysis of the structure of a passive sentence such as *exercitus in Cedrosiae fines perducitur* 'the army is led into the country of Cedrosia' (Curt. IX 10, 17). The passive morphology blocks the verb from theta-marking the subject and case-marking the object:

(16)

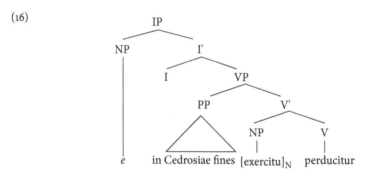

As (16) clearly shows, the subject position of a passive sentence is empty, while the object position is filled by a noun phrase which is theta-marked as Theme by the verb but remains case-less. For this reason, it is represented as a pure stem [exercitu]$_N$ without inflection. However, this is a violation of the Case Filter: the sentence as such is ill-formed and some adjustments are required.

We shall proceed step by step. The first option could be the deletion of the direct object, whose lack of case is responsible for the ill-formedness of the sentence. In this way, the verb becomes intransitive. Intransitive verbs are usually allowed in impersonal passive constructions, as shown in (17):

(17)   Ubi in hostium fines ventum est (Liv. X 14, 5)
       'When they arrived (lit. "it is arrived") at the borders of the enemy'

This is a valid solution for those transitive verbs which admit an intransitive use, e.g. *bibo* 'to drink' can be used intransitively, i.e. *bibitur* 'they drink' (lit. 'it is drunk'). This solution, however, is not possible with *perduco*, which cannot be used intransitively.

   In this case we must find another solution. A sentence with the corresponding active transitive verb could be (18):

(18)   Agricola in fines Borestorum exercitum deducit (Tac. *Agr.* 38, 2)
       'Agricola leads the army into the country of the Boresti'

The structure of the active sentence differs from the structure of the passive one because only the former has two positions where both theta-role and case are assigned. The subject, i.e. *Agricola*, is assigned an Agent theta-role and nominative case, while the object, i.e. *exercitum*, is assigned a Theme theta-role and accusative case. Conversely, the passive sentence has a single position hosting the object, which is theta-marked, and an empty position where nominative case can potentially be assigned. Therefore, a possible way to rescue our sentence could involve the syntactic displacement of the object. Suppose that the noun phrase *exercitus* leaves its base position, where it cannot be case-marked, and moves to the empty subject position, leaving a trace (*t*) in the starting position. The resulting surface structure is shown in (19):

(19)

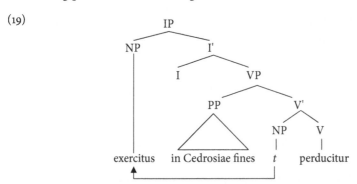

In this structure, the object moves from the complement position of V to the surface subject position, i.e. the specifier of the IP. Through this movement, the noun phrase *exercitus* can be assigned nominative case by the finite inflection of the verb *perducitur*. In this way, the Case Filter is satisfied and the sentence is grammatical.

   In sum, the deep structure of a passive sentence in (16) is modified by the syntactic movement of a constituent, giving rise to the surface structure in (19).

The essential point of this analysis is that the assignment of theta-roles always takes place in deep structure, e.g. *exercitus* is regularly assigned the same Theme theta-role by the verb *perducere* both in the active and in the passive sentence. When the object is displaced to the surface subject position to become case-marked, its theta-role does not change.

The above analysis shows that, in order to understand the functioning of a passive construction, it is sufficient to combine the principles of the thematic theory and of the case theory. Theta-roles, e.g. Agent and Theme, are assigned in deep structure and depend on the intrinsic properties of each individual verb. Structural cases, i.e. nominative and accusative, are, in contrast, assigned in surface structure and depend on the surface position of elements. As shown by the above examples, there may be instances in which some elements need to move in the passage between one structure and the other. While the nodes of the phrase marker remain unaltered in the passage between the two structures (cf. the so-called 'Structure Preservation Principle'), phrases can undergo various instances of movement.

The crucial difference between the two sentences, i.e. active and passive, is that the subject position of a passive sentence is empty in deep structure and is not associated with any theta-roles. The passage from an active to a passive sentence is not properly a transformation, as it was called in the early days of generative grammar, but rather a phenomenon which is internal to the passive construction, which requires a more complex derivation to solve a case-related anomaly. The solution is precisely the movement of a constituent, e.g. in example (19) the NP *exercitus* moves from the object position (deep structure) to the subject position (surface structure), where it can be case-marked.

Moreover, the movement analysis of passive constructions also provides an account for the fact that the semantic relationship between the subject and the passive verb is identical to the one holding between the corresponding active verb and its object. This is due to the fact that the surface subject of a passive sentence is actually base-generated in the object position, where it is theta-marked, hence its object-like semantic relationship with the verb.

The last issue to be considered here is the *by*-phrase of a passive sentence, that is, an adjunct occupying a peripheral position with respect to the verb node, e.g. *exercitus ducitur ab imperatore* 'the army is led *by the general*'. The position of *ab imperatore* radically differs from the position occupied by the subject of the corresponding active construction (*imperator ducit exercitum*). We shall now see why.

We have just mentioned the fact that the subject of an active sentence is assigned nominative case structurally, while its theta-role is assigned by virtue of the intrinsic features of the verb. We also know that the subject of a passive sentence is assigned nominative case, but inherits its thematic role from the object position, where it is base-generated. As a consequence, in the analysis of a passive sentence there is no need to be concerned with the subject of the corresponding active sentence. When uttering a sentence such as *exercitus in Cedrosiae fines perducitur*, whose subject position is empty in deep structure, the speaker does not know or is not willing to reveal the identity of the commander. Conversely, the only thing he or she is concerned about is simply the object, i.e. the army. If he or she wants the Agent theta-role to enter the construction, this can only be expressed by means of an adjunct, which is placed outside the verb node. In other words, the agentive semantics must be expressed by the adjunct of an autonomous constituent, i.e. the so-called *by*-phrase, e.g. *ab imperatore* 'by the general'.

However, it is often the case that an agent-less passive sentence cannot be turned into an active sentence, either because it would be very difficult to express its subject, e.g. in *arma capiuntur* 'weapons are taken', only the context may clarify the identity of the subject of the action, or because the action depends only on the subject of the passive sentence, e.g. *ferri* 'to be carried', that is 'to travel'. Finally, it may also be the case that the action is autonomous and spontaneous, e.g. *verti* 'to turn around'.

Therefore, the passive is also semantically autonomous with respect to the active construction. *Imperator exercitum ducit* is not the equivalent of *exercitus ducitur ab imperatore*, in that the constituents are presented in a different way. In other words, the two sentences follow a different communicative strategy, whereby *imperator* is the centre of the action in the former, and *exercitus* in the latter.

Finally, the distinction between deep and surface structure is fundamental in order to solve the problem of the definition of the notion of subject. Contrary to the traditional definition (the subject is 'the one who performs the action'), the subject of a passive sentence is typically the one who undergoes the action. This paradox can be solved if we consider that each passive sentence is associated with two levels of representation. As a consequence, there are two potential subjects, i.e. the one in deep structure, which is empty, and the one in surface structure, which is a raised object. The subject who 'performs the action' is only the one that is assigned an Agent theta-role in deep structure, as is the case for most active sentences. However, in the deep structure of a passive sentence there is no subject, in that the verb cannot assign a thematic role to it. As a consequence, a passive sentence only has a subject in surface structure, which is nothing but a raised object and therefore does not perform, but rather undergoes, the action.

20.5 Inherent case

In Section 20.2, we said that structural case can be assigned by functional elements, e.g. nominative case is assigned by the functional head I. Moreover, we also showed that the assignment of structural case is disjoined from the assignment of a specific theta-role, in that the only requirement is the relevant structural position, cf. the subject of passive sentences.

In contrast, inherent case can only be assigned by lexical heads, such as nouns, verbs, and prepositions, but not by functional ones. Moreover, while structural cases do not have a basic semantic value, each inherent case can be specified for a given semantic value. In other words, inherent case is the syntactic mark of the assignment of a specific theta-role.

For example, there is a strong correspondence between genitive case and the Possessor theta-role, e.g. *arma hostium* 'enemies' weapons'. Similarly, dative is typically employed to mark theta-roles such as Benefactive, *tibi amicus sum* 'I am your friend' (lit. 'I am friend to you'), or Goal, e.g. *dies conloquio dictus* 'the day established for the talk'. As for the ablative, this typically covers a wide range of semantic values, in that—historically—the case which used to mark the Source, e.g. *Romā* 'from Rome', also absorbed the values of the archaic Instrumental case, e.g. *dentibus* 'with one's teeth', and Locative case, e.g. *Athenis* 'in Athens', because of syncretism.

The description of the possible semantic values of each case is extensively covered by traditional Latin grammars under a section called 'case syntax'. In Chapter 21, we will follow this tradition, but will also try to show that it is actually possible to reduce the extreme variety of semantic values expressed by cases by making a distinction between structural and inherent cases and by grouping the latter category under wide semantic units which correspond to different theta-roles.

21

Case syntax

21.1 Nominative and vocative

Nominative is the prototypical *structural case*, in that it is always assigned to the NP occupying the *subject* position, i.e. the specifier of the IP. Nominative case is assigned by the finite functional head I; if this latter is infinitive, the subject is assigned accusative case. In other words, nominative is only assigned to the subject by the finite inflection of the verb.

The main peculiarity of this case noted by traditional grammars is the so-called 'double nominative', that is, a structure consisting of a nominative subject and a nominal predicate or a predicative subject complement. Therefore, its name comes from the fact that both the subject and the nominal predicate (or the predicative subject complement) of this construction are nominative.

The analysis of the double nominative is quite straightforward. Its structure is based on that of a small clause (cf. Section 19.4). A small clause combines a noun phrase with another noun or adjective phrase in a predicative relationship and the two always agree in case.

The nominal predicate only admits the copula *esse*. Conversely, the predicative subject complement can occur with different categories of verbs, called 'copulative', since their function is similar to the function of the copula in sentences with a nominal predicate.

The most common type of copulative verb refers to a state of being or becoming, such as *nascor* 'to be born', *morior* 'to die', *fio* 'to become', *evado* 'to turn out', *maneo* 'to remain', *discedo* 'to go away', *videor* 'to seem', etc. For example:

(1) Tabulae quidem certe incorruptae atque integrae manent (Cic. *Font.* 3)
    'The accountbooks at least certainly remain uncorrupted and undamaged'

(2) Sol Democrito magnus videtur (Cic. *fin.* I 20)
    'The sun seems vast to Democritus'

On the other hand, some verbs admit the double nominative when they are used in the passive form. They belong to the following classes:

(a) 'appellative' verbs, such as *dicor* 'to be said', *appellor* or *vocor* 'to be called', *nominor* 'to be named', for example:

(3) Rectae animi adfectiones, virtutes appellantur (Cic. *Tusc.* II 43)
     'All the right affections of the soul are called virtues'

(4) Aristaeus [...] olivae dicitur inventor (Cic. *nat. deor.* III 45)
     'Aristaeus is said (to be) the discoverer of the olive'

(b) verbs of 'election', such as *eligor* 'to be elected', *creor* 'to be made', *legor* 'to be chosen':

(5) Ille legatus a suis civibus electus (Cic. *II Verr.* 2, 156)
     'He was elected ambassador by his fellow citiziens'

(c) verbs of 'evaluation', such as *aestimor, existimor* 'to be valued'; *ducor, putor, habeor* 'to be considered', *cognoscor* 'to be known':

(6) Virtus clara aeternaque habetur (Sall. *Cat.* 1, 4)
     'Valour is considered (to be) distinguished and everlasting'

The last peculiarity of the nominative mentioned by traditional grammars is the so-called 'nominative with infinitive' construction. Since this phenomenon involves embedded clauses, it will be illustrated in detail in Section 26.5.

We shall now conclude this section with some remarks about the *vocative*, which is a rather peculiar case, in that it is assigned exclusively to interlocutors to express a request or a command or to catch their attention. The vocative can also be used on its own to address somebody:

(7) Heus, adulescens! (Plaut. *Epid.* 1)
     'Hey, young man!'

More often, the vocative is combined with the imperative of a verb, as in the (8):

(8) Mi gnate, da mihi hanc veniam (Ter. *Hec.* 604)
     'My dear son, do me this favour'

When it is combined with the imperative, the vocative indicates the subject of the verb, while this latter selects its other complements in a regular fashion, e.g. the direct object *hanc veniam* and the indirect object *mihi* in (8).

21.2 Accusative

The first point to discuss is the distinction between structural and inherent accusative case. Just like the nominative, the *structural accusative* is simply a mark of syntactic dependency. Therefore, it does not convey any predetermined meaning, but indicates that the noun phrase occupies the object structural position, i.e. the complement of V. In other words, accusative case is always assigned to the object of transitive verbs.

As its case-assigner is the verb, the only peculiarities of the structural accusative are related to the properties of the thematic structure of some verbs. We have already seen that the thematic structure is part of the grammatical information of each verb and cannot simply be inferred from its meaning. This is shown by the fact that two verbs with roughly the same meaning can have different thematic structures in two different languages, i.e. some verbs are transitive in Latin but intransitive in English, or the other way round.

We report below a short list of verbs which are transitive in Latin, i.e. they take a direct object, but intransitive in English, i.e. they take other complements. The dictionary entry always specifies whether a verb is transitive or intransitive, so we will just report here some of the most important examples:

(a) Lat. *fugio, effugio, refugio,* En. 'to escape from'

(9)   Ut equitatum effugerent (Caes. *civ.* I 65, 4)
      'To escape from the cavalry'

(b) Lat. *deficio,* En. 'to run out of', 'to fail to'

(10) Hostes res frumentaria deficiere coepit (Caes. *Gall.* II 10, 4)
      'Corn-supply began to fail to the enemies'

(c) Lat. *ulciscor,* En. 'take vengeance for'

(11) Quanto satius est sanare iniuriam quam ulcisci (Sen. *de ira* III 27, 1)
      'How much more satisfactory it is to heal a wrong than to take vengeance for it'

A particular case is represented by the verb *dono* 'to give', which exhibits a double argument structure both in Latin and in English. In the first type of construction, i.e. Lat. *donare aliquid alicui,* En. *give something to somebody,* the verb assigns accusative case to the given object and dative case to the receiver (in English this latter is introduced by the preposition *to*):

(12) (Caesar) praedam militubus donat (Caes. *Gall.* VII 11, 9)
      'Caesar gives the booty to his soldiers'

In the second type of construction, in contrast, the receiver in Latin is assigned accusative case and the given object is assigned ablative case, i.e. Lat. *donare aliquem aliqua re.* In English, this type of construction superficially consists of two consecutive noun phrases, where the first one must be the receiver and the second one the given object, i.e. En. *give somebody something* vs. **give something somebody,* hence the expression 'double object construction'. An example is given in (13):

(13)   Scipio [...] Masinissam insignis donibus donat (Liv. XXIX, 35, 3)
        'Scipio [...] gives Masinissa conspicuous rewards'

Furthermore, both in Latin and in English, it is possible to express the direct object of an intransitive verb, provided that the 'inner object' shares its root with the verb, e.g. En. *to live a troubled life, to dream a strange dream*, etc. This is the so-called 'cognate accusative'. An example is given in (14):

(14)   Tu usque a puero servitutem servivisti (Plaut. *Capt.* 543)
        'You were a slave from childhood'
        (lit. 'you have served the servants')

Another peculiar use of the accusative is related to the thematic structure of *impersonal verbs*. We have already seen that the subject of impersonal verbs in Latin is obligatorily a null pronoun, i.e. pro. These verbs typically express a state of mind, e.g. *miseret* 'to feel pity', *paenitet* 'to regret', *piget* 'to be bothered', *pudet* 'to feel ashamed', and *taedet* 'to get bored'. Their thematic structure is the following: the subject is a null pronoun, the verb is inflected for the third person singular, and the object (accusative) is the person who experiences the feeling. Conversely, the Experiencer of the corresponding verbs in English is the subject, as shown by the examples in (15):

(15)   a. me paenitet (Cic. *Att.* III 3, 1)
            'I regret'
        b. me miseret (Cic. *div.* I 66)
            'I feel pity'
        c. te pudeat (Cic. *fin.* II 7)
            'you should feel ashamed'

In Latin, the person or thing towards which the feeling is addressed is expressed by a genitive noun phrase, while in English it is expressed by a prepositional phrase:

(16)   Fratris me piget pudetque (Ter. *Ad.* 391)
        'I feel sick and ashamed of my brother'

(17)   Me miseret tui (Ter. *Eun.* 802)
        'I am sorry for you'

We have already seen that the subject of an impersonal verb is usually a null pronoun, but it can also exceptionally be a neuter pronoun, e.g. *id, hoc*:

(18)   Non te haec pudent? (Ter. *Ad.* 753)
        'Aren't you ashamed of these things?'

Finally, the cause of the feeling can be expressed by an embedded clause, which we shall analyse in detail in the following chapters. For the sake of the present discussion it is sufficient to observe that the embedded clause can be a *causal* clause, i.e. *quod* plus an indicative or subjunctive verb, or—less frequently—an *infinitival* clause or an *indirect question*:

(19)   Paeniteat quod non foveo Carthaginis arces (Ov. *fast.* VI 45)
       'I would repent of not favouring Carthage's walls'

(20)   Paenitet in posterum diem dilatum [esse] certamen (Liv. X 40, 1)
       'He regrets that the struggle has been postponed to the following day'

(21)   A senatu quanti fiam minime me paenitet (Cic. *Att.* I 20, 3)
       'I by no means repent the Senate's estimation of me'

There are some other verbs which admit an *impersonal use*, i.e. verbs which regularly select an explicit nominative subject and an accusative object but which can exceptionally admit a null subject as well. When used impersonally, these verbs are always inflected for the third person singular, e.g. *decet* 'it is proper, suitable', *dedecet* 'it is not proper', *fugit, fallit* 'it escapes', *latet* 'it remains hidden'. We report some examples in (22) and (23):

(22)   Oratorem vero irasci minime decet, simulari non dedecet (Cic. *Tusc.* IV 25, 55)
       'It is most improper for an orator to become angry, but it is not unbecoming to pretend'

(23)   Omnes fontes aestate quam hieme gelidiores esse, quem fallit? (Plin. *nat.* II 233)
       'Who does not know that all springs are colder in summer than in winter?'

Consider now the second type of accusative, i.e. the *inherent accusative*. First of all, the inherent accusative can express the semantic value of circumstantials which indicate the *extent* of space or time, e.g. *dies noctesque cogitans* 'thinking for days and nights'; *quindecim pedes latus* 'five feet long'. A detailed analysis of the usages of the accusative of extension with prepositions will be offered in Section 21.6, when we describe complements of time and place. The remaining semantic values of the inherent accusative are listed below:

The *accusative of exclamation* is used, just like the nominative, to give a particular emphasis to a constituent. It is often accompanied by interjections:

(24)   O miseras hominum mentes, o pectora caeca (Lucr. II 14)
       'O wretched minds of men, o blinded hearts!'

The *accusative of respect or specification* (also known as the synecdochical or Greek accusative) is chiefly confined to poetry and is selected by adjectives and participles indicating the state of being dressed or naked for a part of the body, as in the example (25):

(25)   umeros perfusa capillis (Ov. *fast.* II 309)
       'her hair streamed on her shoulders'

The accusative expressing the person or thing affected is very common with
   verbs expressing states of mind, cf. the so-called *verba affectuum,* such as
   doleo and *maereo* 'to suffer', *horreo* 'to be horrified at', etc. The cause of the
   subject's psychological state can be expressed in the ablative, if it is considered a true cause, or in the accusative, if it refers to the affected object:

(26)   a. Qui sociorum iniuriis doleat (Cic. *II Verr.* 3, 6)
          'He who feels pain for (our) allies' wrongs'
       b. Maxime Dionis mortem doluerunt (Cic. *Cael.* 24)
          'They were very sorry for Dione's death'

In its vocabulary entry, *doleo* is classified as intransitive in a sentence like (26a)
and transitive in a sentence like (26b). According to our classification of the
accusative, i.e. structural and inherent, we should rather consider both (26a)
and (26b) as intransitive. For while the verb *doleo* assigns the theta-role of
Experiencer to its subject, it also assigns a second theta-role to the cause of the
subject's psychological state. This latter theta-role is marked by inherent case,
i.e. accusative or ablative, rather than by a structural accusative, which only
transitive verbs can assign.

   In contrast to the structural accusative, inherent accusative cannot be
turned into a nominative if the verb acquires passive morphology, as shown
by the examples in (27):

(27)   a. Mortem timent
          'They fear death'
       b. Mors timetur
          'Death is feared'
       c. Mortem dolent
          'They regret death'
       d. *Mors doletur
          'Death is regretted'

A transitive verb such as *timeo* assigns structural accusative case, cf. (27a), and
can thus be turned into the passive voice, cf. (27b). A verb such as *doleo,* in
contrast, can assign inherent accusative case, cf. (27c), and therefore does not
admit a passive construction, cf. the ungrammaticality of (27d).

   The last phenomenon that we shall consider in this section is the so-
called 'double accusative'. In fact, this traditional term covers a wide range
of rather heterogeneous phenomena, whose only common feature is the
presence of two accusatives. Three different types of construction fall under
this label.

First of all, a double accusative originates when the main verb selects a small clause as its complement. In this case, both the direct object and the predicative *object complement* are assigned accusative case. Verbs which select a small clause are typically *appellative* verbs, verbs *of election*, and verbs *of evaluation* in the active form. An example is given in (28):

(28)   Is A. Postumium Tubertum, socerum suum, severissimi imperii virum, dictatorem dixit (Liv. IV 26, 11)
       'He appointed A. Postumius Tubertus, his father-in-law, a man of the sternest authority, dictator'

Secondly, a double accusative can be found with *prefixed transitive verbs* incorporating the prepositions *circum-* and *trans-*, e.g. *circumduco* 'to lead around'. Here, the first accusative is the direct object, which is case-marked by the verb, while the second accusative is the complement of place, which is case-marked by the incorporated preposition, as shown by example (29):

(29)   Quos Pompeius omnia sua praesidia circumduxit (Caes. *civ.* III 61, 1)
       'Pompey conducted them round all his garrisons'

Finally, the third type can be found with two groups of special verbs, which assign both *structural* accusative case and *inherent* accusative case, and which represents the prototypical case of 'double accusative', involving a person and a thing. We distinguish between the two classes, whose complete list is reported below:

(a) *verba rogandi*, i.e. verbs meaning 'ask', such as *posco* 'to demand', *reposco* 'to demand back (from someone)', *flagito* 'to plead urgently', *oro* 'to beg', *rogo* 'to implore', *interrogo* 'to interrogate'. These verbs assign inherent accusative case to the object of the request and structural accusative case to its addressee, as in example (30):

(30)   Te hoc beneficium rogo (Cic. *Att.* XIV 13A, 3)
       'I ask you this favour'

(b) The verbs *doceo* 'to teach' and *celo* 'to hide'. These verbs assign structural accusative case to the object of teaching or hiding, and inherent accusative case to the person who is taught or thing which is hidden from something. The structure is thus *aliquem aliquid doceo* 'I teach something to somebody' and *aliquem aliquid celo* 'I hide something from somebody'. Some examples are given in (31) and (32):

(31)   Catilina iuventutem mala facinora edocebat (Sall. *Cat.* 16, 1)
       'Catilina taught many evil actions to the young men'

(32)   Ista flagitia me celavisti (Plaut. *Bacch.* 166)
       'You have hidden these shameful acts from me'

In Latin the passive of *doceo* is usually avoided. In this case, the verb is substituted by synonyms such as *erudior, imbuor, instituor*, which do not have the double accusative, just as German typically avoids *lehren* 'to teach' and resorts to the synonym *unterrichten* 'to educate', e.g. *du wirst in Geschichte unterrichtet* 'you are educated in history'. In those cases in which the use of the passive is admitted, i.e. with the participle *doctus*, the object of the teaching is not assigned accusative case but the ablative of specification in Ciceronian Latin:

(33)   doctus Graecis litteris (Cic. *Brut.* 168)
        'trained in Greek letters'

Thus, in order to exceptionally form the passive with the person who is taught, the verb *doceo* gets rid of the argument marked by the structural accusative, that is, what is taught, to give its place to the other, i.e. the person. In this way, the person can exceptionally be assigned structural accusative case and can then be turned into the subject of the passive sentence. In order to avoid any ambiguities, the object of teaching will be assigned another inherent case, i.e. ablative. In fact, the double accusative construction was probably perceived to be intrinsically ambiguous, because of the difficulty of distinguishing the structural accusative from the inherent accusative. Therefore, it is not surprising that, in their most common use, *doceo* and *celo* assign structural accusative case to the person, while the taught/hidden thing is introduced by the preposition *de* and receives ablative case, i.e. *docere aliquem de aliqua re* 'to teach someone (about) something'.

21.3 Genitive

The genitive typically expresses a *nominal dependency*. As a consequence, the structure we will be concerned with is mainly the noun phrase, although at the end of this section we will also mention its use with adjectives and verbs.

We shall start from the head of the phrase, i.e. the noun. A distinction must first be drawn between object nouns and event nouns (cf. Section 17.2). Object nouns refer to objects and can only assign a theta-role which establishes a relationship between the referred object and something else, such as its Possessor, e.g. *arma hostium* 'the enemies' weapons'. In contrast, event nouns (cf. Latin *nomina actionis*) have a thematic structure which is similar to the one of verbs from which they are derived, e.g. *descriptio* 'description' from *describo* 'to describe'. The structure projected by event nouns shares many features with the structure projected by the corresponding verb forms. However, unlike the verbal construction, where the subject and the object are assigned two different structural cases, one single structural case is assigned within the nominal construction, i.e. the genitive.

As for event nouns then, a further sub-distinction must be drawn between *subjective* and *objective genitive*. This distinction is quite clear in English, where the relative order of subject (S), verb (V), and object (O) in the sentence parallels the relative order of subjective genitive (S), noun (N), and objective genitive (O) in the noun phrase, as shown by the examples in (34):

(34) a. the enemy   destroyed   the city
                S   V   O

      b. the enemy's   destruction   of the city
                S   N   O

      c. *the city's   destruction   of the enemy
                O   N   S

The parallelism between (34a) and (34b) is quite straightforward, in that English distinguishes between a 'subjective' genitive case, i.e. the so-called Saxon genitive, and an 'objective' genitive case, that is, the prepositional genitive. Moreover, the ungrammaticality of (34c) also shows that the assignment of subjective and objective genitive, just like the assignment of nominative and accusative case, is not random.

In contrast, Latin does not make any morphological distinction between the subjective and objective genitives. This means that the distinction between the two will be determined only by the context, as shown in (35):

(35) a. Filii parvi desiderium mei (Cic. *ad Quir.* 8)
          'The yearning of my little son for me'
      b. Laborum dei patientia (Plin. *nat.* XXXIV, 141)
          'The endurance displayed by the god in his labours'

In sentence (35a) the ambiguity is solved by a lexical property of the pronoun *mei*, i.e. the genitive of personal pronouns has an intrinsic objective value. The ambiguity of (35b) can be solved only on a semantic basis, i.e. *labor* is an inanimate noun and therefore cannot be the subject of the verb 'to endure'.

The ambiguity of Latin structures with a double genitive is the main reason why these are generally avoided by exploiting various techniques, e.g. the above-mentioned use of the genitive personal pronouns in the first and second persons, *mei, tui, nostri, vestri,* which are objective, and otherwise must be replaced by the possessive adjectives *meus, tuus, noster, vester.* In most cases, the objective genitive can be replaced by various prepositional phrases, which make its semantic value explicit, e.g. *illius metus in hostes* 'his fear of the enemies'. In other words, Latin generally opts for the use of one single genitive. Statistically, the subjective genitive tends to precede its noun, as shown by the examples in (36) with the noun *descriptio*:

(36) a. Philosophorum descriptiones (Cic. *de orat.* I 221)
      'Philosophers' descriptions'
      ('The descriptions made by philosophers')

   b. Adversariorum descriptio (Cic. *inv.* II 17)
      'The opponents' description'
      ('The description made by the opponents')

   c. Vergili descriptio (Sen. *contr.* VII 1, 27)
      'Virgil's description'
      ('The description made by Virgil')

At the same time, the objective genitive tends to be placed after the noun, as in the examples in (37):

(37) a. Descriptio aedificiorum (Cic. *leg. agr.* 40)
      'The description of the buildings'

   b. Descriptio disciplinae (Cic. *Acad. post.* I 17)
      'The description of the discipline'

   c. Descriptio siderum (Cic. *nat. deor.* II 115)
      'The description of the stars'

The hypothesis that the subjective genitive structurally precedes the objective one is also confirmed by those few cases in which a noun phrase is modified by both genitives, as in (38):

(38) a. Pro veteribus Helvetiorum iniuriis populi Romani (Caes. *Gall.* I 30, 2)
      'For the old outrages done by the Helvetii to the Roman people'

   b. Omnium exspectatio visendi Alcibiadis (Nep. VII 6, 1)
      'Everyone's desire of seeing Alcibiades'

In both (38a) and (38b) the two genitives, i.e. subjective and objective, precede and follow, respectively, the nominal head, that is *iniuriae* in (38a) and *exspectatio* in (38b). Therefore, we can claim that the elements occupy their base position in these examples, as represented in the structure shown in (39):

(39)

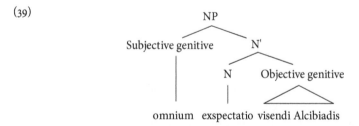

We have already seen that Latin word order is not fixed, so other orders can be derived from the above structure via movement, e.g. the head N can move leftwards, across all the other elements. This is why it possible to find a subjective genitive after a noun.

The displacement of the objective genitive to a prenominal position is a type of movement that is new to our discussion, but its explanation is quite straightforward. Note that in English it is possible to delete the subject and promote the object to the subject position, with a mechanism that is similar to passivization:

(40)   a. The city was destroyed (by the enemy)
       b. The city's destruction (by the enemy)

Just as in a passive sentence the object of the deep structure, i.e. the patient, becomes the subject, in a similar way it is possible to promote the objective genitive to the position of the Saxon genitive of an event noun phrase, with a movement that is parallel to the movement of the subject in a passive sentence. In both cases, the agentive *by*-phrase, e.g. *by the enemy*, can be optionally projected, which realizes the thematic role suppressed by the passivization.

Latin behaves similarly, in that it is possible to promote the objective genitive to the position preceding the noun, as shown in (41):

(41)   Ad artis descriptionem et praecepta tradenda (Cic. *inv.* I 9)
       'To describe the art and to transmit the rules'

In (41), the noun phrase *artis descriptio*, that we claim to be passive, is coordinated with a phrase, i.e. *praecepta tradenda*, that is clearly passive, in that it contains a gerundive. Just as some deverbal adjectives are always passive, cf. the so-called gerundives, we now make the claim that there are some deverbal nouns which can be passive as well.

This view is confirmed by the possibility of inserting a circumstantial expressing the agent, just as in a passive sentence, as shown in (42):

(42)   Alexander gratiarum actionem ab hoste supervacaneam esse respondit (Iustin. *epit.* XI 12, 11)
       'Alexander replied that thanks were unnecessary from an enemy'

In (42), the genitive which functions as the theme of *actionem* has been promoted to the passive subject position, while the agent is expressed by a *by*-phrase, i.e. *ab hoste*, in the adjunct position.

The idea of a passive construction for nouns had already hinted at by some ancient grammarians. For example, Aulus Gellius, in a famous passage, associates the different meanings of *metus hostium*, i.e. 'enemies' fear' or 'fear of the enemies', to the active or passive voice of the corresponding verb:

(43)   Metus hostium recte dicitur, et cum timent hostes et cum timentur (Gell. IX 12, 13)

'For it is correct to say *metus hostium* 'fear of the enemy' both when the enemy fear and when they are feared'

In other words, the genitive *hostium* within the noun phrase can function either as the object of an active transitive verb, i.e. *timent*, or as the subject of a passive verb, i.e. *timentur*.

We shall now consider the semantic values expressed by the genitive of object nouns. The first one is the so-called *possessive genitive*. Its English counterpart is the possessive Saxon genitive, e.g. *domus Ciceronis* 'Cicero's house'. This type of genitive is used especially with kinship nouns (the very noun 'genitive' comes from *genus* 'family') and is sometimes called 'genitive of origin', as shown by (44):

(44)   Hamilcaris filius (Liv. XXVI 20, 6)
        'Hamilcar's son'

As for word order, we have already noted that the possessive genitive can either precede the noun, i.e. *Hamilcaris filius*, or follow it, e.g. *arma hostium*. (cf. Section 18.6). This alternation was explained in the following way. In the base structure of the noun phrase, the possessive genitive which modifies object nouns is generated on the left of the noun, cf. En. *John's book*. The postnominal position of the genitive, in contrast, can be derived via leftward movement of the noun, which is optional in a language like Latin, but obligatory in a language such as Italian. This is the reason why Latin admits both *Ciceronis liber* and *liber Ciceronis*, while in Italian the only possible order is *il libro di Cicerone* (cf. **di Cicerone il libro*). Finally, English admits two orders, like Latin, but it must resort to two different structures, i.e. the Saxon genitive in prenominal position, e.g. *Cicero's book*, and a prepositional phrase in the postnominal one, e.g. *the book of Cicero*.

The genitive which modifies object nouns can also convey some special meanings:

Partitive genitive indicates the division of something into parts, i.e. it refers to a sub-set of some entity. It is assigned by expressions of quantity and numerals. English often omits the partition, as shown by examples (45) and (46):

(45)   Maxima pars vatum (Hor. Ars XXIV)
        'Most (of the) poets'

(46)   Paucae bestiarum (Liv. XXX 33, 14)
        'Few (of the) animals'

Epexegetic genitive, also called 'appositional' genitive or 'genitive of explanation': it explains a generic notion, as shown in (47):

(47)   Flos purpureus rosae (Hor. *carm.* III 15, 15)
       'The purple-coloured blossom of the rose'

Genitive of quality indicates a quality attached to somebody. The structure
of the phrase is always adjective+noun. The genitive typically indicates a
moral quality, while the ablative indicates a physical quality. For example:

(48)   Vir magni ingenii (Cic. *leg.* III 45)
       'A man of great talent'

The genitive of quality may be used as a predicate with the verb 'to be' to
designate the person who is in charge of something (this latter is expressed
by a simple infinitive or by an infinitival clause). In English, it can be
rendered with a periphrasis such as 'it is up to ...'. In fact, the Latin
expression always implies nouns such as *officium, munus* 'duty' as well.
For example:

(49)   Sapientis est consilium explicare suum (Cic. *de orat.* II 333)
       'It is up to the wise to explain his decision'

Sometimes, the person who is in charge of something is expressed by a
possessive pronoun, i.e. *meum, tuum, nostrum, vestrum est* 'it is my/your/
our duty', where expressions such as *officium* or *munus* are always implied:

(50)   Non est tuum de re publica bene mereri (Cic. *Phil.* II 36)
       'Service to the Republic is not your duty'

Finally, we should mention the use of the genitive to express structural
dependency from adjectives and verbs. As we know from the structure of
adjective phrases, the *genitive with adjectives* is used to mark the complement
of the adjectival head, as shown by example (51):

(51)   Cupidus pecuniae (Cic. *I Verr.* 3, 8)
       'Grasping after money'

Example (51) shows that the adjective *cupidus* assigns a Theme role to its
complement and marks it with the genitive case, in order to specify the extent
of the concept expressed by the adjective.

Furthermore, the *genitive with verbs* is also used as a non-prototypical
dependency mark, e.g. there are some peculiar verbs which assign the genitive
to their object, instead of the accusative, in order to express some specific
semantic values. A short list is given below:

Genitive of memory is assigned by verbs such as *memini* 'to remember' and
oblivisci 'to forget', as in examples (52) and (53):

(52)   Vivorum meminerimus (Petr. *Sat.* 43, 1)
       'Let us remember the living'

(53)   Obliviscere caedis atque incendiorum (Cic. *Catil.* 1, 6)
       'Forget the murder and arsons'

Genitive of price is assigned by two types of verbs of rating and buying:

    (a) verbs which refer to a moral value, such as *aestimo* 'to estimate', *habeor* 'to be estimated', *sum* 'to be worth'. In this case, the genitive indicates the quantity of the estimation, e.g. *magni* 'a lot', *pluris* 'more', *plurimi* 'a lot more', *tanti* 'a lot', *parvi* 'little', *quanti* 'how much', *nihili* or *pro nihilo* 'nothing' or 'not at all'. Some examples are given in (54) and (55):

    (54)   Parvi sunt foris arma, nisi est consilium domi (Cic. *off.* I 76)
           'Weapons are of little value outside if there is no wisdom at home'

    (55)   Permittite ut liceat quanti quisque velit tanti aestimet (Cic. *II Verr.* 3, 221)
           'Allow everyone to rate as much as he likes'

    (b) verbs which refer to a commercial value, such as *aestimo* 'to estimate', *emo* 'to buy', *vendo* 'to sell', *veneo* 'to be on sale', etc. These assign genitive case to indicate a generic estimation, e.g. *tanti, quanti, pluris,* or ablative case to indicate a precise estimation:

    (56)   Frumentum tanti fuit quanti Verres aestimavit (Cic. *II Verr.* 3, 194)
           'The corn cost as much as Verres had estimated'

    (57)   Emi virginem triginta minis (Plaut. *Curc.* 343)
           'I have bought a girl for thirty mina'

Genitive of charge or penalty is assigned by a special class of verbs, called verbs 'of judicial action', which express concepts such as 'to accuse' (*accuso, arguo, reum facio, insimulo*), 'to condemn' (*damno, condemno*), 'to discharge' (*absolvo*).

These verbs assign genitive case to the phrase which indicates the offence, e.g. *furti accusare* 'to charge (somebody) with theft', or the punishment, e.g. *furti damnare* 'to convict (somebody) of theft'. The same construction can be found with adjectives conveying the same meaning, such as *reus* '(the) guilty (party)', *insons* 'innocent', etc.:

    (58)   Is est reus avaritiae (Cic. *Flacc.* 7)
           'He is accused of avarice'

    (59)   Caesar repetundarum convictos ordine senatorio movit (Suet. *Iul.* 43, 1)
           'Caesar excluded the people guilty of exaction from the senatorial order'

    (60)   Hunc argenti condemnabo (Plaut. *Most.* 1098)
           'I will condemn him to pay the costs'

Genitive with 'interest' 'it matters', 'it concerns', *and 'refert'* 'it is of importance': the subject is typically a null pronoun and the person concerned is in the genitive, as shown by example (61):

    (61)   Interest Ciceronis (Cic. *Att.* XIV 6, 3)
           'It is interesting to Cicero'

The person can also be expressed by a possessive pronoun in the ablative singular feminine, i.e. *mea, tua, sua, nostra, vestra*, as shown by example (62):

(62)   Magis rei publicae interest quam mea (Liv. XXVI 31, 10)
        'It concerns the state more than myself'

According to ancient grammars, both expressions exhibit ellipsis of the phrase *in re*, e.g *interest Ciceronis (in re)* 'it matters to Cicero's business' and *interest mea (in re)* 'it matters to my business'.

The object of the interest can instead be expressed by a neuter pronoun or by an embedded sentence, either an infinitival clause or an indirect question:

(63)   Mea hoc interest (Cic. *fam.* VI 10a, 3)
        'This is of great importance to me'

(64)   Multum interest te venire (Cic. *fam.* XII 9, 2)
        'It is of great importance that you should come'

(65)   Magni refert hic quid velit (Cic. *Att.* XIV 1, 2)
        'What he wants is of great importance'

Also note that the degree of interest is expressed by adverbs in examples (64) and (65), e.g. *multum, maxime, minime, plurimum*, or by a genitive of quantity, e.g. *magni, parvi, tanti, quanti*.

21.4 Dative

Dative is an inherent case marking the following theta-roles of indirect objects: *Benefactive, Experiencer*, and *Purpose*. As the Latin name itself suggests, this case is typically assigned to the person to whom something is given (cf. Lat. *dare* 'to give'). The dative can convey various semantic nuances, which depend on the assigning verb. Therefore, it is advisable to always look up the meaning of the verb when translating, since dictionaries usually indicate the special meaning of the construction with the dative.

On the other hand, the terminology under which traditional grammars have tried to group the semantic values of the dative is less relevant. First of all, grammars typically identify the dative as the case of indirect objects, used with trivalent verbs in combination with the accusative of direct objects to denote the passage of an object from one person to another, as in example (66):

(66)   Librum tibi celeriter mittam (Cic. *Att.* XV 27, 2)
        'I will send you the book very soon'

When the dative is used to mark an adjunct, it is called of 'advantage' or 'disadvantage' if the person it denotes is involved in the event (cf. Lat. *dativus commodi* or *incommodi*), as in the example (67):

(67)   Sibi vivit (Sen. *epist.* 55, 5)
        'He lives for himself'

Both meanings are actually labelled under the same theta-role of Benefactive. Since the vast majority of values expressed by the dative depend on the assigning verb, it is now worth going through some peculiar sets of *dative with intransitive verbs*. These sets should only be used as a general reference and may be summarized as follows:

(a) verbs of occurrence, such as *fit, accidit, evenit, obtingit* 'to happen', 'to occur':

(68)   Quod cuique obtigit, id quisque teneat (Cic. *off.* I 7, 21)
       'Everyone should retain what has occured to him'

(b) verbs expressing an order (the so-called *verba imperandi*) such as *impero, praecipio* 'to order', to command'. The thematic structure of these verbs includes the addressee of the order, which is marked by the dative, and the content of the order, which is expressed by an embedded clause in the subjunctive mood introduced by the complementizers *ut/ ne* (or by an infinitive or an indirect question):

(69)   Legatis ut exirent [...] praecepit (Nep. VI 5)
       'He ordered [...] the ambassadors to leave'

(c) verbs expressing damage (the so-called *verba nocendi*), such as *noceo* 'to do harm', *obsto, obsisto* 'to stand against':

(70)   Nocentem corporibus metuemus Austrum (Hor. *carm.* II 14, 15)
       'We shall fear the south-wind that harms our bodies'

(d) verbs expressing excellence, such as *antecedo, anteeo* 'to go before', 'to precede', *antisto* 'to stand before', 'to be ahead of', *praesto* 'to stand out', 'to be superior'. The person or thing surpassed are in the dative, while the object of excellence is a simple ablative:

(71)   Crotoniatae multum omnibus corporum viribus et dignitatibus antisteterunt
       (Cic. *inv.* II 1, 2)
       'The men of Croton were ahead of everyone in strength of body and dignity'

(e) verbs expressing trust, such as *fido, confido* 'to trust', *diffido* 'to distrust'; *irascor* 'to be angry at'; *assentior* 'to agree with'; *gratulo* 'to congratulate'; *benedico* 'to speak well of' and *maledico* 'to speak ill of':

(72)   *Adsentior C. Marcello potius quam App. Claudio* (Cic. *div.* II 75)
       'I agree with Gaius Marcellus, rather than with Appius Claudius'

(f) other verbs, such as *suadeo* 'to advise' and *persuadeo* 'to convince', 'to
persuade'; *nubo* 'to marry'; *noceo* 'to do harm'; *parco* 'to spare'; *faveo* 'to
favour':

(73) An C. Trebonio ego persuasi? cui ne suadere quidem ausus essem (Cic. *Phil.* II 27)
      'Did I convince Caius Trebonius? a man whom I should not have dared even
      to advise'

Finally, note that there are some verbs whose meaning varies, depending on
the thematic structure which is projected, i.e. whether they assign accusative or
dative:

(74) a. *caveo*   + dative 'to take care of'
                       + accusative 'to beware of'
      b. *consulo*   + dative 'to take care of'
                       + accusative 'to consult'
      c. *provideo*   + dative 'to look after'
                       + accusative 'to foresee'

A second set of meanings is expressed by a type of dative which is not directly
assigned by verbs, but is rather used to mark autonomous adjuncts. The
complete typology is described below.

Dative of agency: the theta-role of Agent is typically marked by the ablative;
the dative is used with the passive perfect participle and the gerundive in
the so-called passive periphrastic conjugation:

(75) Lucanus [...] magis oratoribus quam poetis imitandus (Quint. *inst.* X 1, 90)
      'Lucan [...] is more to be imitated by orators than by poets'

Dative of possession is used to mark the possessor as Benefactive in the
construction *sum* plus dative (the most frequent expression for possession in Latin is 'this is to me', rather than 'I have this'):

(76) Suus cuique mos est (Ter. *Phorm.* 454)
      'Everyone has his own habits'

Ethical dative (*dativus ethicus*) or 'dative of feeling', cf. also the similar
dative of reference, or of 'person judging' (*dativus iudicantis*): it denotes
the person interested in the verbal process:

(77) Quid mihi Celsus agit? (Hor. *epist.* I 3, 15)
      'What is my Celsus doing?'

Dative of purpose denotes the aim of an event. It is typically used with verbs
such as *venio, mitto, relinquo*:

(78) P. Sulla auxilio cohorti venit (Caes. *civ.* III 51, 1)
      'Publius Sylla came to help the cohort'

Predicative dative or dative of result: some verbs, especially *sum* and *habeo*, assign dative case in order to express the effects or the results of an action. Many of these constructions are almost idiomatic, such as *commodo esse* 'to be beneficial', *exemplo esse* 'to be an example', *usui/utilitati esse* 'to be useful':

(79)   Exemplo debet esse omnibus (Cic. *Brut.* 242)
        'He should be an example for everyone'

Double dative: the first dative denotes the person or thing affected, the second indicates the purpose or effect. We have seen in example (78) the dative of purpose. The same structure may be used with the verb *esse*:

(80)   Libertati tempora sunt impedimento (Cic. *S. Rosc.* 9)
        'The times are an obstacle to freedom'

Finally, Latin also employs the *dative with adjectives*, which is used to mark the complement of adjectives denoting friendliness and nearness:

(81)   Tribuni nobis sunt amici (Cic. *Q. fr* I 2, 16)
        'The tribunes are friendly to us'

21.5 Ablative

Ablative is the inherent case marking the theta-roles of *Source* and *Instrument* of indirect objects, and is also used with a wide range of adjuncts. Diachronically speaking, the ablative is said to be a syncretic case, because it combines two semantic values which were originally marked by three distinct cases, i.e. the Instrumental, the Locative, and the Ablative proper, this last conveying the idea of separation (the word *ablativus* itself derives from the verb *aufero* 'to take away').

Just like the dative, the ablative can express a wide range of semantic nuances, which largely depend on the assigning verb. For this reason, it is always advisable to refer to the dictionary in order to establish the exact meaning of the ablative in a given context. As usual, we report below a short list of its most relevant uses described by traditional grammars, starting from the ablative proper, which marks the theta-role of Source.

Ablative of separation expresses the 'place whence' and is assigned by verbs such as *moveo, amoveo, removeo* 'to take away', 'to remove from'; *avoco, revoco* 'to call off'; *cedo, excedo* 'to give place to', 'to retire'; *defendo* 'to defend'; *secerno* 'to put apart'; *separo* 'to separate'; *divido* 'to divide'. As a general rule, these verbs select a simple ablative or the preposition *a, ab, e, ex, de* and the ablative. Some examples are given in (82) and (83):

(82)   Hostes defessi proelio excedebant (Caes. *Gall.* III, 4, 2)
        'The exhausted enemies retired from the fighting'

(83) Olympus […] qui Macedoniam dividit a Thracia (Hyg. *astr.* II 7)
      'Mount Olympus […] which separates Macedonia from Thrace'

Ablative of origin or source is assigned by verbs such as *nascor* 'to be born' and *orior* 'to arise', especially in their participle forms, e.g. *natus, prognatus, procreatus.* It can be either simple or accompanied by the prepositions *a, ab*:

(84) Equestri loco natus (Cic. *rep.* I 10)
      'Born in an equestrian family'

Ablative of material denotes the material of an object. It is assigned by the prepositions *ex/de* and accompanies verbs such as *facere* 'to construct', 'to build' and *fingere* 'to mould':

(85) Naves factae subito ex umida materia (Caes. *civ.* I 58, 3)
      'Ships which have been built in a hurry and of green timber'

Sometimes the ablative of material can modify a noun, while the meaning of the verb is implied:

(86) Fuit in tectis de marmore templum (Verg. *Aen.* IV 457)
      'A temple (made) of marble stood within the palace'

Ablative to express the *topic*: the topic which is being discussed is expressed by *de*+ablative. It can be found with verbs meaning 'to talk', 'to say', 'to deliberate', 'to reflect', as in example (87):

(87) Sed ego non loquor de sapientia, de impetu animi loquor (Cic. *Cael.* 76)
      'I am not talking about wisdom, but about of the force of the soul'

Ablative of comparison: comparative adjectives are often followed by the ablative, as an alternative to the *quam* 'than' construction:

(88) Lux sonitu (= quam sonitus) velocior est (Plin. *nat.* II, 142)
      'Light is faster than sound'

We shall now list the main semantic values expressed by the ablative marking the theta-role of *Instrument*.

Ablative of means or instrument: if the phrase denotes an animal or thing it is ablative; if it denotes a person it is introduced by *per*+accusative, as shown by examples (89) and (90):

(89) Ferro via facienda est (Liv. IV 28, 4)
      'Your sword must open the way'
      (lit. 'the way must be made with the sword')

(90) Statuerunt iniurias per vos ulcisci (Cic. *II Verr.* 9)
      'They decided to take vengeance against the offences through you'

The reason for this distinction is that only the nouns which are or are perceived to be not human can be assigned the Instrument theta-role, which is marked by ablative case. This is not possible with human nouns, which require an alternative periphrasis, such as *per*+accusative. This is a locative metaphor and literally means 'through somebody'. As a consequence, if the person is exceptionally perceived to be a thing, it can be assigned the theta-role of Instrument and can be marked by the ablative case, as shown by example (91):

(91)   Ea legione quam secum habebat [...] fossam perducit (Caes. *Gall.* I 8, 1)
       'With the legion which he had with him [...] he built a trench'

In (91), the legion is considered a tool in the hands of its commander, and for this reason it is assigned the Instrument theta-role.

Also consider the following special uses of the ablative of instrument:

(a) The verbs *utor* 'to use', *fruor* 'to enjoy', *potior* 'to become master of', *vescor* 'to feed' assign the ablative of instrument to their objects:

(92)   Satis recte oculis uteris (Plaut. *Epid.* 3)
       'Your eyesight is pretty normal'
       (lit. 'you use your eyes pretty correctly')

(93)   Si pace frui volumus, bellum gerendum est (Cic. *Phil.* VII 19)
       'If we want to enjoy peace, we must bear war'

(b) With the phrase *opus est* 'there is need of', 'it is necessary to', the person is dative, while the object is ablative (impersonal construction) or nominative, if it is a neuter pronoun or adjective (personal construction):

(94)   Pace brevi nobis opus est (Ov. *her.* 18, 203)
       'We need a brief reconciliation'

(95)   Quaecumque [...] opus sunt noctu comparantur (Caes. *Gall.* V 40, 6)
       'All the things [...] which are needed are prepared in the night'

(c) The adjectives *dignus* and *indignus* also assign the ablative of instrument:

(96)   Dignus es verberibus multis? (Plaut. *Mil.* 341)
       'Do you deserve many lashes?'

Ablative of agent or cause: the Agent theta-role in passive sentences is expressed by means of the adjunct *ab*+ablative, e.g. *ab amico retentus* 'detained by a friend'. This kind of *by*-phrase is admitted in Latin only if the agent is an animate noun. Otherwise, inanimate nouns are usually expressed by the ablative of instrument, e.g. *tempestate retentus* 'detained by the storm'. In addition to this, the ablative of cause can be used to mark adjuncts of active sentences in the following way:

(a) *simple ablative* denotes a cause which is internal to the subject or which can affect its physical or mental state:

(97)   Laetari bonis rebus et dolere contrariis (Cic. *Lael.* 47)
       'To rejoice at good events and to suffer at the reverse'

(b) with *prae* and the ablative, especially if it expresses an obstructing cause impeding the action:

(98)   Nec prae maerore loqui potuit (Cic. *Planc.* 99)
       'And he could not speak because of the grief'

Causal adjuncts can also be marked by other cases, assigned by special
elements, e.g. the prepositions *ob* and *propter* assign accusative case to
denote an external cause, while the ablative of *causa* and (more rarely)
gratia assign genitive case to indicate the final cause:

(99)   Si honoris causa statuam dederunt, inimici non sunt (Cic. *II Verr.* 2, 150)
       'If they gave this statue to do you honour, they are not your enemies'

The *ablative of accompaniment* marks adjuncts with a semantic value called
   sociativus. It is typically introduced by the preposition *cum*, which can be
   omitted if the phrase consists of a noun accompanied by an adjective or
   by a genitive.

(100) Cum his legatis Commius Atrebas venit (Caes. *Gall.* IV 27, 2)
       'Commius the Altrebatian came together with these ambassadors'

(101) Postero die consul omnibus copiis in aciem descendit (Liv. XXXI 36, 4).
       'The following day the consul went to the battlefield with all his army'

The *ablative of manner* is used to mark adjuncts denoting the manner of an
   action. Just like the ablative of accompaniment, the ablative of manner is
   introduced by *cum* if the phrase consists of a single noun; if this latter is
   accompanied by an adjective, the simple ablative is employed instead:

(102) Metellus saucios cum cura reficit (Sall. *Iug.* 54, 1)
       'Metellus restores the wounded with careful attention'

(103) Verum summa cura studioque conquirimus (Cic. *Acad.* I 7)
       'We seek the truth with the greatest commitment and eagerness'

The *ablative of respect or specification* denotes and delimits the conceptual
   area of the verb or noun. It is expressed by a simple ablative:

(104) Peripatetici Academique re consentientes, vocabulis differebant (Cic. *fin.* IV 5)
       'The Peripatetics and Academics agreed in substance but differed in terminology'

The *ablative of price and measurement* alternates with the genitive of price
   with verbs meaning 'to evaluate', 'to measure', 'to judge' (*aestimo, metior,
   iudico*, etc.), and more generally with expressions whose measure needs
   to be determined:

(105) Redeam ego in patriam, trecentis nummis non aestimatus civis? (Liv. XXII
       59, 18)
       'Should I return to my country as a citizen not reckoned to be worth three
       hundred coins?'

(106) Hibernia insula dimidio minor, ut existimatur, quam Britannia est (Caes.
       Gall. V 13, 2).
       'Ireland is less, as is reckoned, than Britain, by one half'

Ablative of quality: while the genitive of quality denotes a moral quality, the ablative of quality denotes a physical quality. The structure is always adjective + noun:

(107)   Agesilaus statura fuit humili (Nep. XVII 8, 1)
         'Agesilaus was of short stature'

21.6 Time and place

Inherent cases, and in particular the accusative and ablative, are also assigned to adjuncts of time and place, traditionally labelled 'circumstantials', i.e. autonomous phrases (mainly prepositional) which can be freely adjoined to a sentence to add some extra information, such as time and place.

The cases and prepositions selected by this type of phrases are summarized below:

21.6.1 Place

Place where

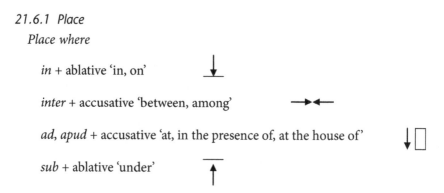

in + ablative 'in, on'

inter + accusative 'between, among'

ad, apud + accusative 'at, in the presence of, at the house of'

sub + ablative 'under'

Special uses:

- The preposition can be omitted in the phrase *locus* + adjective and all the phrases containing the adjective *totus*, e.g. *tota urbe* 'all over the city'. The ablative without preposition is also used in the expression *terra marique* 'on land and sea'.
- With *domus* and *rus* and with names of towns and of small islands of the first and second declension, the *place where* is expressed by the so-called locative case, e.g. *domi* 'at home', *ruri* 'in the country', *Romae* 'in Rome'. All the other names of towns and of small islands are expressed by the simple ablative, e.g. *Athenis* 'in Athens'.

Place to which

ad + accusative 'to(wards)'

in + accusative 'into, onto'

Special uses:

- With *domus* and *rus* and with all names of towns and of small islands the *place to which* is expressed by the simple accusative, e.g. *eo domum* 'I go home'.
- With proper nouns, *in* + accusative denotes hostility, e.g. *in Pisonem* 'against Piso'.

Place from which

a, ab + ablative 'from'

e, ex + ablative 'out of'

de + ablative 'down from'

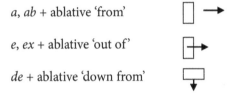

Special uses:

- With *domus* and *rus* and with all names of towns and of small islands, the *place from which* is expressed by the simple ablative, e.g. *Romā* 'from Rome'.

Place through

per, trans + accusative 'through, across'

Special uses:

- With *porta, via, flumen, vadum, pons, campus, terra, mare* the *place through* is expressed by the simple ablative. The movement through a circumscribed place is expressed by *in* + ablative.

21.6.2 Time

Time at which or within which

   (*in*) + ablative: 'on, at'

Time how long

   (*per*) + accusative: 'during'

Special uses:

- *ad* or *in* + accusative: 'until'
- *ab* or *ex* + ablative: 'since'
- (*iam*) + accusative of the ordinal: 'for'
- *abhinc* + accusative: 'how long ago'
- ablative of the ordinal followed by *quoque*: 'how often'
- simple ablative or *intra* + accusative: 'how long it takes'
- simple ablative or *post* + accusative (or ablative): 'in (how much time)'

The construction 'how much time before/after' is expressed by various phrases which include a cardinal number (X) and *ante/post*, respectively. The possible combinations are reported below:

(108) a. ante/post X annos
       b. X annis ante/post
       c. X ante/post annos (annis)

Age is expressed by the following phrases with a cardinal number (X) or an ordinal number (X+1) (this latter increased by one unit with respect to the cardinal):

(109) a. X annos (annis) natus
          'aged X years'
       b. X annorum puer (adulescens, senex)
          'child (young, old man) of X years'
       c. X annum agens
          'being in the X+1 year of one's life', that is, 'X years old'

21.7 Other prepositional adjuncts

We shall now conclude our review of adjuncts by listing the most frequent prepositions of Latin (Tables 21.1 and 21.2), along with the specification of the case they assign, i.e. either accusative or ablative. As usual, we always recommend referring to the dictionary, where all the meanings and cases assigned are reported for each preposition.

TABLE 21.1 Prepositions with the accusative

Preposition	Translation
ad	'to'
adversus	'against'
ante	'before'
apud	'at', 'at the house of'
circa/circum	'around'
contra	'against'
extra	'outside'
inter	'between'
intra	'inside'
iuxta	'near to'
ob	'for', 'because of'
per	'through'
post	'after'
praeter	'beyond', 'besides'
propter	'near', 'because of'
super	'over', 'above' (also with the ablative)
trans	'across', 'to the farther side of'
ultra	'beyond'
versus	'towards'

TABLE 21.2 Prepositions with the ablative

Preposition	Translation
a, ab	'from'
coram	'in the presence of'
cum	'with'
de	'down from'
e, ex	'out of'
prae	'in front of', 'because of'
pro	'in front of', 'on behalf of'
sine	'without'
sub	'under' (also with the accusative)

As already mentioned above, the preposition *in* may be used with the ablative and the accusative in order to express different meanings of time and place (cf. Section 21.6).

22

The compound sentence: coordination

22.1 Coordination and subordination

The syntactic phenomena reviewed so far all belong to the domain of the simple sentence, that is, a sentence containing only one predicate and its arguments. Now that we know the properties of simple sentences, we can turn to the analysis of more complex structures, i.e. compound sentences. The different components of a compound sentence are called 'clauses'. While a simple sentence consists of a single clause, a compound sentence consists of two or more clauses.

There are two ways to combine clauses to form a compound sentence, called coordination and subordination.

Coordination is the easiest procedure and is widely exploited by children, less-educated people, and writers who want to recur to a more colloquial register. In a coordinated structure, the single clauses are independent units placed one after the other and optionally linked by conjunctions.

From a stylistic point of view, a distinction is made between explicit coordination, i.e. clauses combined by conjunctions, e.g. *veni et vidi et vici* 'I came and I saw and I conquered', and implicit coordination, i.e. without conjunctions, e.g. *veni vidi vici* 'I came, I saw, I conquered'. This latter type of coordination is also known as asyndeton, which in Greek means 'without conjunction'. The Greek term 'parataxis' is employed to refer to coordination and subordination without conjunctions, e.g. *volo facias* vs. *volo ut facias* 'I want you to do'.

22.2 Conjunctions

Coordination is a very simple but also very powerful mechanism to create compound syntactic structures. The coordinator is called a 'conjunction' and joins two phrases of the same category together, creating a new complex phrase of the same category. For example, the conjunction *et* 'and' can combine two noun phrases (*mater et pater*), two verb phrases (*venit et vidit*), or two sentences (*Marius dormit et Terentius ambulat*). The phrase marker of a conjunction phrase is shown in (1):

(1)

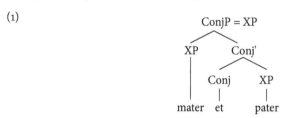

The head of the phrase is the conjunction (Conj), which takes the first conjunct as its specifier and the second conjunct as its complement. The two conjuncts must be two phrases of the same category (XP). Conjunction phrases belong to the same category too, i.e. a ConjP like *pater et mater* combines two noun phrases and is a noun phrase itself.

In terms of linear order, the head obligatorily precedes the complement, in most Latin conjunction phrases, just as in English, e.g. **mater pater et* is ungrammatical, as is the English corresponding form **mother father and*. However, just as with noun and verb phrases, we expect to find some traces of the reverse order in Latin, whereby the complement precedes the head. This is true for the enclitic conjunctions -*que* 'and' and -*ve* 'or', whose structure is shown in (2):

(2)

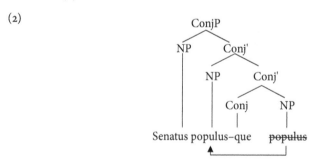

Similarly to noun and verb phrases, we can suppose that the base order of conjunction phrases is head before complement, and that the reverse order is derived via movement.

22.3 Copulative conjunctions

Copulative elements have the logical value of a conjunction connective and can be used to combine both clauses and noun phrases. Copulative conjunctions are divided into two categories, i.e. affirmative and negative.

(a) Affirmative copulative conjunctions:

   et 'and': the most common type of conjunction. It can be used to connect two or more noun phrases or two clauses which belong to the same level.

   -que 'and': used to connect two noun phrases that have a strong internal connection and form a single concept, or which behave like the two opposite ends of a pole, e.g. *senatus populusque Romanus* 'the senate and people of Rome'; *terra marique* 'on land and sea'.

   atque (*ac*) 'and indeed', 'and also': endows the second term with an augmentative value and puts emphasis on it. It can also be reinforced by the following expressions: *atque adeo* 'and in fact', *ac potius* 'and rather'.

   etiam 'even', 'and furthermore': puts emphasis on the second term. It can be reinforced in the following way: *etiam atque etiam* 'again and again'.

   quoque 'also', 'too': places the two terms on the same level. It can be rendered as 'in the same way'.

(b) Negative copulative conjunctions:

   et non (*ac non*) 'and not': used to negate just one of the two terms, in order to contrast two concepts.

   neque (*nec*): means 'and not', just like *et non*, but is used to negate a whole sentence. Note that two negative conjunctions neutralize each other, e.g. *nec non* means 'and also'.

   nedum: intensifies the negation, meaning 'by no means', 'not to speak of'.

Negative copulative conjunctions also frequently occur with pronouns, for example:

   nec quisquam, nec ullus: 'and nobody'.

   ne ... quidem 'not even' (the word which is negated is placed between *ne* and *quidem*).

(c) Correlatives

Both affirmative and negative conjunctions can be used correlatively. A short list of the possible combinations is given below:

   et ... et: 'both ... and'

   tum ... tum: 'at one time ... at another'

   cum ... tum: 'as ... so'

   modo ... modo: 'now ... now'

   neque ... neque: 'neither ... nor'

   non modo ... sed etiam 'not only ... but also'

Also note that while English typically prefers a single connective, Latin has a strong tendency to emphasize antithetical relations and thus often recurs to correlative connectives.

22.4 Disjunctive conjunctions

Disjunctive coordination is based on elements which have the logical value of a disjunction connective. Latin is very precise in the distinction of the various semantic values of this type of coordination.

aut 'or': denotes absolute exclusion.

vel 'or': connects two similar elements, implying a choice between the alternatives, which can also both be present.

-ve: means 'or' in a weaker sense; it denotes an irrelevant difference.

sive (seu): means 'or if' and connects two different aspects of the same concept.

Disjunctive conjunctions can also be used correlatively, as shown below:

aut ... aut 'either ... or': denotes opposite and mutually exclusive alternatives.

vel ... vel 'either ... or': denotes two alternatives which are not mutually exclusive.

sive ... sive 'if ... or if': denotes two alternatives with no certainty about the true one.

22.5 Adversative, causal, and illative conjunctions

Adversative conjunctions introduce a clause whose meaning is in contrast with the preceding one. As usual, Latin can exploit a wide range of terms to express various semantic nuances.

sed 'but': this is the most common adversative conjunction.

at 'but': denotes a stronger contraposition, e.g. 'on the contrary'.

verum and *vero* 'but': denote a weaker contraposition, e.g. 'in fact'.

autem (postposed) 'but on the other hand', 'however': denotes a less precise distinction.

tamen 'yet', 'nevertheless': usually appears in sentence-initial position.

Causal conjunctions connect two clauses which belong to a wider reasoning and introduce a new point.

nam 'for', 'in fact': clause-initial.

enim 'for', 'in fact': identical to *nam* but is placed in second position.

namque, etenim 'for indeed': these are the stronger corresponding forms of *nam* and *enim*.

Illative conjunctions introduce the logical conclusion of an argument, i.e. the sentence which summarizes and concludes the preceding reasoning.

ergo 'therefore', 'accordingly': denotes the logical conclusion par excellence and is endowed with a peculiar argumentative strength.

igitur 'therefore', 'accordingly': introduces the conclusion in a weaker and more generic way.

itaque 'and so', 'accordingly': is more narrative and introduces a natural consequence.

proinde 'therefore': expresses a volitional nuance and introduces an order or a desire.

23

The complex sentence: embedded clauses

23.1 Complementizers

We shall now turn our attention to the structure of subordinate or embedded clauses, which is one of the most interesting areas of Latin syntax. Unlike English and many other modern languages, literary Latin has a strong preference for subordination rather than coordination. Instead of a linear sequence of clauses, variously connected by conjunctions or punctuation marks, Latin typically exhibits highly articulated hierarchical structures consisting of one main clause and one or more embedded ones.

In terms of phrase structure, the sentence is hierarchically superior to the clause, which is in turn hierarchically superior to the phrase. This implies that the internal structure of the sentence can be represented by a phrase marker which is very similar to the one we employed for the analysis of phrases and simple clauses, and this constitutes a very desirable state of affairs. As we shall see below, all syntactic structures, from the smallest phrase to the most complex sentence, exhibit the same properties. More technically, it will be shown that all syntactic structures are recursive.

We can now proceed with the analysis of the subordinate clause. As usual, we will start from the identification of the head of this syntactic construction. If clauses can be embedded, we must assume the existence of something which is hierarchically superior. Traditional grammars use the expression 'subordinate particles' to refer to the elements which introduce subordinate clauses, while formal linguistics employs the term 'complementizers'.

The complementizer is the functional head determining the type of embedded clause. In other words, the complementizer (C) is the head which takes the clause as its complement. As usual, the combination of the head and its complement forms an intermediate constituent (C'). By adding a specifier, whose features we shall discuss below, we obtain the maximal projection CP, i.e. the *complementizer phrase*.

Consider the following example taken from Catullus (*carm.* 66, 48): *ut Chalybon omne genus pereat* '(I wish) that all the race of the Chalybes would perish'. Its structure is given in (1):

(1)

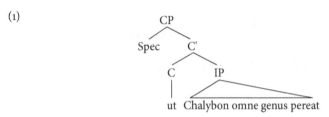

ut Chalybon omne genus pereat

The triangle indicates that the structure dominated by the IP, that is a simple clause, i.e. *Chalybon omne genus pereat*, has not been analysed, for the sake of simplicity. We have already analysed the structure of the IP in Chapter 19. In (1), it is made up of a subject and a verbal predicate. In this chapter, we want to focus our attention on the structure *above* the IP, that is the CP.

The head of this structure is the complementizer *ut*, which takes the IP as its complement. This explains why the type of embedded clause depends on the complementizer, e.g. the complementizer *ut* typically introduces a final or consecutive clause, *quia* introduces a causal clause, *dum* a temporal clause, and so on.

One interesting detail of the analysis in (1) is that it implies the presence of a CP in all clauses, i.e. both embedded and main ones. This can be accounted for by saying that the head and the specifier of the CP of main clauses are usually empty. This is the reason why in Chapter 19 we have not projected a CP node over the IP in main clauses which form simple sentences.

Note that the importance of projecting a number of positions above the IP level in simple sentences as well lies in the fact that these can host different particles which can be inserted in order to modify the sentence in some specific ways, e.g. to turn it into an exclamation-exhortative sentence like the one above, or into an interrogative sentence such as *an ut pro huius peccatis ego supplicium sufferam?* 'Am I to be punished because of his sins?' (Ter. *Andr.* 888):

(2)

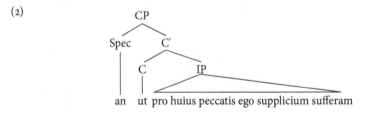

an   ut pro huius peccatis ego supplicium sufferam

In this example, we have also inserted a particle in the specifier of the CP. But in most cases, the complementizer stands alone. There are also a number of cases, in Latin as in English, in which the exclamatory interpretation is obtained without any complementizer.

For this reason, it is possible to think that every IP is located inside a CP layer, which relates the clause to the speaker's attitude, even without the use of overt complementizers. The CP layer is the area where the informational structure of the clause is codified, and may therefore be identified with the area that we called the left periphery in Section 19.8.

To sum up, we claim that every clause has a tripartite structure. The inner layer is the VP, which represents the lexical and semantic relations between the verb and its arguments. The second layer is the IP, which locates the predication in the speech time and is associated with the notion of subject. The third layer is the CP we have introduced in this section. It includes not only the complementizers, but also such notions as illocutionary force (i.e whether the clause is declarative, exclamative, etc.), negation, focus, and topic.

23.2 Main clauses and embedded clauses

We shall now describe the most important use of the complementizer, i.e. introducing embedded clauses. A sentence like *ut veniat!* 'let him come!' can be analysed as a main exclamatory clause. This very same clause can also be embedded, as in (3):

(3)   Patrem orato ut veniat (Plaut. *Asin.* 740)
      'Ask my father to come'

Example (3) is a compound sentence consisting of a main clause, i.e. *patrem orato* 'ask my father', and an embedded one, i.e. *ut veniat* 'to come'. On a superficial level of analysis, it may seem that the two clauses are simply coordinated. One may argue that the two clauses are autonomous sentences placed one after the other, e.g. 'ask my father: come!'. In contrast, a relationship of subordination exists between the two in which the particle *ut* is the complementizer. Consider example (4):

(4)   Pompeius suis praedixerat, ut Caesaris impetum exciperent (Caes. *civ.* III 92, 2)
      'Pompeius had previously ordered his men to await Caesar's attack'

The first step of our syntactic analysis is the identification of two adjacent clauses, i.e. one which is affirmative and one which is exclamatory-exhortative. The structure of the two clauses can be represented as in (5) (for the sake of the present discussion, we shall skip the representation of the original base position of the subject and the object):

(5)

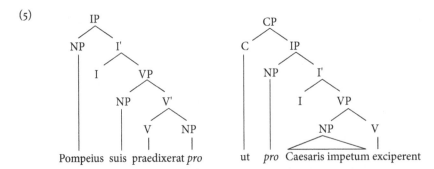

The object of the clause *Pompeius suis praedixerat*, i.e. the thing being asked, is represented by a null pronoun. Similarly, the subject of *ut Caesaris impetum exciperent* is a also null pronoun, which refers to Pompey's soldiers. This is a paratactic analysis, whereby the two clauses are simply placed one after the other. This is probably the historical origin of subordination, too, i.e. there may have been a progressive development in the literary Latin tradition whereby a shift took place from a predominantly coordinating phase to a predominantly subordinating one. In what follows, we shall describe this process in terms of phrase structure.

If there is a relationship of subordination between the two clauses of example (5), this means that they are not simply juxtaposed but are rather embedded one into the other to form a single structure. More precisely, the CP of the embedded clause is inserted in the phrase structure of the main clause. The structure of the compound sentence can be represented as in (6):

(6)

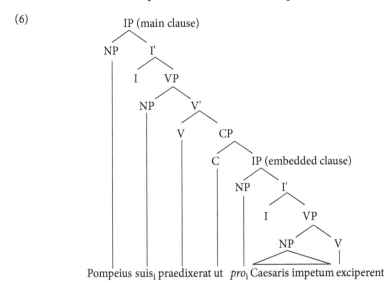

The structure in (6) shows that the sentence contains two IP nodes, i.e. it contains two clauses: the main one and the embedded one. The notion of subordination or embedding is represented by the fact that the main clause is placed above the subordinate clause, which in turn occupies a lower position within the phrase marker.

The internal structure of the IP of the two clauses is identical to the one of simple independent sentences, which we have already described. Each IP contains an NP subject and an intermediate projection I', which in turn contains the inflectional information of the verb (I) and the verb phrase (VP). Finally, this latter contains the verbal head (V) and its complements.

The crucial point for the present discussion is the position of the phrase hosting the complementizer, i.e. the CP. In the structure in (6), the CP is the complement of the VP of the main clause. The embedded clause occupies exactly the same structural position as an NP direct object. This is shown by the fact that the verb *praedico*, for example, can select a NP direct object as well, e.g. *pauca praedixero* 'I will have said a few things before' (Tac. *dial.* 28, 3).

The parallelism between the structural position of the direct object and of the embedded clause is clear also in examples (7) and (8):

(7)   Adulescens petit pecuniam (Quint. *decl. min.* 245, 3)
      'The young man claimed the money'

(8)   Varenus petit ut sibi quoque evocare testes liceret (Plin. *epist.* V 20, 2)
      'Varenus asked that he too should be allowed to summon witnesses'

We can understand why this type of subordinate clause is traditionally called 'substantive', i.e. precisely because it occupies the same position as a noun (substantive), cf. *pecuniam* in example (7).

23.3 Substantive clauses with *ut, quod, quin*

A sentence such as *senatus decrevit ut consules rem divinam facerent* 'the senate decreed that the consuls should perform a sacrifice' (Liv. XXXI 5, 2) contains an embedded clause, whose structure can be analysed along the lines depicted in the previous paragraph:

(9)

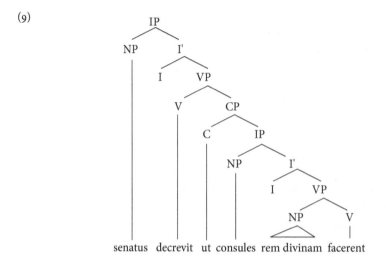

senatus   decrevit   ut   consules   rem divinam   facerent

Substantive clauses in Latin can be introduced by three complementizers, i.e. *ut* (as in example (9)), *quod*, and *quin*, while English mainly resorts to the complementizer *that*.

23.3.1 Ut

The embedded clause is in the subjunctive mood. Embedded clauses introduced by the complementizer *ut* can be divided into two categories, i.e. 'result clauses' (the negation is *ut non*) and 'volitive clauses' (the negation is *ne*).

(a) result clauses: these are mainly selected by the following verbs:
   verbs meaning 'to happen', e.g. *fit ut...*, *accidit ut...* 'it happens that...';
   verbs expressing the result of an action: *facio ut...* 'to make something happen'; *committo ut...* 'to allow'; *oportet ut...* 'it is advisable that...';
   sum with a neuter noun or adjective, e.g. *mos est ut...* 'it is customary that...'; *reliquum est ut...* 'it remains that...'.

(b) volitive clauses: these are mainly selected by the following verbs:
   verbs meaning 'to want', 'to plead', and 'to order', e.g. *velim ut...* 'to wish that...'; *oro ut...* 'to plead that...'; *impero ut...* 'to command that...';
   verba timendi (verbs expressing fear), e.g. *timeo ne...* 'to fear that...'; *vereor ne...* 'to be afraid that...'.

Note that *verba timendi* select *ne* to express something the speaker hopes will *not* happen, e.g. *metuo ne...* 'to fear that...', that is, 'I hope that it is not going to happen', otherwise they select *ut* if the speaker hopes that something will happen, i.e. *metuo ut*...'to fear that...not', that is, 'I hope that it is going to happen'.

23.3.2 Quod

The embedded clause is in the indicative mood. The complementizer *quod* is called declarative (it can be rendered as 'that' or sometimes as 'the fact that', 'as for the fact that'). It is mainly employed to introduce embedded clauses selected by the following verbs:

verbs meaning 'to add' and 'to omit', e.g. *accedit quod*...'adding that...'; *mitto quod*...'to omit that...';
verbs meaning 'to praise' and 'to blame', e.g. *laudo quod*...'to praise for...'; *reprehendo quod*...'to blame for...';
verba affectum (verbs expressing feelings), e.g. *laetor quod*...'to be glad that...'; *doleo quod*...'to suffer (from the fact) that...';
judgements about an action, e.g. *bene fit quod*...'it is good that...'.

23.3.3 Quin

The embedded clause is in the subjunctive mood. Embedded clauses introduced by the complementizer *quin* are selected only by main verbs with a negative meaning, such as the following:

non dubito quin...'not to doubt that...';
verba impediendi et recusandi (verbs meaning 'to prevent' or 'to reject') in the negative form, e.g. *non impedio quin*...'not to prevent someone. from...'; *nihil obstat quin*...'nothing prevents someone/something from...' (in this case the complementizer *quominus* can be employed as well).

23.4 Sequence of tenses *(consecutio temporum)*

We have seen that the mood of the embedded clause depends on the type of complementizer, i.e. *quod* selects the indicative and *ut* and *quin* select the subjunctive. Tense, on the other hand, is determined by the relation to the main clause, in accordance with patterns of contemporaneity, anteriority, or posteriority. The sequence of tenses which is established between the main clause and the embedded one (for those sentences which require an embedded subjunctive), known as *consecutio temporum*, is one of the most important chapters of Latin syntax.

TABLE 23.1 *Consecutio temporum* (subjunctive clauses)

	Contemporary embedded clause	Anterior embedded clause	Posterior embedded clause
Main clause Primary tense	**present**	**perfect**	**future participle with present of** *sum*
e.g. *non dubito* 'I do not doubt'	*quin veniat* 'that he is coming'	*quin venerit* 'that he has come / he came'	*quin venturus sit* 'that he will come'
Main clause Historic tense	**imperfect**	**pluperfect**	**future participle with imperfect of** *sum*
e.g. *non dubitabam* 'I did not doubt'	*quin veniret* 'that he was coming'	*quin venisset* 'that he had come'	*quin venturus esset* 'that he would come'

The mechanism of *consecutio temporum* is summarized in Table 23.1. Firstly, a distinction must be made between two categories of tense in main clauses, i.e. primary tenses and historic tenses. The primary tenses of Latin are the present and the future, while the historic tenses are the perfect, the imperfect, and the pluperfect.

Secondly, the relationship between the main and embedded clause follows three possible patterns, i.e. contemporaneity, anteriority, and posteriority.

The translations show that the *consecutio temporum* is not peculiar to Latin syntax, but also has its parallel forms in English.

24

Interrogative clauses

24.1 Interrogative intonation

A simple sentence can receive an interrogative interpretation by virtue of a specific intonation, which is orthographically rendered by a question mark. In other words, intonation is sometimes sufficient to endow a sentence with an interrogative interpretation, especially in the spoken language, both in Latin and in English, as shown by example (1):

(1)   Tu, verbero, imperium meum contempsisti? (Plaut. *Asin.* 416)
      'You, scoundrel, disdained my order?'

In example (1), a simple question mark, which we may suppose to indicate the action of an abstract operator in the CP area, is sufficient to distinguish the interrogative sentence from its declarative counterpart.

As a general rule, however, the interrogative interpretation is usually expressed by some specific grammatical phenomena other than intonation. In this chapter, we will consider a particular type of clause, i.e. interrogatives, which are characterized by the presence of a CP and by a special type of movement, which will be described shortly.

24.2 Yes-no questions

Interrogative sentences can be divided into two classes, depending on the type of expected answer, i.e. the so-called yes-no questions, whose expected answer is either 'yes' or 'no', and the so-called *wh*-questions, whose expected answer is a whole phrase.

Yes-no questions can be further divided into two classes, characterized by a different semantic value. The first class consists of 'rhetorical questions', that is, questions posed by a speaker who already knows the answer or wants to suggest it. In particular, if the expected answer is positive, Latin employs the interrogative particle *nonne* 'is it not the case that…?'; if it is negative it employs *num* or *an* 'can it be said that…?'. These particles occupy the position of specifier of the CP. As an example, we show in (2) the analysis of the following rhetorical question: *num quia ius civile didicerat?* 'maybe because he had learned law?' (Cic. *de orat.* III 135).

(2)

```
                    CP
                   /  \
              Spec      C'
               |       /  \
               |      C    IP
               |      |    /\
            num quia ius civile didicerat
```

The second class of yes-no questions consists of proper, non-rhetorical questions which are employed when the answer is not already known by the speaker. Many languages achieve this type of interpretation via syntactic movement, whose peculiarities vary cross-linguistically.

For example, English resorts to the systematic anteposition of the auxiliary before the subject, e.g. *John will invite Mary / will John invite Mary?* This type of syntactic movement exhibits some peculiar features in Latin, as shown by examples (3) and (4):

(3) Ego eam sententiam dixi (Cic. *fam.* X 16, 1)
     'I expressed this opinion'

(4) Dixine ego istaec? (Plaut. *Cist.* 295)
     'Did I say these things?'

These examples show that the interrogative sentence differs from the declarative one not only because of the syntactic movement of the verb, but also because of the presence of a clitic element, i.e. the enclitic interrogative particle -*ne*, which attracts the moved element. In other words, the enclitic particle -*ne* occupies the position of the complementizer and attracts a lexical head, which is usually the verb, which gets attached to the clitic, as shown in (5):

(5)

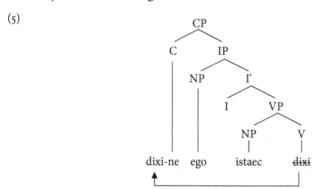

The base position of the verb is signalled by a trace, i.e. ~~dixi~~, while the landing site is marked by the enclitic particle *-ne*, to which the verb gets attached, i.e. *dixine*.

In most examples, the element which is moved and attached to the clitic is the verb. The high frequency of use of such forms explains the fusion and the phonological erosion of the verb and the clitic, which is particularly common with some forms of the second person singular, e.g. *ais-ne* becomes *ain* 'do you say?'; *vides-ne* becomes *viden* 'do you see?'. At the same time, if a sentence contains a nominal predicate, the displaced element is usually the copula, e.g. *est-ne haec patera?* 'is this the bowl?' (Plaut. *Amph.* 780).

It is also possible, albeit less frequent, that the moved element is another lexical head, such as the subject, e.g. *ego-ne istuc dixi?* 'Did I say this?' (Plaut. *Amph.* 747), the object, e.g. *vos-ne senes mirer?* 'Should I admire you, elders?' (Ov. *met* III 538), or an adjunct, e.g. *recte-ne interpretor sententiam tuam?* 'Do I understand your opinion correctly? (Cic. *Tusc.* III 37). In this way, the moved elements achieve a particular emphasis, confirming the fact that not only complementizers but also focus effects typically take place in the CP area.

We shall now conclude this section with an additional note. The reader may have observed that while the particles *num* and *nonne* are placed in the specifier of the CP, the particle *-ne* occupies the head position of the same projection. This fact is not surprising, in that the two types of question have a different interpretation. Nonetheless, there is another argument in favour of this structural analysis. This analysis predicts that while rhetorical questions could admit a complementizer, this is not possible with genuine yes-no questions, whose C position is already occupied by the interrogative particle. This prediction is borne out by the data, i.e. while the former type of question allows the insertion of a complementizer such as *quia* (cf. example (2), *num quia ius civile didicerat*), the latter type is incompatible with complementizers, e.g. **dixine quia ego istaec?*

24.3 *Wh*-questions

The second type of interrogative sentence is represented by the so-called *wh*-questions. When the speaker needs some specific information, a peculiar strategy is adopted which does not involve the simple insertion of interrogative particles, such as *num, nonne,* or *-ne*, but rather the *substitution* and *movement* of phrases. This implies that each interrogative sentence must be associated with two distinct levels of representation, which are connected by an operation of substitution and movement, just like passive sentences.

The constituent which is unknown to the speaker is substituted by an interrogative phrase. Interrogative phrases in Indo-European languages are characterized by the presence of an interrogative word, either a pronoun, adjective, or adverb, whose root originally contained a labiovelar stop. For example, Latin interrogative phrases begin with *qu-*, e.g. *quis, qui, qualis, quantus, quot* (originally also *cur, uter,* and *ubi* contained a labiovelar), while in English they begin with *wh-* (which is also the result of the evolution of an original labiovelar stop), hence the name '*wh*-phrases', which is employed in modern linguistics.

The *wh*-phrase substitutes the unknown phrase and is then displaced to a sentence-initial position, in the specifier of CP. Consider example (6):

(6)   Quid is dicit? (Cic. Q. Rosc. 42)
      'What does he say?'

Assume that the starting point for the interpretation of this sentence is the deep structure of the corresponding declarative sentence containing the answer to the question, i.e. *is hoc dicit* 'he says this' (Gell. X 16, 2). In order to form the corresponding interrogative sentence, the unknown constituent, i.e. *hoc*, must be replaced by the interrogative pronoun *quid*, which is assigned the same theta-role and the same case—accusative—by the verb *dicere* as the replaced element, i.e. *hoc*. Finally, an instance of *wh*-movement takes place, whereby the element bearing the *wh*-feature, i.e. *quid* in our example, is displaced to the specifier of the CP, which is endowed with a *wh*-feature. The resulting structure is represented in (7):

(7)

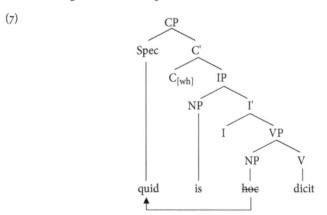

This analysis captures the peculiar logical value of the interrogative pronoun, which replaces the unknown element but, above all, also performs the function of a logical operator, in that it identifies the domain in which the specific value will be determined. The logical form of example (7) can be represented as in (8):

(8)   For which element x is it true that he has done *x*?

The logical value of the interrogative explains why the displacement of *x* in a sentence-initial position is necessary.

Another advantage of the above analysis is that case-assignment can be explained straightforwardly. The interrogative pronoun bears the same case as the one assigned by the verb to the trace of the unknown constituent, i.e. ~~hoc~~. This can be explained by saying that the pronoun *quid* in (7) has inherited the accusative case assigned by the verb *dico* to the pronoun *hoc*, which occupies the object position.

In contrast, in a question such as *quis hoc fecit?* 'who did that?' (Cic. *II Verr.* 3, 168), the interrogative pronoun *quis* inherits nominative case from its trace. This case is assigned by the finite inflection of the verb *facere* to its subject *is*, as shown in (9):

(9)

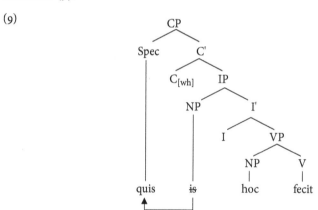

The structure of an interrogative sentence can be more complex. There are some cases in which the interrogative pronoun does not replace a whole constituent, as in the above examples, but only its specifier, before undergoing the usual movement. Consider example (10):

(10)   Quem tu parasitum quaeris? (Plaut. *Men.* 285)
       'What sponger are you looking for?'

As in the previous examples, the underlying structure of example (10) is that of the sentence containing the answer to the question, i.e. *tu illum parasitum quaeris*. However, the unknown element is now only the demonstrative *illum*, and not the whole phrase *illum parasitum*, because we know that the interlocutor is looking for a sponger, but we do not know its qualities. As a consequence, *illum* is replaced by the interrogative pronoun *quem*, while *parasitum* remains in its base position. Finally, the interrogative pronoun moves to a sentence-initial position, in the usual way:

(11)

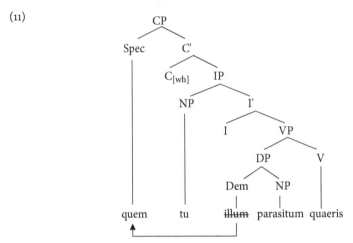

The interrogative pronoun *quem* in this case is replacing only the demonstrative of the object noun phrase, before being displaced to the specifier of the CP.

24.4 Indirect questions

In Section 24.3, we saw that one the main features of interrogative sentences is the presence of a CP. We also know that the main function of the CP is to allow the embedding of one clause into another.

This means that an interrogative sentence, which inherently contains a CP node, can be easily embedded in a matrix clause, that is, the clause which dominates and selects the embedded one. More precisely, this is possible when the main clause contains a verb such as 'ask', 'understand', 'doubt', etc. The verb *intellego* 'to understand', for example, can select a so-called indirect question, e.g. *illi intellegunt quid Epicurus dicat* 'they can understand what Epicurius says' (Cic. *fin.* II 4, 13), which has the structure in (12):

(12)

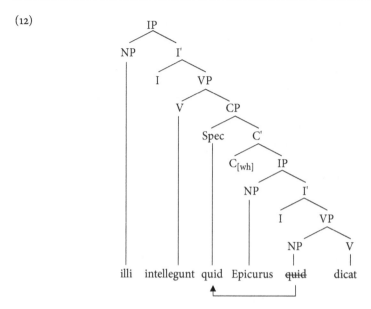

In the structure in (12), the CP of the embedded interrogative clause occupies the position of the direct object of the main VP, whose V is *intellegunt*. The structure of a complex sentence containing an indirect question is thus the same as the structure of a sentence containing an embedded clause introduced by a complementizer such as *ut* (cf. Section 23.3). Indirect questions exhibit a subjunctive verb and obey the *consecutio temporum* (cf. Table 24.1).

TABLE 24.1 *Consecutio temporum* (indirect questions)

	Contemporary embedded clause	Anterior embedded clause	Posterior embedded clause
Main clause Primary tense	**present**	**perfect**	**future participle with present of** *sum*
e.g. *nescio* 'I don't know'	*quid agat* 'what he is doing'	*quid egerit* 'what he has done / did'	*quid acturus sit* 'what he will do'
Main clause Historic tense	**imperfect**	**pluperfect**	**future participle with imperfect of** *sum*
e.g. *nesciebam* 'I didn't know'	*quid ageret* 'what he was doing'	*quid egisset* 'what he had done'	*quid acturus esset* 'what he would do'

Table 24.1 is almost identical to the one presented in Section 23.4 for substantive sentences introduced by *ut, ne*, and *quin* (cf. Table 23.1).

The analogy between substantive clauses introduced by *ut* and indirect questions is further confirmed by the fact that some verbs, such as *video*, can select either an indirect question, e.g. *vide quid postulet* 'see how much he asks for' (Ter. *Heaut.* 871), or a substantive clause such as *vide ut sis fortior* 'make sure that you are braver' (Sen. *contr.* X 2, 16).

Also note that indirect questions can be either *wh*-questions, introduced by a *wh*-element, as in the above examples, or yes-no questions, introduced by particles such as *num, nonne*, or *-ne*, as in examples (13) and (14):

(13)   Animadverte rectene hanc sententiam interpreter (Cic. *fin.* II 20)
       'Notice whether I understand this maxim correctly'

(14)   Nescires utrum inter decemviros an inter candidatos numerares (Liv. III 35, 3)
       'One would not have known whether to count him among the decemvirs or the candidates'

Example (14) contains an example of a 'disjunctive interrogative', where the first element is introduced by *-ne* or *utrum*, while the second one is introduced by *an* and expresses an alternative option to the first element.

Relative clauses

25.1 Movement of relative pronouns

Relative clauses have a structure similar to interrogative clauses. They are introduced by the relative pronoun *qui*, by relative indefinite pronouns such as *quisquis* and *quicumque*, or by relative interrogative pronouns such as *qualis* and *quantus*. These relative elements have a morphological structure similar to interrogative elements, as they are introduced by the same labiovelar root *qu-*. Therefore, it is assumed that they belong to the same category of *wh*-elements.

However, the analogy between these two types of structure, i.e. relative and interrogative clauses, is in fact related to the presence of *wh*-movement. The relative pronoun, just like the interrogative one, replaces a phrase and moves to the specifier of the CP, leaving a trace in its base position. Just like the interrogative pronoun, it also inherits case from its trace, i.e. the element it replaces.

There are two main differences between relatives and interrogatives. The first is that a relative clause cannot stand alone as a simple sentence but must always be embedded in a matrix clause, unlike interrogatives.

The second difference is that a relative clause and an interrogative clause stand in a different relation to the matrix clause. While the latter (an indirect question) occupies the object position of the matrix verb, the former (a relative clause) occupies the position of adjunct of a noun phrase of the matrix clause. This means that relative clauses occupy the same position as adjectives, i.e. adjuncts of a nominal phrase. For this reason, traditional grammars often label them as adjective clauses.

We shall now analyse the phrase marker of a compound sentence containing a relative clause. The matrix clause will contain a noun phrase consisting of a head and an adjunct. We shall call the head of this noun phrase the 'antecedent' of the relative pronoun. It is commonly held that the relative pronoun refers to its antecedent, that is the two are co-referential, which means that they refer to the same person or thing. Consider, for example, sentence (1):

(1)   Germani, qui trans Rhenum incolunt, in Helvetiorum fines transierunt (Caes. *Gall.* I 28, 4)
'The Germans, that live across the Rhine, crossed the Helvetian borders'

The subject of the main clause is the noun phrase *Germani qui trans Rhenum incolunt*. The relative clause occupies the position of adjunct of the head *Germani*, as shown in (2):

(2)

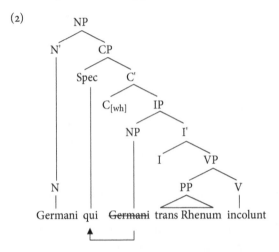

The structure in (2) shows that the CP of the relative clause typically occupies an adjectival position, as shown by the fact that the relative clause *qui trans Rhenum incolunt* could be easily substituted by an adjective such as *Transrhenanus*, giving rise to the NP *Germani Transrhenani* 'the Germans living across the Rhine'.

The relative pronoun bears the same meaning and case as its trace (*Germani*). It moves from the subject position of the embedded clause, i.e. the specifier of the IP, to the position of introductory element of the embedded clause, i.e. the specifier of CP, as shown by the arrow.

In example (2), the movement of the relative pronoun can be observed only in the phrase marker, as no other element intervenes between the moved element and its trace. However, there are many cases in which such a movement becomes 'visible', since the relative pronoun has to cross over some other elements during its displacement. In sentence (3), for example, the relative pronoun has been extracted from the object position:

(3)   Germani [$_{CP}$ quos [$_{IP}$ Romani ~~Germanos~~ timent]] fortissimi sunt

'The Germans, whom the Romans fear, are the strongest'

In this case the relative pronoun *quos*, which inherits accusative case from its trace in the direct object position, has to cross the subject *Romani* on its way to the specifier of the CP. The crossing of the subject also takes place when the relative pronoun is extracted from the position of indirect object:

(4)   Germani [$_{CP}$ quibus [$_{IP}$ Romani ~~Germanis~~ laudem tribuunt]] fortissimi sunt

'The Germans, for whom the Romans reserve their praise, are the strongest'

In this case, too, the relative pronoun *quibus*, which inherits dative case from its trace, crosses the subject *Romani* on its way to the specifier of the CP.

It should also be pointed out that the antecendent of the relative pronoun is not necessarily the head of the subject NP of the matrix clause, such as *Germani* in the above examples, but it can also be the head of the object NP:

(5)   Germanos [$_{CP}$ qui [$_{IP}$ ~~Germani~~ trans Rhenum incolunt]] primus Caesar vicit

'Caesar was the first to defeat the Germans that live across the Rhine'

Otherwise, the antecedent can be any other NP in the matrix clause, as shown by example (6):

(6)   Belgae proximi sunt Germanis [$_{CP}$ qui [$_{IP}$ ~~Germani~~ trans Rhenum incolunt]]

'The Belgians are the closest to the Germans, who live across the Rhine'

The relative pronoun is the link between the main and the embedded clause. It agrees in gender and number with its antecedent in the main clause, but inherits case from its trace in the embedded clause.

This means that there is a structural tension in the relative pronoun between agreement with the antecedent and case inherited from the trace. Such a tension can exceptionally result in a phenomenon of 'attraction', which may follow two directions. If the relative pronoun, contrary to the common rule, also agrees in case with its antecedent, a phenomenon of 'direct attraction' of the relative is invoked. In this case, the agreement with the antecedent is extended from gender and number only to include case, as shown by example (7):

(7)   In his libris quibus (= quos) dixi (Gell. X 23, 2)
      'In those books which I have mentioned'

In example (7), the trace of the relative pronoun is the object of the verb *dixi*. Consequently, we expect the relative pronoun to bear accusative case. However, as a consequence of the phenomenon of attraction, the pronoun receives dative case from its antecedent *libris* instead.

A more rare option is the so-called 'inverse attraction', which takes place when the antecedent agrees in case with the relative pronoun, as shown by example (8):

(8)   In navi non erat Naucratem (= Naucrates) quem convenire volui (Plaut. *Amph.* 1009)
       'Naucrates, whom I wanted to meet, was not on the ship'

In example (8), the antecedent is the subject of the matrix clause, i.e. *in navi non erat Naucrates*. However, its case, which should accordingly be nominative, is attracted by the case of the relative pronoun, i.e. the accusative *quem*, whose trace is the object of the verb *convenire*. In other words, the subject *Naucratem* exceptionally gets accusative case as a consequence of the inverse attraction of the relative.

25.2 Free relative clauses

After discussing the structure of relative clauses, we can now consider those cases in which the relative pronoun seems to lack an antecendent, i.e. the so-called 'free' relative clauses. Although they are introduced by a relative pronoun, it seems that these sentences are not adjoined to a noun phrase, as shown by example (9):

(9)   Deum colit qui novit (Sen. *epist.* 95, 47)
       'God is worshipped by those who know Him'

In example (9), the relative *qui novit*, lit. 'who knows', seems to be the postverbal subject of *Deum colit*, lit. '(he) worships God'. If this analysis were correct, we should reject the description of relative clauses in terms of their peculiar kind of adjunction to the main clause, that is as adjective clauses. But clearly the correct analysis must be another one. The subject position of the main clause *Deum colit* is already occupied by an understood element, i.e. a null subject: (*is*) *colit*, or more precisely [pro *colit*].

If this analysis is correct, we can now understand the correct structure of the whole sentence *Deum colit qui novit*. If the relative clause is always an adjective clause, it follows that in example (9) it will occupy the adjunct position of the null subject. Indeed, if the subject position is occupied—and therefore a substantive clause is banned—the adjunct position is free and can host the relative clause, as shown in (10):

(10)   Deum colit (is) qui novit

Note that in the English translation 'God is worshipped by those who know Him', the subject is expressed by the pronoun *those*, as English does not admit null subjects.

Therefore, we can conclude that relative clauses always perform the function of nominal adjuncts, i.e. they are true adjective clauses and cannot perform the function of subject or object.

Free relative clauses are typically used with a null pronoun when the antecedent and the relative bear the same case, e.g. instead of *is qui* only *qui* is employed. On the other hand, if the antecedent and the relative bear a different case, the antecedent is usually expressed by a demonstrative pronoun, i.e. *is*, which is called 'correlative'. However, there are many exceptions to this rule and grammars often mention cases of implicit correlatives, as in (11):

(11)   Xerxes praemium proposuit (ei), qui invenisset novam voluptatem (Cic. *Tusc.* V 20)
       'Xerses offered a reward to anyone who would discover a new pleasure'

The translation shows that in English it is not possible to omit the antecedent, i.e. **to who* instead of *to anyone who*, while the demonstrative pronoun *ei* can be replaced by a null pronoun in Latin.

Finally, note that relative pronouns differ from demonstrative pronouns with respect to two properties. Firstly, relative pronouns do not have a deictic function, that is, identifying a referent in the extralinguistic context, but rather an anaphoric one, that is, referring to a linguistic antecedent. Secondly, given that demonstrative pronouns too can have an anaphoric function, the peculiar feature of relative pronouns is that they function as embedding elements, just like complementizers, but such that they always identify the adjunct of a noun phrase.

25.3 Pseudo-relatives and the relative nexus

We shall now briefly introduce a syntactic structure which is similar to the relative clause and is traditionally known as a 'pseudo-relative'.

A pseudo-relative clause is a stylistic means which is very common in historiographical prose and is used to create the effect of an embedding relation between two sentences which are in fact independent and simply juxtaposed, as shown by example (12):

(12)   Helvetii legatos de deditione ad eum miserunt. Qui, cum eum in itinere convenissent, [...] paruerunt (Caes. *Gall.* I 27, 1)
       'The Helvetii sent ambassadors to him to surrender. And these, after meeting him on the march, obeyed'

The relative pronoun *qui*, which introduces the second sentence, after the full stop, performs the same anaphoric function as a demonstrative preceded by a conjunction, i.e. *et ii* (also shown by the translation 'and these'). For this reason, traditional grammars interpret the relative pronoun *qui* in example (12) as a 'relative nexus', which is equivalent to *et ii*, that is a coordinating conjunction followed by a demonstrative pronoun.

The reason why the relative nexus is preferred to the combination of a conjunction and a demonstrative is that the presence of a relative pronoun gives the idea of an embedded structure, which is usually preferred in the literary style, as it is perceived to be more refined than simple coordination.

25.4 'Improper' or adverbial relative clauses

We have already seen that relatives are adjective clauses in that they describe an inherent feature of the element they modify. Relative clauses typically exhibit the indicative mood.

However, relative clauses can exceptionally be used as adverbial clauses, whose different semantic values will be described in Chapter 28 (cf. final or purpose, consecutive or result, temporal, causal, conditional, and concessive). In this case, relative clauses typically exhibit a verb in the subjunctive mood.

We will now describe an example of a relative clause with a purpose meaning. Consider sentence (13):

(13)   Romulus legatos circa vicinas gentes misit, qui (= ut ii) societatem conubiumque novo populo peterent (Liv. I 9, 2)
'Romulus sent ambassadors round among the neighbouring nations in order to ask for an alliance and the privilege of intermarrying for the new people'

Note that in the English translation it is preferable to replace this type of relative clause with the corresponding adverbial clause (in this case 'in order to ask for' and not 'which should ask for').

Finally, it is important to bear in mind that the use of the subjunctive is not sufficient to identify this peculiar meaning of the relative clause. In Latin, it may be the case that the verb of an embedded clause (and in particular of a relative) switches from indicative to subjunctive if the higher verb is subjunctive or infinitive. This phenomenon is known as 'attraction of mood' or *perseveratio modorum* (also known as 'subjunctive by attraction'). This is due to the fact that the indicative, which is the objective mood, is not appropriate in an embedded context. Consider example (14):

(14)   Accidit, ut nonnulli milites, qui lignationis munitionisque causa in silvas discessissent, repentino equitum adventu interciperentur (Caes. *Gall.* V 39, 2)
'It happened that some soldiers, who had gone into the woods to get timber for entrenching, were cut off by the sudden arrival of the horsemen'

In this case the relative clause *qui...discessissent* exhibits a subjunctive verb because it depends on a subjunctive embedded clause, i.e. *ut...interciperentur*, so the indicative mood of the relative is attracted to the subjunctive. Also note that in example (14) the attracted subjunctive is 'distinctive', whereas in other contexts it is often of the 'oblique' type, because it is used to express the thought of someone other than the speaker.

26

Infinitival clauses

26.1 Accusative and infinitive (*accusativus cum infinitivo*)

Case theory (cf. Section 20.2) predicts that nominative is the case assigned by the finite inflection of the verb to the subject NP. As a consequence, if the verb is non-finite, it is not able to assign nominative case to its subject. This is the reason why the subject of infinitival clauses exhibits accusative rather than nominative case.

We now have to identify the structural configuration which allows the assignment of accusative case to the subject of an infinitive, and the element responsible for this. As a starting point, consider the analysis of a simple infinitival sentence:

(1) Fateor eam esse importunam (Plaut. *Asin.* 62)
     'I believe her to be harsh'

If we translate this structure into Italian, the infinitival clause must be replaced by a finite embedded clause introduced by the complementizer *che* 'that':

(2) a. *Confesso lei essere insopportabile (It.)
     b. Confesso che lei è insopportabile (It.)

This is due to the fact that infinitival clauses with an explicit subject are quite rare in Italian, where they are restricted to only some verbs of perception, e.g. *ho visto due persone fuggire* 'I saw two people running away'. In English, in contrast, it is possible to translate example (2b) by using an infinitival clause with an accusative subject:

(3) I believe [her to be harsh]

However, English also differs from Latin. Although the use of an infinitival embedded clause is admitted with a transitive verb such as *to believe*, this very same construction is banned with deverbal nouns, such as *belief*, and with passive or impersonal verbs, such as *it was believed*:

(4) a. *The belief [her to be harsh]
     b. *It was believed [her to be harsh]

Conversely, Latin easily permits the replacement of a transitive verb with a deverbal noun and a copula, e.g. *rumor erat* can replace *dicebant* and select an infinitival clause:

(5) [Rem te valde bene gessisse] rumor erat (Cic. *fam.* I 8, 7)
     'It was rumored that you had handled the matter very well'

Moreover, the infinitival clause in Latin can also be selected by a passive or impersonal verb, as in example (6):

(6) Traditum est [etiam Homerum caecum fuisse] (Cic. *Tusc.* V 39, 114)
     'It is said that even Homer was blind'

The above translations show that English has to replace the Latin infinitival clause with a finite *that*-clause.

On the basis of the different syntactic behaviour of Latin and English, we can formulate the following hypothesis about the assignment of accusative case to the subject of an infinitival clause. In English, the subject of the infinitival clause is assigned accusative case by the higher verb. Accordingly, this has to be a transitive verb. In generative grammar, this phenomenon is known as 'Exceptional Case Marking'. In Latin, in contrast, the subject of the infinitival clause is assigned accusative case in an autonomous way, within the very same infinitival clause. This explains why there are no restrictions on the transitivity of the higher verb in Latin.

If the above analysis is correct, it naturally follows that the element responsible for the assignment of accusative case to the subject of Latin infinitival clauses is an abstract complementizer, which performs the same function as the English complementizer *for* in sentences such as (7):

(7) a. [$_{CP}$ For [$_{IP}$ him to invite Mary]] would be stupid
     b. It is important [$_{CP}$ for [$_{IP}$ customers to read the instructions carefully]]

In the examples in (7), *for* is both a preposition assigning accusative case (witness the fact that the correct form is *for him* and not *for he) and a complementizer, similar to *that*, although while the latter introduces a finite clause, the former introduces an infinitival one.

In this sense, it is reasonable to claim that the structure of Latin infinitival clauses is similar to the structure of the other substantive clauses that we have already described in Section 23.3. These are introduced by various complementizers. Those introduced by *quod* typically exhibit an indicative verb; those introduced by *ut, ne, quin, quominus* typically exhibit a subjunctive one:

(8) a. gaudeo [$_{CP}$ quod [$_{IP}$ ille venit]]
     b. impero [$_{CP}$ ut [$_{IP}$ ille veniat]]

Infinitival clauses, which have exactly the same value as substantive clauses, are also introduced by a special complementizer, i.e. an abstract complementizer which selects an infinitival verb and assigns accusative case to the subject of the infinitival clause, just like English *for*. This abstract complementizer is a phonologically null element and will be graphically represented as $\emptyset_C$:

(9)   dico [CP $\emptyset_C$ [IP illum venire]]

The phrase marker of a sentence such a *Hermagoras dixit procuratorem clamare* 'Hermagoras said that the agent was shouting' (Sen. *contr.* VII 5, 15) is as shown in (10):

(10)

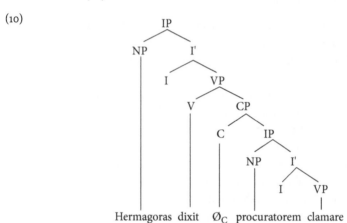

Just like other substantive clauses, the infinitival clause occupies the object position of the matrix verb. However, in this kind of structure the subject receives accusative case from the null complementizer and not from the matrix verb.

Null complementizers are quite common cross-linguistically. Both in Italian and in English, for example, the explicit complementizers *che* and *that* can alternate with null complementizers, as shown by examples (11) and (12):

(11)   a. credo [CP che [IP sia bene]] (It.)
           'I think that it is good'
        b. credo [CP $\emptyset_C$ [IP sia bene]] (It.)
           'I think it is good'

(12)   a. he said [CP that [IP he would go]] (En.)
        b. he said [CP $\emptyset_C$ [IP he would go]] (En.)

Latin as well allows the omission of the complementizer *ut* in subjunctive embedded clauses selected by verbs such as *impero, oro, volo*, as shown in (13):

(13) a. volo [$_{CP}$ ut [$_{IP}$ veniat]]
          'I want him to come'
          (lit. 'I want that he comes')

      b. volo [$_{CP}$ Ø$_C$ [$_{IP}$ veniat]]
          'I want him to come'
          (lit. 'I want he comes')

Now the questions arise as to why there is no explicit counterpart to the null complementizer which introduces infinitival clauses, and why this is allowed only in Latin. The answer lies in the different morphological properties of the infinitive in Latin and in English, as we shall see in Section 26.2.

26.2 Sequence of tenses in infinitival clauses

In contrast to English, the Latin infinitive can morphologically express the whole tense sequence of present/past/future, both in the active and the passive voice (cf. Sections 14.6.8 and 14.7.7) (Table 26.1).

These morphological properties of the Latin infinitive are systematically organized in the syntax in order to express an anterior/contemporary/posterior relationship between the selecting clause and the infinitival one, in a parallel fashion to the organization of the tenses of the subjunctive in finite embedded clauses (cf. *consecutio temporum* in Section 23.4).

The sentences in (14) to (16) exemplify the use of the three tenses of the active infinitive of *laudare* in order to express an event which is contemporary, anterior, and posterior with respect to the main clause:

(14) Voluntatem se laudare Maharbalis ait (Liv. XXII 51, 3)
      'He said he praised Maharbal's goodwill'

(15) Laudavisse hasce ait architectonem (Plaut. *Most.* 760)
      'He says some architect had praised that (house)'

(16) Noluisti facere: laudaturum me putas? (Sen. *contr.* IX 4, 15)
      'You did not want to do it: do you think I am going to praise you?'

TABLE 26.1 Tenses of the infinitive

Voice	Tense	Example
Active	Present	laudare
	Perfect	laudavisse
	Future	laudatur-um (-am, -um; -os, -as, -a) esse
Passive	Present	laudari
	Perfect	laudat-um (-am, -um; -os, -as, a) esse
	Future	laudatum iri

The sequence of tenses in infinitival clauses is summarized in Table 26.2 (cf. Table 23.1 for the *consecutio temporum* of the subjunctive).

If the verb lacks the supine (and therefore the future infinitive), the periphrasis with the future infinitive of 'to be' is used instead, i.e. *fore ut* + subjunctive. This very same periphrasis is also used instead of the passive and (sometimes) active future infinitive if the speaker wants to emphasize the idea of something happening.

Note that the main difference between the sequence of tenses with the subjunctive and with the infinitive is that, unlike subjunctive embedded clauses, infinitival embedded clauses are not affected by the fact that the higher clause displaces a primary tense or a historic one, in that the only kind of relationship which is expressed is contemporaneity (present infinitive), anteriority (perfect infinitive), and posteriority (future infinitive).

When we described the structure of the complementizer phrase (CP), we noted that there is a strong relationship between the complementizer (C) and the embedded clause (IP). This implies that the complementizer must be compatible with the inflection of the verb. This is the reason why, for example, it is impossible to combine the complementizer *ut* with an indicative embedded clause, e.g. **impero ut ille venit*.

As a consequence, it is reasonable to argue that the null complementizer $\emptyset_C$ is only compatible with an infinitive whose inflection can exhaustively express a present, past, or future temporal relationship.

TABLE 26.2 *Consecutio temporum* (infinitival clauses)

	Contemporary embedded clause	Anterior embedded clause	Posterior embedded clause
Main clause Primary tense	**present**	**perfect**	**future**
e.g. *dico* 'I say'	*te venire* 'that you are coming'	*te venisse* 'that you have come / you came'	*te venturum esse* 'that you will come'
Main clause Historic tense	**present**	**perfect**	**future**
e.g. *dicebam* 'I said'	*te venire* 'that you were coming'	*te venisse* 'that you had come'	*te venturum esse* 'that you would come'

This explains why the Latin null complementizer is banned from languages such as English or Italian, where the only attested infinitive is present (in both languages the past infinitive is periphrastic and mainly conveys an aspectual meaning, while the future infinitive does not exist). In other words, the null complementizer is incompatible with the inflection of the infinitive of such languages, as this is not able to morphologically express the complete sequence of present, past, and future exhaustively.

This analysis also explains why, in the development from Latin to Romance, infinitival clauses gradually disappeared and were replaced by finite embedded clauses, such as those introduced by *quod* (from which It. *che*, Fr. *que*, Sp. *que*, etc. are derived). This was due to an impoverishment of the temporal paradigm of the infinitive. In particular, the perfect infinitive was lost at a very early stage, gradually affecting the whole system of infinitival inflection.

26.3 Simple infinitive

In the previous sections we have reviewed the use of embedded infinitives with an accusative subject, that is, the so-called 'accusative and infinitive' (*accusativus cum infinitivo*). This is the most common use of infinitival clauses in Latin. Nevertheless, there also exist cases of subject-less infinitives which traditional grammars call simple infinitives. In fact, we will see that these structures also exhibit a subject, albeit a special non-lexical one.

We shall start with the so-called 'nominal use' of the infinitive. A nominalized infinitive can be used as a proper NP and can occupy the subject or predicate position of the clause, as shown by example (17):

(17) Ridiculum est currere ad mortem tedio vitae (Sen. *epist.* 24, 22)
      'It is silly to run towards death because you are tired of life'

This kind of structures raise an interesting issue, i.e. the verb *currere* 'to run', despite its nominalization, retains the need to assign its thematic role to the subject. Therefore, it is reasonable to claim that a nominalized infinitive also has its own null subject, that we shall call PRO, as shown in (18):

(18) ridiculum est [$_{NP}$ PRO currere]

The main difference between 'big pro' (PRO) and 'little pro' (pro) is semantic. We have already seen that little pro is nothing but a personal pronoun which is used as the understood subject of finite clauses, e.g. in It. [pro *parlo*] 'I speak' pro means 'I', while in [pro *parliamo*] 'we speak' pro means 'we'. In more technical terms, little pro is able to find a referent in the linguistic context (an antecedent) or in the extralinguistic context (a given person or thing). On the other hand, PRO is not able to refer to a precise person or thing, e.g. in Lat.

[PRO *currere*] it is not possible to identify a specific referent, such as 'I' or 'you'. Whenever there is no linguistic antecedent, PRO can only receive an arbitrary interpretation. This means that the subject of *currere* in example (18) can be any individual which is arbitrarily chosen. In Section 26.4 we shall consider different examples in which PRO refers to a linguistic antecedent.

26.4 Control sentences

The so-called 'control sentences' consist of a control verb selecting a simple infinitive, as shown in example (19):

(19)   Galli obsides Caesari dare intermiserant (Caes. *Gall.* IV 31, 1)
       'The Gauls had stopped giving hostages to Caesar'

The matrix clause *Galli intermiserant* introduces an embedded clause, i.e. *obsides Caesari dare*, which looks like an *accusativus cum infinitivo*, with the exception that the subject is silent. This is due to the fact that the infinitive *dare* assigns the theta-role Theme to *obsides*, the Benefactive to *Caesari* and the Agent to PRO, which is a null element. This means that the subject position of the embedded clause must be filled by PRO, as shown by the structure in (20):

(20)   [$_{IP}$ PRO obsides Caesari dare]

In (20), PRO does not have an arbitrary interpretation. Instead, its referent is a linguistic antecedent placed in the main clause in (19), e.g. *Galli*, as shown by the indexes in (21):

(21)   Galli$_i$ intermiserant [PRO$_i$ obsides Caesari dare]

In this case, PRO is said to be controlled by its semantic antecedent, that is the controller, e.g. *Galli* in example (21). This type of infinitive is therefore considered a 'control' infinitive.

   One important feature of this kind of structure is that PRO inherits from its controller not only its semantic referent but also its gender, number, and case. This is particularly clear whenever PRO is the subject of a nominal predicate. If the controller is the subject of the selecting clause, then PRO receives nominative case, as shown by example (22):

(22)   ego$_i$ volo [PRO$_i$ esse bonus]
       'I want to be good'

On the other hand, if the controller is the object of the selecting clause, PRO will receive accusative case:

(23)   iubeo te_i [PRO_i esse bonum]
      'I order you to be good'

Another important feature of this kind of structure is that no tense variation is admitted, i.e. the infinitive must always be inflected for present tense. For example, it is possible to say *iubeo te esse bonum* but not **iubeo te fuisse bonum* or **iubeo te futurum esse bonum*.

To sum up, the *accusativus cum infinitivo* always has a lexical subject (which is assigned accusative by the abstract complementizer $\emptyset_C$) and admits tense variation on the infinitive. On the other hand, control infinitives have a null subject, i.e. PRO, which is not directly assigned case but inherits it from its controller, and do not admit any tense variation on the infinitive.

The choice between an *accusativus cum infinitivo* and a control infinitive depends on the lexical properties of the selecting verb and is always encoded in dictionaries, which report whether a verb admits an *accusativus cum infinitivo*, a simple infinitive, or both constructions.

We shall now consider some additional examples, which show again the necessity to resort to a non-linear analysis in order to understand linguistic structures. Consider the sentences in (24), which are apparently similar:

(24)   a. dicunt me venire
        'They say that I am coming'

      b. hortantur me venire
        'They order me to come'

On a superficial level of analysis, both sentences consist of the linear sequence verb+accusative+infinitive. However, the hierarchical structure of these two sentences is radically different.

First of all, consider the lexical properties of the selecting verbs, i.e. *dico* and *hortor*. These two verbs have a different thematic structure. The verb *dico* assigns the theta-role Agent to the null subject (pro) and the Theme to what is being said, i.e. the infinitival clause *me venire*. In contrast, the verb *hortor* assigns the Agent to the null subject (pro), the nominal Theme to the individual who is being exhorted, i.e. *me*, and the clausal Theme to the action, i.e. the infinitive *venire*.

This analysis implies that *me* will occupy a different position in the two clauses. In (24a), the pronoun occupies the subject position of the infinitival clause with accusative subject, as shown in (25):

(25)   dicunt [$\emptyset_C$ me venire]

In contrast, in example (24b) the pronoun *me* occupies the object position of the matrix verb and functions as controller of the infinitival clause:

(26)   hortantur me_i [PRO_i venire]

This difference between the two structures in (25) and (26) is responsible for the different properties of the two infinitival clauses in (24a–b). In the first case, i.e. an *accusativus cum infinitivo* in (24a), the tense of the infinitive can be modified:

(27) a. dicunt me venire (present)
      b. dicunt me venisse (perfect)
      c. dicunt me venturum esse (future)

In contrast, in the second example, i.e. a control structure (24b), PRO does not allow any tense variation on the infinitive, i.e. the infinitive of a control structure only can be present, while the perfect and the future are excluded:

(28) a. hortantur me venire
      b. *hortantur me venisse
      c. *hortantur me venturum esse

Note that the difference between *dicunt me venire* and *hortantur me venire* can only be captured by a structural analysis, which also allows us to predict the different behaviour of these apparently identical sequences of words.

This discussion has also shown the importance of resorting to abstract elements such as the null complementizer $\emptyset_C$ and the null subject PRO, which give grammar more explicative power. In conclusion, the use of underlying abstract forms is necessary to account for the concrete grammatical relations that we can observe.

26.5 Raising structures (*nominativus cum infinitivo*)

In this section we shall describe the last type of infinitival clause, which shares some properties both with the *accusativus cum infinitivo* and with control structures.

Its name, 'raising structure', comes from the fact that the subject of the embedded clause is raised to the subject position of the main clause. This implies that the subject of this infinitival bears nominative case. For this reason, this structure is traditionally called 'nominative with infinitive' (*nominativus cum infinitivo*).

The starting point of our analysis is again the structure of the verb heading the main clause. In order to select a raising structure, the verb has to be passive and it has to belong to a specific category of raising verbs.

In Latin, the most important raising verb is *videor* 'to seem', which is the passive of *video* 'to see'. Consider example (29):

(29) Flamma videtur ardere (Plin. *nat.* XXXVII 189)
      'The flame seems to burn'

As usual, we will start our analysis by looking at the thematic grid of the selecting verb. The verb *video* means 'to see' and assigns the theta-role Experiencer to the subject and the Theme to the action. For example, in a sentence such as *video flammam ardere* 'I see the flame burning', the subject is a null pronoun, i.e. pro, and the object is an *accusativus cum infinitivo*, i.e. *flammam ardere*:

(30)   [$_{NP}$ pro] video [$_{CP}$ Ø$_C$ [$_{IP}$ flammam ardere]]

We have already seen that, in this case, the null complementizer Ø$_C$ is required to assign accusative case to the subject of the infinitive, i.e. *flammam*.

    Consider now the passive *videor*. We know that a passive sentence does not contain the subject of the corresponding active sentence. This is due to the fact that a passive verb, in this case *videor*, absorbs the subject theta-role, which means that the subject position remains empty in the deep structure, as shown in (31):

(31)   [$_{NP}$ e] videtur [$_{IP}$ flamma ardere]

This structural configuration contains an empty position which can be assigned nominative case. Therefore, the subject of the infinitive, i.e. *flamma*, which cannot be assigned nominative case by the non-finite inflection of *ardere*, can receive nominative case by leaving its base position and raising to the subject position of *videtur*, as shown in (32):

(32)

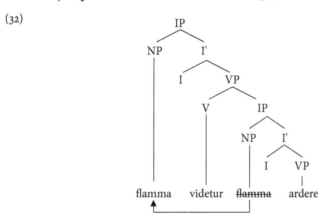

Just like a passive sentence, e.g. *flamma videtur* 'the flame is seen', this structure contains a raised element which has the same landing site, i.e. the subject position. The difference lies in its base position. In a simple passive sentence, the raised element is the object, e.g. *flamma videtur* 'the flame is seen'. In a structure with an infinitival embedded clause, in contrast, the raised element is the subject of the infinitival clause, i.e. *flamma videtur ardere*. The trigger of the movement is the same, i.e. the need to find a case-marked position. In addition, the landing site coincides, i.e. the empty subject position of the passive verb.

This analysis captures the similarities and differences between passives and infinitival raising structures in an economical way, and it also accounts for the fact that the final result of a raising structure is an infinitive with a nominative subject. Although this result may sound parodoxical, in that a non-finite inflection is not able to assign nominative case, this structure is not exceptional, in that the subject is not assigned nominative case by the infinitive but by the passive verb in the matrix sentence, where the subject of the infinitive is displaced.

This analysis also explains why—in addition to raising structures, which represent the so-called 'personal constructions' of *videor*—another 'impersonal' construction exists, with no raising, in which the subject of the infinitive bears accusative case. This is again linked to the semantic properties of the verb heading the sentence. In addition to its first meaning, i.e. 'to seem', the verb *videor*—accompanied or not by a neuter adjective such as *utile, iustum,* etc.—can acquire a meaning such as 'it seems convenient', which is associated with a different theta-grid. This latter does not contain an empty subject position, in that *videor* in this case behaves like an impersonal verb, whose subject position is obligatorily filled by a null pronoun, i.e. pro. The only empty position is, in fact, a clausal theme, that is, an embedded infinitival clause expressing the thing which it is convenient to do. Therefore, the verb *videor* inflected for the third person singular can be accompanied by a control structure or by an *accusativus cum infinitivo*, but not by a raising structure:

(33)   Mihi est visum de senectute aliquid ad te conscribere (Cic. *sen.* 1)
       'It seemed to me appropriate to write something on old age for you'

(34)   Tibi videtur utile esse nos colloqui (Cic. *fam.* IV 1, 2)
       'It seems advantageous to you that we should talk'

This very same analysis also applies to the other copulative verbs inflected for the passive, which we discussed when we described the double nominative (cf. Section 21.1). Some of them can also be used with the nominative and the infinitive, i.e. they admit a raising structure.

The first group includes the so-called *verba iubendi*, that is verbs meaning 'to order', 'to allow', 'to forbid', etc. When they are passive, e.g. *iubeor, prohibeor, vetor,* etc., they become raising verbs, i.e. they select an infinitive with a nominative subject, as shown by example (35):

(35)   Otacilius cum classe proficisci iussus est (Liv. XXIV 11, 7)
       'Otacilius was ordered to depart with his fleet'

The second group includes the so-called *verba narrandi*, that is narrative verbs such as *dico, trado, puto,* etc. We have already seen in Section 26.1 that, when these verbs are active, they select an *accusativus cum infinitivo*. When they are passive, by contrast, they admit the same two possibilities as *videor.* The personal option, i.e. the raising structure, such as En. *John is said to be good,* is preferred with the present, as shown by example (36):

(36) Homerus fuisse ante hanc urbem conditam traditur (Cic., *Tusc.* V 7)
      'Homer is said to have lived before the foundation of Rome'

The impersonal option, in contrast, i.e. a third person singular neuter verb selecting an *accusativus cum infinitivo,* is preferred with perfect forms, as shown by example (6) in Section 26.1, repeated here as (37):

(37) Traditum est etiam Homerum caecum fuisse (Cic. *Tusc.* V 39, 114)
      'It is said that even Homer was blind'

We shall now conclude this section with a cross-linguistic observation. It may be argued that the empty subject position that we have posited in the above examples for Latin verbs such *videor* is rather ad hoc. However, there is a strong empirical argument in favour of this empty subject position coming from verbs which correspond to *videor* in non-null-subject languages, such as English, i.e. *to seem,* and French, i.e. *sembler.* Unlike *videor,* English and French verbs typically select a finite embedded clause introduced by an overt complementizer, i.e. En. *that* and Fr. *que.* In such a configuration, no raising is required, in that the subject of the finite embedded clause is directly assigned nominative case by the finite inflection of the embedded verb. However, in English and French the subject position of 'to seem' is also empty in this case, and—crucially—has to be filled by an expletive, i.e. En. *it,* Fr. *il.,* as shown by the examples in (38):

(38) a. It seems that John has arrived (En.)
      b. Il semble que Jean est arrivé (Fr.)

These verbs can also select a non-finite clause. In this case, the subject of the embedded infinitive is raised to the empty subject position of the matrix clause, just as in Latin:

(39) a. John seems to have arrived (En.)
      b. Jean semble être arrivé (Fr.)

This comparative analysis provides strong arguments in favour of the existence of abstract syntactic elements, such as null subjects in Latin. Abstract concepts represent a necessary component of a formal grammar, provided that their existence is rigorously constrained.

27

Participial clauses

27.1 Syntactic uses of the participle

Broadly speaking, the participle is a verbal adjective, in that it exhibits both adjectival and verbal behaviour. In particular, it expresses prototypical verbal information, i.e. tense (present, perfect, and future), but—at the same time—has an adjectival type of inflection expressing gender, number, and case.

The verb *laudo*, for example, has three participle forms, which express three different tenses, i.e. the present participle (*laudans*), which is inflected like a second class adjective, and the past (*laudatus, -a, -um*) and future (*laudaturus, -a, -um*) participles, which are inflected like first class adjectives.

There are four possible syntactic uses of the participle. In the first two, the adjectival nature of the participle prevails, whereas in the last two it is its verbal nature that predominates. In the following sections, each of these uses will be described.

27.2 Attributive participle

Consider first the purely adjectival use of the participle, which traditional grammars call 'attributive'. In this case, the participle simply behaves like an attribute, i.e. an adjective, as shown by example (1):

(1)   Praetor aequus et sapiens dimitti iubet senatum (Cic. *II Verr.* 4, 146)
      'Our fair and wise governor orders to dissolve the senate'

In this case, the present participle of *sapere*, i.e. *sapiens*, lit. 'knowing', that is, 'wise', is on the same level as the adjective *aequus* 'fair' and simply behaves like an adjectival adjunct of the head of the noun phrase *praetor*.

This kind of participle can be attached to any noun phrase. In example (1), the participle is attached to subject noun phrase, i.e. *praetor*, but it can equally modify an object noun phrase, as shown by example (2):

(2)   Adice incertos oculos, gradum errantem (Sen. *epist.* 83, 21)
      'Besides the unsteady eyes, the hesitating step'

In this case, too, it is clear that the object noun phrase modified by an adjective, i.e. *incertos oculos*, is equivalent to the one modified by a participle, i.e. *gradum errantem*.

27.3 Predicative participle

The second adjectival use of the participle is traditionally called 'predicative'. This term underlies the analogy between this kind of participle and the predicative complement described in Section 19.4.

The predicative complement is a small clause which combines a noun phrase and an adjective phrase, or two noun phrases, establishing between the two the same predicative relation as the one holding between a subject and a nominal predicate. Consider example (3):

(3)   Hannibal princeps in proelium ibat (Liv. XXI 4, 8)
      'Hannibal was the first to enter battle'

In example (3), the phrase *Hannibal princeps* is not simply a noun phrase consisting of a noun and an adjective. If this were the case, its meaning should be 'the first Hannibal'. Instead, the correct meaning is 'Hannibal (was) the first'. This implies that there must exist a predicative relationship within the phrase *Hannibal princeps*, such as the one which is expressed by the sentence 'Hannibal was the first'. In other words, *Hannibal princeps* must be a small clause, that is, a pure predicative nucleus, which can be analysed as in (4):

(4)

$$
\begin{array}{c}
\text{SC} \\
\diagup\diagdown \\
\text{NP} \quad \text{AP} \\
| \qquad | \\
\text{Hannibal} \quad \text{princeps}
\end{array}
$$

This kind of structure is identical to the one which underlies simple clauses with a nominal predicate, such as *Hannibal princeps erat*.

Having said that, note that the participle, too, being an adjective, can perform a predicative function, i.e. it can be part of a small clause. Accordingly, this use of the participle is known as predicative. A sentence such as *Hannibal currens vēnit* 'Hannibal arrived running' will thus include the structure in (5):

(5)

$$
\begin{array}{c}
\text{SC} \\
\diagup\diagdown \\
\text{NP} \quad \text{PartP} \\
| \qquad | \\
\text{Hannibal} \quad \text{currens}
\end{array}
$$

First of all, we can now understand why the predicative participle can function as subject or object complement. The phrase *Hannibal currens* in (5) contains an example of a subject complement. Consider example (6):

(6)   Te sapientem et appellant et existimant (Cic. *Lael.* 6)
      'They both call you and consider you wise'

The phrase *te sapientem* contains an example of a participle in the position of predicative object complement. This use is particularly frequent with verbs of perception, such as *video* and *audio*:

(7)   Parasitum tuum video currentem (Plaut. *Curc.* 277)
      'I can see your sponger running'

The predicative participle is used instead of an *accusativus cum infinitivo*, e.g. *video parasitum currere* 'I can see your sponger running', in order to empha-size the immediacy and the dynamism of the event, while the infinitival clause represents the simple and unmarked way to describe the same event.

   Secondly, when the predicative participle combines with a copula, it can give rise to a simple clause with a nominal predicate. Consider example (8):

(8)   Qui, si dediticius est, profecto iussis vestris oboediens erit (Sall. *Iug.* 31, 19)
      'And he, if he has surrendered, will be obedient to your commands'

In this case, too, it is clear that the structure of the nominal predicate, consisting of a predicative participle and the copula, i.e. *oboediens erit*, is identical to the one consisting of an adjective phrase and the copula, e.g. *dediticius est*. This is due to the fact that they both share the same small clause structure.

27.4 Appositive participle (*participium coniunctum*)

This section will be devoted to the description of a use of the participle in which its verbal nature prevails over the adjectival one. It is called 'appositive', a term which underlies the fact that this use is an extension of the appositions mentioned in Section 19.4 as typical uses of the small clause.

   The distinction between the predicative participle described in Section 27.3 and the appositive participle described here lies in the fact that the predicative participle in a small clause performs the same function as an adjective phrase:

(9)   SC
                                      ╱╲
                                 NP   PartP = AP

while the appositive participle is similar to a verb accompanied by its direct object or other complements or adverbial adjuncts. In other words, the appositive participle, too, is inserted within a small clause, but its structure is rather that of a verb phrase:

(10)   SC
                              NP   PartP = VP

The appositive participle represents the verbal head of a complex structure which contains not only the participle but also the complements selected by the thematic grid of the verb. Consider example (11):

(11)   Caesar, transgressus Visurgim, indicio perfugae cognoscit delectum ab Arminio
       locum pugnae (Tac. *ann.* II 12, 1)
       'After crossing the Weser, Caesar learns from the indication of a deserter the
       ground chosen by Arminius for battle'

Example (11) clearly shows that, on the one hand, the appositive participle, i.e. *transgressus* 'having crossed', is an apposition of the subject of the main clause, i.e. *Caesar cognoscit*, but on the other hand it also constitutes the verbal nucleus of a clause containing a direct object, i.e. *Visurgim*.

For this reason, the appositive participle may be considered a subordinate clause, whose structure is similar to that of a relative clause, in that it is adjoined to a constituent of the main clause as apposition, but also expresses a meaning which is similar to the one expressed by adverbial embedded clauses with a temporal meaning, which will be discussed in Section 28.4. Although the appositive participle is not completely unknown in English, the best way to render a Latin *participium coniunctum* is through an embedded clause, e.g. 'after crossing the Weser'.

The appositive participle can often be found in sentences with a complex embedding structure, such as (12):

(12)   Is, cohortatus milites, ut copiam pugnae in aperto faceret, aciem pro castris
       instruit (Tac. *Ann.* III 20, 2)
       'After encouraging his men to offer battle in the open plan, he drew up his line in
       front of the encampment'

Example (12) consists of a main clause, i.e. *is aciem pro castris instruit*, a higher embedded clause containing an appositive participle with a temporal meaning, i.e. *cohortatus milites*, which literally means 'having encouraged the soldiers', and a lower embedded clause introduced by *ut*, selected by the thematic structure of *cohortare*.

This type of construction is particularly frequent in Latin. While English would more naturally recur to coordination, e.g. 'he encouraged his men and drew up his line', Latin prefers embedded structures, e.g. 'having encouraged his men, he drew up his line'. The embedded clause will typically be either a relative, e.g. 'he that had encouraged his men', or an appositive participle, as in the example in (12), or an ablative absolute, which we shall discuss in Section 27.5.

27.5 Ablative absolute

The ablative absolute is the last type of verbal use of the participle. This structure is very frequently used to express subordination, as an alternative to the appositive participle.

Instead of modifying one phrase of the main clause, the ablative absolute is a modal adjunct which modifies the whole clause, e.g. *legionibus transductis* literally means 'with the troops led across', which is in fact rendered as a temporal embedded clause, e.g. 'after leading the troops across'. Consider example (13):

(13)   Caesar, legionibus transductis, ad oppidum constitit (Caes. *civ.* I 16, 3)
       'Caesar, after transferring his troops, stopped outside the town'

The underlying structure is again a small clause:

(14)   SC
                                   / \
                                 NP   PartP
                                  | |
                            legionibus transductis

This is also confirmed by the fact that the participle of an ablative absolute, e.g. *legionibus transductis*, can often be replaced by a noun or adjective phrase, e.g. *Cicerone consule* 'under Cicero's consulate', *natura duce* 'with nature as a guide', *dis invitis* 'against gods' will', *Hannibale vivo* 'while Hannibal was alive', and so on. Here follows one example:

(15)   De me senatus ita decrevit, Cn. Pompeio auctore (Cic. *Pis.* 35)
       'Upon me, the senate decreed this, on the motion of Gnaeus Pompeius'

This and the previous examples contain instances of small clauses and allow us to gain a better understanding of the notion of 'small clause', which is nothing but a pure predicative nucleus, as shown by the structures in (16):

(16)   SC   SC
                 / \   / \
               NP   AP   NP   NP
                | | | |
           Hannibale vivo   Cicerone consule

We have already seen that a small clause may turn into a sentence with a nominal predicate or a predicative participle. Now we shall consider the small clause by itself.

The ablative absolute is a pure small clause which is used as a circumstancial, as exemplified by *urbe capta* in the clause in (17):

(17)

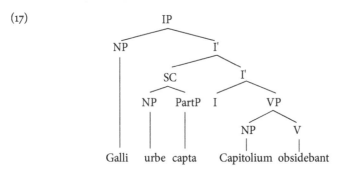

'The Gauls, having conquered the town, beset the Capitol'

In (17), the adjunct *urbe capta* functions as an adjunct to the main clause (the traditional term ablative absolute indicates the fact that this lacks any links with the remainder of the sentence). The ablative case, which marks both components of the small clause, typically marks the adjuncts of time and place, to which the ablative absolute can be assimilated.

We shall now end this section with a number of concluding remarks about the nature of the participle heading the ablative absolute. First of all, we shall focus our attention on the single theta-role assigned by the verb *capio* in example (17), which appears in the ablative absolute inflected in its passive past participle form, i.e. *capta*. We have already seen that the passive voice allows the verb to assign only the Theme theta-role to its internal complement, which is *urbe* in this case. This theta-role is the same one that the active verb *capio* would assign to its object, while the Agent theta-role, which is typically reserved to the subject, is not assigned, as a consequence of the passive voice of the verb.

The peculiar structure of the ablative absolute, i.e. a small clause in which the participle assigns the object theta-role but not the subject one, which would be assigned by the corresponding active form, allows us to understand why in Classical Latin this structure is almost exclusively employed with active transitive verbs and intransitive deponents.

As for active verbs, the explanation is pretty straightforward. In example (17), the apparent subject of the ablative absolute, i.e. *urbe*, is actually assigned the same theta-role as the object of the corresponding transitive verb, i.e. *urbem capere*, just like the subject of a passive clause headed by a finite verb, e.g. *urbs capitur* 'the town is conquered'. If the verb were intransitive, e.g. *fremo, strepo, tremo*, this role could not be assigned. In other words, intransitive verbs cannot occur in ablative absolute structures because they lack passive voice.

We shall now turn our attention to intransitive deponent verbs, e.g. *morior* 'to die' and *orior* 'to rise', which are frequently used as ablative absolutes, e.g. *Cicerone mortuo, sole orto*, etc., unlike transitive deponent verbs, e.g. *hortor* 'to exhort' and *arbitror* 'to decide', which rarely appear in this kind of structure, cf. **hortatis militibus, *sententia arbitrata*. The participle of a transitive deponent verb assigns two theta-roles, i.e. the Agent and the Theme, e.g. *Caesar, hortatus milites*. This means that the thematic structure of the participle is incompatible with the syntactic structure of the ablative absolute, which allows only one theta-role. However, the most interesting case is represented by intransitive deponent verbs. The analysis of active transitive verbs that we have just proposed suggests a simple hypothesis, i.e. the 'subject' of the ablative absolute of an intransitive deponent verb is also assigned the theta-role of an object. This in turn suggests that, in a clause such as *Cicero moritur* 'Cicero dies', the surface subject is originated in the object position.

In the modern linguistic tradition, verbs such as *morior* are called unaccusatives, cf. Section 14.9. The term indicates that these verbs are not able to assign accusative case to their object. This category is not unique to Latin, and was first identified in languages such as Italian, where unaccusative verbs such as *morire* 'to die' exhibit a number of peculiar features, such as the selection of the auxiliary *essere* 'to be' instead of *avere* 'to have'.

In Italian, too, the absolute use is not admitted with all kinds of intransitive verb, but only with unaccusatives, as shown by the contrast in (18):

(18)   a.   Arrivato   Gianni,   l'affare   poté   essere   concluso
            Arrived   John   the deal   could be   concluded
            'After John had arrived, they could complete their deal'

       b.   *Telefonato Gianni,   l'affare   poté   essere   concluso
            Telephoned   John   the deal   could be   concluded
            'After John had telephoned, they could complete their deal'

In Latin, the analogy between unaccusatives and passives is quite straightforward. Unaccusative verbs always exhibit passive endings, e.g. *nascor, morior*, etc., and their subject is base-generated in the object position, just as with passive sentences.

Therefore, in a sentence containing an unaccusative verb, such as *Cicero moritur*, we must posit that the surface subject is a deep object which has been moved, just as in a passive sentence. The structure of a sentence headed by an unaccusative verb is therefore as in (19):

(19)

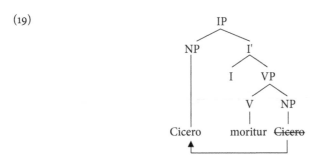

Note that the syntactic structure of *Cicero moritur* is identical to the one of *exercitus perducitur*, in that the surface subject is actually generated in the object position. In other words, the subject of an unaccusative verb is not displaced from the specifier of the VP, as the subject of a transitive verb is, but rather from the object position of V, just like the subject of a passive sentence.

For this reason, we shall also introduce in Latin the distinction between unaccusative verbs (intransitive deponents) and the remaining deponent verbs, which have acquired active meaning. The very term 'deponent' was coined by ancient grammarians to indicate that the verb has 'deposited' its active morphology, without adding anything about the nature of the verb. A transitive deponent verb such as *hortor* now preserves only a shadow of the original Indo-European middle morphology and has instead acquired the same value as an active verb. Conversely, the passive morphology of an unaccusative verb such as *morior* is part of the very structure of this verb, which allows only one object in its deep structure (which becomes the subject of the surface string). In other words, these verbs witness the fact that one of the functions of the original middle morphology was the codification of unaccusativity.

28

Adverbial clauses

28.1 Classification of embedded clauses

Traditional grammars classify embedded clauses according to the position that they occupy within the selecting clause. For example, we have already seen that embedded clauses introduced by *quod, ut*, and *quin*, indirect questions, and infinitival clauses are classified as 'substantive' clauses, in that they occupy the same position as a subject or object noun phrase. Relative and (most) participial clauses, in contrast, are considered to be 'adjectival', as they occupy the same position as an adjective within a noun phrase. The last category of embedded clauses includes the so-called 'adverbial' clauses, which occupy the same position as adverbs, i.e. adjuncts which are not selected by the thematic grid of the predicate. The ablative absolute is an example of an adverbial clause.

Consider the example in (1):

(1) Cervus, cum bibisset, restitit (Phaedr. I 13, 3)
     'The deer, after drinking, stopped'

The matrix clause consists of a subject noun phrase, i.e. *cervus*, and a verb phrase headed by an intransitive verb, i.e. *restitit*. These two elements would be sufficient to determine the well-formedness of the sentence and to guarantee a complete meaning, i.e. 'the deer stopped'. As a consequence, the embedded clause introduced by the complementizer *cum* can only occupy an adjunct position, as if it were simply an adverb such as *segniter* 'lazily', as shown by the structure in (2):

(2)

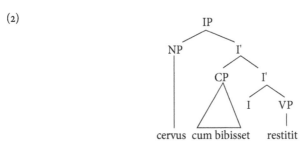

Traditional grammars employ various labels to refer to such embedded clauses, such as 'adverbial', 'indirect', or 'circumstantial'. All these labels are meant to indicate the fact that this kind of embedded clause is always adjoined to the same position as adverbs or prepositional phrases not selected by the thematic structure of the predicate, e.g. *cervus cum cura restitit* 'the deer stopped with care'.

Both adverbial and prepositional adjuncts are inserted to express some additional information regarding the time, the place, or the manner of the event. This means that the semantic value of this kind of embedded clause is the same as that of adjuncts. As we shall see in the next paragraphs, this value can be final or purpose, consecutive or result, temporal, causal, conditional, concessive and of wish or proviso.

In the following paragraphs, each type of adverbial clause will be discussed, with special reference to its dedicated complementizers, moods, and tenses.

28.2 Final or purpose clauses

Complementizer: *ut* (negative *ne*)

Mood: *subjunctive*

Tenses: they follow the contemporary slot of the *consecutio temporum*, i.e. present if selected by a primary tense; imperfect if selected by a historic tense.

English translation: 'so that', '(in order) to' + infinitive.

Examples:

(3) Non ut edam vivo, sed ut vivam edo (Quint. *inst.* IX 3, 81)
    'I do not live to eat, but eat to live'

(4) Paucis absoluit, ne moraret diutius (Pacuv. *trag.* fr. 181)
    'He spoke briefly so as not to waste too much time'

Other expressions of purpose:

- *Quo* + subjunctive, before a comparative:

(5) Classis petere altum visa est, quo facilius superaret promunturium (Liv. XXV 27, 11)
    'The fleet seemed to be heading out to sea to go past the promontory more readily'

- Relative clause with final interpretation (*relative clauses of purpose*):

(6) Ad tyrannum legatos miserunt qui admonerent foederis Romani (Liv. XXXV 13, 2)
    'They sent ambassadors to the tyrant to remind him of the Roman alliance'

- Future participle:

(7)   Legati ad regem descenderunt veniam petituri (Curt. VIII 10, 33)
      'The deputies came down to the king to ask for pardon'

- *Ad* + gerund or gerundive:

(8)   Non satis tutus est ad narrandum hic locus (Ter. *Phorm.* 817)
      'This place is not safe enough to speak'

(9)   Ille ad defendendam causam adest (Ter. *Phorm.* 266)
      'He is here to defend the case'

- Simple gerundive:

(10) Diviti homini id aurum seruandum dedit (Plaut. *Bacch.* 338)
      'He has given that gold to a wealthy man to keep it for him'

- ablative of *causa* or *gratia* + gerund or gerundive:

(11) In Siciliam sum inquirendi causa profectus (Cic. *II Verr.* 1, 6)
      'I went off to Sicily to collect evidence'

(12) Ptolomaeus petendi auxilii gratia Romam venerat (Val. Max. V 1, 1)
      'Ptolemy had come to Rome to ask for help'

- Supine, with verbs of motion:

(13) Bituriges ad eum legatos mittunt auxilium petitum (Caes. *Gall.* VIII 4, 2)
      'The Bituriges sent ambassadors to him to seek help'

28.3 Consecutive or result clauses

Complementizer: *ut* (negative: *ut non*)
Mood: *subjunctive*
Tenses: present to indicate the present consequence of a past event; imper-
    fect (progressive) or perfect (punctual) to indicate a past consequence;
    pluperfect to denote anteriority
English translation: 'so that', 'that'.

The consecutive clause is often preceded by adverbs or other expressions
which anticipate its semantic value, giving rise to the correlative structures
illustrated in Table 28.1.
    Examples:

(14) Tam autem eras excors, ut tota in oratione tua tecum ipse pugnares (Cic. *Phil.* II 18)
      'And you were so senseless that throughout your speech you were fighting with
      yourself'

(15) Delenitus sum profecto ita, ut me qui sim nesciam (Plaut. *Amph.* 844)
      'I am so bewitched that I do not know who I am'

TABLE 28.1 Correlative structures with *ut*

Correlative structure	Translation
sic . . . ut . . .	'so . . . that . . .'
ita . . . ut . . .	'so . . . that . . .'
tam . . . ut . . .	'so . . . that . . .'
usque adeo . . . ut . . .	'to such an extent . . . that . . .'
is (or *talis*) *. . . ut . . .*	'of such a kind . . . that . . .'
tantus . . . ut . . .	'so great . . . that . . .'

Other expressions of result:

- Relative clauses of result:

(16)   Ego non sum dignus qui bibam? (Petr. *Sat.* 20, 5)
       'Do not I deserve to drink?'

28.4 Temporal clauses

(a) Generic concomitance (*cum* plus subjunctive).
   The embedded clause introduced by the complementizer *cum* plus the subjunctive expresses a concomitant circumstance, with a generic value which can be either temporal or causal, especially if there is a concatenation of facts within a historical narration (for this reason, this use of *cum* is also known as *cum narrativum* or *historicum*).

   Complementizer: *cum*
   Mood: *subjunctive*
   Tenses: they follow the *consecutio temporum*
   English translation: 'when' or 'as', 'because'. Note that the choice between the temporal value and the causal one is not always neat but the two tend to overlap (as also suggested by the Latin saying *post hoc, ergo propter hoc* 'after this, therefore because of this').

   Examples:

(17)   Ibi eum Caesar cum vidisset, nihil aspere, nihil acerbe dixit (Cic. *fam.* XIII 29, 4)
       'When Caesar saw him there, he said nothing rough, nothing bitter'

(18)   Nimis abes diu, praesertim cum sis in propinquis locis (Cic. *fam.* II 1, 4)
       'You have been away for too long, especially because you are so near'

(b) Semantic value of 'when' (*cum* plus indicative).

   Complementizer: *cum*
   Mood: *indicative*
   Tenses: the same as in English.

Examples:

(19)   Cum Caesar in Galliam venit, alterius factionis principes erant Haedui, alterius Sequani (Caes. *Gall.* VI 12, 1)
'When Caesar arrived in Gaul, the leaders of one party were the Haedui, of the other the Sequani'

(20)   Virum bonum cum laudabant, ita laudabant: bonum agricolam bonumque colonum (Cato *agr.* 2, 6)
'When they praised a good man, they praised him in this way: a good farmer and a good tiller of the soil'

The temporal clause is often introduced by adverbs or other expressions which anticipate a temporal interpretation, giving rise to correlative structures such as (21):

(21)   a. tum...   cum...
           'then...   when...'
        b. nunc...   cum...
           'now...   when...'

Examples:

(22)   Tum eras consul, cum in Palatio mea domus ardebat (Cic. *Pis.* 26)
'You were consul when my house on the Palatine burned'

Other special uses:

• *cum inversum*: the expressions *cum subito, cum repente* and sometimes just *cum* mean 'when all of a sudden', 'suddenly':

(23)   Vix haec dicta dederat, cum Romani equites [...] pedestres acies turbarunt (Liv. XXIX 2, 12)
'He had just said this, when suddenly the Roman horse [...] threw the infantry lines into confusion'

• *cum iterativum*: it means 'every time that':

(24)   Mirari soleo, cum video aliquos tempus petentes (Sen. *dial.* X 8, 1)
'I am usually astonished every time that I see some men asking for time'

• *cum coincidens*: means 'the moment when', 'for the reason that'. The expression *cum primum* means 'as soon as':

(25)   Cum primum potuit, imperium deposuit (Nep. *Timol.* 3, 4)
'As soon as he could, he laid down his command'

(c) Semantic value of 'while' (*dum* plus indicative).

Complementizer: *dum*
Mood: *indicative*
Tenses: the same as English.

Examples:

(26) Homines, dum docent, discunt (Sen. *epist.* 7, 8)
      'Men learn while they teach'

(27) Nunc animum advortite, dum huius argumentum eloquar comoediae (Plaut. *Amph.* 95)
      'Now give me your attention while I declare the argument of this comedy'

Other special uses:

• *cum adversativum*: it means 'while', 'on the other hand' and is used with the subjunctive:

(28) Ibi forum agit, cum ego sim in provincia (Cic. *Att.* V 17, 6)
      'He holds court there, while I am in the province'

28.5 Causal clauses

Complementizers: *quod, quia, quoniam* 'because', 'since'
Mood: *indicative* when the reason is that of the writer or speaker; *subjunctive* when the reason is viewed as that of another (cf. the so-called 'oblique discourse')
Tenses: the same as English.

Examples:

(29) Nec haec idcirco omitto quod non gravissima sint, sed quia nunc sine teste dico (Cic. *prov. consul.* 6)
      'I do not omit these facts because they are not most serious, but because now I speak without witnesses'

(30) Noctu ambulat in publico Themistocles, quod somnum capere non posset (Cic. *Tusc.* IV 44)
      'Themistocles walked by night in a public place because he was unable to sleep'

The causal clause is often preceded by adverbs or other expressions which anticipate its semantic value giving rise to correlative structures such as those in Table 28.2.

TABLE 28.2 Correlative structures with *quod*

Correlative structure	Translation
id ... quod ...	'for this ... because ...'
idcirco ... quod ...	'for this ... because ...'
propterea ... quod ...	'for this ... because ...'
non quod ... sed quia ...	'not because ... but because ...'
magis quia ... quam quod ...	'more because ... than because ...'

Examples:

(31)   Ego ad te propterea minus saepe scribo, quod certum non habeo ubi sis (Cic. *Att.* VI 9, 8)
        'For this I write to you less frequently, because I do not know exactly where you are'

(32)   Et primo magis quia improviso id fecerat, quam quod par viribus esset, anceps certamen erat (Liv. XXVII 28, 16)
        'And at first the battle was uncertain, rather because he had done that unexpected action than because he was a match in (armed) forces'

Additional expression:

- a causal relative clause, introduced by *quippe, utpote, ut*:

(33)   Neque eo magis cupido Iugurthae minuebatur, quippe qui totum eius regnum animo iam invaserat (Sall. *Iug.* 20, 6)
        'Jugurtha's longing did not diminish at all, because in his mind he had already seized all (Adherbal's) realm'

28.6 Conditional sentences

Complementizer: *si* 'if'

Moods and tenses: borrowing this terminology from Greek dialectics, traditional grammars divide the conditional sentence into two clauses: the protasis 'condition', i.e. the conditional embedded *if*-clause, and the apodosis 'conclusion', i.e. the matrix clause. The different use of moods and tenses depend on the fact that, from a semantic point of view, there are three types of conditional sentence:

Type I: *Real* or *Logical* Conditional Sentences (the fulfilment of the condition is the logical result)
Type II: *Ideal* Conditional Sentences (the matter is open to question)
Type III: *Unreal* Conditional Sentences (conditions contrary to fact).

It is up to the writer to judge the degree of possibility of the conditions, i.e. it is a completely subjective judgement. The tense and mood of the apodosis and protasis depend upon the above classification, as shown by Tables 28.3–28.5.

28.6.1 Independent apodosis

Examples:

(34)   a. Si docent, philosophi sunt (Sen. *epist.* 89, 19) (Type I)
            'If they teach, they are philosophers'

TABLE 28.3 Tense and mood of the protasis and apodosis (independent apodosis)

	Protasis	Apodosis
Type I (Logical)	Indicative *si hoc dicis* 'if you say this'	Indicative *erras* 'you are mistaken'
Type II (Ideal)	Present and perfect subjunctive *si hoc dicas* 'if you were to say this'	Present and perfect subjunctive *erres* 'you would be mistaken'
Type III (Unreal)	Imperfect and pluperfect subjunctive *si hoc diceres* 'if you said / were saying that (but you did not)'	Imperfect and pluperfect subjunctive *errares* 'you would be mistaken'

b. Dies deficiat, si velim paupertatis causam defendere (Cic. *Tusc.* V 102) (Type II)
   'Time would fail me if I wanted to maintain the cause of poverty'

c. Si timidus essem, tamen ista epistula mi omnem metum abstersisses (Cic. *fam.* XI 24, 1) (Type III)
   'If I were fearful, you would have wiped away all my fear with this letter'

28.6.2 Dependent apodosis

(a) Infinitival apodosis

TABLE 28.4 Tense and mood of the protasis and apodosis (infinitival apodosis)

		Protasis	Apodosis
Type I		Subjunctive, according to *consecutio*	Infinitival, according to *consecutio*
puto te 'I think that (you)'		*si hoc dicas* 'if you say this'	*errare* 'you are mistaken'
Type II		Subjunctive, according to *consecutio*	Future infinitive (*-urum esse*)
puto te 'I think that (you)'		*si hoc dicas* 'if you were to say this'	*erraturum esse* 'you would be mistaken'
Type III		Imperfect and pluperfect subjunctive	Irrealis future infinitive (*-urum fuisse*)
puto te 'I think that (you)'		*si hoc diceres* 'if you said / were saying that'	*erraturum fuisse* 'you would be mistaken'

In order to express the irrealis future infinitive of verbs lacking the supine, the periphrasis *futurum fuisse* + imperfect subjunctive is employed.

Examples:

(35) a. Neque ego umquam bona perdidisse dicam, si quis pecus aut supellectilem amiserit (Cic. *parad.* 8) (Type I)
       'I will never say that someone has lost goods, if they have lost cattle or furniture'

      b. Negat Cicero, si duplicetur sibi aetas, habiturum (esse) se tempus, quo legat lyricos (Sen. *epist.* 49, 5) (Type II)
       'Cicero said that if his life was doubled, he would not have time to read the lyric poets'

      c. Ariovistus respondit, si quid ipsi a Caesare opus esset, sese ad eum venturum fuisse (Caes. *Gall.* I 34, 2) (Type III)
       'Ariovistus replied that if he had needed something from Caesar, he would have come to him'

(b) Subjunctive apodosis

TABLE 28.5 Tense and mood of the protasis and apodosis (subjunctive apodosis)

	Protasis	Apodosis
Type I	Subjunctive, according to *consecutio*	Subjunctive, according to *consecutio*
non dubito quin	*si hoc dicas*	*erres*
'I do not doubt that'	'if you say this'	'you are mistaken'
Type II	Subjunctive, according to *consecutio*	Subjunctive, according to *consecutio* (but also forms ending in -*urus sim* or *essem*)
non dubito quin	*si hoc dicas*	*erraturus sis*
'I do not doubt that'	'if you were to say this'	'you would be mistaken'
Type III	Imperfect subjunctive Pluperfect subjunctive	Imperfect subjunctive Pluperfect subjunctive (but also forms ending in -*urus fuerim*)
non dubito quin	*si hoc diceres*	*errares*
'I do not doubt that'	'if you said / were saying that'	'you would be mistaken'

Examples:

(36) a. Neminem sequentium laudare ausus est, veritus, credo, ne multos offen-
          deret, si paucos excerpsisset (Tac. *dial.* 26, 7) (Type I)
          'He did not dare to praise any of their successors because he was afraid,
          I believe, of offending many if he had specified only a few'

      b. Neque dubitare debeant, quin, si Helvetios superaverint, Romani una cum
          reliqua Gallia Haeduis libertatem sint erepturi (Caes. *Gall.* I 17, 4) (Type II)
          'They should not doubt that if the Romans were to beat the Helvetii, they
          would have taken their freedom away from the Haedui, together with the
          rest of Gaul'

      c. Adeo citato agmine ducti sunt ut, si via recta vestigia sequentes issent,
          haud dubie adsecuturi fuerint (Liv. XXVIII 16, 2) (Type III)
          'They were led to march so quickly that, if they had gone along the right track,
          following the enemy's track, they would undoubtedly have overtaken them'

Additional conditional expression:

• a conditional relative clause, limited to the expression of Type II and III:

(37) Haec et innumerabilia ex eodem genere qui (= si quis) videat, nonne cogatur
      confiteri deos esse? (Cic. *nat. deor.* II 12)
      'If someone considered these and countless similar facts, would they not be
      compelled to acknowledge that the gods exist?'

28.7 Concessive clauses and clauses of wish or proviso

(a) Concessive clauses
    Complementizers:
    quamquam + indicative
    quamvis, licet, ut + subjunctive
    etsi, etiamsi, tametsi + indicative or subjunctive
    English translation: 'even if', 'although', 'granted that'.

Example:

(38) Medici, quamquam intellegunt saepe, tamen numquam aegris dicunt illo
      morbo eos esse morituros (Cic. *div.* II 54)
      'Doctors, although they often know, yet they never tell their patients they are
      going to die of that disease'

Additional concessive expression:

• a concessive relative clause:

(39) Namque egomet, qui (= quamvis) sero ac leviter Graecas litteras attigissem,
      tamen cum pro consule in Ciliciam proficiscens venissem Athenas, complures
      tum ibi dies sum propter navigandi difficultatem commoratus (Cic. *de orat.* I 82)

'For, although I came into touch with Greek literature late and lightly, still, when I reached Athens on my journey to Cilia as proconsul, I remained there for several days because of the difficulty in sailing'

(b) Clauses of wish or proviso:

Complementizers: *dum, modo, dummodo*
Mood: *subjunctive*
Tenses: in accordance with the *consecution temporum*
English translation: 'provided that'.

Examples:

(40) Oderint, dum metuant (acc. *trag.* 203)
'Let them hate, provided they fear'

(41) Genus hoc numerorum, dummodo ne continui sint, in orationis laude ponetur (Cic. *de orat.* III 185)
'This kind of rhythm is placed in prose with merit, provided that it is not uninterrupted'

28.8 Indirect discourse (*oratio obliqua*)

The easiest way to refer someone else's speech is by using direct speech (*oratio recta*), which consists of the exact quotation of the speaker's words, as signalled by quotation marks. However, both Latin and English have recourse to a more stylistically refined technique, known as *oratio obliqua* 'indirect discourse', which allows a more nuanced and varied expression of the reported speech.

Indirect discourse is introduced by an implicit main clause containing a generic subject and a *verbum dicendi* or *sentiendi*, that is, a verb roughly meaning 'he/she said or thought' or 'they said or thought'. The actual indirect discourse instead consists of a number of embedded clauses which report somebody else's speech or thought.

The use of moods and tenses in the indirect discourse is governed by a number of simple rules. There are two types of clauses which can be used to express the indirect discourse:

(a) infinitival clauses (*accusativus cum infinitivo*), which have a pure declarative value. In English, they are typically rendered with the indicative.
(b) subjunctive clauses, which have a volitional value, either exhortative or concessive. In English, they are typically rendered with a modal verb.

Examples:

(42) Sibi semper primam fuisse dignitatem (Caes. *civ.* I 9, 2)
'For him, dignity was always of first importance'

(43)   Iret, ea consulibus nuntiaret (Liv. II 36, 2)
       'He should go and inform the consuls'

Any further embedded clauses are always subjunctive, while their tense is determined by the *consecutio temporum* (this is also the case for clauses that are indicative in the corresponding direct speech, such as relative clauses). In English they are typically rendered with the indicative, as shown by examples (44) and (45):

(44)   Populi Romani imperium Rhenum finire; si se invito Germanos in Galliam transire non aequum existimaret, cur sui quicquam esse imperii aut potestatis trans Rhenum postularet? (Caes. *Gall.* IV 16, 3–4)
       'The Rhine marked the border of the Roman empire: if he thought it unfair that the Germans should cross into Gaul against his will, why did he claim that he had any power or authority across the Rhine?'

(45)   Namque absentia legati remoto metu Britanni agitare inter se mala servitutis, conferre iniurias et interpretando accendere: nihil profici patientia nisi ut graviora tamquam ex facili tolerantibus imperentur. Singulos sibi olim reges fuisse, nunc binos imponi, e quibus legatus in sanguinem, procurator in bona saeviret (Tac. *Agr.* 15, 1–2)
       'Their fear removed by the absence of the deputy, the Britons began to discuss the evils of their slavery, to compare their wrongs and inflame their significance by commenting on them: nothing was gained by submission, except that heavier burdens were imposed, as if they found them easy to bear. In the old days they had only one king, now two were imposed: a deputy to wreak his fury on their lifeblood, a procurator on their property'

Note that in the indirect discourse, interrogative clauses are typically subjunctive, e.g. *cur postularet* in Caesar's example (44), while irrealis questions, e.g. *quid facturum fuisse* (Liv. VIII 31, 5), exhibit the infinitive.

   As for personal pronouns, the first person of the direct speech is substituted by the third person in the indirect discourse, just as in English, e.g. direct speech *he said: 'I will do it'* → indirect speech *he said that he would do it*. However, note that Latin employs *ipse* for the third person nominative and the reflexive *se* for the remaining cases, as shown by example (46):

(46)   Perfacile factu esse illis probat conata perficere, propterea quod ipse suae civitatis imperium obtenturus esse. [...] se suis copiis suoque exercitu illis regna conciliaturum confirmat (Caes. *Gall.* I 3, 6–7)
       'He convinces them that it is easy enough to accomplish such endeavours, because he himself is about to secure the sovereignty of his own state. [...] He confirms that he will win them their kingdoms with his own supplies and his own army'

Conclusion

Through the analysis of increasingly complex structures, we have reached the end of our description of Latin grammar. It goes without saying that many other questions remain to be explored and that other analyses could be offered for the topics that we did investigate. Indeed, it may well be the case that our proposals will end up being a simple initial approximation of a far more complex picture that we have not yet fully grasped. In this sense, we hope that this work will be perceived not as a conclusive examination but rather as a starting point for further research. However, even if approximate, the system has turned out to be rather consistent. Looking back at this work, we can note that many phenomena which looked heterogeneous or odd at first sight have finally found their place within a unitary and simple theory.

Needless to say, 'simple' does not mean 'easy'. Within the scientific realm, the notion of simplicity amounts to the possibility of accounting for the highest number of empirical facts using the smallest number of theoretical principles. Through the syntactic analysis of many different structures, we have achieved a more consistent and detailed explanation than traditional grammars, whose initial empirical observations remain extremely valuable.

One of the most interesting results of this approach is the fact that it managed to explain some of the most varied features of Latin grammar by combining a small number of universal principles with a few specific parameters, which have been described throughout the discussion. These very principles have also been identified in some modern languages, such as English and Italian. All in all, Latin has been treated as a natural language, governed by largely universal rules, rather than the artificial product of some arbitrary prescriptive rules. This general state of affairs finally allows us to understand one of the most comprehensive principles of universal grammar, that is, 'structure dependency'. On a superficial level, language is a continuous flow of sounds which are perceived as a linear string. In fact, language is nothing but the combination of a small number of distinct minimal units, whose hierarchical structure is more important that their linear ordering. Complex structures are created by combining basic units in accordance with well-defined structural rules. The study of these structures is essential in order to understand the functioning of the grammar, by means of which speakers can endlessly create new architectures of words.

Bibliography

Introduction: from traditional grammar to modern linguistics

1.1 The teaching of Latin

Balbo, A. 2007. *Insegnare latino. Sentieri di ricerca per una didattica ragionevole.* Novara: UTET Università.

Benincà, P. & R. Peca Conti 2003. 'Didattica delle lingue classiche e linguistica teorica.' *Università e Scuola* 8(2).38–53.

Bortolussi, B. 2011. 'Generative grammar and the didactics of Latin: the use of examples'. *Formal Linguistics and the Teaching of Latin*, ed. by R. Oniga, R. Iovino, & G. Giusti, 319–342. Newcastle upon Tyne: Cambridge Scholars Publishing.

Cardinale, U. 2011. 'Linguistics and the teaching of classical languages'. *Formal Linguistics and the Teaching of Latin*, ed. by R. Oniga, R. Iovino, & G. Giusti, 343–353. Newcastle upon Tyne: Cambridge Scholars Publishing.

Cardinaletti, A. 2011. 'Linguistic theory and the teaching of Latin'. *Formal Linguistics and the Teaching of Latin*, ed. by R. Oniga, R. Iovino, & G. Giusti, 429–444. Newcastle upon Tyne: Cambridge Scholars Publishing.

Giusti, G. & R. Oniga 2011. 'Why Formal Linguistics for the Teaching of Latin?' *Formal Linguistics and the Teaching of Latin*, ed. by R. Oniga, R. Iovino, & G. Giusti, 1–20. Newcastle upon Tyne: Cambridge Scholars Publishing.

Gwosdek, H., ed. 2013. *Lily's Grammar of Latin in English: An Introduction of the Eyght Partes of Speche, and the Construction of the Same.* Oxford: Oxford University Press.

Gruber-Miller, J., ed. 2006. *When Dead Tongues Speak: Teaching Beginning Greek and Latin.* Oxford: Oxford University Press.

Lister, B. 2007. *Changing Classics in Schools.* Cambridge: Cambridge University Press.

Lister, B., ed. 2008. *Meeting the Challenge: International Perspectives on the Teaching of Latin.* Cambridge: Cambridge University Press.

Oniga, R. 1991. 'Grammatica generativa e insegnamento del latino.' *Aufidus* 14.83–108.

Oniga, R. 1998. 'Teorie linguistiche e didattica del latino'. *Estudios de lingüística latina*, ed. by B. García-Hernández, 613–626. Madrid: Ediciones Clásicas.

Oniga, R. 2007. 'Grammatica latina e linguistica contemporanea'. *Quaderni Patavini di Linguistica* 23.67–83.

Oniga, R. 2012. 'Insegnare latino con il metodo neo-comparativo.' *Lingue antiche e moderne dai licei alle università*, ed. by R. Oniga & U. Cardinale, 101–121. Bologna: Il Mulino.

Oniga, R. & U. Cardinale, eds. 2012. *Lingue antiche e moderne dai licei alle università.* Bologna: Il Mulino.

Penello, N. 2006. 'Applicazioni di elementi di linguistica formale alla didattica del latino.' *Atti della Giornata di linguistica latina*, ed. by R. Oniga & L. Zennaro, 159–178. Venezia: Cafoscarina.

Schmude, M. P. 2012. 'Die Didaktik der Alten Sprachen und ihr Beitrag zum Mehrsprachigkeit im Fächerkanon des Gymnasiums in Deutschland.' *Lingue antiche e moderne* 1.37–54.

Short, W. M. 2011. 'Metaphor and the teaching of idioms in Latin.' *Formal Linguistics and the Teaching of Latin*, ed. by R. Oniga, R. Iovino, & G. Giusti, 227–244. Newcastle upon Tyne: Cambridge Scholars Publishing.

Stray, C. 1998, *Classics Transformed: Schools, Universities, and Society in England, 1830–1960*, Oxford: Oxford University Press.

Vedovato, D. & N. Penello 2012. 'Descrizione dei dati linguistici e prassi didattica: riflessioni e proposte.' *Lingue antiche e moderne* 1.89–117.

1.2 A generativist perspective

Bortolussi, B. 2006. 'La grammaire générative et les langues anciennes.' *Lalies* 26.57–102.

Chomsky, N. 1957. *Syntactic Structures*. The Hague: Mouton.

Chomsky, N. 1965. *Aspects of the Theory of Syntax*. Cambridge, Mass.: MIT Press.

Chomsky, N. 1975. *Reflections on Language*. New York: Random House.

Chomsky, N. 1988. *Language and Problems of Knowledge*. Cambridge, Mass.: MIT Press.

Chomsky, N. 1995. *The Minimalist Program*. Cambridge, Mass.: MIT Press.

Chomsky, N. 2000. *The Architecture of Language*. Oxford: Oxford University Press.

Chomsky, N. 2012. *The Science of Language*. Cambridge: Cambridge University Press.

Cook, V. J. & M. Newson 1996[2]. *Chomsky's Universal Grammar: An Introduction*. Oxford: Blackwell (1988[1]).

Haegeman, L. 1994[2]. *Introduction to Government and Binding Theory*. Oxford: Blackwell (1991[1]).

Haegeman, L. ed. 1997. *The New Comparative Syntax*. London: Longman.

Hornstein, N., J. Nunes, & K. Kleanthes 2005. *Understanding Minimalism*. Cambridge: Cambridge University Press.

Jackendoff, R. 1994. *Patterns in the Mind: Language and Human Nature*. New York: Basic Books.

Kiss, K. É., ed. 2005. *Universal Grammar in the Reconstruction of Ancient Languages*. Berlin: Mouton de Gruyter.

Larson, R. 2010. *Grammar as Science*. Cambridge, Mass.: MIT Press.

Piattelli-Palmarini, M., & R. C. Berwick 2012. *Rich Languages from Poor Inputs*. Oxford: Oxford University Press.

Latin reference grammars

Hofmann, J. B. & A. Szantyr 1965. *Lateinische Syntax und Stilistik*. München: Beck (Italian partial translation *Stilistica latina*, ed. by A. Traina, updated version by R. Oniga. Bologna: Pàtron, 2002).

Kühner, R. & C. Holzweissig 1966[4]. *Ausführliche Grammatik der lateinischen Sprache*, I, *Elementar-, Formen- und Wortlehre*. Hannover: Hahn (repr. 1989; 1912[2]).

Kühner, R. & C. Stegmann 1976[5]. *Ausführliche Grammatik der lateinischen Sprache*, II 1–2, *Satzlehre*, ed. by A. Thierfelder. Hannover: Hahn (repr. 2012; 1914[2]).

Leumann, M. 1977[2]. *Lateinische Laut- und Formenlehre*. München: Beck (1926[1]).

Meiser, G. 1998. *Historische Laut- und Formenlehre der lateinischen Sprache*. Darmstadt: Wissenschaftliche Buchgesellschaft.

Weiss, M. 2009. *Outline of the Historical and Comparative Grammar of Latin*. Ann Arbor & New York: Beech Stave Press.

Recent Latin grammars from specific linguistic perspectives

Bortolussi, B. 2008. *Bescherelle Grammaire du latin*. Paris: Hatier.

Kienpointner, M. 2009. *Latein – Deutsch kontrastiv. Vom Phonem zum Text*. Tübingen: Groos.

Panhuis, D. G. J. 2006. *Latin Grammar*. Ann Arbor: University of Michigan Press.

Pinkster, H. & C. Kroon 2006. *Latein. Eine Einführung*, trans. by R. Hoffmann. Heidelberg: Winter (original Dutch edition 1989).

Touratier, C. 2008. *Grammaire latine. Introduction linguistique à la langue latine*. Paris, Sedes (German ed. by B. Liebermann 2013).

Latin etymological dictionaries

de Vaan, M. A. C. 2008. *Etymological Dictionary of Latin and the Other Italic Languages*. Leiden & Boston: Brill.

Ernout, A. & A. Meillet 1959[4]. *Dictionnaire étymologique de la langue latine: histoire des mots*. Paris: Klincksieck (repr. 1967; 1932[1]).

Walde, A. & J. B. Hoffman 1956[4]. *Lateinisches etymologisches Wörterbuch*. Heidelberg: C. Winter (1906[1]).

Part I   Phonology

2.2 The letters of the Latin alphabet

Devine, A. M. 1971. 'Language and alphabet. Further parallels.' *Orbis* 20.347–355.

Gatzemeier, M. 2009. *Unser aller Alphabet. Kleine Kulturgeschichte des Alphabets*. Aachen: Shaker.

Traina, A. 1973[4]. *L'alfabeto e la pronunzia del latino*. Pàtron: Bologna (1957[1]).

Wallace, R. 2011. 'The Latin alphabet and orthography.' *A Companion to the Latin Language*, ed. by J. Clackson, 9–28. Oxford: Wiley-Blackwell.

3. Phonemes

Marotta, G. 1981. 'Contributo all'analisi fonologica del vocalismo latino classico.' *Studi e Saggi Linguistici* 21.85–131.

McCullagh, M. 2011. 'The sounds of Latin: Phonology.' *A Companion to the Latin Language*, ed. by J. Clackson, 83–91. Oxford: Wiley-Blackwell.

Mignot, X. 1975. 'Phonologie pragoise et phonologie générative dans la description du latin.' *Bulletin de la Société de Linguistique* 70.203–231.

Niedermann, M. 1953[4]. *Phonétique historique du latin*. Paris: Klincksieck (1906[1]).

4. Pronunciation

Allen, W. S. 1978[2]. *Vox Latina: A Guide to the Pronunciation of Classical Latin*. Cambridge: Cambridge University Press (1965[1]).

Collins, A. 2012. 'The English pronunciation of Latin: its rise and fall.' *Cambridge Classical Journal* 58.23–57.

Marouzeau, J. 1955. *La prononciation du latin: Histoire, théorie, pratique*. Paris: Les Belles Lettres.

5. Prosody and metrics

Allen, W. S. 1973. *Accent and Rhythm*. Cambridge: Cambridge University Press.

Bernardi Perini, G. 1986[4]. *L'accento latino: Cenni teorici e norme pratiche*. Bologna: Pàtron (1964[1]).

Boldrini, S. 1992. *La prosodia e la metrica dei Romani*. Rome: La Nuova Italia Scientifica.

Devine, A. M. & L. D. Stephens 1980. 'Latin prosody and meter: brevis brevians.' *Classical Philology* 75.142–157.

Devine, A. M. & L. D. Stephens 1984. *Language and Metre*. Chico, Calif.: Scholars Press.

Fortson, B. W. 2011. 'Latin prosody and metrics.' *A Companion to the Latin Language*, ed. by J. Clackson, 92–104. Oxford: Wiley-Blackwell.

Janson, T. 1977. 'Latin vowel reduction and the reality of phonological rules.' *Studia Linguistica* 31.1–17.

Lehmann, C. 2005. 'Latin syllable structure in typological perspective.' *Papers on Grammar* 9. 127–147.

Marotta, G. 1999. 'The Latin syllable.' *The Syllable: Views and Facts*, ed. by H. v.d. Hulst & N. Ritter, 285–310. Berlin & New York: Mouton de Gruyter.

Marotta, G. 2000. 'Sulla massimalità dei piedi trocaici: il caso del latino.' *Lingua e Stile* 35.387–416.

Marotta, G. 2006. 'L'algoritmo accentuale latino nel confronto di due teorie fonologiche.' *Atti della Giornata di linguistica latina*, ed. by R. Oniga & L. Zennaro, 133–158. Venezia: Cafoscarina.

Mester, A. 1994. 'The quantitative trochee in Latin.' *Natural Language and Linguistic Theory* 12.1–61.

Oniga, R. 2010. 'Metrica latina arcaica e fonologia prosodica', *Latin Linguistics Today*, ed. by P. Anreiter & M. Kienpointner, 45–56. Innsbruck: Universität.

Probert, P. 2002. 'On the prosody of Latin enclitics.' *Oxford University Working Papers in Linguistics, Philology and Phonetics*, ed. by I. J. Hartman & A. Willi, 7.181–206.

Zirin, R. A. 1970. *The Phonological Basis of Latin Prosody*. The Hague: Mouton.

Part II   Morphology

6. Words, roots, and stems

Aronoff, M. 1976. *Word Formation in Generative Grammar*. Cambridge, Mass.: MIT Press.

Aronoff, M. 1994. *Morphology by Itself: Stems and Inflectional Classes*. Cambridge, Mass.: MIT Press.

Aronoff, M. & K. Fudeman 2011[2]. *What is Morphology?* Chichester: Wiley-Blackwell (2005[1]).

Booij, G. 2012[3]. *The Grammar of Words: An Introduction to Linguistic Morphology*. Oxford: Oxford University Press (2005[1]).

Di Sciullo, A.-M. & E. Williams 1987. *On the Definition of Word*. Cambridge, Mass.: MIT Press.

Fruyt, M. 2001. 'Réflexions sur la notion de "mot" en latin: les verbes du type *calefacio*.' *De lingua Latina novae quaestiones*, ed. by C. Moussy, 81–94. Leuven: Peeters.

Graffi, G. 2008. 'La parola tra "unità concreta" e "unità astratta".' *Incontri Linguistici* 31.41–75.

Granucci, F. 2008. 'Per una definizione di "parola" in latino.' *Autour du lexique latin*, ed. by G. Viré, 50–61. Bruxelles: Latomus.

Matthews, P. H. 1991[2]. *Morphology*. Cambridge: Cambridge University Press (1974[1]).

Scalise, S. 1984. *Generative Morphology*. Dordrecht: Foris.

7. Parts of speech

Baker, M. C. 2003. *Lexical Categories: Verbs, Nouns, and Adjectives*. Cambridge: Cambridge University Press.

Brøndal, V. 1948. *Les parties du discours*. Copenhagen: Munskgaard.

Caramazza, A. & C. Finocchiaro 2002. 'Classi grammaticali e cervello.' *Lingue e Linguaggio* 1.3–37.

Matthews, P. H. 1967. 'Latin.' *Lingua* 17.153–181.

Salvi, G. 2013. *Le parti del discorso*. Rome: Carocci.

Vogel, P. M. & B. Comrie, eds. 2000. *Approaches to the Typology of Word Classes*. Berlin: Mouton De Gruyter.

8. A theory of inflection

Carstairs, A. 1984. 'Paradigm economy in Latin.' *Transactions of the Philological Society* 82.117–137.

Clackson, J. 2011. 'The forms of Latin: inflectional morphology', *A Companion to the Latin Language*, ed. by J. Clackson, 105–117. Oxford: Wiley-Blackwell.

Dressler, W. U. 2002. 'Latin inflection classes.' *Theory and Description in Latin Linguistics*, ed. by M. Bolkestein, C. Kroon, H. Pinkster, H. W. Remmelink, & R. Risselada, 91–110. Amsterdam: Gieben.

Ernout, A. 1953[3]. *Morphologie historique du latin*. Paris: Klinckieck (1914[1]).

Oniga, R. 1989. 'Morphological theory and Latin morphology.' *Cahiers de l'Institut de Linguisitique de Louvain* 15.333–344.

Pultrová, L. 2006. *The Vocalism of Latin Medial Syllables*. Prague: Karolinum Press.

Roberts, P. 2012. 'Latin rhotacism: a case study in the life cycle of phonological processes.' *Transactions of the Philological Society* 110.80–93.

Touratier, C. 1975. 'Rhotacisme synchronique du latin classique et rhotacisme diachronique.' *Glotta* 53.246–281.

9. Noun declensions

Buzássyová, L. 2005. 'The Latin third declension in the scope of natural morphology.' *Papers on Grammar* 9.15–24.

Devine, A. M. 1970. *The Latin Thematic Genitive Singular*. Oxford: Blackwell.

Gonzalez Rolán, T. 1971. 'Estudio sobre la primera declinación latina.' *Emerita* 39.293–304.

Hamp, E. P. 1997–1998. 'Fides and the Latin 5th declension.' *Glotta* 74.54–56.

Janson, T. 1971. 'The Latin third declension.' *Glotta* 49.111–142.

Mignot, X. 1974. 'Sur les alternances dans les thèmes consonantiques de la 3ème déclinaison latine.' *Bulletin de la Société de Linguistique* 69.121–154.

Porzio Gernia, M. L. 1986. 'Latin declension. A theoretical and methodological approach.' *Papers on Grammar* 2.1–18.

Touratier, C. 1989. 'La 3ème declinaison latine. Essai de morphologie synchronique.' *Cahiers de l'Institut de Lingusitique de Louvain* 15.435–446.

10. Adjective declensions

Brachet, J.-P. 2003. 'Normalisations morphophonologiques dans la flexion des adjectifs latins et dans leurs dérivés.' *Latomus* 62.261–274.

Fugier, H. 1972. 'Le système latin des comparatifs et superlatifs.' *Revue des études latines* 50.272–294.

Sánchez Salor, E. 1979. 'Apuntes para un estudio formal del adjetivo latino.' *Revista española de lingüística* 9.23–57.

11. Adverbs

Cupaiuolo, F. 1967. *La formazione degli avverbi in latino*. Naples: Libreria Scientifica Editrice.

Pinkster, H. 1972. *On Latin Adverbs*. Amsterdam: North-Holland.

Ricca, D. 2010. 'Adverbs.' *New Perspectives on Historical Latin Syntax*, II, ed. by P. Baldi & P. Cuzzolin, 109–191. Berlin: Mouton de Gruyter.

Strati, R. 1996. *Ricerche sugli avverbi latini in -tus*. Bologna: Pàtron.

12. Pronouns

Baldi, P. & A. Nuti 2010. 'Possession.' *New Perspectives on Historical Latin Syntax*, III, ed. by P. Baldi & P. Cuzzolin, 239–387. Berlin: Mouton de Gruyter.

Bertocchi, A. & C. Casadio 1980. 'Conditions on anaphora: an analysis of reflexive in Latin.' *Papers on Grammar* 1.1–46.

Bertocchi, A. & M. Maraldi 2008. 'Universal quantifiers in Latin: some remarks on ambiguity.' *Autour du lexique latin*, ed. by G. Viré, 9–21. Brussels: Latomus.

Fruyt, M. 1987. 'Interprétation sémantico-référentielle du réfléchi latin.' *Glotta* 65.204–221.

Orlandini, A. 1981. 'Semantica e pragmatica dei pronomi indefiniti latini.' *Lingua e Stile* 16.215–234.

Orlandini, A. 1989. 'Les pronoms possessifs et personnels en latin.' *Indogermanische Forschungen* 94.177–189.

Pierluigi, S. 2007. 'Latin third-person possessives in a GB approach.' *Ordre et cohérence en latin*, ed. by G. Purnelle & J. Denooz, 143–152. Geneva: Droz.

Pieroni, S. 2006. 'Per un ordinamento paradigmatico dei dimostrativi. Spunti dal latino.' *Atti della Giornata di linguistica latina*, ed. by R. Oniga & L. Zennaro, 179–201. Venice: Cafoscarina.

Pieroni, S. 2010. 'Deixis and anaphora', *New Perspectives on Historical Latin Syntax*, III, ed. by P. Baldi & P. Cuzzolin, 389–501. Berlin: Mouton de Gruyter.

Ros, H. 2001. 'Binding Theory and valency grammar in Latin.' *Glotta* 77.244–261.

13. Numerals

Bertocchi, A., M. Maraldi, & A. Orlandini 2010. 'Quantification.' *New Perspectives on Historical Latin Syntax*, III, ed. by P. Baldi & P. Cuzzolin, 19–174. Berlin: Mouton de Gruyter.

De la Villa, J. 2010. 'Numerals.' *New Perspectives on Historical Latin Syntax*, III, ed. by P. Baldi & P. Cuzzolin, 175–238. Berlin: Mouton de Gruyter.

Galmiche, M. 1977. 'Quantificateurs, référence et théorie transformationnelle.' *Langages* 48.3–49.

Keyser, P. 1988. 'The origin of the Latin numerals 1 to 1000.' *American Journal of Archaeology* 92.529–546.

14. Verbal inflection

De Melo, W. D. C. 2007. *The Early Latin Verb System*. Oxford: Oxford University Press.

Embick, D. 2000. 'Features, syntax and categories in the Latin perfect.' *Linguistic Inquiry* 31.185–230.

Fruyt, M. 1992. 'Le paradigme verbal: un ensemble flou.' *La validité des catégories attachées au verbe*, ed. by C. Moussy & S. Mellet, 21–36. Paris: PUPS.

Magni, E. 2010. 'Mood and modality.' *New Perspectives on Historical Latin Syntax*, II, ed. by P. Baldi & P. Cuzzolin, 193–275. Berlin: Mouton de Gruyter.

Matthews, P. H. 1972. *Inflectional Morphology: A Theoretical Study Based on Aspects of Latin Conjugation*. Cambridge: Cambridge University Press.

Pinkster, H. 1983. 'Tempus, Aspect and Aktionsart in Latin (Recent Trends 1961–1981).' *Aufstieg und Niedergang der römischen Welt* II. 29(1).270–319.

Touratier, C. 1971. 'Essai de morphologie synchronique du verbe latin.' *Revue des études latines* 49.331–356.

Touratier, C. 1972. 'Morphophonologie du verbe latin.' *Bulletin de la Société de Linguistique de Paris* 67.139–174.

Touratier, C. 1983. 'Analyse d'un système verbal (les morphèmes grammaticaux du verbe latin).' *Latin Linguistics and Linguistic Theory*, ed. by H. Pinkster, 261–281. Amsterdam: Benjamins.

15. Derivation

Bertocci, D. 2011. 'Tipi di preverbazione in latino: la funzionalità aspettuale.' *I preverbi. Tra sintassi e diacronia*, ed. by D. Bertocci & E. Triantafillis, 3–34. Padua: Unipress.

Brachet, J.-P. 2000. *Recherches sur les préverbes* de- *et* ex- *du latin*. Brussels: Latomus.

Fruyt, M. 1986. *Problèmes méthodologiques de dérivation à propos des suffixes latins en . . .* cus. Paris: Klincksieck.

Fruyt, M. 1991. 'Complex lexical units in Latin.' *New Studies in Latin Linguistics*, ed. by R. Coleman, 75–91. Amsterdam: Benjamins.

Fruyt, M. 2011. 'Word-formation in Classical Latin.' *A Companion to the Latin Language*, ed. by J. Clackson, 157–175. Oxford: Wiley-Blackwell.

Gaide, F. 1988. *Les substantifs masculins latins en . . .* (i)ō, . . . (i)ōnis. Leuven: Peeters.

García-Hernández, B. 1989. 'Les préverbes latins. Notions latives et aspectuelles.' *Cahiers de l'Institut de Lingusitique de Louvain* 15: 149–159.

Haverling, G. 2000. *On* -sco *Verbs: Prefixes and Semantic Functions. A Study in the Development of Prefixed and Unprefixed Verbs from Early to Late Latin*. Göteborg: Acta Universitatis Gotheborgensis.

Heslin, T. P. 1987. 'Prefixation in Latin.' *Lingua* 72.133–154.

Jekl, Á. 2011. 'Verbal prefixation in Classical Latin and in Italian: the prefix *ex-*.' *Formal Linguistics and the Teaching of Latin*, ed. by R. Oniga, R. Iovino, & G. Giusti, 201–214. Newcastle upon Tyne: Cambridge Scholars Publishing.

Kircher-Durand, C. 1982. *Les noms en* -nus, -na, -num *du latin classique*. Nice: Centre de recherches comparatives sur les langues de la Méditerranée ancienne.

Kircher-Durand, C. 1991. 'Syntax, morphology and semantics in the structuring of the Latin lexicon, as illustrated from the -lis derivatives.' *New Studies in Latin Linguistics*, ed. by R. Coleman, 111–127. Amsterdam: Benjamins.

Mignot, X. 1969. *Les verbes dénominatifs latins*. Paris: Klincksieck.

Oniga, R. 2000. 'La création lexicale chez Pétrone.' *La création lexicale en latin*, ed. by M. Fruyt & C. Nicolas, 155–166. Paris: PUPS.

Oniga, R. 2005. 'Composition et préverbation en latin: problèmes de typologie.' *La composition et la préverbation en latin*, ed. by C. Moussy, 211–227. Paris: Presses de l'Université de Paris-Sorbonne.

Perrot, J. 1961. *Les dérivés latins en* -men *et* -mentum. Paris: Klincksieck.

Pultrová, L. 2011. *The Latin Deverbative Nouns and Adjectives*. Prague: Karolinum Press.

Quellet, H. 1969. *Les dérivés latins en* -or. Paris: Klincksieck.

Sblendorio Cugusi, M. T. 1991. *I sostantivi latini in* -tudo. Bologna: Patron.

Van Laer, S. 2010. *La préverbation en latin: étude des préverbes* ad-, in-, ob-, *et* per- *dans la poésie latine républicaine et augustéenne*. Brussels: Latomus.

16. Composition

Benedetti, M. 1988. *I composti radicali latini. Esame storico e comparativo*. Pisa: Giardini.

Brucale, L. 2012. 'Latin compounds.' *Probus* 24.93–117.

Fruyt, M. 2002. 'Constraints and productivity in Latin nominal compounding.' *Transactions of the Philological Society* 100.259–287.

Lindner, T. 2002. *Lateinische Komposita. Morphologische, historische und lexikalische Studien*. Innsbruck: Innsbrucker Beiträge zur Sprachwissenschaft.

Lindner, T. 2011–2012. 'Komposition.' *Indogermanische Grammatik*, IV/1.1–2, ed. by J. Kuryłowicz, M. Mayrhofer, A. Bammesberger, & T. Lindner, 1–148. Heidelberg: Winter.

Lindner, T. & R. Oniga 2005. 'Zur Forschungsgeschichte der lateinischen Nominal-komposition – Per una storia degli studi sulla composizione nominale latina.' *Papers on Grammar* 9.149–160.

Nielsen Whitehead, B. 2011. 'The alleged Greek influence on Latin compounding.' *Formal Linguistics and the Teaching of Latin*, ed. by R. Oniga, R. Iovino, & G. Giusti, 215–224. Newcastle upon Tyne: Cambridge Scholars Publishing.

Oniga, R. 1988. *I composti nominali latini. Una morfologia generativa*. Bologna: Pàtron.

Oniga, R. 1992. 'Compounding in Latin.' *Rivista di Linguistica* 4.97–116.

Scalise, S. & I. Vogel 2010. *Cross-disciplinary Issues in Compounding*. Amsterdam: Benjamins.

Part III   Syntax

17. Preliminary notions: valency and theta-roles

Baños Baños, J. M., ed. 2009. *Sintaxis del latín clásico*. Madrid: Liceus.

Grimshaw, J. 1990. *Argument Structure*. Cambridge, Mass.: MIT Press.

Happ, H. 1976. *Grundfragen einer Dependenzgrammatik des Lateinischen*. Göttingen: Vandenhoeck & Ruprecht.

Horrock, G. 2011. 'Latin syntax.' *A Companion to the Latin Language*, ed. by J. Clackson, 118–143. Oxford: Wiley-Blackwell.

Lehmann, C. 1973. *Latein mit abstrakten Strukturen*. Munich: Fink.

Pinkster, H. 1990. *Latin Syntax and Semantics*. London: Routledge.

Tesnière, L. 1959. *Éléments de syntaxe structurale*. Paris: Klincksieck.

Touratier, C. 1994. *Syntaxe latine*. Leuven: Peeters.

18. Phrases

Bloomfield, L. 1933. *Language*. New York: Holt Rinehart & Winston.

Fugier, H. 1983. 'Le syntagme nominal en latin classique.' *Aufstieg und Niedergang der römischen Welt* II. 29(1).212–269.

Gianollo, C. 2007. 'The internal syntax of the Nominal Phrase in Latin. A diachronic study.' *Ordre et cohérence en latin*, ed. by G. Purnelle & J. Denooz, 65–80. Geneva: Droz.

Giorgi, A. & G. Longobardi 1991. *The Syntax of Noun Phrases*. Cambridge: Cambridge University Press.

Giusti, G. & R. Oniga 2007. 'Core and periphery in the Latin noun phrase.' *Ordre et cohérence en latin*, ed. by G. Purnelle & J. Denooz, 81–95. Geneva: Droz.

Graffi, G. 1990. 'L'analisi in costituenti immediati prima di Bloomfield.' *Lingua e Stile* 25.457–469.

Graffi, G. 2001. *200 Years of Syntax*. Amsterdam: Benjamins.

Iovino, R. 2011. 'Word order in Latin nominal expressions: the syntax of demonstra-tives.' *Formal Linguistics and the Teaching of Latin*, ed. by R. Oniga, R. Iovino, & G. Giusti, 51–64. Newcastle upon Tyne: Cambridge Scholars Publishing.

Iovino, R. 2012. *La sintassi dei modificatori nominali in latino*. Munich: Lincom
  Europa.
Jackendoff, R. 1977. *X'-Syntax: A Study of Phrase Structure*. Cambridge, Mass.: MIT
  Press.
Kayne, R. 1994. *The Antisymmetry of Syntax*. Cambridge, Mass.: MIT Press.
Luraghi, S. 1985. 'The relationship between prepositions and cases within Latin prep-
  ositional phrases.' *Subordination and Other Topics in Latin*, ed. by G. Calboli,
  253–271. Amsterdam: Benjamins.
Luraghi, S. 2010. 'Adverbial phrases.' *New Perspectives on Historical Latin Syntax*, II,
  ed. by P. Baldi & P. Cuzzolin, 19–107. Berlin: Mouton de Gruyter.
Mignot, X. 1989. 'Système X-barre et description du syntagme nominal latin.' *Cahiers
  de l'Institut de Linguistique de Louvain* 15.285–296.
Renzi, L., ed. 1988. *Grande grammatica italiana di consultazione*, I, *La frase. I sintagmi
  nominale e preposizionale*. Bologna: Il Mulino.
Renzi, L. & G. Salvi, eds. 1991. *Grande grammatica italiana di consultazione*, II, *I
  sintagmi verbale, aggettivale, avverbiale. La subordinazione*. Bologna: Il Mulino.
Risselada, R. 1984. 'Coordination and juxtaposition of adjectives in the Latin NP.'
  Glotta 62(3).201–231.
Wharton, D. 2009. 'On the distribution of adnominal prepositional phrases in Latin
  prose.' *Classical Philology* 104.184–207.

19. The simple sentence

Bauer, B. 1995. *The Emergence and Development of SVO Patterning in Latin and
  French*. Oxford: Oxford University Press.
Bauer, B. 2009. 'Word order.' *New Perspectives on Historical Latin Syntax*, I, ed. by
  P. Baldi & P. Cuzzolin, 241–316. Berlin: Mouton de Gruyter.
Cabrillana, C. 2011. 'Theoretical and applied perspectives in the teaching of Latin
  syntax: on the particular question of word order', *Formal Linguistics and the
  Teaching of Latin*, ed. by R. Oniga, R. Iovino, & G. Giusti, 65–84. Newcastle upon
  Tyne: Cambridge Scholars Publishing.
Cardinaletti, A. & M. T. Guasti, eds. 1995. *Small Clauses*. San Diego, Calif.: Academic
  Press.
Devine, A. M. & L. D. Stephens 2006. *Latin Word Order: Structured Meaning and
  Information*. Oxford: Oxford University Press.
Graffi, G. 1997. 'Frasi complete e frasi ridotte.' *Lingua e Stile* 32.273–291.
Ledgeway, A. 2012. *From Latin to Romance: Morphosyntactic Typology and Change*.
  Oxford: Oxford University Press.
Luraghi, S. 1997. 'Omission of the direct obiect in Latin.' *Indogermanische Forschungen*
  102.239–257.
Maraldi, M. 1985. 'Null subjects: some implications for Latin syntax', *Syntaxe et latin,
  Actes du IIème Congrès international de linguistique latine*, ed. by C. Touratier, 41–53.
  Aix-en-Provence–Marseille: Université de Provence.
Moro, A. 1997. *The Raising of Predicates: Predicative Noun Phrases and the Theory of
  Clause Structure*. Cambridge: Cambridge University Press.
Moro, A. 2009. *Breve storia del verbo essere*. Milan: Adelphi.

Ostafin, D. M. 1986. *Studies in Latin Word Order: A Transformational Approach.* Unpublished PhD dissertation, the University of Connecticut, Storrs.

Panhuis, D. 1982. *The Communicative Perspective in the Sentence: A Study of Latin Word Order.* Amsterdam: Benjamins.

Polo, C. 2004. *Word Order between Morphology and Syntax.* Padua: Unipress.

Rizzi, L. 1986. 'Null objects in Italian and the theory of "pro".' *Linguistic Inquiry* 17. 501–558.

Rizzi, L. 1997. 'The fine structure of the left periphery.' *Elements of Grammar: Handbook in Generative Syntax,* ed. by L. Haegeman, 281–337. Dordrecht: Kluwer.

Salvi, G. 2004. *La formazione della struttura di frase romanza.* Tübingen: Narr.

Salvi, G. 2005. 'Some firm points on Latin word order: the left periphery.' *Universal Grammar and the Reconstruction of Ancient Languages,* ed. by K. É. Kiss, 429–456. Berlin: Mouton de Gruyter.

Salvi, G. 2011. 'A formal approach to Latin word order.' *Formal Linguistics and the Teaching of Latin,* ed. by R. Oniga, R. Iovino, & G. Giusti, 23–50. Newcastle upon Tyne: Cambridge Scholars Publishing.

Spevak, O. 2006. 'Recent studies on word order in Latin.' *Mnemosyne* 59.434–453.

Spevak, O. 2010. *Constituent Order in Classical Latin Prose.* Amsterdam & Philadelphia: Benjamins.

Sznajder, L. 1998. 'Verbes transitifs en latin sans objet.' *Estudios de Lingüística Latina,* ed. by B. García-Hernández, 791–808. Madrid: Ediciones Clásicas.

Zubizarreta, M. L. 1998. *Prosody, Focus, and Word Order.* Cambridge, Mass.: MIT Press.

20. Case theory

Borgato, G. 1982–1983. 'I casi del latino.' *Quaderni Patavini di Linguistica* 3.55–75.

Calboli, G. 1975[2]. *La linguistica moderna e il latino. I casi.* Bologna: Pàtron (1972[1]).

van Kemenade, A. 1987. *Syntactic Case and Morphological Case in the History of English.* Dordrecht: Foris.

Viparelli, V. 1993. 'Il problema del caso nell'antichità classica e nella linguistica moderna (I).' *Bollettino di Studi Latini* 23.401–444.

21. Case syntax

Baldi, P. 1977. 'Morpho-syntax and the Latin genitive.' *Folia Linguistica* 11.93–108.

Bortolussi, B. 1987. *Considérations sur l'accusatif latin.* Unpublished thesis, Université Paris-VII.

Bortolussi, B. 1988. 'L'accusatif d'objet interne.' *Linguistik Parisette* (Akten des 22. Linguistischen Kolloquiums), ed. by R. Zuber & H. Weber, 73–81. Tübingen: Niemeyer.

Bortolussi, B. 1992. 'Passif, agent et sujet en latin.' *Recherches linguistiques* 21.21–33.

Colucci, L. 1981. *Prospettive per una reinterpretazione del dativo in Virgilio.* Rome: Signorelli.

De Carvalho, P. 1985. *Nom et déclinaison.* Bordeaux: Presses Universitaires.

Espinilla, E., P. E. Quetglas, & M. E. Torrego, eds. 1995. *Sintaxis del dativo latino.* Madrid: Universidad Autónoma; Barcelona: Universitat de Barcelona.

Hoecke, W. van 1996. 'The Latin dative.' *The Dative*, I, ed. by W. van Belle & W. van Langendonck, 3–37. Amsterdam & Philadelphia: Benjamins.

Taraba, J. 1985–1986. 'Valeurs d'ensemble des cas et rôles sémantiques avec application aux nominatifs et accusatifs latins.' *Graecolatina et Orientalia* 17/18.67–87.

Tikkanen, K. 2011. 'Comparative grammar and the genitive case: Latin syntax and the Sabellian languages.' *Formal Linguistics and the Teaching of Latin*, ed. by R. Oniga, R. Iovino, & G. Giusti, 173–186. Newcastle upon Tyne: Cambridge Scholars Publishing.

Touratier, C. 1978. 'Quelques principes pour l'étude des cas (avec application à l'ablatif latin).' *Langages* 12.28–116.

Vairel, H. 1981. 'The position of the vocative in the Latin case system.' *American Journal of Philology* 102.438–447.

22. The compound sentence: coordination

Bortolussi, B. 1990. 'Coordination, négation et structure de la proposition en latin.' *L'information grammaticale* 46.40–43.

Calboli, G., ed. 1989. *Subordination and Other Topics in Latin*. Amsterdam: Benjamins.

Kroon, C. 1995. *Discourse Particles in Latin: A Study of* nam, enim, uero *and* at. Amsterdam: Gieben.

Longrée, D. 2001. 'Aux frontières de la coordination: du fonctionnement des termes "corrélatifs" chez Tacite.' *De lingua Latina novae quaestiones*, ed. by C. Moussy, 395–407. Leuven: Peeters.

Orlandini, A. 2001. '*Nec, neque* ou de la disjonction.' *De lingua Latina novae quaestiones*, ed. by C. Moussy, 525–537. Leuven: Peeters.

Orlandini, A. & P. Poccetti 2008. 'Les relations sémantiques entre la coordination connective, adversative et disjonctive en latin et dans les langues de l'Italie ancienne.' *Papers on Grammar* 10.179–203.

Torrego, M. E. 2009. 'Coordination.' *New Perspectives on Historical Latin Syntax*, I, ed. by P. Baldi & P. Cuzzolin, 443–487. Berlin: Mouton de Gruyter.

Traina, A. 1966. 'Appunti per la storia del termine "paratassi".' *Atene e Roma* 11.169–174.

23. The complex sentence: embedded clauses

Bodelot, C. 2000. *Espaces fonctionnels de la subordination complétive en latin*. Leuven: Peeters.

Bodelot, C. 2003. *Grammaire fondamentale du latin. Tome X. Les propositions complétives en latin*. Leuven: Peeters.

Bolkestein, A. M. 1977. 'The difference between free and obligatory *ut*-clauses.' *Glotta* 55.321–350.

Bresnan, J. 1970. 'On complementizers: towards a syntactic theory of complement types.' *Foundations of Language* 6.297–321.

Danckaert, L. 2012. *Latin Embedded Clauses: The Left Periphery*. Amsterdam: Benjamins.

Espinilla, E., P. E. Quetglas, & M. E. Torrego, eds. 1999. *La consecutio temporum latina*. Madrid: Universidad Autónoma; Barcelona: Universitat de Barcelona.

Fleck, F. 2008. *Interrogation, coordination et subordination: le latin 'quin'*. Paris: PUPS.

Lakoff, R. T. 1968. *Abstract Syntax and Latin Complementation*. Cambridge, Mass.: MIT Press.

24. Interrogative clauses

Bodelot, C. 1987. *L'interrogation indirecte en latin*. Leuven: Peeters.

Brown, H. P., B. D. Joseph, & R. E. Wallace 2009. 'Questions and answers.' *New Perspectives on Historical Latin Syntax*, I, ed. by P. Baldi & P. Cuzzolin, 489–530. Berlin: Mouton de Gruyter.

Orlandini, A. 1980. '*Unius figurae crudelis eventus*, or on rhetorical questions.' *Papers on Grammar 1*, 103–140.

Risselada, R. 2005. 'Particles in questions.' *Papers on Grammar* 9.663–679.

Stephens, L. D. 1986. 'Indirect questions in Old Latin.' *Illinois Classical Studies* 10.195–207.

25. Relative clauses

Bortolussi, B. 2005. 'Subordination seconde du relatif. Contraintes d'emploi.' *Papers on Grammar* 9.479–492.

Chomsky, N. 1977. 'On wh-movement.' *Formal Syntax*, ed. by P. S. Culicover, T. Wasow, & A. Akmajian, 71–132. New York: Academic Press.

Lavency, M. 1998. *Grammaire fondamentale du latin*. V/2. *La proposition relative*. Leuven. Peeters.

Lehmann, C. 1984. *Der Relativsatz*. Tübingen: Narr.

Pompei, A. 2011a. 'Relative clause.' *New Perspectives on Historical Latin Syntax*, IV, ed. by P. Baldi & P. Cuzzolin, 427–548. Berlin: Mouton de Gruyter.

Pompei, A. 2011b. 'Relative clauses of the "third type" in Latin?' *Formal Linguistics and the Teaching of Latin*, ed. by R. Oniga, R. Iovino, & G. Giusti, 227–244. Newcastle upon Tyne: Cambridge Scholars Publishing.

Touratier, C. 1980. *La relative*. Paris: Klincksieck.

Vester, E. 1989. 'Relative clauses: description of the indicative—subjunctive opposition.' *Subordination and Other Topics in Latin*, ed. by G. Calboli, 326–350. Amsterdam: Benjamins.

26. Infinitival clauses

Bolkestein, M. 1976. '*A.c.i.*- and *ut*-clauses with Verba Dicendi in Latin.' *Glotta* 54.263–291.

Bolkestein, M. 1979. 'Subject-to-object raising in Latin?' *Lingua* 48.15–34.

Bortolussi, B. 2000. 'L'infinitif substantivé.' *La création lexicale en latin*, ed. by M. Fruyt & C. Nicolas, 61–73. Paris: PUPS.

Cecchetto, C. & R. Oniga 2002. 'Consequences of the analysis of Latin infinitival clauses for the theory of case and control.' *Lingue e Linguaggio* 1.151–189.

Cecchetto, C. & R. Oniga 2004. 'A challenge to null case theory.' *Linguistic Inquiry* 35.151–159.

Szilágyi, I. 2011. 'Control and AcI in Classical Latin: structural interpretation problems and innovative tendencies', *Formal Linguistics and the Teaching of Latin*, ed. by R. Oniga, R. Iovino, & G. Giusti, 85–100. Newcastle upon Tyne: Cambridge Scholars Publishing.

27. Participial clauses

Benedetti, M. 2002. 'Radici, morfemi nominali e verbali: alla ricerca dell'inaccusatività indeuropea.' *Archivio Glottologico Italiano* 87.20–45.

Lavency, M. 1986. 'Le paradigme syntaxique de l'ablatif absolu,' *Hommages à J. Veremans*, ed. by F. Decreus, & C. Deroux, 184–191. Brussels: Latomus.

Levin, B. & M. Rappaport-Hovav 1995. *Unaccusativity: At the Syntax-Lexical Semantics Interface*. Cambridge, Mass.: MIT Press.

Maiocco, M. 2005. *Absolute Participial Constructions: A Contrastive Approach to the Syntax of Greek and Latin*. Alessandria: Edizioni dell'Orso.

Perlmutter, D. M. 1978. 'Impersonal passives and the unaccusative hypothesis.' in *Proceedings of the 4th Annual Meeting of the Berkeley Linguistic Society*, 157–189.

Pompei, A. 2004. 'Propriétés nominales et propriétés verbales du participe.' *Studi Italiani di Linguistica Teorica e Applicata* 33(2).31–48.

28. Adverbial clauses

Bãnos, J. M. 2011. 'Causal clauses.' *New Perspectives on Historical Latin Syntax*, IV, ed. by P. Baldi & P. Cuzzolin, 195–234. Berlin: Mouton de Gruyter.

Baratin, M. 1981. 'Remarques sur l'emploi des temps et des modes dans le système conditionnel latin.' *Bulletin de la Société de Linguistique* 76.249–273.

Bermudez Ramiro, J. 2004. *El estilo indirecto en latín (oratio obliqua)*. Amsterdam: Hakkert.

Bertocchi, A. & M. Maraldi 2011. 'Conditionals and concessives.' *New Perspectives on Historical Latin Syntax*, IV, ed. by P. Baldi & P. Cuzzolin, 93–194. Berlin: Mouton de Gruyter.

Cabrillana, C. 2011a. 'Adverbial subordination: introductory overview.' *New Perspectives on Historical Latin Syntax*, IV, ed. by P. Baldi & P. Cuzzolin, 11–18. Berlin: Mouton de Gruyter.

Cabrillana, C. 2011b. 'Purpose and result clauses.' *New Perspectives on Historical Latin Syntax*, IV, ed. by P. Baldi & P. Cuzzolin, 19–92. Berlin: Mouton de Gruyter.

Heberlein, F. 2011. 'Temporal clauses.' *New Perspectives on Historical Latin Syntax*, IV, ed. by P. Baldi & P. Cuzzolin, 235–372. Berlin: Mouton de Gruyter.

Luraghi, S. 2001. 'The discourse function of *cum* with the subjunctive in narrative texts.' *De lingua Latina novae quaestiones*, ed. by C. Moussy, 409–426. Leuven: Peeters.

Maraldi, M. 1998. 'Concessive *ut*: parataxis, hypotaxis and coordination.' *Estudios de Lingüística Latina*, ed. by B. García-Hernández, 487–501. Madrid: Ediciones Clásicas.

Maraldi, M. 2001. 'Forms of concession in Latin.' *De lingua Latina novae quaestiones*, ed. by C. Moussy, 427–445. Leuven: Peeters.

Pasoli, E. 1966². 'Per una trattazione sistematica del periodo ipotetico.' *Saggi di grammatica latina*, 91–124. Bologna: Zanichelli (1961¹).

Tarriño, E. 2011. 'Comparative clauses.' *New Perspectives on Historical Latin Syntax*, IV, ed. by P. Baldi & P. Cuzzolin, 373–426. Berlin: Mouton de Gruyter.

Torrego, M. E. 2001. 'Typologie sémantique des propositions finales latines.' *De lingua Latina novae quaestiones*, ed. by C. Moussy, 627–639. Leuven: Peeters.

Traina, A. 1959. 'Due questioni di sintassi latina: l'attrazione modale e le interrogative nel discorso indiretto.' *Athenaeum* 37.258–278.

Traina, A. 1961. '*Idola scholae*. 9. La "logica" della grammatica e le concessive latine.' *Atene e Roma* 6.214–219.

Vester, E. 1994. 'The internal structure of adverbial *ut*-clauses.' *Linguistic Studies on Latin*, ed. by J. Herman, 269–279. Amsterdam: Benjamins.

Index